D0153114

Winners and Losers

Winners and Losers
Social and Political Polarities in America

Irving Louis Horowitz

Duke Press Policy Studies
Duke University Press
Durham, N.C.   1984

© 1984 Duke University Press, all rights reserved

Printed in the United States of America on acid-free paper

Library of Congress Cataloging in Publication Data

Horowitz, Irving Louis.
  Winners and losers.

  (Duke Press policy studies)
  Includes index.
  1. Sociology—Addresses, essays, lectures.
2. Political sociology—Addresses, essays, lectures.
3. United States—Politics and government—1945–
4. Ideology—Addresses, essays, lectures. 5. Polarity
(Philosophy)—Addresses, essays, lectures. I. Title.
II. Series.
  HM33.H67   1984   306′.2′0973   83-25353
  ISBN 0-8223-0495-3
  ISBN 0-8223-0602-6 pbk.

306.20973
H816w

To the Memory of Two Friends:
Kalman Silvert and Gino Germani

Contents

Acknowledgments

Since Montaigne and Bacon an essay has come to mean the composition, in relatively brief form, of writings that contain moral thrust no less than empirical substance. Social science is blessed with some outstanding essayists who, for the most part, are trained or have received supplemental education in fields somewhat removed from their presumed professional vocation. Indeed, I am struck by the social worth of miseducation for becoming a social scientist.

Whatever the weaknesses in this literary genre, and however much my admission stimulates rather than lays to rest fears that essays, unlike research papers or professional articles, are really not truly social scientific, professional people seem fascinated with this genre quite beyond any single "profession." Trying to make sense of the whole in a brief space is both a risk and a challenge. The essay form provides opportunities for superficiality and also possibilities for new intellectual directions. I will neither claim to have escaped the former nor insist that herein I have uniformly achieved the latter.

Yet it does seem to be my good fortune that the essays offered here have been sufficiently well regarded to merit this third collection. My first collection, *Professing Sociology: Studies in the Life Cycle of Social Science*, included essays written from 1955 through 1967. My second collection, *Ideology and Utopia in the United States*, included essays written from 1968 through 1976. And this volume before you, *Winners and Losers*, covers the period up to the present, that is, from 1977 through 1983, with a few earlier essays never before reprinted but strongly evocative of the work as a whole.

Let me frankly deal with the charge that I have changed my political orientation, becoming more "mainstream" (whatever that means in the context of social science Balkanization). The obvious caveat is that if one were wedded to every single utterance made over three decades, one would be either divine or mad. Alfred N. Whitehead cleverly combined the two into divine madness. While I must admit to a disenchantment with political tests for social science values and a corresponding enchantment with social science as an end in itself—just as reason is an end in itself—after reviewing my essays over this span of nearly three decades, I must still conclude that the world has changed far more dramatically than have my words or ideas about society.

Social science is both more exact in its evidentiary demands and less likely to give fatuous advice to those who would make "wars" against poverty, ignorance, hunger, militarism, communism, or what have you. The triumphal spirit has given way to a well-deserved modesty—one grounded in the simple observation that our intellectual synthesis of empirical research and critical theory remains a distant goal. To recapture past grandeur is impossible. The fragmentation of knowledge prevents this from taking place. But the potential for a new synthesis based on the inner history of social science, rather than the often passing and frivolous claims of external interest groups, is now coming into focus. *Winners and Losers* is one effort, joined by many others to be sure, to locate the sources of such a synthesis and discuss the consequences of the inevitable reintegration of society and culture that will follow the present demiurge.

The changes made vary from essay to essay, from mere cosmetic changes in grammar and tense to quite substantial changes in style and substance. My essays as originally conceived are not cast in stone. They are moral but not necessarily sacral. They are empirical and tentative, not necessarily fixed in time and space. The opportunity to give decennial reflection is just that: an opportunity. I have not changed their moral thrust or their sociological sensibility. This work stands or falls on how well the parts add up to form a worthy whole. That I shall leave to my readers to determine and define.

Let me then gratefully acknowledge permissions granted by the following publications to use materials from articles originally published elsewhere. The citations are to the original article titles, with the chapters of *Winners and Losers* containing material from these articles given in parenthesis following citations. As I have already noted, these original materials have been revised, either slightly or substantially, depending on their vintage and their applicability to the overall design of the book:

"On the Expansion of New Theories and the Withering Away of Old Classes." *Society* 16, no. 2, January/February 1979 (chapter 1).

"Race, Class, and the New Ethnicity: The Holy Ghost of Social Stratification." From *The American Working Class: Prospects for the 1980s*, edited by Irving Louis Horowitz, John C. Leggett, and Martin Oppenheimer. New Brunswick and London: Transaction Books, 1979 (chapter 2).

"The Environmental Cleavage and Social Ecology." *Social Theory and Practice* 2, no. 2, Spring 1972 (chapter 3).

"Social Welfare, State Power, and the Limits of Equity." From *Growth in a Finite World*, edited by Joseph Grunfeld. Philadelphia: The Franklin Institute Press, 1979 (chapter 4).

"Winners and Losers: The Limits of Pragmatism and Moralism in Politics." *New Literary History* 13, no. 3, Spring 1982 (chapter 5).

"Autobiography as the Presentation of Self for Social Immortality." *New Literary History* 9, no. 2, Autumn 1977 (chapter 6).

"On Alienation and the Social Order." From *Dialogues on the Philosophy of Marxism*, edited by John Somerville and Howard L. Parsons. Westport, Conn.: Greenwood Press, 1974 (chapter 7).

"Sociology and Futurology: The Contemporary Pursuit of the Millennium," *Berkeley Journal of Sociology* 19, no. 1, Winter 1974–75; and "International Studies and the Pursuit of the Millennium," *International Studies* 8, no. 1, Winter 1981 (chapter 8).

"Beyond Democracy: Interest Groups and the Patriotic Gore." *The Humanist* 32, no. 5, September/October 1979 (chapter 9).

"Slouching Toward the Brave New World: Bureaucracy, Administration, and State

Power." *Marxist Perspectives* 3, no. 1 (whole number 9), Spring 1980 (chapter 10).

"Economic Equality as a Social Goal." *Journal of Economic Issues* 14, no. 4, December 1980 (chapter 11).

"From the New Deal to the New Federalism." *American Journal of Economics and Sociology* 42, no. 2, April 1983 (chapter 12).

"Transnational Terrorism, Civil Liberties, and Social Science." From *Terrorism: Interdisciplinary Perspectives*, edited by Yonah Alexander and Seymour Maxwell Finger. London: McGraw-Hill Book Co., 1977 (chapter 13).

"The Routinization of Terrorism and Its Unanticipated Consequences." From *Terrorism, Legitimacy and Power: The Consequences of Political Violence*, edited by Martha Crenshaw. Middletown, Conn.: Wesleyan University Press, 1983 (chapter 14).

"The Penal Colony Known as the Soviet Union," *Society* 11, no. 5, July/August 1974; and "Revolution, Retribution, and Redemption," *Society* 15, no. 6, September/October 1978 (chapter 15).

"Open Societies and Free Minds," *Contemporary Sociology* 8, no. 1, January 1979; "From the End of Ideology to the Beginning of Morality," *Contemporary Sociology* 10, no. 4, July 1981; and "Talmon's Genius," *Present Tense* 10, no. 2, Winter 1983 (chapter 16).

"Left-Wing Fascism: An Infantile Disorder." *Society* 18, no. 4, May/June 1981 (chapter 17).

"Socialism and the Problem of Knowledge." From *The Concept of Socialism*, edited by Bhikhu Parekh. London: Croom Helm, 1975 (chapter 18).

"Radical Politics and Sociological Research: Observations on Methodology and Ideology" (with Howard S. Becker). From *Varieties of Political Expression in Sociology*, edited by Robert K. Merton. Chicago and London: University of Chicago Press, 1972 (chapter 19).

"The Sociology of Development and the Ideology of Sociology." From *Societal Growth: Processes and Implications*, edited by Amos H. Hawley. New York: Macmillan/The Free Press, 1979 (chapter 20).

"Social Research and Political Advocacy" (with Jeanne Guillemin). From *Ethics, the Social Sciences, and Policy Analysis*, edited by Daniel Callahan and Bruce Jennings. New York: Plenum Press, 1983 (chapter 21).

"Language, Truth and Politics." *The Washington Quarterly* 6, no. 1, Winter 1982–83 (chapter 22).

"Moral Development, Authoritarian Distemper, and the Democratic Persuasion." From *Moral Development and Politics*, edited by Richard W. Wilson and Gordon J. Schochet. New York and London: Praeger Publishers/Holt, Rinehart & Winston, 1980 (chapter 23).

"Moral Implications of Social Science Disputations." Published for the first time in *Winners and Losers*. Durham: Duke University Press, 1984 (chapter 24).

Irving Louis Horowitz

Introduction

Those familiar with my work are aware that I am essentially an essayist rather than a writer of lengthy tomes. With exceptions, such as *Radicalism and the Revolt Against Reason*, my work of a quarter century ago on Georges Sorel, and much more recently, *C. Wright Mills: An American Utopian*, my major works are essentially composites of essays, articles, and short monographs. That certain thematic consistency emerges in my work is due more to the integral nature of the issues that concern me and the traditions within which I work rather than intent. Only infrequently is scholarship served by holistic notions, at least with respect to my own work, and I daresay with respect to many others as well.

The main pivots about which my efforts have revolved are clear enough: socio-economic development, *Three Worlds of Development* (1965, 1972), *Beyond Empire and Revolution* (1982); public policy, *The Rise and Fall of Project Camelot* (1967), *Social Science and Public Policy in the United States* (1975), *Constructing Policy* (1979); and political sociology, *Professing Sociology* (1968), *Foundations of Political Sociology* (1972), and *Ideology and Utopia in the United States* (1976). If one reads these books it becomes evident that even these distinctions are roughhewn and uncast in stone. The interplay of persons, organizations, and ideologies in the structure of classes and the performance of politics has consistently occupied my attention and focused my writings.

Winners and Losers, a work in a similar vein, had its origins in many recent essays and articles I have produced over the past decade, or since *Ideology and Utopia in the United States*. It takes up issues of struggle in the social, ideological, and political contexts. Each chapter centers on the variables that give substance and structure to the political dynamics of social interaction. Many of these chapters have been substantially rewritten; others have had more cosmetic changes; and a few have been left virtually intact. Preparing a book for publication allows for revision in the exact sense of the word—to look again with fresh perspective upon phenomena examined in an earlier period. Events change theories. Ontology wins out over the epistemology. And this is necessarily the case. The alternative is fanaticism disguised as principle, dogmatic assertion that realities must be bent to the will of doctrinal purities. All this ever serves is intellectual vanity. One struggles to preserve theoretical consistency only when one cannot accept that events have made theories obsolete. To avoid being labeled a damned fool, or worse, an eclectic, some social scientists turn superrationalistic. They construct explanations for why their theories have not been understood by critics, or worse, understood improperly. As a result, a tradition, more like a cult, grows around those individuals for whom the preservation of intellectual perfection comes to mean more than the analysis of practical imperfections.

Those who stake much on a unified picture of the world end up obscuring the blemishes of the world—those very elements that make the life and work of social research both fascinating and worthwhile. While I would like to think my perspectives are consistent, I am much more concerned with describing and explaining events so as to help social researchers lend coherence to the world of social relations. Whether the dreams of social physics can ever be reached, putting what we know about society into formulas like the general and special theories of relativity strikes me as intellectual hubris. Likewise, putting every belief we have to work through a notion of social engineering, as if society were a tabula rasa upon which people's lives were ordered, strikes me as the opposite side of that same coin: intellectual impertinence.

But this is not intended to be a statement about what the book before you is not, or even a peroration on the state of the sociological arts. Few of the materials included here show much concern for such weighty issues as the state of the disciplines or the state of its practitioners. Rather, my concerns are with the larger picture: with fissures and factions in society, cleavages and conflicts in the political system, and varieties of ideological formation that inform actual behavior and disturb assumptions. I believe that these essays, built up over time and space, result in a theoretically meaningful entity, an approximation of a unified theory of society. One must, however, clear away much intellectual rubbish to make possible the consideration of larger holisms. If this work does not establish a great chain of being guided by little pieces of interlocking necessities, it at least helps us to appreciate how winning and losing intersect in a pattern of behavior consistent with our observations.

Some scholars write in a terribly arid way as if people simply did not exist or play a part in the drama of life. Others write as if people were free spirits, unencumbered by systems, structure, and/or collective conscience and unconscious alike. For my part, the tension, the drama, the stuff of life, and why I chose as a title *Winners and Losers* (in addition to its being the title of an essay in the book) is to show that the best social science is done by those who recognize the existence of polarities (chance and necessity, systems and individuals, past and future, good and evil, and yes, winning and losing) without deciding on behalf of one or the other; indeed, recognizing that these ontological categories often blend into each other, or even convert into each other.

The social scientific standpoint can survive only when its advocates appreciate sincerely the many-sided claims on historical truth. Rationalizations are common to all. Claims of divine sanction are common to all. Self-righteous posturing is common to all. Identification with God and History are common to all. If rationalization is difficult to detect, it is even more difficult to realize. Claims are not facts. Some claims are better than others; some people are better than others; and some explanations are superior to others. The good social scientists cannot stop at pure relativity, or an empty dialectical vessel, without implicitly surrendering their role as interpreters of experience. The good social scientist is obligated to stake a claim for the better against the lesser, for larger truths against intimate lies, for the better social and political system against the lesser social and political system. Putting all these themes to work is no easy task.

Whether one ends up a winner or a loser is a function of who is in the audience. The recipient of information and evidence is very much a factor in prediction no less than description. Rationalization being what it is, we all begin with a presumption of moral virtue no less than empirical fact. Are there measures beyond the market, does the audience speak as masses or as elites, or is the work vouchsafed by numbers and markets at all? Does a larger metaphysical entity determine when and if one is adjudicated a success or a failure, or even when a game is terminated? We are touched by vanities as well as ambitions, a search for personal verification no less than intellectual explanation. Because of these crosscutting currents, the experience of producing a new work is always an adventure. And just as it is foolish to ask if the tenth-born is more or less of a thrill than the firstborn, so too is this the case with books.

With a deep sense of adventure no less than pride, I present this volume for public inspection. The book contains the best writing in essay form of which I am capable. In many ways it represents a sequel to *Professing Sociology* (1968) and *Ideology and Utopia in the United States* (1976), prepared in a postsociological universe. I hope it will stimulate large-scale reconsideration from my friends, and only small-scale consternation from foes. There is a danger in resubmitting, however much in an altered state, materials from previous years and other contexts. Inevitably, the questions asked are not only about the empirical or theoretical worth of each contribution, but whether its republication constitutes a sinful act of pride or a contrite act of faith. I leave my readers to make this complex judgment for themselves.

Princeton, New Jersey
15 March 1983

Part I. Society

1. Class Composition and Competition

The most fascinating aspect of the current revival of interest in the character and conduct of the American class system is that the source, the impulse, for such renewed analysis derives more from a neoconservative movement interested in the expansion of new theories and the withering of old classes than from any neoradical mood that might once again doom America by drowning it in class warfare. Indeed, the very sterility of much present-day sociological analysis permitted the subject of stratification to lie fallow at least since the fine essays by Riesman and Mills in the mid-1950s.[1] One might even argue that the disinterest of much sociology in genuine class analysis, in favor of millenarian beliefs in parties, foci, and sheer spontaneity, permitted this vacuum to be filled by more traditional types of historical researchers. This exercise in criticism of the new theories of new classes should therefore not diminish any sense of the breakthrough effort at construction represented by the current wave of writings on the changing character of class composition and class competition in American society.

There is such a plethora of contradictory signals and approaches with respect to the constitution of the "new class" that with some profit we might briefly review outstanding European contributions to class analysis. In this way the analysts of the new class can be traced back to one or the other of these older viewpoints.[2] Time has obscured the fact that not only were there theories and doctrines rivaling class—racial analysis, ethnic factors, religious groundings, etc.—but within class analysis itself profound divisions quickly surfaced. It is, or rather was, characteristic of nineteenth-century social thought to take a variable, latch on to it for what it was worth, then exaggerate its meaning. All other visions and variables were excoriated as worthless. Nineteenth-century social stratification assumed conflict and contradiction even when none was found. Dialectical reasoning went on a mad spree so that every idea was seen to be at war with every other idea. Class struggle for the intellectual class gave rise to struggles over the meaning of classes.[3] One can examine in its pristine forms the sort of theorizing prompting new class advocates to recreate in a livelier rhetoric, and within an American framework, the same sorts of confusion and confounding.

Class is a sufficiently pervasive term that constructing a new class is a simple enough operation. All one has to do is select one or several classical visions of class and make a pronouncement of novelty. Any stratum or sector of society can be so isolated. But then again, this may be said of other crucial variables in social science, for example: power, race, ethnicity, profits. The fatal fly in the ointment of all single variable analyses is that ultimately they suffer from an intolerable reductionism, which explains little and promises so much. This being the case, we can at least clear up some of the ambiguity surrounding the term *class*.

The Classical Visions of Social Class

The oldest and perhaps still the most serviceable notion of class relates to *class as station*, to a specific position in the economic hierarchy, such as proletariat, peasant, bourgeois. In such a view, class is relational and functional at the same time. Class is defined with respect to control of mechanisms of production or lack thereof. A social class is also an aggregate of persons who perform the same function in the organization of production. In such an economic view, common to Smith, Ricardo, and Marx, labor is the basis of human self-realization. What distinguished Marx was not his idea of class, but his idea of class struggle as the essential motor of social development; and beyond that, class as an instrument of political transformation. But to infuse the concept of class with such dynamism is to move from class as a station to class negation and transformation of that station. To make such an assumption is finally to distinguish a class acting as an objective entity in its own right from class serving a subjective belief in its own rights.[4]

Max Weber well understood this peculiar ambiguity in the class variable. He recognized that classes are not communities; they merely represent potential bases for communal activity. Weber thus introduced a notion of *class as opportunity*. One can speak of a class when a number of people have in common a specific causal component of their life chances. Classes are defined specifically by economic interests as indicated by possession of goods and opportunities for income, rather than by the economic station occupied by an individual. Weber introduced an element of skill and education as part of the definition of class. Hence, he came close to a belief in occupation as an essential part of what constitutes a class. What made Weber's modifications particularly intriguing was his effort to explain why sectors of society behave in a certain way. The values of any given cluster of people help to determine their position in the social hierarchy. If a group perceives its position in a social system as essentially hopeless, the potential for volatile, revolutionary change is high; but if it views its position as poor but constantly improving, then expectations for rapid revolutionary change are simply not going to materialize because they evaporate as economic goals are met. Hence, for a class to act for itself and not just subsist in itself, it must have aspirations no less than actualities.[5]

Emile Durkheim, the third figure in the trinitarian cosmos of European social theory, sought to broaden the notion of class even further. For him and his followers, *class as logical order* was the key factor in any definition. The first logical categories for Durkheim were social in nature. Classes of things were related to classes of people into which natural and manufactured things were integrated. People were grouped by others, and perceived themselves as real in terms of groups. They assembled other things in similar group terms. For Durkheim the notion of class was virtually antithetical to that of struggle. Rather, as Robert Nisbet has accurately pointed out, Durkheim's notion was that the way in which groups fit into one another permits the evolution of society through creation of law, clan, and group. The way social relations fit into each other determines the efficacy and longevity of a class. Social classes change and emerge in the process of legalization, and more basically, in the organic and contractual processes that establish the essential nature of any society. The Durkheimian view of class is far from the economic realm; the essential dynamism of the concept becomes subsumed under an essential orderliness. In such a vision the abolition of classes is akin to the end of civilization, and not a higher stage in the evolution of humanity. Durkheim differed profoundly from the Germanic school of Marx and probably of Weber as well. Class is part of nature, and hence a permanent part of human relations. Injustices are adjudicated through law, custom, and morality. In such a view, as manifested in the final two chapters of the *Division of Labor*, class conflict ends not in liberation, but in the destruction of law, custom, and morality.[6]

In substituting a legal and political notion of class for the older social and economic definitions, Durkheim opened a Pandora's box not so easily capped by a vision of essential natures and order. For in the very imperfection of creation, classes, like other things, were created uneven in size and unequal in strength. For Gaetano Mosca two classes of people appear in all advanced civilizations: one class that rules and another that is ruled. The class that rules is generally small, enjoys the privileges and prestige of monopolizing power, controlling political functions, and managing public affairs. The class that is ruled tends to be large, amorphous, and is directed and also often oppressed by the ruling class. For Mosca, the real worth of a concept of *class as political rule* lies in the fact that the varying structure of ruling classes has a preponderant importance in determining the political type and the political formula. Such a notion of class blends with one of elites, the special carriers of civilization of any given people. With Mosca stratification analysis comes full cycle: from class as a special preserve preventing the forward march of civilization, to class as a natural manifestation of elites preserving and extending a civilization.[7]

It remained only for Ferdinand Toennies to take the final steps, and reverse Mosca's faith in elites, by a definition of *class as mass*. In this sense, a class is authentic only when it develops effective power through the strength of the mass, that is, through large numbers that make up a meaningful collectivity. Far from being a simplifier or vulgarizer of Marx, Toennies took full account of developments in stratification and appreciated that the sorts of political and administrative elites that define the state could only be dealt with by a vision of class as mass participation, and not as a special magical preserve of one segment in the industrial process. Classes were characterized by animosity and enmity; what Durkheim referred to as classes were for Toennies really estates or social orders.

The process of social mobility had inextricably been fused to that of political allocation. All sorts of problems emerged by the early twentieth century: how does a class make revolution, when in fact only organized groups ("vanguards") make changes of a structural sort? How does class analysis solve problems of racial, ethnic, or sexual variety; and if it does not, why should class analysis merit a special place in stratification theory? How does a class cope with its own leadership, or with military groups seizing power, or party factions intent upon a coup? In reducing class to basic common denominators, to an elite or to a mass, to apocalyptic visions of a utopian future rather than analytic concepts of present utility, the burden of class analysis shifted dramatically from a search for new classes to a search for more specific carriers of civilization if one is conservative, or to new sources of revolution if one is radical.[8]

A serious problem with class analysis generally, and with analysis of the new class specifically, lies in predicting behavior. Even if there may be a slight ambiguity as to the morphological contours of this new class, there has been little serious effort to correlate new class membership with specific forms of behavior. Is the new class more Democratic than Republican? Well, in some elections it is, but in others it is not. Is the new class more inclined to liberalism than other classes? Well, some intellectuals are, but not necessarily the best or the brightest. Is the new class inclined to internationalist or isolationist postures? Well, it depends on the situation and the period of time. Precisely at the level of predictability class theory can be seen at its most vulnerable. It is not simply incomes and occupations that are at stake, but specific behaviors that presumably can be inferred from specific class affiliations. At this level of moving from classes to behaviors class theory crumbles. It was precisely the inability to make grandiose inferences from membership to behavior that represented the Achilles heel of classical social theorists. The nineteenth century thus bequeathed not only its problems, but its doctrines as well.

Current Visions of Social Class

If one takes the position that the new class consists largely of intellectuals, of a cultural apparatus made up of middle-class disenchanted figures of the 1950s and 1960s, then we are left with the fact that the new dissidents, as Norman Podhoretz calls them, comprise cohorts drawn from the same social and economic stratum. If this adversary culture is busily at work undermining the Protestant ethic and the business establishment, then an equal number of new dissidents are at work defending the economic system and the social order. The intellectual community, now as in earlier times, cleaves along major lines: equity versus equality, ascription versus achievement, quota systems versus meritocracy, and so on. But this approach tends to undermine the notion of a new class and to reestablish the classical idea of Marxism: that the cultural apparatus reflects the major class currents, and is not itself the trend setter.

The new class can be defined more broadly in terms of bureaucrats, administrators, evaluators, and policy makers, an entire cluster of people for whom the arguments in defense of high culture are a luxury item within democratic society. The defense of middle class values as the source of liberty, democracy, and human decency is a far simpler task than the defense of the middle class as an operational class. Here the problem lies clearly in the conflict between the actual interests of a bourgeois class and its self-proclaimed ultimate values. This sort of disjunction has long been recognized, and has long been a source of irritation, even friction, among the intelligentsia. They are forced to choose between a dominant economic class engaged in debaucheries of all sorts and a class whose very laissez-faire attitudes toward others could be interpreted as more liberal than those of any other class, and hence they become a superior element within the new class.

If one takes Peter Berger's position that members of the new class are largely characterized by their secularity, and that the new class represents simply an adversarial vision, in which every anticapitalist bias becomes a socialist vision, then one must enquire as to why this intellectual community is so silent about that socialist vision, leaving such musings to the remnants of the old left. Even if we assume the correctness of the correlation between pluralism and modernization, secularism and the distribution of knowledge through agencies of planning and administration (or childhood health and cultural permissiveness), it is difficult to assess how this adds up to a new class, much less to a class which is subject to a particularly vehement form of the cognitive effects of modernism. What in fact seems to occur is that these groups tend to cleave sharply on nearly all serious issues. The resurgence of religiosity, even the emergence of a civil religion as a dominant hallmark of American civilization, argues strongly against the concept of class, since no strong evidence exists to indicate how the new class becomes a class for itself. Indeed, the evidence indicates a set of contradictions emerging in new class theory even before the conditions of class ripening have been fully explored. We are faced with a new class that not only eludes definition at the economic level, but is, if anything, even more ambiguous at the ideological level. The new class is both a product of, and a rebellion against, secularity and modernity. The disjunction between class as membership and class as behavior casts a grave pall over the concept, and reduces it to a cry of conscience of conservative intellectuals against radical intellectuals. Although the new class does not fit old definitions of class, it can be understood without taking recourse to a general revision of class analysis.

To speak of the new class in terms of a theory of privilege, and to see privileges in terms of environmental cleanliness, transportation advantages, household assistance, and finally, political advantage is reasonable enough. The problem, even when posed in hypothetical form as it is by Aaron Wildavsky, returns to meanings and classes. Nonetheless, one can and usually does speak of interest groups or advantages in quite the same terms as some would speak of classes. Likewise, tens of millions of taxpayers pay for the privileges of the few. But this sort of Mosca-like vision of class, i.e., the division between those who rule and those many who are ruled, disguises the emergence of new forms of interest groups. It can be observed that new agents have entered the political arena: lawyers, social activists, lobbyists, to effect the sorts of changes they want. It is even correct to note that stupidity and sloth may have a greater role in permitting these people to gain access than conspiracy; but how is this different from elite politics of a conventional sort? It might be argued that new class theory is regressive in that the political context of stratification becomes muted rather than strengthened.

A characteristic of antidemocratic tendencies in our times, aristocratic and populist varieties alike, is to seek a measure of power through the courts and lobbying agencies rather than through direct political participation. At this level, the politics of sociological statistics becomes clearest. For to the extent that a manufacture of classes can take place, a manufacture of class struggles can also occur, followed by a manufacture of class revolutions. However, in this process, the new class quickly dissolves into a series of practical interest groups. Purported new class members, along with society as a whole, must decide upon the worthiness of particular kinds of struggle: violence versus nonviolence, restoration versus revolution, coalitions versus autonomous party politics, aboveboard versus underground. At such levels, the notion of a new class seems to lose much of its potency, or at least urgency. What seems to be the case is that the new class is simply an emerging educated group penetrating an already greatly enlarged bureaucracy. Education may indeed be an ever more important filtering device for public service, but this results in a more potent bureaucracy, rather than any observed new class alignment.

Those who treat the new class in terms of a set of labels or ideologies—for example, public sector advocacy, bureaucratic regulation, upsurge of planners and experts, media violence and pornography, societal permissiveness, racial and social engineering, displacement of military safeguards by health and welfare boondoggles—are rendering an oversimplified model of American reality. Was it the reaction to such new class antics, or to its emergence, that won elections for Republicans in 1968 and 1972? What led to its losses four years later? To develop an ideological cluster and then label this a belief system of a new class, as Kevin P. Phillips suggests, is only to repeat the shortcomings of a new majority notion. Oversimplified politics lead to electoral disaster. In point of fact, to identify a new right as archetypical enemy of the new class is simply not to take seriously that, increasingly in the 1980s, many members of the new right, at least in electoral terms, are drawn from the very segments of society that presumably generate a new politics or a new class. To speak of the explosiveness of the new right outside party channels is difficult enough; but it also exaggerates the weaknesses of party politics in America. For example, even as party identification might dwindle, the absence of the sort of mass disaffection from the voting syndrome is equally conspicuous. Elections in which issues are sharply focused command wide voter response. Neither of these phenomena can be explained by new class approaches.

Legitimacy is not uniquely a function of party support, but of system maintenance. Such support has not diminished in American society. To further postulate a götterdämmerung of new right versus new class, is to ignore the interpenetration of the bureaucratic networks extending from the suburban courthouse to the federal Congress. The inability to influence interest groups plagues many Americans. Hence, the failure of a so-called new class or new dissident elements ever to rise beyond the status of a narrow social stratum, often attached to a tolerant Schumpeterian university, is constantly repeated. The intelligentsia is hardly capable of exercising the sorts of class power one usually claims as the basis of revolutionary regimes. Their cleavage is all too apparent in the current policies of both major parties. This is not to deny a strain of competition in American history between elitism and populism; but even in this, no consistent class pattern is evident. The carriers of radical ideas shift as often as is in the interests of the combatants—without any apparent overriding metaphysic of class membership.

When one deals with specific segments of a new class one sees how difficult it is for that class to expand its membership. With the legal profession, for example, there is the irritating factor that Nathan Glazer adduces: namely, lawyers, by the nature of an adversarial system, tend to be located on both sides of any issue. Hence, this profession cannot as a whole represent or lead a new class. Beyond this technical point, the number of lawyers consciously identified with a new class is quite small. Attorneys involved in public affairs or ombudsmen services are a fraction of the law profession. There are few lawyers servicing public interest causes, and a great many lawyers servicing business and corporate interests, that is, established class frameworks. The key word for lawyers is service rather than power. Even if we restrict ourselves to public interest law, we find advocates of expanding and retrenching government power. Likewise, public interest attorneys seek decriminalization and deinstitutionalization as a standard mode of operating. Then how will the new class expand its membership? The new class attorneys are in a small minority. American society is moving in a more specialized direction. There are ever expanding numbers of lawyers, and precious few public interest advocates. The great paradox becomes that public interest lawyers will need an ever increasing supply of new public interest claims involving a coterie of planners, social workers, and city planners.

We are offered an unusual argument about lawyers critical of government, while they urge its expansion. Only if we divide the world into professional classes, into an interventionist, public interest, bar association on one side, and the older more powerful nonactivist segments of the legal profession on the other, does the problem begin to surface. It seems far simpler, and more precise, to say that public interest attorneys, all two thousand of them, represent a small fraction of a profession which has been far more tied to an old class of commerce and a new breed of politicians than any new class as a force unto itself. The emergence of a small group of public service lawyers can be viewed as a class phenomenon only if Glazer is willing to argue that the great multitudes of Americans require no legal counsel. It might be conceptually neater and intellectually sounder to consider the law profession in the post-Watergate era as a trifle more responsive to public needs than in the past, precisely because at least this small segment of professional life is drawn from a wider social and sexual stratum than in the past. While it is proper to infer that lawyers might be more responsive to broad public issues than in the past, this hardly adds up to a vanguard sector of the new class.

To speak of the new class as a potent force in middle management or middle echelons of government is again to raise questions of demographic definitions of who is or who is not a member of the new class. Jeane Kirkpatrick is obviously correct to note that this is not simply a choice between Marxian and Paretan political standards of class, but more, whether a notion of new class is being smuggled in to represent a middle management and middle bureaucratic tyranny of power. However, to attribute to this new class, as Kirkpatrick does, a decline in national consensus or a collapse in progressive involvement in national politics raises a question of whether this new class urging noninvolvement is the same as the other new class urging the centrality of the political process, especially among the reforming sectors. If the new class is reduced to intellectuals who are symbolic rulers of the spoken and written word, then one is drawn to an obvious dilemma: why is this new class so thoroughly and profoundly divided on every central issue? Moreover what constitutes even its political unity?

America never rested on a single normative base. Therefore, to uphold a Platonic model against the new class is little else than a charade, a denial that American society has lacked a firm sort of intellectual consensus for nearly the entire length of its independent history. Aside from the fact that such consensus may not be a positive value, consensus generally is high only in crisis periods, when war threatens the social system or scandal threatens the legitimacy of the political regime. Hence, this old Federalist view of the new class ultimately reveals itself to be an attack on intellectuals as such; specifically, an attack on their liberalism. But once we translate phrases like rationalistic, moralistic, and reformist approaches into concrete attitudes, say attitudes toward Israeli treatment of the Palestine issue or aid to the apartheid government of South Africa, this sort of psychologizing of class analysis, in which class position determines sociopolitical orientation, becomes vague and largely lacking in serious predictive value. Kirkpatrick offers shrewd and penetrating remarks on the 1950s as a germinal period in the confrontation of grass-roots conservatism with elitist liberalism. Such historical distinctions are generally accurate and helpful. But why are they encumbered by new class theory as a new event? Cultural polarization is real. It takes place now in a highly bureaucratized context. But that bureaucracy, far from representing a new class, represents the largest growing segment of society as a whole. The bureaucratic segment of society is most clearly attuned to the preservation of the status quo, not to social innovation. Germany, the United States, the Soviet Union have each witnessed a huge growth in the bureaucracy, of which the intelligentsia might well be a special vanguard. But that bureaucracy has been a force for preservation and not transformation.

The effort by Everett Carll Ladd to redirect class analysis is both suggestive and imaginative: to correlate changes in social strata with new ideological tendencies as recorded by survey data. The main thrust of this work is to chart a "new liberalism" and a "new conservatism." Then Ladd works his way back to demonstrate the existence of a basic form of new class conflict. In this case, an upper middle class intelligentsia confronts a lower middle class–working class alliance with their bourgeois counterparts. The very necessity to force the language of class into a mold that might easier be dealt with in coalition formation and interest group terms than in class terms indicates a critical problem in this correlational analysis. Quite beyond this, any sort of cross tabulation of data indicates much lower rates of steady class differentiation than would make it feasible to speak of new fundamental forms of class conflict.

At a general level of values, differences between the college bred and others, between the new class and the old class, are perceptible. But when questions shift to homeowners versus apartment dwellers, black versus white, intervention versus isolation, then differences in the same data seem to melt. One could draw different conclusions from the same data: First, the retention of a high degree of system legitimation in America as a whole despite party disaffection; second, the failure of strong value differences to translate into equally clear policy distinctions; third, the discovery that changing educational requirements and economic participation create as much convergence as cleavage between administrative and managerial elites. As the intelligentsia moves into administrative roles and business partnerships, one might see the stratum itself change and create new fusions.

In a somewhat different context, in a study of methodological dilemmas in studying social development, I earlier noted a basic problem in research which shows high degrees of similarities in attitudinal data and equally high degrees of dissimilarities in structural variables. With the data presented on the new class, the data is reversed but the problem remains the same. The dilemma between attitude "waves" and structural "particles" remains fully intact.[9] There is a high degree of differentiation on questions of basic values between a new class intelligentsia and old class proletarians, but overarching structural similarities still require measurement. For example, the extent to which professions and occupations are meshing, the degree to which unionization (the basic blue-collar organizational form) is penetrating the academic world (the basic intellectual community) requires further study. Then there are foreign policy issues such as the Middle East conflict or attitudes toward intervention in formerly accepted enemy spheres of influence—items short of all-out combat—that might reveal very high crossover patterns between old and new classes. A failure to do this leads to a renewed emphasis on abstractions claiming magically to have observed working-class democratization. This is not to discount the critical importance of survey data, especially so imaginatively rendered and clustered by Professor Ladd; it is to caution strongly against broad-ranging inferences and extrapolations of new class versus old class struggles that prima facie evidence has failed to make evident.

The work of Seymour Martin Lipset on the intelligentsia in America travels along by now well-known turf. It is fascinating how the intellectual community can represent itself in such polarized expressions: one group seeing the academy as a bastion of left opposition to the society as a whole, another group seeing this same community of scholars as virtually impervious to demands for social reform and social justice. We can see that the subjective position of the professoriate does not necessarily satisfy critics that such self-positioning is little more than self-delusion. For the phrase "liberal" in our age has itself become an essential ideological battleground. For some, a majority at this point, liberalism does not signify left politics, but the dominant American value strain; whereas for survey researchers, liberalism is part of a statistical continuum very much part of the left. It is fascinating to note that university life, like American society generally, shows a pattern of greater liberal identification in higher class institutions, and less liberal sentiments among mass institutions. This explanation in terms of commitment to research (more liberal) versus commitment to teaching (less liberal) is similarly suggestive of new research tasks for social stratification, rather than new class formations as such.

When it comes to statements of class, the intellectuals in the academy can boast of little other than Mandarinism, that is, supply services vitally needed by various social collectivities and their elites. But this service role is exactly the source of denial that the intellectuals are a class, or even a vanguard stratum. Admittedly, supplying data or ideas to others is a vital chore, and has been since Platonic and Confucian eras in the West and East. But how does this help provide a definition of a new class? It is one thing to speak of knowledge-producing occupations, but quite another to transform such an amorphous cluster into a class either in itself or for itself. Some elite groups of intellectuals probably do hold a set of views that can be characterized as left-oriented, anticapitalist, and sympathetic to social change. But it is not simply the Schumpeterian premise of a bourgeois class sheltering its latent opponents which is at work, but the changing intellectual values of the business community, which has generated much intellectual support. This is well understood by Lipset and his colleagues. The legitimacy of the social system is not called into question by the intellectuals, and hence the basis of a protracted class conflict along intellectual-worker lines becomes doubtful. One must note that using roughly the same data, Ladd and Lipset, who have worked so closely together in the past, have yet managed to draw radically different conclusions about the American stratification hierarchy. This points to the porous nature of new class theory; it further suggests the weakness of class analysis extrapolated from other central elements in the stratification network.

Daniel Bell's desire to parcel out new social strata from new cultural attitudes is a major first step to get beyond the "muddle" of new class theory. Bell offers a meaningful corrective to the general idea that intellectuals are somehow uniformly more radical than the rest of society. Certainly, the British and Russian intelligentsia belies such a belief. More pointedly, when we move from the realm of statistical samples and averages to crucial political personages in contemporary intellectual life, we find that a good many, if not most, intellectuals are antitotalitarian and even anticommunist. True enough, writers and scholars like Silone, Camus, and Spender, remained liberal, even radical, but resisted the totalitarian temptation. How this differed from the classical posture of intellectuals becomes itself hard to fathom. Indeed, if we break out statistically tenured from untenured, senior from junior, professors, the level of radicalization shows a marked downward shift with increased seniority. The more interesting question is whether the new information technology, with its emphasis on data as opposed to theory, simply cancels out any sort of conventional left-right dichotomy.

Changes in the class structure of industrial and postindustrial societies have been duly and frequently noted: shifts to white-collar occupations; decline in blue-collar occupations; the veritable disappearance of the farming class as a major force in America. In such a situation, the potential for militant student or academic minorities to organize and protest expands. But why this is not simply part of interest group politics, why one needs a theory of the new class remains largely unexplained. One then gets into the now familiar arguments about meritocracy versus egalitarianism. Daniel Bell is on solid ground in raising doubts that the knowledge stratum has a sufficient community of interest to form a class—at least in any sense of class spelled out earlier. His careful delineation of the new men and women of knowledge represents a remarkable advance over Florian Znaniecki's formalistic typology of some forty years ago. Such distinctions are at the very root of new approaches to social stratification. Classification according to social strata, functional roles, professional estates, and institutional locations, assuredly represents a major step forward in the study of changing occupation and stratification networks in American society. It does this precisely by taking account of the new technology instead of imposing a new class.

Bell's position begins to dissolve as a solid package in the effort to save new class theory by calling the new class a "mentality" rather than a "class." For when a whole series of assumptions about individualism, traditionalism, and anti-institutionalism are brought into play, they only serve to confound issues in stratification theory. If the root and branch of the new class are not in the adversarial culture, but in the people who have "carried the logic of modern culture to its end," and this endpoint is a "culture in disarray," then any effort at juxtaposing new class liberals to old class conservatives simply ends in an intellectual nullity. Indeed, Bell's analysis quickly turns to the role of the state as that mechanism whose primary responsibility is controlling resources. To the degree that this allocational mechanism is termed a new class, which is part of state power, then new class theory may have some relevance. But the "deeper currents" are what remain to be discussed. It is highly suggestive to speak of the unraveling of character and social structure under capitalism during its bourgeois phase. But does this mean that a free market system can survive and endure as a capitalist system in a post bourgeois phase? Does it even make sense to speak of a capitalist society without a capitalist class? This is not intended as rhetorical or disputatious, because Bell's analysis compels such questions. One would hope that these questions form the next round in the scholarly discussion of the future of social class in a postindustrial world.

The argument advanced by Michael Harrington that late capitalism is a precursor to authoritarian society, and that the new class will only advance that trend, carries with it a further belief that socialism is the answer to such authoritarian developments. What is involved is a neat distinction between socialism and collectivism, between the processes of distribution on one side and those of repression on the other. But while Harrington properly notes that not all collectivisms are socialist—Brazil and Taiwan, for example—it is nonetheless the case that all socialist states thus far have been collectivist; and this he is less candid to state. Whatever the status of the new class either in theory or practice, it is hard to envision how the solution to this issue can help sustain a classical belief in socialism. I am not entirely sure how Harrington's listing of notables, or any pinpointing of elites, can lead to a solution of class issues. More likely, it will evoke mirth; especially with Harrington prominently placing his name on the agenda of world history as both "good" and "left." It is difficult to imagine that a decade from now this list of dignitaries will even be remembered in name, much less in deed. Further, any sense of elites must be mediated by nationality, region, profession, and a host of such considerations.

It is certainly true that the new classes are not primarily a new economic royalty, but is that really the issue? The possession of wealth and the acquisition of power have for long now been sharply differentiated in the United States. But because Harrington represents the last hurrah of utopian socialist orthodoxy, his analysis in the 1980s is burdened by precisely the notions of the 1960s, down to including the community-organizing projects, which are more pyrrhic than real. It is fair to say, as Harrington does, that the rhetoric of the new class is to utilize socialist language for antisocialist ends; but is this much different than the equally commonplace course of using antisocialist rhetoric for socialist ends? After the proper deferential remarks to the "right people" Harrington himself ends with a plea for this new class, which only a few pages earlier in his text was declared to be nonexistent. Why or how such a new class of intellectual bureaucrats necessarily "must" provide nonauthoritarian solutions to inevitable collectivisms in any future left-wing movement remains a mystery wrapped in a mythic united front.

The views of Andrew Hacker can all too easily (and improperly) be dismissed as iconoclastic. His position, its linguistic volte-face notwithstanding, provides an important contribution in showing how new classes are manufactured. Hacker's intriguing view is that the new class is composed not of a left or right cluster of ideologists, but of symbolists removed from actualities: petroleum executives who have never seen a drop of oil, army officers promoted on the basis of literary skills in preparing a dissertation rather than trained for combat duty. The new class is being paid to produce symbols, while middle management is left minding the store. Ideological persuasions and passions, arguments between left and right for possession of the soul of the new class, all of this is puffery to disguise a formalistic rationality. Not a new class, but a new search for a place in the occupational ladder becomes decisive. The new symbolists produce words and numbers rather than goods and services. The systematic incapacity of postindustrial society to absorb meaningful labor forms produces new ideologists rather than new classes. The new is directed toward outflanking technology, instead of solving unemployment. We now have misemployment. The new class, Hacker writes, are "bit players who don't even write their own lines."

The paper by Hacker offers a devastating set of truths that places the causal sequence between class and work in proper revisionist order. First comes the structure, then comes the person to fill the slot. It is not only a case of rationality in the symbolic sense, but rationalizing one's position in a present structure of incompetence and obsolescence. Although the rhetoric of Hacker is cast in Marxian terms, the faint glimmer of a fin de siècle anti-intellectualism hangs over this argument; more a harkening to Sorel and Mosca than to Marx or Weber. From an attack on the intellectual as symbolist, Hacker quickly moves to a critique of intellectual work as even remotely meaningful. It might well be that bravery of the soldier no less than the knavery of the intellectual goes up in the smoke of advanced technology. In consequence, early retirement will be the fate of members of the academic class, no less than the managerial class. But that one group is inferior to the latter remains a doubtful article of faith. What is more likely is that new meanings of work will be located in new moorings of information systems. The new technology may yet create a new class; but what to do with the older classes will not easily disappear as a social problem.

The Withering Away of Old Classes and the Expansion of New Theories

How did it come about that a stellar gathering of largely conservative analysts have chosen this moment in time and this aggregate variable to deal with the social environment? It is no secret that class analysis is not characteristic of most classical writings from the conservative persuasion. True enough, figures like Brooks Adams and Alexis de Tocqueville did employ class in a central way. However, for the most part, the rhetoric of conservatism has been a rebellion against the secularization of ideas which class analysis represents. Norms, values, laws, communities, even racial and ethnic groups, are more common denominators representative of conservative viewpoints. The earlier conservatives who employed class analysis were reflecting more an animus toward the turn of the century rapacious bourgeoisie who were culturally "barbarous" rather than any full blown effort at progressive social science analysis.

The history of twentieth-century conservatism might well be summed up as a strong identification with nation over and against the history of radicalism with its equally impassioned pleas on behalf of class. One would have thought that conservatives would rest content with the series of victories achieved by national interests over class interests, and the state over society. In World War I, Germany and France in particular were compelled to choose nation over class, and did so with immense and unambiguous gusto, at least until the end of the war was in sight. Every major settlement in the post–World War II phase was made on the basis of national boundaries rather than class affiliations. The Third World is a conceptual framework residing in the United Nations. The nations of that Third World are a practical reality. The Second World is a vague affiliation and disaffiliation of varieties of socialism, but the national boundaries between China and Russia, or between Albania and Yugoslavia are as ironclad as any legal edifice which exists in the capitalist sector. This only deepens the mystery; for instead of celebrating the soundness of its general vision on the significance of nationalism, of building upon the vision and wisdom of Hans Kohn and Hans Morgenthau, the new conservatives have embarked upon a search for the new class.

Interest-group theory, linked as it is with the pluralistic model of political science, has been rejected by new class theorists for the same reason it was rejected by old class theorists: it failed to make sense of the big picture. Pluralism assumed a sense of social harmony and political melioration increasingly difficult to locate "out there." Interest group analysis, tied as it is to liberalism, and supportive of the establishment, proved unable to generate enthusiasm and excitement. But in fact, it is interest group theory that still stubbornly prevails: whether in the form of Morgenthau's vision of national interest groups being the essence of foreign policy; Dahl's thesis about pluralistic elites engaged in countervailing networks of governance rather than conspiratorial theories of rule; or V. O. Key's notion of party politics and coalitional frameworks bargaining away power in exchange for social goods.[10]

The same anger felt in the past by old class theorists at the interest group vision of

America has now been transported to the new class theorists: psychologically, both groups share a quest for reductionistic certainty in place of a quest for truth. The need for order and security replaces older beliefs in community and risk taking. Exposés of the weaknesses in bourgeois democracy become the property of the new conservatives of the 1980s as it was the eminent domain of the new radicals of the 1960s. True enough, the present crop of conservative theorists are considerably brighter than their radical counterparts of an earlier generation. Still, there is a lingering suspicion raised by their works that the quest for certainty, the attack on pragmatics not because it is wrong, but because it fails to provide emotional satisfaction, underlines the theory and practice of authoritarian distempers—right and left. Class analysis thus becomes a chimera behind which to rage against the present moment in history, to insist that it cannot last because of its corruption, sloth, divisiveness, or giganticism. It might be the case that the center cannot hold, that the defenders of the present moment, with their pragmatic, positivist, pluralist biases will yield power with public mumblings and a private sigh of relief. The problem is then whether it will do so to a right that preserves rather than to a left that destroys. This effort to translate class shifts into effective political messages thus seems to be the main agenda of this search for a new class.

In the light of the seeming potency of classical conservative arguments it still remains somewhat puzzling to see the neoconservatives leap to arguments based on the new class. This incongruity would seem to be as much a function of biography as it is of history. Many neoconservatives share a common background in socialism as an ideology and in academic politics as a style. The movement from socialism to sociology never quite extinguished their intellectual commitment to varieties of marxisms that informed their present activities, whether in science or criticism.[11] What has taken place is a transvaluation of values, but not necessarily a corresponding maturation of social analysis. As a result, the impulse toward class analysis becomes a natural discursive style for explaining current events. Even if there is a fierce opposition to left-wing socialism or Soviet-styled totalitarianism, the residual common denominator would appear to have a deeper basis of common urgings than the temporary divisions in political opinions and persuasions.

If there is a general ideological impulse towards using a class model for thinking about social ailments, there is also a practical and quite specific target population: new groups of intellectuals, bureaucrats, professionals, or whatever the new class turns out to be, that simply would no longer accept the view that liberalism would or could remain the lingua franca of politics in America. This new class has thus taken the conventional rhetoric of the age and expropriated it for its special ends. Pluralism in politics, functionalism in sociology, positivism in philosophy, experimentalism in science, caution in bureaucracy; this entire concatenation of values hangs together to cause deep anguish in the hearts and minds of the new conservatives. Daniel Patrick Moynihan, writing a decade earlier, was first and perhaps best in setting the agenda for this 1980s assault on modernity from the standpoint of class analysis:

We need to break the Marxist spell that has immobilized so much twentieth century social thought and has now returned to our campus in a vulgarized but appallingly virulent form. . . . But most of all we need a sense that our mission is the maintenance of social stability as well as the facilitating of social change. The optimizing rationalism of the past has been dissolved. The times are tragic and will be surmounted only, I should think, by men capable of accepting that fact. Our politicians have been better about this than have our professors. [12]

The general tone as well as the specific target of this mission underlies a good deal of ideological opposition to new class analysis. Without getting into the niceties of this argument, the object of this analysis, or better the subject of this assault, is not some vague general new class, but a quite specific clustering on the left, presumably bent on the destruction of the American social order through centralization at home and capitulation overseas. As the campus threat of the 1960s diminished, as vulgar Marxists receded into other forms of vulgarity, it became apparent that the American civilization was still not enduring; that the tragic times are not a product of rampaging students, but of the very Washington politicians and established leaders dedicated to system maintenance. In this sense the new class is a new bogeyman, a handy scapegoat for our failures and frustrations—and more practically, the presumed cause of inflation and taxation.

The rage against modernity, a veritable revolt against modernity, helps to explain why a group of scholars, themselves largely representative of an interest group that might be called a subsection of the new class, have banded together. The attack on the new class calls forth a combination of populist resentment, appealing to the deepest and darkest fears of everyone from truck drivers to militarists, and an elitist attack on the accessibility of the good things in life to all: higher education, party influence, maximum leisure, and new sources of upward mobility. It is not only the huge numbers of outsiders and minorities that have penetrated the ranks of educators and bureaucrats, but their *trahison*, their betrayal of fundamental traditional values in the process. The new class, to the extent that it is real and under attack, is not simply an enlarged aristocracy of mind such as the Southern conservatives of the antebellum epoch; rather, it denies that mind must necessarily be aristocratic. The accessibility of education for the masses carries within itself claims that egalitarian premises are perfectly compatible with the present needs of American society. The problem is that this expanded sector still can claim the special benefits of society accruing formerly only to the educated few wherein lies the contradiction of the new class; it wants privileges and prestige on the basis of arguing for equality of ends.

The search for the new class, like that for the holy grail, is based on a monistic set of premises that simply will not hold up under investigation. New classes, strata, sectors, segments, are constantly being formed and reformed; but more pointedly, their power to influence events is limited by the extraordinary degree to which American society, and postindustrial societies generally, have become integrated along interest group lines and have consequently disintegrated along class lines. The nation, in such a scheme, is basically a residual, near passive category. It derives its momentum from times of crisis and threat, and mobilizes only when it must, not in response to cajolings or mobilizations or rallies or general strikes. Hence, the operational frameworks become extremely brittle, even fragmented.

The primary frameworks include interest group formations, which gather around ascriptive societal features, such as race, ethnicity, gender, or religion. These assume ever larger potencies in group life. Beyond that, at a secondary level are organizing frameworks like families, trade unions, or voluntary associations; these provide networks for action that permit ends to be closely meshed with means. Beyond the plethora of professional associations are temporary coalitions for broad political or economic goals, such as taxpayer rebellions or local agencies of control. As a result an individual can be a member of any number of organizations, such as the American Association of University Professors, the American Association for the Advancement of Science, the American Political Science Association, the International Studies Association, the American Association for Peace in the Middle East, the New Jersey Political Science Association, the Democratic Caucus, and ad infinitum. Levels of participation, intensity, and commitment will vary person by person, intellectual by intellectual, new class member by new class member. Until it can be reasonably shown that concrete actions uniformly flow from membership in a new class, and that membership supervenes all other membership categories, the search for a new class must remain an ambitious, but flawed analytical goal; a statistical cluster rather than a political cluster.

On the other hand, before advocates of the old class arise and dismiss new class theory, it might be appropriate to note that the potency of intellectuals and academics to establish policy and evaluative guidelines at all echelons is a very real phenomenon. Throughout the current period, academics have been trading gowns for towns at an accelerated pace. They have moved from the academic arena to the policy arena, and in the process discovered that without their presence in greasing the wheels of change or rationalizing the ideologies of such change, not much can take place. There simply is too little happening below. The labels used in this sort of compendium may be awkward, but the observations are often sound and worthy, even if the theoretical premises remain open to doubt.

Old class theorists have a more difficult time. They are left with old truths and new deceptions. They tend to be more skilled in ideological combat, in collapsing an adversarial position, but they lack a sensitivity to new events, and as a result their work tends to become stagnant and rhetorical; a movement from Marxism to dogmatism. The end of class as an organizing premise for advanced society is by no means restricted to new class theorists. The expansion of ascriptive factors and the corresponding disaggregation of class variables cut both ways; the scimitar is rougher on old class theorists. For they continue to act as if nothing really has happened to the West in the past one hundred years except the increasing decadence of world capitalism. But the utter failure of socialism to take up the slack and lift up libertarian hearts makes their observations and hatreds sterile. The near total inability to operate within a class analysis in understanding or predicting the varieties of socialisms around the world—from Yugoslavia to Cambodia—dooms old class theory more emphatically than paradigmatic weaknesses doom new class theory, which at least has not abandoned a libertarian goal.

This should in no way be interpreted as a plague on both old and new varieties of stratification analysis. Rather, it is a plea that the house of class itself should be reexamined and cleansed. What may be required is a new house altogether, built on stronger intellectual grounds. It is time to let class take its rightful place in the hall of intellectual history, and move on to the tasks of examining how American and other societies work, and beyond that, what the master concepts of this epoch are, so that we can begin to predict major dilemmas of the next era.

2. Holy Ghosts in Ethnic Closets

Recent attitudes and behavior of working-class Americans, sometimes called the "new ethnics," have deeply shocked and bewildered many acute commentators. The supposed return to militant self-identification has led one radical to claim that "the working-class white man is actually in revolt against taxes, joyless work, the double standard and short memories of professional politicians, hypocrisy and what is considered the debasement of the American dream."[1] The same display of muscular working-class behavior has led an equally radical critic to assert that

> the hard-hat labor unionists, and they are by no means limited to the building trades, have joined with the military elite and their political spokesmen. This suggests the great danger of the rise of a proto-fascist workers' movement in the United States. Whatever social and cultural forces may be invoked to explain this development, it is already manifesting itself in a variety of ways. The racist hard-hats from many unions are the potential street fighters of American fascism.[2]

From the foregoing statements it is difficult to surmise who is in greater need of depolarization: the working class or its intellectual saviors.

Who Is an Ethnic?

Whatever actual evidence we have is considerably more ubiquitous and nondescript than either projections for an ethnic-based fascism or for an ethnic-based new socialism. At the level of attitudes, we can make several generalizations. First, working-class ethnics for most part are neither more nor less prejudiced against the black community than the wealthier classes.[3] Second, classical aspirations of upward mobility and geographic relocation along class rather than ethnic lines still permeate working-class ambitions.[4] Third, traditional class allegiances to the party system remain essentially as fluid or as fixed as they have been for other classes.[5] Fourth, it has been questioned whether feelings of alienation and anomie have affected the working class any more than other social sectors. The working class in general continues to favor government welfare and income maintenance programs, at least those affecting them in particular.[6]

Even at this late date, there remains no clear definition of the phrase "working class"; no statement, even at a statistical level, of any special economic squeeze against the working class; and finally, there remains the highest doubt that economic problems specific to blue-collar workers or to white ethnics as such exist. Such problems seem universal, affecting blue-collar and white-collar people alike. In short, economic problems are endemic to the United States of America, and the ethnic aspects of these problems are simply expressions of such universal class dilemmas.[7]

Whether or not the general wisdom is accurate, the rise of a new literature on blue-collar ethnics does herald something novel in the social sciences. At the least,

earlier analyses based on the end of class interests, class ideologies, and class politics have receded to the point of either a memory or a whisper, only to be replaced
by a verbal celebration of ethnic interests, ethnic ideologies, and ethnic politics.
The only certainty is that such exaggerations too will pass.

Any attempt to define ethnicity raises at least three sociological problems: who is
an ethnic; how can ethnicity be distinguished from other social variables and character traits; and what can ethnicity predict—what are its behavioral consequences?
Before coming to terms with the current ideological and political uses of ethnicity, it
may be worthwhile to describe the ideological sources of the current celebration of
ethnicity. The general characterization of ethnicity in the social science literature
can be summarized under seven headings.

1. It is frequently claimed that ethnics are neither very rich nor very poor, nor
part either of the ruling class or of the underclass. Rather, they are often identified
either with the blue-collar working class or with the lower middle class.
2. The current literature presents highly selective idiosyncratic definitions of ethnicity. Jews and Japanese are often excluded by intellectual fiat from the ethnic
category on the basis of their middle- or upper-class position and on the basis of
their upward mobility through education; at other times, they are included as a
political category of an anti-WASP sort.
3. Ethnicity *within* lower-class groups or racial groups such as blacks seems to be
excluded from discussion. Thus, for example, distinctions and differences between East African blacks and Jamaican blacks are very rarely spoken of by those
defining or employing the term ethnicity.
4. There is a strong tendency to describe white ethnics in terms of those living in
the urban complex or the inner city in contrast to other whites living in suburban
or nonurban regions.
5. A distinction is often made between nativists and ethnics, that is, between
people who have Protestant and English-speaking backgrounds and those with
Catholic and non-English-speaking backgrounds, although in some cases (for instance, the Irish) ethnics may be identified solely on the basis of religion.
6. Ethnics are said to have in common a vocational orientation toward education,
in contrast to a liberal arts or humanities orientation. They tend to be non-
academic, anti-intellectual, and highly pragmatic. Interestingly, although blacks
are perhaps the best illustration of a vocationally oriented subculture, they are not
generally categorized as ethnics.
7. Ethnics are usually said to possess characteristics and attitudes identified with
those on the political right: strong patriotic fervor, religious fundamentalism, authoritarian family patterns, and so forth. Characterizations of social ethnicity and
political conservatism show such a strong correlation that one is led to conclude
that it is the combination of class and ethnic factors that uniquely accounts for
political attitudes.[8]

Determining who is an ethnic has more to do with sentiment than with science.
The concept defines a new, positive attitude toward those who fit the model. One
now hears "them" spoken of as middle class, lower middle class, or working class

in contrast to lower class. "They" are said to be part of a great new wave of populism: the struggle against opulence on the one hand and welfare on the other. As such, the concept of ethnicity claims a political middle ground. It does not celebrate a national consensus nor does it accept the concept of a class struggle. Its ideologists perceive of ethnics as a series of interest groups rather than a social class. There is an unstated kinship between classical liberalism and the ideology of ethnicity. Ethnic groups promote the theme of cultural pluralism and cultural difference more distinctly than they do specific forms of social change or social action,[9] which helps to explain why dedicated civil libertarians have moved their attentions and affections from the black underclass to the white ethnic class.[10]

One of the more customary ploys in refocusing attention away from blacks and toward ethnics is to point to quantitative parity. The new ethnics take note of the fact that there are nearly as many Americans of Italian and Irish extraction as there are of African extraction. The supreme difficulty in this sort of quantitative exercise is the absence of qualitative commonsense. The blacks have a unique and special history in America that provides them with a solidarity and a definition quite apart from other Americans; whereas the Italians and Irish, and other ethnic groupings as well, have a far weaker sense of delineation and definition. The blacks (and this they share uniquely with the Jews) represent a group apart; the new ethnics represent groups that would like the future payoffs, but not the historic penalties, of becoming a group apart.[11] Now it might well be the case that even blacks will be rent by sharpening class divisions to the point where racial commonalities dwindle. If this should be the case, then it is more likely that class factors rather than ethnic factors would become the beneficiary of such economic cleavages.[12] But thus far such a collapse of racial identification seems remote.

The Roots of Ethnicity

The rise of ethnicity as a separate factor reflects the existence in the United States of a crosscutting culture that reduces any sense of common identity among those who comprise the ninety million members of the total working class, of whom fewer than one-fourth are organized into unions. Observers have discussed the persistence of ethnic identity from this vantage point. Michael Parenti has observed that in a single weekend in New York separate dances for persons of Hungarian, Irish, Italian, German, and Polish extractions were advertised in the neighborhood newspapers and the foreign language press. Herbert Gans and Gerald Shuttles have discussed the persistence of a tightly knit network of relationships among Italians living in Boston and in Chicago. Occupationally, the $5,000 to $10,000 category embraces secretaries and assembly-line workers, senior clerks and cab drivers. Geographically, workers spread out over the South with its racially dominated politics, the Midwest where fear of communism is a serious sentiment, and the Northeast where problems of traffic congestion and state financial support for parochial schools excite political passions.[13]

Ethnicity refers then to a cluster of cultural factors that define the social profile of the person beyond or apart from the racial or class connections of that person. It defines the binding impact of linguistic origins, geographic backgrounds, cultural and culinary tastes, and religious homogeneity. In this sense, the concept of ethnicity is not only distinguished from class, but in a certain respect must be considered its operational counterpart. It provides the cultural and theological linkages that cut through class lines and form new sources of tension and definition of inclusionary-exclusionary relationships in an American society grown weary of class perspectives on social reality.

In part, the renewed emphasis upon ethnicity signifies the decline of the achievement orientation and the return to an ascriptive vision. Generational success can no longer be measured in terms of job performance or career satisfaction. Therefore, new definitions of group membership are sought in order to generate pride. These often take the form of a celebration of ethnic origins and a feeling that such origins somehow are more significant to group cohesion than is class or race.

The notion of ethnicity, like other barometers of disaffection from the nation-state, is indicative of problems in self-definition. Americans have long been known to have weak class identification. Most studies have shown that class identification is weak because class conflict is thought foreign to American society; nearly everyone claims to be a middle-class member.[14] Few see themselves at either end of the class spectrum. In fact, one analyst suggested that "it is not implausible to suggest that the 1980 census data will show that greater numbers of Americans will be living in $25,000-plus households than in poverty."[15] As a result, class as a source of status distinction is strong, but as a source of economic mobilization it is weak.[16] In a sense, the concept of ethnicity closely emulates the concept of race; for race, unlike class, is based upon ascription rather than achievement. However, ethnicity defines a community of peoples having language, religion, and race in common. For some, it further entails a commonality of tastes, what Novak has termed "gut issues."[17] For example, Poles and Italians share religious similarities, but they clearly do not share language backgrounds. The church has long recognized ethnicity on the basis of linguistic and national origin as an element in the universal ministerial claims of Catholicism.

Determining the behavioral consequences of ethnicity entails the difficulty of establishing whether there are common political demands or even common economic conditions that all national and linguistic minorities share. Aside from the fact that a bare majority of ethnics participate in Democratic party politics, there is little evidence that ethnics do in fact share common political goals. There seem to be greater gaps between first- and second-generation Irish and Poles than Irish and Poles of the same generation. Hence the actual power of ethnicity as an explanatory variable must be carefully evaluated and screened.

In large measure, the new ethnicity reflects rather than shapes the new politics. The present era represents a new kind of emphasis. The collapse of federalism, the strain on the American national system, and the consequent termination of the melting pot ideology have led to a situation where ethnicity in a sense fulfills the thirst for community—a modest-sized community in which the values of rural America as well as rural Europe could be simulated in the context of a postindustrial world, yet without the critique implied by the radical and youth movements.

Disillusionment with the American system and its inability to preserve a universal series of goals has led to a reemergence of community-centered parochial and particularistic doctrines. Indeed, the positive response of the American nation to the historic injustices heaped upon the black people has made it seem that ethnicity could achieve the same results by using a similar model of social protest.

There has been a notable shift of attitudes at the ideological level. What once appeared to be a minority problem with its attendant drives toward integration into the American mainstream has now become an ethnic problem with its attendant drives toward self-determination apart from the American mainstream. To be more precise, there has been an erosion of that mainstream. With the existence of twenty to thirty million first- and second-generation Italian-Americans, nine to ten million Spanish-speaking Americans, some thirteen million Irish-Americans (these often overlapping with forty-eight million Catholics), who in turn share a country with six million Jews and twenty-three million blacks, the notion of majority status for white Protestant America has been seriously eroded. The notion of the WASP serves to identify a dominant economic group but no longer a political or cultural group that is uniquely gifted or uniquely destined to rule. Thus, ethnicity has served to express a genuine plurality of interests, without necessarily effecting a revolution in lives or attitudes. Increasing at the same time is the desire to be different and to express a genuine plurality of interests, also without necessarily effecting a revolution in life-styles or attitudes. Equality increasingly becomes the right to be different and to express such differences in language, customs, and habits, rather than a shared position in the white Anglo-Saxon Protestant ethos that dominated the United States up to and through the end of World War II and the Cold War period.

Ethnicity is also an expression of the coming into being of new nations throughout the Third World: African nations, Asian nations, Latin American socialist states, Israel as a Jewish homeland, the reemergence of Irish nationalism. The international trend toward diversified power bases has had domestic repercussions on minority standing in the United States. The external reinforcement of internal minorities has changed the self-image of those internal minorities. The new ethnics are, in part at least, the old minorities in an era of postcolonialism, in an era of capitalism on the defensive, at least as a cultural ideal, if not as an economic reality. Thus, whether ethnicity takes revolutionary or reactionary forms internally, its rise to conceptual and ideological preeminence is clearly a function of the breakup of the old order in which Anglo-American dominance went uncontested.

Race, Religion, and Ethnicity

The concept of ethnicity is not only an attempt to simulate the strategy of the blacks for gaining equality through struggle, it also is patterned after the main tactic of the Jews for gaining equality through education. Whether such simulation or imitation will be successful depends on whether ethnicity is an overriding concept or simply a word covering differences of a profound sort between linguistic groups and religious groups. The fact of being Irish may be of binding value, but the fact of being Protestant Irish or Catholic Irish certainly would take precedence over the ethnic unity. Similarly, being a Ukrainian may be of binding value as long as Ukrainians are defined exclusively in nonreligious terms. For the Ukrainian Jews certainly do not participate in the same ethnic goals as other Ukrainians despite a shared geographic and linguistic background. Hence, the concept of ethnicity may explain little in the way of behavior unless it can be demonstrated that it forms the basis of social solidarity and political action and is not simply a residual category.

The new emphasis on ethnicity is distinguishable from the old emphasis on minority groups in the United States primarily because it represents a repudiation of the melting pot ideology or the singularity of American ideology as uniform. Majorities are now a function of coalitions and not uniformities. It is terribly difficult to have minority studies in a world where the major impulse is weak, nonexistent, or defined as another minority. Hence, the rise of ethnicity as a rallying point seems to be in inverse proportion to the decline of white Anglo-Saxon Protestantism as a consensus framework. The latter, too, has turned ethnic. Ethnicity has become a relative concept instead of a subordinate concept.

The call for ethnic power, modeled as it is upon the past decade of civil rights struggles, provides a perfect illustration of the limits of model construction. It involves a blurring of the special circumstances of blacks in the United States. It would not be entirely amiss to recall that the black presence in the United States was largely involuntary, whereas the ethnic minority presence was largely voluntary. Moreover, the black experience in America was linked to the plantation as a total institution and connected to blacks' degradation as a people; white immigration (ethnic immigration) involved participation in the building of America and particularly in the building of its industrial life. Thus, while models for ethnic separatism are premised on the black movement, at the same time they display little awareness of the different circumstances of black participation in American affairs throughout the last one hundred years.

A latent function of current appeals to a new ethnicity is directly related to the great white hope, to the theme of ethnics preventing blacks from becoming the major power bloc in urban America. As such, ethnicity becomes not just a response to present superordinate traits of the dominant American sectors. Ethnicity becomes a euphemism for the fight against crime in the streets and for the fight to maintain a white foothold in the major urban centers. Support for the claims of ethnicity must also be viewed as a reaction to the flight of huge sectors of the middle class to suburban America, thus leaving the white working-class ethnics to absorb the full impact of black militants and black organizations in the American cities.

The celebration of ethnicity is not so much a recognition of the special contribution of Europeans to America as it is the manufacturing of a new conservatism. Ethnicity gives expression to an organized group of white working-class Americans dedicated to the maintenance of their comparative class positions. As such, ethnicity becomes yet another hurdle for black Americans to jump in order to gain equity in this society. An overt struggle between whites and blacks is intellectually impalatable; hence ethnicity emerges to defuse racial tension by shifting the struggle to the loftier plane of downtrodden blacks and denigrated ethnics.

At an entirely different level the celebration of ethnicity has brought about strange new alliances or the potential for new coalitions. After years of struggle in support of black egalitarianism and in particular of black institutions of higher learning, Jews are now being criticized as never before by their black colleagues. Whatever the roots of black nationalism, its first contact is with the Jew as landlord, shopkeeper, and realtor. Whether the turn of the Jewish community to ethnicity will resolve their problems with blacks is difficult to ascertain. In fact, what is being jeopardized is the special philanthropic relationship that has existed throughout the twentieth century between the black and Jewish communities and that perhaps is epitomized by such established black leaders as the late Reverend Martin Luther King and such Jewish leaders as the late Rabbi Stephen Wise. But this was bound to end, as blacks established their own sources of political power and Jews discovered others, especially Israelis, in dire need.

The middle-class character of the alliance between blacks and Jews has long been understood. Its focus on education as the main source of upward mobility rules out the possibility of revolutionary coalition.[18] And as young blacks move more conscientiously toward success through education, and as an older generation of Jews moves with equal rapidity toward reformist goals, the historic alliance between these two peoples becomes seriously jeopardized as they come to compete for the same goals and essentially the same skills. The educational model proved efficacious for the postwar blacks, more so than has been anticipated. As a result, blacks turned toward a political participatory model, operationally defined by a direct challenge to, and search for, a share in government power. Be that as it may, declaration of support by the Jewish community, or its self-declared representatives, on behalf of the ethnic urban white working class, has little more than symbolic significance. Class barriers between peoples continue to be clearly more durable than the commonality of race.

Various organizations' efforts to sensitize and depolarize, although well-intentioned and intellectually sincere, start from a fundamentally erroneous premise; namely, that the key polarity is presently between black America and ethnic America. Such a formulation does permit various organizations, especially Jewish middle-class organizations, to perform their historic role of honest broker and friend at both courts. However, the likelihood is that, despite the differences between Poles and blacks in cities like Detroit or Gary, their problems arise from common sources—a lack of steady jobs, poor upgrading procedures, lack of meaningful retraining programs, and a breakdown of urban development—all of which could create the basis for class solidarity rather than ethnic separation along racial or religious lines. However, the uneven pattern of job dismissals, personal savings, and historical rivalries make such coalitions possible, but not necessary.

It can be understood why some organizational leaders of the Jewish community would seek rapprochement with ethnic groups. However, since white ethnics themselves often, implicitly at least, define the Jews as outside ethnicity and since the class formations that separate ethnic America from Jewish America continue unabated, the possibility of alliance seems remote and, when executed, tenuous. It may represent a tactical side bet in a specific community where Jewish-ethnic interaction is high, but little else. Again, the crosscutting characteristics of race, class, and ethnicity tend to make nonpolitical coalitions exceptionally difficult to maintain over any period of time.

The special tactical relationships between blacks, Jews, and ethnics is the crux of any potential working-class consensus in the United States. In terms of social stratification the United States has become a three-track nation. The blacks are identified as being either on the government payroll or on the government dole. The Jews are identified as being entrepreneurial kingpins in America. The ethnics are seen, or perceive themselves, as the true heirs of the working-class spirit.[19] In this sense, the growing tendency of communist parties throughout the world to accept, if not adopt outright, anti-Semitic postures is a very real response to its working-class and black constituencies, which see Jews very much as the exploiters rather than the exploited, and likewise see them as elements unwilling to participate in the American way of life by virtue of their alleged dual allegiance to Israel. In this sense, Soviet anti-Semitism is a convenient ideological pose for prearranged policies.

Even the executive director of the National Association for the Advancement of Colored People has recognized that blacks subconsciously apply a higher standard in the expectations of Jewish attitudes than any other group and hence become deeply disturbed when Jewish behavior is like that of other whites. Similarly it is evident that Jewish response to manifestations of black anti-Semitism is often in terms of the European holocaust rather than the American ghetto experience.

> There is a positive factor at work in Negro-Jewish relations—above and beyond the close and analytical scrutiny which both are accustomed to render to the issue of their relationship. This is the working partnership which has developed among professionals in their respective organizations and among officials and academicians, whose daily pursuits bring them into close and continual contact. The antennae of representatives in those categories are highly sensitive; they respond to warning signals with consultations; efforts to mediate tension spots; and attempts to achieve formulations which will accommodate at either end.[20]

This kind of "adaptive prophylaxis" offsets respective levels of apprehension, or irritation, in the different constituencies. Leading black and Jewish organizations have worked to reach agreement on equal employment opportunity: the troublesome issue of whether federally imposed guidelines and timetables would or should assume the aspect of preferential quotas. The type of radical and religious compromise that will be reached will clearly not only defuse the issue of employment for minorities but largely determine the ethnic posture.[21]

Black-Jewish competition has been defused, perhaps more among religious leaders than ordinary citizens. Black Christians and more liberal Jewish organizations have assumed leadership in overcoming the intense racial-religious dichotomies of the past decade. To this extent the tactic of accommodating a new ethnicity will lose its impulse. The more traditional alignments of blacks and Jews on a liberal axis will confront the white ethnic on a conservative axis. It might be argued that such competition is merely illustrative of false consciousness and that the real issue remains economic. Such a point of view automatically and mechanically assumes a primacy of the economic. This unwillingness to take seriously the competition of race, ethnicity, and religious clusters is in part responsible for the renaissance of ethnicity to begin with.

The Strategic Uses of Ethnicity

Ethnicity is at least as much a political tactic as a stratification network. The new ethnicity is a statement of relatively deprived sectors seeking economic relief through political appeals. Traditionally, such relief was found through the trade union movement. However, the growing bureaucratization of trade unions has signified a parallel decline of faith in class warfare. To seek relief from factory owners or managers has come to seem less efficient than appeals or, if necessary, threats leveled directly at the federal government. For example, during the 1973 energy crisis, the mass representatives of the teamster workers, over and above either trucking managers or union officials, demanded directly from the government wage benefits corresponding to the new price hikes. The political apparatus provided such fiscal compensation due to rises incurred from higher operating costs. Collective bargaining became transformed into state decision making. This process has only accelerated during the entire 1970s.

Direct bargaining processes between an outside group and the federal administration are not new. The essential tactic of black organizational life, certainly since the New Deal, and intensified after World War II, was precisely a direct negotiation with the political system, in this manner circumventing the economic subsystem. The efficacy of this newer political model is attested to by health and welfare legislation, civil rights rulings, Supreme Court decisions on educational opportunity, and the presidential commissions on minority rights. Negotiations between mass outsider groups and state officialdom achieved more results than the previous search for economic quality through class struggle. This shift from economic to political realms has come to be shared by ethnic representatives, by those who seek to obtain from the government for Americans of Polish, Italian, or Irish extraction similar rights to those achieved by the blacks' leadership.

The dilemma of this approach arises not so much in the model; indeed, to extract promises and seek restitution from federal agencies does seem more promising than to achieve wage benefits from industry. Rather, the dilemma resides one step further back in time: in the differential histories of the black people vis-à-vis the ethnic groups who seek to emulate this racial style within American politics. Even the most ardent defenders of the new ethnicity admit to substantial differences between race and ethnicity on this score.

The new ethnicity does *not* entail: (a) speaking a foreign language; (b) living in a subculture; (c) living in a "tight-knit" ethnic neighborhood; (d) belonging to fraternal organizations; (e) responding to "ethnic" appeals; (f) exalting one's own nationality of culture, narrowly construed. Neither does it entail a university education or the reading of writers on the new ethnicity. Rather, the new ethnicity entails: first, a growing sense of discomfort with the sense of identity one is supposed to have—universalist, "melted," "like everyone else"; then a growing appreciation for the potential wisdom of one's own gut reactions (especially on moral matters) and their historical roots; a growing self-confidence and social power; a sense of being discriminated against, condescended to, or carelessly misapprehended; a growing disaffection regarding those to whom one had always been taught to defer; and a sense of injustice regarding the response of liberal spokesmen to conflicts between various ethnic groups, especially between "legitimate" minorities and "illegitimate" ones. There is, in a word, an inner conflict between one's felt personal power and one's ascribed public power; a sense of outraged truth, justice, and equity.[22]

The new ethnicity is thus a strategic matter of discomfort, dissatisfaction, and disaffection. It is not a question of oppression and subjugation. As a result, it is hard to avoid the conclusion arrived at by Myrdal: that the new ethnicity is not a populist movement, but an elitist demand by a rootless third-generation intelligentsia.

In addition to a missing urge to reach the masses for whom they pretend to speak, the writers on historical identity rather systematically avoid the problem of poverty and all that is related to it. To this also belong the limited horizons, the lack of a rational perception of themselves and the nation, and a reluctance to organize with other groups having the same interests to press their demands through the means freely provided by a democratic America. It is poverty and all this, not the lack of historical identity, that holds American ethnics down. At the same time, it permits the formation of policies that run counter to the American dream of a free and democratic society that creates happiness for all its people, from wherever they come.

The "enemy" the ethnic intellectuals commonly put up as a target—i.e., those people in America who believe in the perfection of the melting pot—is the straw man. For several decades I have been closely following events in this country, and I have seldom met any fairly well-educated American who subscribed to the melting pot with the naivete customarily attributed to those who supposedly held that idea.

That America is a pluralistic society where people with different cultural backgrounds have to live together and mold a nation is an obvious fact. And that this creates problems and difficulties is also obvious. But America in general has shown great capacity to absorb cultural patterns from diverse sources.[23]

This set of demands made by "voluntary ethnics" may very well not be representative of the wishes or desires of Americans of Polish, Italian, Irish, or other European extractions. The newer ethnic consciousness often comes with a hidden agenda concerning the weaknesses in American values and American history not shared by these earlier dominant groups. In its most sophisticated form, the strategy of ethnicity is made in terms of the migration, absorption, and identification of new groups. In its celebrationist form it is said that America has been uniquely able to incorporate all new groups into its social life and political experience.[24] The current charge is that such integration and incorporation are largely chimeric in nature. The evidence for this lies in the understated culture costs of immigration, no less than in the class exploitation of ethnic groups.

Lost in the ethnic interstices of the American social structure, the larger question of class is never engaged, nor is even at issue. This kind of ethnic reductionism forces us to accept as predetermined what society defines as truth. Only through ethnicity can identity be securely achieved. The result is that ethnic questions which could, in fact, further our understanding of the relationship of individuals to social structures are always raised in a way that serves to reconcile us to a common heritage of miserable inequities. Instead of realizing that the lack of well-defined stratification structure, linked to a legitimated aristocratic tradition, led Americans to employ the language of ethnic pluralism in exchange for direct divisions by social class, we continue to ignore the real factors of class in our society.[25]

The same crosscutting problem exists in the current sophisticated expression of ethnicity no less than earlier forms. While blacks are included among the ethnics in the sophisticated version, the politics of ethnicity tend to counterpose their own needs over and above the racial requirements of blacks. Beyond that, the extent of the failure or success of cultural pluralism to modify the culture of monism of American industrialization is an empirical issue not easily decided in terms of the moral superiority of pluralism over monism.

Weighing the ethnic factor with respect to race, religion, and class remains a theoretical issue not only in terms of the identification that people have with ethnicity, but also in its galvanizing impact. Implicit in a great deal of literature on ethnicity is an automatic assumption that ethnicity and working-class membership are axiomatic, while the blacks are identified as lower class, or outside the system of the working class. Sociologists have often exaggerated the idea of a lower-class culture.[26] More to the point, there has been a profound misreading of the actual distribution of the blacks in American society—for if they have a distinctive culture, they nonetheless form an essential human core in the United States labor force, particularly in service industries, government work, and heavy-duty labor.[27] They represent between 15 and 16 percent of the labor force in contrast to 11 percent of the population as a whole. They are becoming unionized at a more rapid rate than their white ethnic colleagues.[28] They also are a crucial factor in assembly-line activities such as steel and auto manufacturing. What sets them apart is not that they are lower class while the white ethnics are working class, but that the bulk of black labor (because of its historical marginality and nontechnical characteristics) remains nonunionized, while a larger percentage of white ethnic labor (also deriving from historical sources such as immigrant syndicalist backgrounds and specialized craft forms of labor) is and has been for some time largely unionized. Accentuating the gap between lower-class black culture and working-class white ethnicity is a profoundly conservative reading of actualities—one that disguises the acute responsibilities of an American labor force sharply divided between one-fifth that is highly organized into trade unions in contrast to the four-fifths that are poorly organized, if organized at all.

This concept of ethnic organization as a precondition for class solidarity is a theme struck by a number of commentators. Richard Krickus has summed up this sentiment with particular force:

> With rising self-awareness, the appearance of vigorous leadership, and the evolution of organizational structures, many black communities can meet the minimum requirement necessary for coalitions. Because similar structures do not exist in most white ethnic communities, a coalition with blacks is not yet feasible. Until the white ethnics, through heightened group identity, generate new leaders and develop new organizational props, the precondition for coalition activities will not materialize in their communities.[29]

The author of these sentiments makes it clear that the purpose of such organizational pluralism is not simply to enhance cultural diversity but to achieve political clout.

> If the white ethnics are to cooperate with and work toward common goals with their nonwhite neighbors, they must acquire the means to articulate their demands in a more effective fashion. Through this process of articulation a clear view of their own self-interest will surface. This in turn is a precondition to their working together with other groups that share many problems in common with them.[30]

The assumption is often made that there is a lockstep arrangement between ethnic identification with black causes, followed by confrontation, which in turn will presumably create the basis for ethnic and racial harmony. The notion of collective self-interest or group self-interest, so important in the development of the black civil rights movement, thus becomes the strategic model for ethnic self-improvement. The dilemma exists nonetheless since it might well be that distinctions and differences between Catholics and Protestants, or for that matter, ethnic enclaves with Catholicism, will exert far more influence than the simple consensus required to make ethnicity a successful strategy and response to racial identity. Hence, mechanistic parallels have precious little worth.

Ultimate class identities can readily become blurred by the immediate ethnic pluralities. The rhetoric of racial and ethnic antagonism may be heightened rather than lessened by the assumption that separate organizations are now required for both black and ethnic groupings. To define tensions between ethnics and blacks without clearly demarcating the similarity of their class interest, which might also involve an identity of class hostilities, serves to exacerbate rather than eliminate tensions. Such a strategic error assumes that specialized groups and momentary tactical considerations must always prevail over long-run trends in the class composition of

American society. It is also to assume that Jews, for example, as ethnic types have a sameness that also makes them part of this solution based on ethnicity. It might just as easily be the case that Jews, too, reveal profound antagonism within their numbers based on considerations of class and religion. For example, there remains a considerable spread in the class and occupational ladder among Jews, and perhaps an even wider disparity among orthodox, reformed, conservative, reconstructionist, and other varieties of Jewish religious practice. Further, on the grounds of national and ethnic backgrounds, Jews of East European and Asian or Middle Eastern origins show wide disparities. Of course beyond that are the gulfs of a more political sort, between Zionists, non-Zionists, and even anti-Zionists. To perceive Jews as one unified phalanx thus credits them with far greater unity than they in fact possess. It also assumes that the world of Jews is necessarily forged exclusively by threat mechanisms from outside groups, and deprives them of the very organic integrity said to be an identifying hallmark of other ethnics.

The world of ethnicity is filled with strategies based upon models largely derived from other groups. The selective and subjective method of defining membership in an ethnic group permits the concept to be employed in any number of political contexts. It might well be that however flawed the concept of ethnicity may be at the theoretical level, it can nonetheless serve as a rallying cry for those groups who are dismayed and disturbed by the breakup of ethnic communities in American society. The Jews, in particular, are castigated for being the first to abandon the urban ship in favor of suburbia; but why ethnicity must, perforce, take an urban rather than a suburban form is rarely examined, much less, critically dealt with.

Within the political framework of American mass society, it might be that ethnicity functions as a conservative manifestation against the breakup of community. In substance, although clearly not in form, this is similar to left-wing radical and racial nationalist groups who likewise exhibit tendencies toward communal separateness, and racial and religious efforts at firm exclusionary-inclusionary relationships. The difference is that the new ethnicity seems to be more concerned with order than community.

Patterns of disaffiliation have found expression throughout all sectors of American society. Those who identify with the past, like those who trust only in the future, have similar problems with the present system of affluence; but quite clearly, they have posed different solutions. It is plain that forms of social change will be scarcely less painful in the United States than they have been elsewhere. Such forms involve coalitions and consolidations of a type that may, in the long run, lead to racial harmony and class unity. However, the more likely immediate outcome will be a forging of ethnic sensitivity that will tend to minimize and mitigate against such efforts at unification and national integration.

There are those who look forward to a great age of unification between lower-class blacks and working-class whites. However, unification, even on the basis of expediency and political coalition, still seems remote. Not only is the social system unable to provide much hope for such a coalition, but the structure of unionism on the one hand and racial separatism on the other conspire to frustrate race-class fusion.[31] That the concept of ethnicity has created one more large-scale strain in the two-hundred-year history of American society is a reflection of the growing intensity of separatist politics and industrialist economics. The ultimate fruit of a policy of racial supremacy has been the intensification of interest-group politics. Race and ethnicity have both threatened the survival of the social system and yet neither seems prepared to offer an option for all peoples living within the United States. In addition to class and race, ethnicity now must be seen as a measure of disintegration in the American sociopolitical system. Indeed, however weak this variable might be, the fact that it has left the sociology texts for the neighborhoods is indicative of the tragic ruptures in a nation unable to overcome the collapse of federalism at home and the shrinking of imperialism abroad.

Ethnicity is in substance a surrogate concept, an expression of disintegration and deterioration of the national economic system and national social priorities. Like other notions of a particularistic nature, its importance derives more from who are excluded than who are included. It is a response to a collective anomie, an era in which the halcyon days of confident national priorities and arrogant international goals have become remote. Representative government has turned unrepresentative. Large factory management and large factory unionism have joined forces to present the ordinary laborer with an unresponsive structure. The drive for economic nationalization has led to the multinational corporation and international cartelization of an accelerated rate. This conglomerate push has underscored the economic impotence of the ordinary person; and the tendency toward subsystemic approaches is reflected in the turn toward ethnicity.

The revival of ethnicity as a working-class value is paralleled by the middle-class return to race, sex, property, and other definitions for surmounting the vacuity and vapidity of postindustrial capitalist life. The weakness of the success ethic and the achievement orientation is revealed in middle-class youths' emphasis on rurality, fundamentalism, psychologism, and other forms of the gemeinschaft community of fate that presumably was left behind with the old world and its feudal relationships. Those groups identified with the blueing of America[32] are no more content with the progress of this nation than are those who are part of the greening of America.[33] That expressions of discontent should take different forms in different classes is certainly not without precedent, but what is surprising is the uniformity of the demand to get beyond the present malaise, the widespread resentment that makes clear that the old sociological consensus and the old political checks and balances are no longer effective mechanisms against disaffection of large portions of American society.

If ethnicity is a surrogate concept, it remains necessary to make plain what it is a surrogate for. Politically, it represents a demand for higher rewards for physical labor at the expense of mental labor; and culturally, it is a statement of the rights of groups to their distinctive life-styles. Beyond that, however, are the historic dimensions: the return to ethnicity, insofar as it is more than an intellectual pipedream, is also a return to community—a pristine era in American life, before the melting-pot ideology boiled out the impurities of the immigrant generation with a weird mixture of external pressure and internalized guilt.

The return to ethnicity is more than a restatement of ascribed values; it harkens back to a period in which family allegiances, patriarchal authority, foreign languages, and the meaning of work itself had a certain priority over career and monetary achievement. On this point there can be little question that the prime targets are the blacks, who have employed the welfare model in order to gain a measure of influence and even self-respect, and the Jews, especially those of the second and third generation, who have employed the educational model to create the basis for rapid upward mobility. The problem is that the new ethnics have a hard time thoroughly identifying with the former model, and an equally hard time gaining access through the latter model. Tragically enough, they lack a model of their own.

By extension, it might be claimed with justification that Jews have largely employed the concept of social class both to explain the American system and to live within its parameters.[34] The blacks have generally employed a concept of racial nationalism to explain why, despite the appearance of wealth, they have been kept out of the advantages of the class network. It is predictable, under the circumstances, that the rise of an ethnic consciousness would lead to a search for large-scale explanations as to why many people of Catholic faith, of Polish, Italian, Irish, and Ukrainian ancestry, and members of the working class seemed to be inexorably locked into the American system at its lower, but not lowest, points. Ethnicity provides a sense of homogeneity without attempting to impose either a class or racial analysis on a conservative set of ethnic workers.

Tendencies toward individualization and privatization have evolved into a loose counterculture *within* ethnic America: on one side are students, blacks, and chicanos; while on the other are Poles, Catholics, day laborers, and all the whites who have failed to melt into the system. Whether the response has been to lean to the left or right is less important than the impulse to resist encroachments on little people— the public turned ethnic with a missionary vengeance.The making of the new minorities points up the huge shift in the United States from a nation of factory workers to a nation of marginals, or at least service-oriented personnel. The response, in some measure, whether put in terms of racial politics or ethnic politics, is a demand for a populist politics of scale in which the possibility for the control of decision making and policy making would be restored to communities of responsibility. This impulse toward community is a possible source of new coalitional efforts, whether under the label of populism or welfarism, that might provide some hope for a reinvigorated politics. For the present ethnicity as a basic concern and a root concept should be neither dismissed nor celebrated.

Since a critical part of my argument is that ethnicity is an important, but nonetheless supplemental, variable in the analysis of American social structure and social stratification, it is entirely fitting to conclude this chapter with a brief explanation of ethnicity and its impact on American foreign policy. Too often, a phenomenon such as class, race, or ethnicity is dealt with exclusively as a domestic issue, hence reducing the frame of analysis to the most obvious and conventional. In point of fact, by examining how ethnicity functions in foreign policy, the researcher is better able to assess the relative no less than absolute worth of any given stratification variable. And I do believe that such an examination will bear out my contention that ethnicity is a strategic as much as a structural phenomenon, one whose measurable importance is subject to policy initiatives at least as often as to political reflexes.

The Politics of Ethnicity

The amount of research and theorizing that has gone forth concerning ethnicity in this recent period is of such a magnitude that one must wonder why so little has been done thus far on the impact of ethnic and national minority groups in the formation of United States foreign policy. Sometimes the most obvious aspects of an issue elude us precisely because of their prima facie character. In this instance, the overseas origins of most ethnics, presumably their continuing concern with events taking place in their country of origin, in large measure explain the importance of the subject at hand: the impact of ethnic groups on United States foreign policy.

Interestingly enough, the consensus among researchers seems to be that the actual amount of impact has been minimal; far less than one would predict given the large number of immigrant peoples involved in gross aggregate terms. A number of papers come perilously close to suggesting that the independent and dependent variables should be reversed: that United States foreign policy serves to stimulate ethnic sentiments as much, if not more, than the other way around. If for no other reason than to articulate these data in a systematic manner for the first time, one would have to say that discussions about ethnicity have been raised to a new level of coherence and intelligence.

Rather than burden these remarks by nit-picking, or suggesting specific methodological strategies or theoretical remedies that might strengthen (or for that matter weaken) ongoing research efforts, I would like to address myself to eleven points which might help to explain the rather weak and even confused impact that ethnic groups have had in forging United States foreign policy, or at least in conceptualizing foreign policy. Six of these points can be considered in the realm of political inquiries and five in the realm of sociological concerns. If the impact of ethnics has been somewhat ambiguous in congressional quarters, there can be no ambiguity about the relative absence of ethnic impact at the judicial and executive levels.

First, inter-ethnic group rivalries—an extremely important factor in ethnic politics—tend to minimize any interest-group impact by creating a cancellation or veto effect; that is, one ethnic group becomes hostile or remains indifferent to the needs of another. For example, the specific demands for national independence and autonomy by Lithuanians, Latvians, and Poles are rarely, if ever, coordinated with demands from Jewish circles seeking to emigrate from the Soviet Union. Although they may have a shared animosity toward the Soviet system, and although some leaders within these émigré groups have sought collaboration, at the same time they retain their own deep inherited animosities toward each other. Similarly, differences among religious subvariables within ethnic groups may mediate or vitiate the impact of ethnic politics. In considering the extent to which the structure of Catholic churches in certain industrial parts of the United States is divided along national lines—that is, Italian Catholics, Polish Catholics, Irish Catholics, and so on—one can see what a formidable obstacle it is to generate ethnic politics that would have sufficient impact to moderate, much less cancel, established United States foreign policy. In short, when the aggregate numbers are further refined, we have a problem of a critical mass, an absence of a hegemonic standpoint that would make ethnics speak with a united voice toward common ends.

A second aspect that vitiates ethnic group politics is the complex nature of struggles being waged overseas. The conflicts between Biafra and Nigeria had the earmarks of a fundamental schism: Biafra asserting the right of each nation to self-determination, confronting Nigeria with its claims of the necessity of national cohesion over and against separatist demands. There are no absolute rights or wrongs at this racially hegemonic level, just decisions and choices that American blacks had to confront and clearly did by choosing different sides of that struggle. Similarly, and more recently, the Angolan struggle pitted Soviet-backed Cuban armed forces against military groups supported by the United States and even South Africa. One might say that the blacks in America were caught between the devil and the deep blue sea: a choice between superpowers at one level, and white satellites sending in guerilla forces at quite another level—but such is the world of overseas struggles. To make ethnic solidarity, even black solidarity on Third World matters, obvious or prima facie is to miss the point of the complexity of real events. Another example of the American black dilemma is Haiti, where one finds a black republic, but also a dictatorial regime that is clearly anathema to most American black citizens. This would indicate that the racial variable, even at its most compelling levels, probably remains less compelling and less pronounced to its adherents than other variables such as class, religion, or nation.

Related to dissent is a third factor that contributes to the survival of ethnic politics, whatever the strengths or weaknesses of specific ethnic formations: the absence, or at times the breakdown, of national American goals. We are clearly at the end of an era based upon national celebration and perennially rising expectations. The reappearing ghost of Malthus haunts Marx and Keynes alike. Shortages, boycotts, resource shortfalls: all raise the specter of falling expectations. Whatever measure social researchers use, it is clear that a sense of cohesion has given way to a sense of separation. But such separation often is limited to survivalist goals of the ethnic groups within their adopted nation, without much possibility of expanding such goals to overseas policy-making contexts.

Fourth, it might be argued that a breakdown of a national consensus has led to a balkanization of values, a pluralism emerging accidentally as a secular nationalism rather than as a planned goal. In the nineteenth century, pluralism really meant the proliferation of a plethora of Protestant church groups. The pluralism of the early twentieth century meant the opening up of economic valves to new groups, including new levels of mass participation in social movements aimed to stimulate the voluntary improvement of American life. One might say that the emergence of ethnicity represents a third-stage rocket in the takeoff of pluralism: one that is based on the importance of secular national concerns in decision making at personal levels, that is, marriage partners, work establishments, and so on. Again, such a pluralism, while strengthening the American capacity to insure its own survival, even in the face of its current collective anomie, hardly adds up to a unified ethnic power bloc capable of influencing United States foreign policy.

A fifth problem concerns the strategy hidden behind the phrase "hyphenated peoples." How long, in spatial and temporal terms, is the hyphen between the terms "Greek-Americans," "Afro-Americans," and "Jewish-Americans"? Or, to be more specific, what weight does the ethnic factor prior to the hyphen assume in relation to the American after the hyphen? For the answers to this strategic question determine in large measure not only attitudes toward United States foreign policy but ultimately issues of allegiance to America in a time of absolute conflict. We need only remind ourselves how rapidly support for German-American Nazi bunds evaporated in 1940–41 once the United States entered World War II. Thus, even when ethnic groups in America receive strong overseas reinforcements and endorsements, when ethnicity is a clear obstacle to United States foreign policy, it collapses under the weight of national interest.

Sixth, we should also be aware that political decisions involve not just a strident defense of overseas interests of ethnic groups, but also some careful calculations of what America means to these groups. For example, just as Afro-American groups have to decide on the importance of African language, culture, and customs, vis-à-vis participation in American affairs, Jewish groups must strike a balance between allegiance to the United States and commitment to the national goals and destinies of Israel. For ethnic groups to run the risk of complete isolation from an American foreign policy context is to insure defeat and frustration; nonetheless, they are constantly faced with pressure that at the very least weakens, if not entirely cancels, their impact on forging United States foreign policy. Even when there is relative solidarity in the goal orientation of such ethnic groups, only a concomitant drive by the national policy can effectuate changes in a desired way. Thus we are faced with converting a problem of punctuation—the hyphen—into a problem of social science: How do groups organize their politics in order to maximize both American and ethnic ends? Without showing what is in it for America, ethnic pressure groups are foredoomed to failure.

Let us now turn to the sociological variables of the ethnic factor in United States foreign policy, which are equal in importance, if fewer in number, to problems posed by ethnic politics. They should at least be employed and categorized so that no misinterpretation of the limits of ethnicity is permitted to filter through the analytic grids being offered.

The seventh, sociological, factor in ethnic politics often involves generational solidarity. Common language, a shared culture, and a struggle to maintain and transmit that inheritance to subsequent generations born and reared within a strictly American context provide the basis for ethnic solidarity. The problem here is nearly insurmountable because it involves the maintenance of dual cultures within a political and economic system that most often rewards high participation in the American culture and maximum utilization of the English language. There are so many crosscurrents among the young that a considerable amount of ethnic political force is drained off in maintaining ethnic loyalties rather than extending such ethnicity to the policy-making arena. In this sense, the ethnic factor can be sharply contrasted to membership in the trade union movement. There is no ethnic personage comparable to George Meany, nothing in ethnic politics that witnesses one leader coughing and fifteen to eighteen million members sneezing. That, in a sense, is exactly what the ethnic factor lacks in sociological terms because the purpose of ethnicity is to distinguish not just the ethnic subculture from the larger culture, but the ethnic group from other ethnic groups. The search for distinction and distinctiveness serves to weaken, on sociological grounds, any overall political impact on international grounds.

The divisiveness of religion, an eighth factor in ethnicity, also serves to weaken dramatically any direct ethnic impact on political affairs. The needs of a religious grouping are by no means isomorphic with those of an ethnic grouping. The Catholic church, which often reveals clear lines of ethnic demarcation among Irish, Polish, Italian, and other ethnic forces, still registers a general orientation that overrides, to some extent at least, specific nationalities that the church represents. This is true to an even greater extent in the Greek community, where, for example, the power of the Greek Orthodox church served, and in many instances still serves, to dampen opposition to the Greek military junta, despite the obvious sentiments of the Greek-American community for democratic government in the old country. Similarly, in the Jewish world, the pluralization process has gone on unabated. Orthodox, conservative, reformed, and reconstructionist temples and synagogues compete with each other for membership loyalties and affections. They provide a particularistic flavor to Jewish-American life that limits a singular Jewish impact on United States foreign policy, even with respect to Israel. Thus, the crosscutting impact of religiosity and ethnicity must be viewed as a major deterrent to an organized expression of ethnic politics in America.

Ninth, there is a clear problem of organization involved in ethnic politics. In decades earlier in this century, and even in the mid-nineteenth century, ethnic groups were social rather than political in character. Their concerns were insurance policies, bank loans to the landsman, services to specialized charities that did not trust the larger culture, burial plots to insure cultural continuity as well as eternal salvation. All of these activities were worthwhile, but have been readily absorbed by the general culture in more recent years. Jewish fraternal organizations, for example, can no longer compete with New York Life or Metropolitan Life in terms of insurance policy benefits. Hence, they are faced with either going out of business or finding new causes. Given Roberto Michels' iron law of oligarchy,[35] we know that organizations do not voluntarily remove themselves from the world simply because they have no social function. What they do is find new functions. Chief among these are the causes of brethren less favored by fortune and fate, living in Europe, Asia, or the Third World. This clear differential permits the ethnic and fraternal societies and clubs to mobilize moral sentiments as well as muster economic support for these less fortunate ethnic groups. In other words, what we have, in part at least, is a change in function in order to guarantee organizational continuity, and not simply a response to daily tragedy and travail taking place in an overseas context.

The tenth factor affecting ethnic politics is the end of the achievement society and the recent emergence of the ascription society. As traditional forms of mobility based on immigration begin to shut down, new social distinctions emerge. Social mobility comes upon the hard fact that the engineer cannot aspire to anything more than his or her parental generation in economic terms. One might argue that the generational revolt of the 1960s was a backhanded recognition that going up on the occupational ladder of mobility no longer made sufficient sense to merit the effort. As a result, there has been a huge return to ascribed features of social life: to matters of race, sex, and religion, as well as to national origin. Ethnicity has become a telling differentiation among people who in a previous generation were marked only by competing on the way up the occupational ladder of success. Now that the ladder has been opened wide, the bases of differentiation must clearly shift. It becomes pointless to discuss America in terms of the theory of the melting pot, given the absence of achievement as the common denominator. The pot has already melted. The question becomes, in effect: What form of solidification remains to be tapped? This is an extremely important sociological aspect of the current ethnic revival, especially the search for ethnicity as a factor in the formation of interest-group politics at home rather than abroad.

Finally, a serious factor inhibiting the expansion of ethnic politics is the potency of the United States as a centrifugal force—even in the absence of older gemeinschaft forms of authority. We must never ignore either the factors that pushed people out of their native lands or the factors that pulled them to America. Ultimately, the passions for exercising a decisive influence in United States policy toward other nations are dampened by a foreknowledge that the country of origin was not so perfect when these people emigrated and is of dubious improvement years later. Often the literature recites animosity for ethnics who have forgotten their ancestral hunting grounds. Regrettably, these same critics have more precisely forgotten the reasons for the century of immigration between 1850 and 1950. If America did not always turn out to be a promised land, there was little doubt in the minds of the émigrés that they were moving from lands often without any promise of equity, justice, or freedom. Thus, the limited capacity for affecting foreign policy is not necessarily a sign of confusion or weakness, nor the absence of will or interest on the part of the ethnic peoples to shape relevant policy.

In the act of forging pluralistic doctrines of political behavior, ethnic groups have carried over the ideology of pluralism to the inner workings of their own organizational life. In the process of such democratization they have become linked with general American interests, norms, and values. As a consequence, ethnicity has probably contributed more to the forging of an American consensus than it has to the erosion of that consensus that seemingly characterizes other critical pivots such as class, race, and sex in the hierarchy of social stratification.

3. Environmental Options versus Economic Imperatives

Contrary to the customary view that the ecology movement is a radical response to dirt, filth, sex, and sin, it is my belief that environmentalism is basically a product of traditional social sentiments that lurk deep in the minds of many Americans—especially those who still harbor faith in rural ideas and troglodytic values. Indeed it is probable that these rural ideas are more firmly and fervently held by those who have never been on a farm and never encountered an honest-to-goodness farmer than by farmers themselves. The present mood was well summed up by the quasi hero of *Easy Rider*, who said to the Arizona farmer with a wife and nine children, "You have quite a stake here—quite a spread—you have everything together, man, and if I had it, I would stay here too." Environmentalism as an ideology is indicative of a fundamental reaction and response to problems posed by a new technological and urban environment.

It is an open secret that the ecology movement has at its core an essentially middle-class constituency. Environmental politics has rapidly become an electoral pressure group.[1] It emerged as a movement out of the efforts of the early sixties to "keep America beautiful" and before that, from nature-loving conservation organizations such as the Sierra Club that saw in the establishment of every factory, airport, or trailer court an affront to the American myth of rurality.[2] The middle classes changed from rural to urban styles between 1860 and 1920, and from 1920 to 1970 they increasingly moved to suburban styles; but the problem since then has been that the lines of communication and transportation have become overextended. Lacking adequate mass transportation networks to the major urban centers, city residents cannot move farther out. Thus the move is back toward center cities, but with the new twist of having them cleaned up for proper bourgeois reentry—and that means working-class relocation and industrial renovation.

So pronounced has been the trend of middle-class suburbia surrounding a working-class inner city that the emergence of the new trend of gentrification in the inner city is perhaps not yet as noticeable as it might otherwise be. The culprits in this urban drama are both the indolent factory owners and the indifferent factory workers, in short, the keys to the industrial system itself. Further, as the middle classes increasingly are linked to service-sector activities rather than productive-sector activities, the tempo and tide of the assault upon urban economic development increase. When the middle classes were pushed out of urban sectors by the polarized expressions of wealth and poverty that have come to characterize our major cities, the resentment over environmental pollution seemed to quicken. Now that the reverse migration has begun, this resentment has become a veritable cascade of ideological assault.

In the past we identified Ludditism with the machine breakers of proletarian origin, but today's enemies of industrial expansion are the middle sectors arguing for environmental purity. This bourgeois Ludditism, resting as it does on a wide network of ideologists, politicians, intellectuals, lawyers, and people occupying middle ranges of power, has thrown up the challenge to those who pollute; but thus far the challenge has taken a specifically middle-class turn: namely, consumerism.[3] And what one finds is a linkage between consumer needs, clean products, and a healthy environment. This very linkage to the consumer sector, however, reveals the essentially middle-class characteristics of the ecological movement.

The ecological movement is not only middle class in character; more, it is a religious drive toward hygiene and cleanliness in which every home becomes a Howard Johnson's replica; and in which cleanliness is not only next to godliness, but often indistinguishable from it. The religious variable and the class variable often overlap. This convergence of class and religion ought not to escape our attention. The working class is in large measure populated by ethnics and Roman Catholics. Therefore how a person lives intersects with what work that person performs to make the ecology movement something less than a universally regarded activity; in fact, for most people it scores far less in importance than unemployment in the factories and crime in the streets.

The ecology movement is also a suburban movement. The demand for cleanliness in the inner city lest the foul air waft its way into suburban American homes has become a central city concern. Of course the high cost of environmental reform often involves severe dislocation within the inner city and even the dismemberment of factory life in the inner city. The anomaly is that those who presumably suffer most from pollution are least involved in its reform, while those least directly affected are demanding changes in the nature of factory management and control.

The most pronounced aspect of the literature on the ecology movement is that assaults from left and right are equally plausible and made with equal ferocity. Consider the following passages from a recent paper by Lee Thayer, professor of communication and director of the Center for the Advanced Study of Communication at the University of Iowa, on the subject of "Man's Ecology, Ecology's Man."

> Our social policies move steadily in the direction of survival of the unfittest. We have confused freedom with self-indulgence. We have martyred the ill-formed, polarized mind. We have put mere existence before living to some end. We have enthroned tastelessness. We have mocked greatness and deified the put-on. We have made anything but short-sightedness appear "too philosophical." We have substituted the capacity to talk for the ability to say something worthwhile. We have made irresponsibility over into a state religion. We have outlawed success, made failure illegal. God is a piece of technology, like a light switch. Love is an illicit or novel orgasm. Mediocrity has become a socially-sanctioned and government-subsidized life's work. Perhaps most insidiously, our social ideologies and policies increasingly penalize competence and reward incompetence. We take from the capable and diligent student to give to the incapable or indif-

ferent student. Our popular moves lionize the inept, the ignorant, the incapable, the purposeless (e.g., "The Graduate"). Competence and purposefulness are the butt of jokes; they are fit themes only for farce and satire. Excellence is rapidly becoming unconstitutional. "Security" is our social-policy answer to incompetence, incapacity and indolence. We have made a tacit choice between being exploited by competence and being exploited by incompetence, and have chosen the latter. . . . Humanity will not expire in a noble fight against extinction by its natural environment. With but a whimper, humanity will simply grind to a halt, ignominiously, having ingeniously created and nurtured, in its man-made environment, the seeds of its ultimate irrelevance. That is the ecological crisis we must eventually face. The diminishing of man by his own hand is the greater cause, just as it is the surer end.[4]

It is quite obvious that the social ecology for Thayer is but a stepping-stone to biological eugenics. Of course the history of eugenic movements in the twentieth century, particularly in its pristine Nazi variety, should caution anyone on this course of action.

Now let us turn to the left-wing critic on the ecological crisis. Professor Barry Commoner of Washington University, a distinguished biologist, writes:

I believe that the system of science and technology, as practiced in the United States and in all other developed countries, is in many ways unsound and unfit as a guide to the nature of man and the world in which he lives. We live in nature; society operates in nature, and our ability to exist in the natural world depends on our knowledge of it. Science should provide that knowledge and technology guide our application of it. But we are failing in these aims. In New York harbor the sewage bacterial count has risen a hundredfold in the last decade, even though marked improvements in the extent of sewage treatment have been made. Apparently there is something wrong with the technology of sewage treatment, which after all was designed to get *rid* of bacteria. . . . Increasing environmental pollution is evidence that our technology is, in important ways, incompetent. Behind this incompetence is an intrinsic weakness in science.[5]

It is evident that Commoner believes the culprit to be science and not, as in the case of Thayer, society. But here a dilemma arises: If the problems are scientific in nature, should not the resolutions be scientific in nature? The social control that many ecologists insist upon seems to blunt, rather than enhance, scientific efforts to resolve the problem of environmental and atmospheric pollution.

I am not suggesting that there is no ecological problem or that the environment is as clean as it should be, or that any of the many studies conducted showing the damage from water, air, and soil pollution are in any way improperly diagnosed; rather, that the ideology that has come to be identified with this ecology movement has ignored the general context of economic development within which problems of pollution have been generated.

The ecology movement can be viewed as a coalition of economic conservatism and scientific narrowness that is often masked by radical slogans and by a secularized vision of the religious life. At every period economic progress reveals social chaos and negative consequences usually unforeseen. The more rapid the rate of change, the more monumental and even monstrous some of these developmental consequences appear to be. But if in fact the levels of pollution in the United States are much higher, so too are the comforts of living superior to anything known in the past. It seems fruitless to enter into a metaphysical debate over the nature of progress. For example, how does one measure the worth of automobile transportation to the urban-industrial complex in contrast to the polluted atmosphere created by poorly designed engines and high-lead fuels? While the answer may be theoretically ambiguous and open to discourse from the practical point of view, there are few people who would give up a single airport and fewer people still who would give up their family automobile for the sake of cleansing the atmosphere.

The fact that the ecology movement has spawned an enormous industry of scientific by-products—from clean detergents to clean gasoline to noncarcinogenic but calorie-free soft drinks—indicates that a kind of American entrepreneurial shrewdness has taken hold of the movement and has capitalized on its fears. We now have stock portfolios based exclusively on environmental values. Such trends are a consequence of a sophisticated awareness that any ecological improvement must take place within the framework of developmental ambitions and market expectations. The American public will accept stagnation but will not long endure lower standards of income, or a return to more primitive economic forms, in exchange for either a clean atmosphere or clean water. Cleanliness may be next to godliness, but it is far removed from industrialism and the expectations it engenders about progress and wealth.

The conflict between ecological and developmental modes is not simply a matter of ideology, but has been incorporated into the structure of legal relations affecting environmental pollution. Nearly every recent state statute claims, as does Missouri's, that its intent and purpose is "to maintain purity of the air resources of the state, to protect the health, general welfare and physical property of the people, maximum employment and full industrial development of the state." A similar statute in the state of Illinois claims that the pollution law requires the board governing such matters "to consider technical feasibility and economic reasonableness" in making its rules and recommendations.[6] The law commands both an ecological solution and an unimpeded, highly developmental economy. As a result, environmentalists claim that the laws as written have loopholes, while developmentalists claim that the laws enacted pave the way for court challenges of pollution control rules that they feel are too restrictive or severe.

State laws fostering economic development have long been on the books, but with the challenge of environmentalists, officials of the state political network could make rules so harsh that they would put many companies out of business. Some corporate lawyers have argued that the environmentalists must be curbed, since otherwise they could ultimately argue for confiscation of industrial property and thus create a bias for riot and rebellion. Even the federal government has taken an ambiguous tack on the relationship of ecology to economy. President Nixon in his water quality legislation spoke of "taking into account the practicability of compliance." This phrase did not occur in the legislation as originally drafted by the Environmental Protection Agency. But by the time the measure was sent to Congress for approval in 1971, this executive phrase had been inserted into the bill in three places. The modifying phrase indicates that the developmentalists were mustering considerable opposition to the environmentalists—and with great effect.

People in this country want and feel entitled to both development and a clean environment: they want to have their cake and eat it too. That has always been a seminal genius of the American conscience and it has uniformly been the source of frustration of most protest movements, whatever their class origins. What the ecologists condemn, the economists celebrate. It may have taken a year, but calorie-free soft drinks went back on the market, and without cyclamates. High-test gasoline is now lead free, and plans for an electric automobile, noiseless jets, and other major technological innovations have as their starting points the existing levels of technology, not a retreat from them.

It is hard to avoid sounding a celebrationist note on this matter; quite the contrary. The problem with developmental programming is its utter disregard of social needs in its linear pursuit of technological goals. As Frank M. Coffin points out:

> Aid has been administered as if there were only one objective—measurable economic gain in the foreseeable future. Projects were evaluated largely from a single-purposed point of view. Housing was financed in overcrowded areas. Saw mills were aided with no thought of the wisdom of cutting down the forest. Ports were exploited with no thought given to the ruin of nearby recreation areas. Steel mills were erected with no consideration given to the discharge of wastes or accumulation of slum areas. Fishing industries were promoted without asking whether overexploitation was being encouraged. Pesticides were made available for crops with no thought of their effect on insects, animals, birds, or humans. Highways were planned for the shortest route from here to there without considering what this would do to the pattern of life on the land in between. Dams were built to produce a certain power capacity on the strength of a cost-benefit analysis which left out the costs to fish in the river, human beings in the valley, communities in the area. . . . There is no study of the costs of a new fertilizer industry needed to desalinate the soil, of a massive medical program needed to combat new diseases, of a soil reclamation program, of relocating displaced fishermen, or of fighting widespread community problems. In short, we have all too often wrongfully assumed that we could do merely one thing, without affecting a multitude of other things.[7]

To avoid this kind of misplanning, we should examine the consequences of an ideology, especially when it so easily affects many diverse sectors which otherwise have very little in common with each other. Therefore, if the ecology movement is to have a positive payoff, it can no longer be perceived as a movement against the city or as a movement against technology, but rather as a protest against exaggeration, excess, and absurdities within urban living and a technological society.

The essential need is not for the restricted and restrained ecological movement, but rather a movement that once and for all recognizes the need for planning in American society as a global need. This means getting beyond the present consumerist stage, in which a box of low-enzyme soapsuds is equated with ecological reform. The historic animosity in America for planning, the irrational linkage of any attempt at the regulation of people with a communist conspiracy, or, at the very least, with an affront on the free enterprise system, has resulted in the special American problem of overdevelopment—which is often equated with the ecology crisis, but is rather a function of an economic system which still has not resolved the poles of wealth and poverty, overproduction and underconsumption, too little work for too many people.

The problems of American society are linked to issues of too much rather than too little, of allocational decisions rather than production norms. The issue of the quality of product, while real, is less significant by far than is the problem of the distribution of already available goods in the society. The emphasis among environmentalists on quality of life issues reads like a series of consumer reports; it indicates a failure of nerve on their part to face up to the heavy burdens of wealth in American society and the need to address the economic cleavages that still exist. In some measure, environmentalism as an ideology accounts for the sharpened struggle of races, ethnic minorities, and outsiders to participate in the "good life" already attained by middle classes now seeking to protect such privileges. These classes resist ecological deterioration without facing up to the socially exclusionary aspects of such environmental protection.

From a technical point of view, the distinct advantage of urging sound principles of planning and regulation is the restoration of confidence in the full development of American society, a development that accounts for an optimal ration of ecological and environmental conditions, but within the larger context of the quantity of available goods and not simply the quality of the environment. Unless it is possible to get beyond a piecemeal attack on problems of pollution, the environmental movement must fail in its noble goals, since solutions based on sentiment must yield to those based on economics. The demand for atmospheric and oceanic cleanliness must yield to more urgent demands for full employment and maximum production. The laissez-faire approach encourages an almost irreconcilable contradiction between costs and prices, quantity production and quality control. As Lewis M. Branscomb pointed out in a recent article:

> Market forces are not satisfactory to allocate these secondary costs. We can't sell air, we don't sell frequencies, and we shouldn't sell the citizen's right to peace and quiet. Only recently have we begun to face this problem of the allocation and regulation of the environment through public stewardship. The individual wants good transportation and clean environment. But when the benefit (clean air) only follows from everyone assuming the cost (a more expensive car), a collective market decision or a social decision is required. The individual's market behavior will not justify any manufacturer's effort to make a more expensive nonpolluting car. The chemical manufacturer is in the same boat. If he makes a unilateral effort

to take care of the problem of wastes in the public interest, he has no protection from his less civic-minded competition. Thus, uniform standards are required.[8]

The purpose of planning is both to assign a meaningful ordering of priorities and to develop a two-pronged attack on social inequality and ecological destruction. Obviously, the physical environment cannot be ignored or abused in the distant expectation of a resolution of social inequality. But just as certainly, the physical improvement of the quality of life will mean precious little if it assists only the precious few.

Times change and so too do attitudes. While for most of the 1960s, the environmental movement was primarily middle class in character, by the 1970s strong negative feelings about hazards and waste materials permeated working-class attitudes as well.[9] Unions, especially those in chemical and electrical fields became acutely conscious of environmental and ecological damage. Legal suits halting asbestos manufacturing reached widespread proportions, and working-class towns no less than middle-class enclaves became involved with the social aspects of the ecological movement.

But the class elements caught up with such working-class–middle-class fusions in the early 1980s. Declining employment opportunities resulting from job loss, plant closings, and a general deterioration of older industries once again compelled the fault line on ecological issues to be drawn in class terms. Uranium plants were welcomed back in Colorado. Low-level nuclear waste sites were established in South Carolina. Slaughterhouse facilities, which were hurried out of small towns in Illinois in the early 1970s, were welcomed back in the 1980s. Not only ecologically hazardous industries, but socially undesirable institutions such as prisons and mental health facilities became not only acceptable but sought after with tax abatements and land concessions.

What this indicates is that the ecological movement, emerging in an affluent period and advanced by an affluent economic sector, lost its momentum not through any loss of moral force but through a loss of economic momentum in the larger society. Indeed, if in the first phase of the ecological movement, the working classes were oblivious to working-class needs, and in the second phase, the working class, with some deep reservations, accepted environment as a broad social issue, in the third phase, middle sectors of the economy, joined by political elites at local and federal levels, have begun to appreciate the force of economic imperatives for those who work for a living.

Imperatives become contingencies over time. The necessity for environmental protection is mediated by the hope for economic improvement. It requires no tedious lessons in social theory to appreciate the fact that so much intellectual bombast about the need to protect environment became ideological ballast only two decades later. It is not that ecology as a movement in the 1980s has failed—not by any means. The economic situation simply preempted human attention. If there is a hierarchy of values, there is also a hierarchy of structures that undergirds and underwrites such values.

4. Unlimited Equality and Limited Growth

The Club of Rome's discourse on the limits to growth has been transformed into a free-for-all on the limits to equity. Simply put, analysis of technological limits to further progress has been supplanted by renewed examination of sociological limits to the egalitarian model that has governed Western society and law in this century.

Equity Demands

The limits to growth debate has led certain commentators to conclude, in no uncertain terms, that "without rather radical changes in the consumption patterns in the rich countries, any pious talk about a new world economic order is humbug."[1] The trouble is that the discussion of changes in consumption is often coupled with talk about the finite nature of physical and productive capabilities.[2] Onto this balance sheet must be placed increased demands for radical changes in the distribution of wealth. When all these elements are calculated, the result is a new equation: the more limited the levels of production, the less inhibited are demands for redistribution of present wealth.

The marshaling of data to support special interests is an old and venerable lobbying technique; the mobilization of such information by have-nots is less venerable but no less compelling. Since these outsider groups have the benefit of social science forces that, if anything, are more sophisticated than older lobbies in collating data for their clientele, the impact of their demands is even greater.[3] As long as the clamor for a greater share of the mythical pie occurs in a context of zero or limited growth, such demands on the larger society are potentially volatile. In the past American society met incremental demands by outsiders (that is, blacks, women, youth, ethnic groups, and the like) by expanding both productivity and consumption. Now such demands are accelerated, while productivity is curbed by class interests and consumption is curbed by environmental interests. Some examples of this phenomenon are in order.

There is a newfound struggle between the Snowbelt and the Sunbelt—between those states of the Midwest and Northeast that are experiencing population decline or stagnation with no corresponding decline in demands for services. These states are beginning to organize to retrieve some of the regions' federal tax money from the Sunbelt states of the South and West. Citing federal tax and spending policies that are shifting an enormous flow of wealth from the North to the South, former Governor Daniel Walker of Illinois said that the time is over for federal subsidies to southern and western states. He was joined by the former governor of Wisconsin, Patrick Lucey, in his call for "a common cause with the Northeast."[4]

The voices of small town and rural people also are being heard, asserting a demand for more equity. These groups constitute 31 percent of the nation's population, account for 44 percent of the poor and 60 percent of substandard housing, yet receive only 27 percent of federal outlays for welfare and poverty. Critics add that rural America contains 29 percent of the national labor force but receives only 17 percent of federal outlays for employment and manpower training programs. The list of complaints and demands for redress of grievances is unending but generally accurate.[5]

Another phenomenon has been the growth of special-interest centers, such as the Center for American Women and Politics. This center cites facts and figures indicating that women constitute more than 50 percent of the voting population and 40 percent of the U.S. labor force, but hold only 4 to 7 percent of all public offices. Few women serve in cabinet posts, only one woman has ever been appointed to the Supreme Court, and very few women have been governors or senators. These patterns of discrimination, the center claims, hold at the level of county, city, and state commissions as well.[6] Again, the demands and appeals of equity are perfectly justifiable on statistical grounds.

In short, there is an overriding pattern of accelerated demands for equity. Because demands for zero growth in industry and population are occurring at the same time, one must expect an intense struggle for the redistribution of the American pie. As the nation slows or stops its creation of a larger pie, concern inevitably shifts to the size of the slices.

Limits to Growth, or Limits to Equity?

Recommendations of the Club of Rome indicate how clearly the sociological message of the limits to equity underlies the technological rhetoric of the limits to growth. First, the club presents an image of a "fixed pie," which assumes nonrenewable or limited resources for further growth. As a result there are few mechanisms available to prevent the rich from growing richer or the poor from becoming poorer. Second, it assumes diminishing returns in the sense that new technology and additional capital investment necessary to extract marginal resources will vastly increase pollution and exhaust resources. Diminishing marginal returns require an effort toward zero growth to reestablish the "natural" balance. Third, the club assumes that the rapidity of change involves growth in the complexity of problems; hence, the resolution of conflicts is difficult, and the management of resources is impossible. The club recommends simplifying issues and centralizing decision making, even if that entails limiting democracy. Fourth, the club presents the notion of uncontrollable expansion in population, which presumably doubles every thirty years. This, too, will mean exhaustion of resources and an inability to cope with the distribution of goods and services. As in so many areas, the Club of Rome's views about population are analogous to stopping the action on a film; they do not argue for the alternative—redistribution of the gross world product. Fifth, the club strongly hints that progress may postpone the need for immediate drastic action, but the final collapse is inevitable. Furthermore, its arrival may be hastened and its effects made even more severe by our efforts to forestall it. Again, the demand is for restraint, even cutback. Sixth, income gaps are widening, rendering worldwide class war or political warfare imminent. Again, the club postulates freezing the current situation, and that means retaining the current inequities rather than redistributing or redividing wealth. The Club of Rome's recommendations range from maintaining the status quo, to planning controlled growth, to implementing harsh and even repressive measures to prevent worse actions in the future.

To date, the social science literature primarily concerns the debate over whether the energy crisis is a reality or a fabrication. Only recently has there been a realization that sociological issues emerge from genuine shortages and that ideological issues are at stake beyond those concerning inequity. The environmentalists have been slow to take into account the social and economic effects of the policies they support. An important social science conference recently constructed a list of two hundred areas in which the energy crisis affects society and that require research.[7] The conference attempted to exchange views with environmentalists, who, for the most part, saw little value in the social science itinerary and were skeptical of an economic view of the energy crisis. The environmentalists believed the solution would come from hard scientific data, that is, from the biological and natural sciences.

Other parties to the dispute, namely, special-interest groups demanding equity, have tended to discount the current energy crisis. Leon Keyserling[8] notes that oil shortages and high electricity costs have resulted from policies of economic scarcity—tight money and fantastically high and rising interest rates—which bear down especially hard on public utilities. Other groups fail to connect the limits to growth with the limits to equity and see the problem as temporary—as a result of current governmental and industrial policy making.

From a political viewpoint, what has taken place is a fragmentation of old coalitions at the mass as well as the intellectual level. Economic clusters, from factory workers to factory owners, see the environmental coalition as a veritable conspiracy to prevent the exercise of free enterprise, free markets, and free labor. The relative reluctance of blacks and other working-class minorities to participate in the environmental alarums is indicative of the intense difference in feelings. A body of folklore has grown up that blames environmentalists, Arabs, and oil companies for the higher costs of fuel to operate and maintain automobiles and to heat homes, costs that are more readily borne by environmental interest groups drawn from the middle class than by economically hard-pressed groups within the working class.

For the most part, environmental groups have labored long and hard to convince sectors of the population that environmentalism means new jobs, above all in poor neighborhoods, and that higher costs are relatively temporary and, even so, worthwhile. Beyond that, they argue that they are drawing attention to problems, such as oil and fuel shortages, so that solutions may be found to prevent the breakdown of the social system.

The recent discussion of the limits to growth and the limits to equity is original. Its contribution to the literature of stratification is to take far greater cognizance than in the past of the costs of equity programs as well as the benefits of growth programs. Equity becomes a goal rather than a reality, albeit one that in absolute terms is unreasonable.

The Development of Equity Concepts

However fervent the sociological debates of the 1950s about the tragedy of human inequality, in retrospect there was a virtual consensus that stratification was a permanent feature of all economies. Hence, the issue was not so much one of establishing egalitarian principles as it was of lessening the extremities of inequality.[9] The 1960s witnessed an almost unanimous repudiation of this position, arguing that social equality is both realizable and a practical necessity. Movements pleading for equity and justice employed an array of statistics showing the income and occupational lag of racial, sexual, and religious minorities and made veiled threats that equity might entail parity of wealth, goods, and services.[10]

The 1970s witnessed neither a return to an early imagery of inequality nor abandonment of the goal of perfect equality. What took place was a clarification between what is and what ought to be, between the facts of inequality and the goals of equality. There was a growing realization that equality is a costly process and, like growth itself, is subject to constant refinement. If equality can be guaranteed only by growth and growth can be secured only by differential rewards and specialized incentives (at least within market economies), then the problems of stratification and equality are dialectically mixed. This fact may contribute to the inability to forge new policies that anticipate new contingencies.

If there is a trend for the 1980s and beyond, it is clearly toward the universal acceptance of equality as a goal and the parallel delegitimation of inequality. Earlier principles of self-regulation and self-interest have clearly fallen on hard times. Even those who still maintain a fervent belief in individualism as a way of life admit the need for state regulation and social interests. The practical legal issues invariably concern how much regulation, how much supervision. In a most perceptive observation, Fred Hirsch has called attention to this particular dialectic:

> The principle of self-interest is incomplete as a social organizing device. It operates effectively only in tandem with some supporting social principle. While the need for modifications in laissez-faire in public policies has been increasingly accepted, the need for qualifications to self-interested behavior by individuals has been increasingly neglected. Yet correctives to laissez-faire increase rather than decrease reliance on some degree of social orientation and social responsibility in individual behavior. The attempt has been made to erect an increasingly explicit social organization without a supporting social morality. The result has been a structural strain on both the market mechanism and the political mechanism designed to regulate and supplement it. In this way, the foundations of the market system have been weakened, while its general behavioral norm of acting on the criterion of self-interest has won ever-widening acceptance.[11]

Thus we have a social system that generates strong contradictions without providing mechanisms for conflict resolution. In this context, making the stakes of success smaller, arguing that "small is beautiful," and urging limits to growth have the overriding effect of reducing tensions without necessarily altering structures. Let us see, then, how the new egalitarianism confronts the new conservatism.

Herbert Gans emphasizes that the black movement provided a new model for equity demands. He presents three major causes of the new egalitarianism originating from the black movement:

1. First, many Americans are now beginning to realize that the frontier, by which I mean the opportunity to strike out on one's own and perhaps to strike it rich, is closing down. 2. Second, as people have voiced more political demands, they have also become less patient with political inequality, particularly with their increasing powerlessness as bureaucracies or corporations continue to get bigger. 3. Third, the affluence of the post-World War II era has enabled many Americans to raise their incomes to a point where they are no longer occupied solely with making ends meet. As a result, new expectations have emerged, not only for a higher standard of living, but also for improvements in the quality of life and for greater power to control one's destiny.[12]

These three points are important, although primarily they are precipitating factors made possible by underlying structural changes. These precipitating factors require further elaboration, but before doing so we must examine the underlying changes that brought them about and gave them force.

The foremost structural change in twentieth-century U.S. society has been in the size, role, and legitimation of state power. The federal government has become a large, complex organization, and most of its growth has taken place in this century. Growth in size alone would not provide a structural basis for delegitimation of state power, but the changing role of the state and changing bases of legitimation have been important factors. Initially, the major responsibility of the federal government was to provide an environment for business activity. The first action taken in pursuit of this goal was the creation of a stable currency and a stable legal order to ensure the rights of exchange and contract. After establishing this basic framework, government also provided services and facilities, such as national roadways and waterways, for economic activities that individuals and firms could not provide for themselves. Government supports may include indirect subsidies, such as protective tariffs and import quotas, and direct subsidies, such as those for the railroads. This legal-rational government provides a predictable environment for the growth of business and capitalist activity. The government legitimated itself by presenting its activities as favorable to economic growth and industrial expansion. As Calvin Coolidge said, "The business of government is business." Even reform groups, such as the Progressives, sought to use the state to provide a better business atmosphere. Antitrust legislation was intended to check the evils of monopoly in relation to business activities.

During the Great Depression and the New Deal, the role of government began to change. In its new framework, it sought not only to improve business conditions but also to better the condition of the population as a whole. Government not only created a framework for business activity through which individuals could benefit by upward mobility but also attempted to intervene more directly in the economy to uplift entire groups. Its first actions were to recognize labor unions and pass favorable laws to their activities. Another indicator of this change was the growth of social welfare programs during and after the New Deal. By these actions, the government indicated that inequality did not result from individuals' failure to take advantage of opportunities but from social factors beyond their control. It began to legitimate itself not only by acting as a protector of the business community but also by assuming a responsibility for improving the status of all groups. The presentation of its goals in these terms further delegitimated existing inequalities by implying that they are not natural and hence are correctable.

Alice Rossi has shown that there is a movement from the lowest or "pluralist" level to the highest or "hybrid" level as equality demands increase. Most equality movements create rising expectations. In describing these patterns, Rossi shows their efforts not only upon women but also upon racial and ethnic minorities:

> 1. *Pluralist model*: This model anticipates a society in which marked racial, religious, and ethnic differences are retained and valued for their diversity, yielding a heterogeneous society in which it is hoped cultural strength is increased by the diverse strands making up the whole society. 2. *Assimilation model*: This model anticipates a society in which the minority groups are gradually absorbed into the mainstream by losing their distinguishing characteristics and acquiring the language, occupational skills, and lifestyle of the majority of the host culture. 3. *Hybrid model*: This model anticipates a society in which there is a change in both the ascendant group and the minority group—a "melting pot" hybrid requiring changes not only in blacks and Jews and women, but white male Protestants as well.[13]

Previously, equality movements were directed against individual firms, groups, or opposing classes in society. The best-documented example is the working-class union movement. Unions directed their activities against corporations or businesses by means of strikes, organizing campaigns, or product boycotts. Initially, unions feared and opposed government intervention in this conflict. Today women, blacks, and others seeking equality attempt to achieve their aims through the state more than through any other part of society. The women's movement is trying to achieve equality through legislation or judicial review by means of lobbying or electoral politics. Action against firms is not taken directly, as unions did, but through a third party, the government, by means of the courts or human rights commissions. When steps are taken directly against a firm, this is often done to provoke the state into action. Strains resulting in demands for equality are not created by the closing of opportunities but by the opening of the state as a new avenue for such demands.

S. M. Miller and Pamela Roby have stated that power is an important aspect of the drive for equality:

> In the "welfare state," in particular, many important elements of the command over resources become available as public services. The distribution and quality

of these public services affect the absolute and relative well-being of all individuals. Considerable inconsistency *may* exist between the incomes and basic services of persons or groups. While the two are fairly closely linked in the United States, poor basic services are *not* associated with low income in Sweden. A larger issue is also involved. As Marshall has argued, the welfare state approach breaks the links between the market and well-being.[14]

As the state attempts to legitimate itself as a service organization, political power enters into the equation as a factor in inequality.

Associated with the rise of state power and questions of equality are the expansion of citizenship to lower classes and the participation in the state of more groups. Initially, it was believed that this expansion of citizenship would introduce a new era of political democracy and consensus, an "end of ideology." Paradoxically, while a nonideological period may have prevailed for a limited time, these developments laid the foundation for a new ideological period.[15]

The increased role of the state as mediator of class claims, rather than the simple legal expression of the dominance of one class over others, converted the state from a superstructural reflex to an initiator. The class state yields to the service state, and the delegitimation of inequality in this way sets the stage for greater political struggle as the arena shifts from the factory or the workshop to legislatures and the community. In short, if economic exploitation remains the source of inequality, the democratic state must become the source of relief from such conditions.

Economic Dysfunctions and the Social Cost of Inequality

It has been a central premise of sociology and economics that inequality is a functional necessity for any society. Even Marxism states that classes are necessary for capitalist development and hence are a precondition for the development of socialism. In sociology, the basis of this argument has been presented by Kingsley Davis and Wilbert Moore: "The main functional necessity explaining the universal presence of stratification is precisely the requirement faced by any society of placing and motivating individuals in the social structure. As a functioning mechanism, a society must somehow distribute its members in social positions and induce them to perform the duties of these positions."[16] A similar view is found in neoclassical economics. Within a market system, inequalities in rewards are necessary. Without them, people would lack motivation to incur the costs involved in leaving present positions and taking on socially important positions that are unoccupied. It is thought that unequal rewards motivate economic growth by spurring investment and entrepreneurship and hence a better society. Neoclassical economists cite the cost of equality in terms of declining efficiency. Attempts to achieve more equality, the neoclassicists believe, result in a less efficient economy due to a decline in motivation, a drop in investment funds, and the rise of costly bureaucracies to ensure equality.

Most arguments against inequality have generally relied upon assumptions about the moral or ethical value of equality or, in its Marxist form, the iron laws of history (the Marxist argument also carried with it a moral vision). Most of these arguments cite the impoverishment or deprived conditions of the lower classes and speak of the right to happiness or to a better life. Christopher Jencks exemplifies this type of argument: "Why, after all, should we be so concerned about economic equality? We begin with the premise that every individual's happiness is of equal value. From this it is a short step to Bentham's dictum that society should be organized so as to provide the greatest good for the greatest number." [17]

Another argument against inequality, one that avoids the pitfalls of moral dictums or assumptions about historical laws, is to point out that while inequality *may* be functional, it is also dysfunctional. There are disadvantages not only for those who hold unequal positions but also for society as a whole. Most arguments concerning inequality, whether pro or con, fail to cite its possible costs in the social as well as the economic realm. Despite many arguments to the contrary, inequality may lead to malintegration in a society. As John Goldthorpe points out, "The existence of inequality, of an extreme, unyielding, and largely illegitimate kind, does mitigate seriously against any stable normative regulation in the economic sphere—because it mitigates against the possibility of effective value consensus on the distribution of economic and other resources and rewards." [18]

The malintegration that is associated with inequality is not simple Marxist class conflict; it is far more complex. There is no clearer example of this complexity than the relationship between inequality and crime. Although the literature does not agree about what is meant by class or status, a standard proposition in criminology is that certain types of crime, particularly violent kinds, are negatively correlated with class or status. The lower the class or status, the higher is the incidence of violent crime: "A 1960 Milwaukee study indicated that the slum or inner core area of the city, comprising 13.7 percent of the population, had 38 percent of the arrests for burglary, had 69 percent of the aggravated assaults, 47 percent of other assaults, 60 percent of the murders, 72 percent of the arrests for commercial vice, 22 percent of the drunkenness, and 67 percent of the narcotics arrests." [19] In a similar vein, large cities have a higher rate of violent crime than small ones. Large cities are more likely to contain concentrations of poor and minority groups. These higher crime rates are an indicator of the relationship between crime and inequality.

Differences between small and large cities cannot be explained simply by greater objective inequality in large urban areas. Goldthorpe spoke of illegitimate inequality, which raises the concept of relative deprivation. As Jackson Toby states: "Analyzing the relationship between objective deprivation and subjective expectation is more complicated than was at first thought. Poverty cannot cause crime but resentment of poverty is more likely to develop among the relatively deprived of a rich society than among the objectively deprived in a poor society." [20] Relative deprivation is more likely to form in large heterogeneous cities than in small homogeneous ones. In large cities, interaction among groups is more likely to take place, allowing for the formation of reference groups and the delegitimation of one's own lower status.

From 1960 to 1973, numerous social changes and social movements were taking place in the United States. The two most important were the black movement and the War on Poverty. Both questioned the social order and gave rise to "new minorities" with rising expectations and new equity demands, who in general did not accept existing inequalities. The easiest way to measure the cost of crime resulting from this delegitimated inequality (and not from poverty alone) is to calculate the cash value of damage done by crime and expenditures by government in combating or correcting the damage.[21] These costs and their relationship to inequality become clearer when the businesses affected are controlled for location. By establishing the categories of ghetto, nonghetto (inner city), and suburbs, one can almost create a scale for levels of inequality. The lowest level is the ghetto, where economic inequality and racial discrimination exist. Next are nonghetto areas, with economic inequality but a generally white population. The last group, the suburbs, does not necessarily consist of W. Lloyd Warner's upper-upper class, but it is the most prosperous of the three. As one moves up this scale, crime decreases in most categories. This supports our proposition about the relationship between inequality and instances of crime.[22] As inequality becomes delegitimated, its cost increases. Other costs of crime are federal outlays for crime reduction ($2,839 million in 1975) and state and local police expenditures ($6,535 million in 1973).[23]

These indicators only take into account the direct monetary costs of crime. Two other costs should be considered. The first are opportunity costs incurred in the expenditure of funds as a result of crime. Government funds are limited, and monies spent on criminal justice programs and police activities cannot be used for other programs. The second cost is noneconomic, namely, the social disruption resulting from crime. Emile Durkheim may have been correct—some levels of crime are functional by virtue of their shock value and reinforcement of social norms—but present crime is far beyond this level. The existing high crime rate inflicts costs in terms of fear among noncriminal members of society. These costs are hard to quantify, but included are such manifestations as the fear of leaving home after dark, crowding in the middle cars of subway trains, and lost sleep from the strange noises outside a window at night.

Another dysfunctional effect of inequality is felt in economic production. The disadvantages of inequality in the workplace have been obvious since Marx's writings on alienation and class conflict. Although no class consciousness or large-scale class conflict as described by Marx exists in the United States, inequalities still impose costs upon the production of goods and services. Workplace inequalities are not defined only by income but in other terms. Ely Chinoy's study of automobile workers[24] demonstrated that workers rank their positions by income plus type of work done, physical demands, health and safety conditions, and authority relations. There are numerous sources of inequality in such multidimensional work. Since these inequalities were pointed out by the workers, their legitimacy is in question.

The consequences of workplace inequality are obvious. One easy means of measuring the cost is work hours lost due to labor disputes.[25] Work stoppages for various causes, ranging from general wage dissatisfaction to plant administration, indicate the degree to which differential rewards lower economic output, quite apart from the "ethical" question of differential payment for different kinds of work. Other costs of inequality in work are harder to measure. Examples are the inefficiency and

poor quality of work resulting from discontent among producers. An indirect measure of these costs is time lost from the job due to illness. Of importance here is the
difference between *disease* and *illness*. Charles Kadushin notes that "disease is an
abnormal structure or function; illness is the feeling of discomfort which arises out
of disease." [26] Kadushin shows that there is little or no association between social
class and *disease*, yet there is a high correlation between social class and *illness*.
What is important is the relationship between income and time loss for illness. [27] A
plausible hypothesis to explain the greater absenteeism among lower as opposed to
other income groups is discontent with work and its inequalities. There are also
other costs, such as sabotage on assembly lines, general apathy regarding the
quality of products manufactured, and a breakdown of creative performance as a
result of routinization.

There are few empirical data on the effect of no-growth policies upon employment or on the effect of increased employment upon the environment. Environmentalists and those supporting increased employment live in different ideological realms
and have little contact with one another. Environmental groups view problems in
terms of biology and physics and have little insight into the social consequences of
their policies. Proponents of full employment and increased equality believe the
world has infinite resources. Many economists concerned about the environment
stress the negative effect of growth upon "spaceship earth" and show little interest
in the consequences of no-growth upon employment patterns and equity demands. [28]
In contrast, Bayard Rustin thinks we are facing a historic national crisis.

> There is mass unemployment, a sizeable and expanding black underclass com-
> prising persons whose lives were scarcely touched by the civil-rights revolution,
> and a declining standard of living for millions of working people. Yet many of
> those who profess concern about unemployment and poverty also actively sup-
> port the concept of limiting economic growth in order to protect the environment.
> That notion, if translated into conscious policy, would measurably worsen the
> nation's—and the world's—economic plight. And its promoters would bear the
> responsibility for having shattered the hopes of those who have never had a nor-
> mal role in the world economy, among whom the darker-skinned people of the
> world rank most prominently. [29]

Clearly, the line between problems of production and consumption is thin indeed.
Perhaps it would be more fruitful to conceptualize the issue as one of redistributing
the present products and consumer patterns.

Environmental protection policy has a direct and an indirect effect upon employment and equality: the direct effect is felt when an operation or industrial plant is
closed due to violation of pollution laws. This results in lowered employment and
economic depression in the surrounding area. A major example is the Environmental Protection Agency's closing of an ore-processing plant that was depositing
chemical waste into Lake Superior. The cost of correcting the problem was beyond
the profits of the operation, and the local economy suffered severely. Older industrial cities bear the brunt of environmental laws. They generally have the worst air-

and water-pollution problems, and hence the laws are enforced stringently. These cities have also become centers for low-income and minority populations. Industries in the area either must add expensive pollution control devices or move to communities where incremental increases in emissions have less effect upon air and water quality. The result is limited increases or actual decreases in employment in the older city. It should be noted that jobs lost are generally unskilled or semiskilled entry-level positions.

The indirect effect of environmental policy has been manifested through structural changes in the U.S. economy. The shift, as outlined by Daniel Bell,[30] has been from energy-intensive productive industries to knowledge-intensive service industries. No-growth in manufacturing, in contrast to accelerated growth in service industries, is a social fact. As Bell states, this process is already going on, and environmental laws will only hasten it. There are several implications for employment and equality. First, high-level positions in service industries require considerable skill and knowledge; entry into them requires certified education and professional standing. The result will be a small professional elite and a vast class of unskilled workers with little opportunity for advancement. Second, concerning the wage structure and productivity of service industries, that sector suffers from low productivity and lacks the means for increasing it. Since wage gains will not be connected to productivity gains, they will be harder to obtain. This is particularly true when the employer is the government and the wages are drawn from taxes. Third, there will be a relative decline of labor unions, which historically have been a force working for equality. With the decline of the industrial sector, where they are strongest, the relative power of unions will diminish.

Other Characteristics and Consequences of Inequality

Thus far we have been discussing costs of inequality in a limited circumstance, that is, when existing inequalities are perceived as illegitimate. Both crime and work conflict are costs inflicted by actors who perceive their inequality as being unnatural or wrongly and injustly imposed upon them. There are other costs that do not require either the delegitimation of inequality or the conscious action of those in unequal conditions. These costs center around the less than optimal distribution and use of resources for which there is an inelastic demand. They are particularly important in a world of limited resources and economic growth, and they are highest for a market economy. Mark Kelman[31] presents this case in terms of medical services, the demand for which is virtually inelastic but the supply of which is limited. Consequently, physicians and hospitals are located in high-income areas, and low-income areas suffer from a lack of services. A direct cost to society is the general rise in the price of all medical services due to this pattern. In high-income areas, large sums of money are spent upon nonessential services, such as cosmetic surgery. This drain of resources and personnel raises the cost of essential and life-sustaining services for all users.

An equitable policy for the distribution of funds for medical care would limit demand for nonessential services and increase the supply of resources and personnel for other important uses. Growth alone would not reduce medical costs, but might increase them. Given a product with inelastic demand, such as medical care, economic growth without redistribution of purchasing power would only increase the demand for medical services across all groups. There would be greater demand for nonessential services, and resources would be drained off from essential services. This may be the reason that the United States has the most used (some claim the most overused) medical system and yet the most costly and inefficient delivery system. Kelman's model of the social costs of inequality can also be applied to other limited resources with inelastic demand. A few examples are energy, food, and certain environmental amenities. All are in limited supply, yet high-income groups demand and can command a greater share of them: heated pools, higher quality protein, and quiet neighborhoods. The limited supplies mean higher costs across the board. For the most part, questions related to equity have been considered within a domestic context. Increasingly, a group of economists and sociologists, among whom Gunnar Myrdal is typical, have argued that a more appropriate framework for the discussion of these issues is the international arena and that problems of redistribution of wealth can only be understood within that larger scope.

> The blunt truth is that without rather radical changes in the consumption patterns in the rich countries, any pious talk about new world economic order is humbug. It is legitimate for an economist to analyze the rational inferences in regard to economic policy based on what is in people's true interests and their acclaimed ideals. But if, instead, we raise the problems of what is actually going to happen, it is difficult to believe that rational policy conclusions will be followed in the practical policies of the developed countries. In the tradition of Western civilization we are quite well trained to combine base behavior with high ideals.[32]

Leaving aside the feasibility of Myrdal's solution based on "rational national planning," which has as its end product a "curtailment of consumption," the fact that such desperate theorizing is taking place highlights the reemergence of Malthusian doctrine.

The current stratification of nations is being questioned. This means not only the creation of a Fourth World, a *lumpenproletariat* of nations, but also major shifts in relations within and between the other three worlds. Relations based upon ideology are being reevaluated, and dependency relations are being reversed. The major characteristics of this neo-Malthusian world are the growth of power based upon raw materials and the decline of power based upon technology or military position. Ideology no longer functions as either a basis of or a barrier to alliance. The Organization of Petroleum Exporting Countries (OPEC) is a case in point. All its members have Third World social organization, yet differ in many other respects. Although we generally consider OPEC to be an Arab cartel, it includes such non-Arab countries as Iran, Indonesia, and Venezuela. Members represent not only diverse religions and cultures but also ideologies. Even among the Arab members are radical Algeria and conservative Saudi Arabia. Norman Girvan has outlined the dynamics of this emerging phenomenon: "Nor is Third World economic nationalism seen as stopping at attempts to control prices for the primary products upon which the export incomes and the economic livelihood of these countries depend. Market power is seen as only one component in a general strategy for securing control over marketing and ultimately over production of the natural resources that sustain the Third World economies."[33] This philosophy is adaptable to either a socialist or capitalist economy, or to the range of mixed market systems that falls between the two.

Accompanying these new nonideological developments in the Third World has been the breakup of ideological alignments in the First and Second Worlds. The behavior of NATO and OECD (Organization for Economic Cooperation and Development) countries in response to OPEC is an illustration. These First World countries failed to agree on common action during or after the oil embargo. Similarly, the Second World, which also exports petroleum, has acted in a nonideological manner. During the embargo, the Soviet Union voiced full support of Arab actions, yet it continued to sell to target countries. In 1973, the year of the embargo, Soviet exports to Japan and the Netherlands doubled, and the cash value of those exports tripled.[34] This represents a pragmatic nonideological world view on the part of the Second World.

More important than the breakdown of ideology has been the shift in the basis of power, until recently based upon either technology or military strength. Within this framework, the First and Second Worlds were in a superior position to the Third World. With unlimited raw materials, industrial nations were able to set the price for those materials and finished products. The increased awareness of limited resources has altered this relationship. Japan is an example. Prior to the 1973 oil embargo, many predicted that Japan would be the power of the next century. Although heavily industrialized and technologically advanced, Japan must import both fuel and food; it was nearly destroyed by the embargo and has yet to recover fully from its economic effects. Although oil is in short supply, manufactured goods are available to OPEC nations at competitive prices. The position of OPEC nations has improved as a result of their cartel activities, but Third World nations lacking in natural resources have declined economically. The prices they pay for imports, both raw and finished, are forced upward, but the prices they receive for their limited exports are unchanged. As these nations decline, the size of the Fourth World increases.

Nathan Keyfitz has discussed the effect on poor countries:

Price increases such as those of the Organization of Petroleum Exporting Countries can have little overall effect on the number of middle class people in the world (although they have some effect on whether the newly middle class will speak Spanish or Arabic or English). Who ultimately bears the burden of such price raises is not clear. Some of the burden is carried by poor countries that are not endowed with materials; when the repercussions have worked themselves out, India may find it has contributed a higher proportion of its income to Saudi Arabian opulence than the U.S. has. Certainly some U.S. fertilizer that would have gone to India before 1973 now goes to the Middle East; German chemical-plant investments are similarly diverted. The offsetting of oil price rises by French arms sales to Iran has everything to do with national power and little to do with the total distribution of poverty or even the national distribution. The main point is that only a small fraction of the world population is in the resource-rich areas.[35]

In those countries that do have raw materials, there is a question as to whether the OPEC model can be followed. Superficially, it appears it may yet be feasible.

Four poor countries—Chile, Peru, Zambia, and Zaire (Congo)—supply most of the world's exportable surplus of copper. Three others—Malaysia, Bolivia, and Thailand—account for 70 percent of all tin entering international trade channels. Cuba and New Caledonia have well over half of the world's known reserves of nickel. The main known reserves of cobalt are in Zaire, Cuba, New Caledonia, and parts of Asia. And Mexico and Peru, along with Australia, account for 60 percent of the exportable supply of lead.[36]

Some of these groups, for example, coffee, copper, and bauxite exporters, are trying to form cartels and gain more control over the marketing of their raw materials.

It is by no means clear that the policies of OPEC can be adopted successfully by other Third World countries. Petroleum is an unusual product in that demand is nearly inelastic and substitution is difficult. A Brookings Institution study sets three conditions for a successful cartel: "(a) The group must control a sufficiently large share of world exports, world production, and, for mineral resources, world reserves; (b) the price elasticity of demand for the commodity in question, including the cross-elasticity with possible substitutes, must be sufficiently low; (c) the group itself must be sufficiently cohesive to prevent individual members from pursuing their own advantage through unilateral action in the market."[37] Rarely can these conditions be met. Most nonfuel resources have very elastic demand curves; they can be easily substituted or done without. Two examples are coffee and copper. Coffee can be forgone with no major effect on the life-style of the user. In contrast, for both economic and social reasons, other energy sources cannot easily replace petroleum.

What is of interest for the First World is that advanced technology does not fit this model. The power of the First World has largely rested upon its technological ability and control. Hans Morgenthau has shown that technology does not fit the framework discussed above in two areas: monopoly and inelasticity of demand.[38] William Schneider has also pointed out that "(1) the United States does not have a monopoly on advanced industrial and scientific technology. The expertise and production capability for a wide range of advanced technology products exist in most of the West European countries and Japan. Over time, the ability of a target nation to procure advanced technology from nations other than the United States is likely to increase. (2) There are few examples of advanced technology that are both essential and unique (that is, for which no substitutes are feasible)."[39]

Since Schneider is speaking only of the United States, a third point should be noted. The First World has not been sufficiently cohesive to prevent individual members from pursuing their own advantage. Three examples of the failure of technological power are the U.S. trade embargo of Cuba; its embargo of Iran; and the UN embargo of Rhodesia. In fact, Schneider's argument for using food as an economic weapon is symptomatic of the failure of technology and industry to form a base of power in a neo-Malthusian world.

Given this outline of the effects of a no-growth policy upon international stratification, it is possible to point out major implications for both First and Third World countries: a decreased standard of living for much of the First World and increased standards for those fortunate Third World countries able to exploit cartels. Since the Third World differs from the Fourth because of its "concept of emergence" and since the possibility of emergence is limited because all Third World countries cannot play the cartel game (given their limited resources), the size of the Fourth World will expand, augmented by former members of the Third World.

Conclusion

As I have tried to show elsewhere,[40] the presumed "crisis" in world capitalism is largely a fictitious extrapolation from American conditions, that is, from the past disproportionate utilization of resources and energy by the United States. As we enter the 1980s, more, not fewer, nation-states are in advanced stages of capitalist development, or at least have a mixed market-welfare system that can boast of a sizable, even expanding, private sector. Hence, the limits-to-economic-growth model is a response to the specific American situation, and it should be so perceived before the world is reduced to the manufacture of windmills.

The subtle transformation from the limits-to-growth model to the limits-to-equity type has considerable dangers, and these at least should be addressed, if not resolved. First, in shifting the emphasis to economic equilibrium and away from social stratification, certain structural deformities in U.S. society are hardened, and the attendant risk of class polarization and ultimately class warfare is enhanced. Second, to speak of limits to equity as an absolute physical requirement invites the state to turn a deaf ear to the needs and aims of the less economically advantaged sectors of society, which also risks polarization. Third, in order to deal with such heightened polarization, it is not improbable that ever-increasing repressive measures will be used in domestic affairs. Fourth, such repression would inevitably risk a growing isolation from the international community. Fifth, the ultimate consequence of a limits-to-growth policy would be an absolute decline in the United States as a world power; it would mean acceptance not only of the redivision of the world's resource and energy base but also a redistribution of profits so that new wealthy and exploiting classes on the world scene would and could act with impunity against the United States. This would aggravate the growing internal fissure between haves and have-nots in the domestic economy.

The limits-to-equity model is simply a mechanistic response to structural changes in the balance of forces in the international economy and technology. To accept uncritically a model that accepts the international status quo and categorically denies the major impulses that have guided U.S. society throughout the century is to invite a solution that would only sharpen the inner tensions of that society. It would be made more vulnerable to contradiction and collapse. Those who take their theorizing as axiomatic rather than problematic would do well to ponder these risks of the limits-to-growth ideology before seeking to impose it on U.S. society as a general theory of the future direction of its domestic and foreign policy.

5. Winners and Losers

To study winners and losers is only to make an old problem personal: the gap between politics as a science and politics as a vocation. We too often treat the political world as possessed of self-evident properties apparent to any who study it. In point of fact, politics is anything but self-evident and hardly systematic; although dogmatists and model builders may think otherwise. There are simply too many possibilities, options, and choices to permit consistent adherence to a normative framework. Efforts to do so may prove idiosyncratic no less than reductionist. Just as there is a perennial gap between social facts and theoretical possibilities, there is a similar range of discrepancies between human actors and political systems.

A distinct motif of this essay is to follow up and deepen an earlier essay, "Autobiography as the Presentation of Self for Social Immortality."[1] For what is involved in each of the four cases—Thomas Hutchinson, Leon Trotsky, George Plunkitt, and Joseph Stalin—are varieties of career justification, and not simply advice or instruction to others. Each of these figures exemplifies ideological messages, indicating ways in which winning in politics is possible. They are themselves exemplars of certain approaches. Despite the cynicism and instrumental approaches of George Plunkitt and Joseph Stalin, their examples assert techniques for victory in both the personal and larger collective senses. And despite the exile and humiliation of Thomas Hutchinson and Leon Trotsky, their examples also assert forms of struggle and techniques for political survival that have meaning in some ill-defined long run. Again, let me emphasize that I do not intend an exercise in power or nationality. Rather, I will show how through the ideological remains of four distinctive characters, two very distinct forms of political morality emerge: pragmatism and moralism.

Some two decades ago, in an essay on war gaming, I asserted that continuing conflicts in military encounters depend, in the long run, on convincing one's own side, and sometimes the other side as well, that one has both averted catastrophe and gained victory.[2] This is accomplished by selecting and developing different criteria of winning. Here I wish to extend that earlier argument. In politics, a crude index of victory is party control of the ability to exercise raw power. But all regimes and leaders necessarily come to an end. Antagonists willing and able to continue their opposition to the party in power, choosing exile, even humiliation, are able to do so because they do not accept defeat, certainly not as an internal matter. Instead, like Jehovah's Witnesses they shift the date of their expected victory to a more distant future. Political decisions are justifications for, as much as informed by, moral posture. Whether politics issue into ethics, as Aristotle held, or whether ethical propositions define political issues, as Plato tended to advocate, is less critical a concern than the reasons which are offered for a near universal association of the two in the conduct of public affairs.

To analyze this association between politics and morality, I have chosen to look at the careers of two pairs of figures, pairs as different from each other as each member is from the other member of the pair. A pragmatist and a moralist pair are each selected from America and Russia. While the Russian pair, Stalin and Trotsky, are well-known leaders of the Soviet Revolution and Marxist theory, the American pair, Plunkitt and Hutchinson, represent different centuries as well as distinctive approaches. This pairing therefore is less self-evident.

George Washington Plunkitt was one of a small, exclusive group of leaders of Tammany Hall during its halcyon days at the turn of the century. The son of Irish immigrants, he spent his lifetime in the service of Manhattan's Fifteenth Ward. Joseph Djugashivili (Stalin) was the last born, only surviving child of Georgian (Russian) parents of peasant stock who were descendants of serfs. Stalin was himself educated as a seminarian in the Orthodox church. Thomas Hutchinson was the son of Protestant merchants, born in prerevolutionary Boston. He entered Harvard at twelve, and led a life of commerce, learning, and politics. Leon Bronstein (Trotsky) was the son of a Jewish couple engaged in farming in the southern Ukraine. He was schooled at a Jewish-German colony and then at a secular institution in Odessa. As a youth he was more taken with the Narodniks than the Marxists.

These spare biographical sketches are not so much intended to explicate as to undermine emphasis on background variables as a tool of analysis. The moral choices politicians make have precious little to do with the moral strictures of their origins. Those one anticipates in childhood to rebel, often grow up to conform, while those who might be expected to conform, rebel against authority and system.

It might be argued that a more natural antagonist for Plunkitt of Tammany Hall than Hutchinson of Massachusetts would have been Tammany's earnest critic, the Reverend Charles Henry Parkhurst. While it is true that Parkhurst led the forces for reform, he did so as a moralist rather than as a political figure willing to run moral risks. It seems to me that some firm criteria, such as exile and loss of rank, are far more important than temporal or even occupational symmetry. This is not to deny the significant role played by Parkhurst in exposing the venality and corruption of Tammany, but his refined dream of an Atlantic civilization in which the United States is appointed "to be able permanently to communicate impulses . . . of a finer type . . . to the heathen" makes him both uninteresting and unimpressive in terms of our search for a keener understanding of winners and losers battling in the political trenches.[3]

The pairings present wildly different literary styles in addition to different political ideologies: coarse versus sophisticated, earthy versus austere, crudely self-interested versus lofty other-interested, and Jesuitical versus Talmudic. But my concern is not with the history of ideas as an abstract enterprise, or devolution of literary manners. It is to illustrate the conduct of the political process at its polarized extremes, and in so doing to demonstrate how politics determines the fate of moral credos, rather than, as is often presumed in the classical tradition, the other way around.

Plunkitt

Plunkitt gives us a series of recommendations and propositions which are clearly closer to Machiavelli than to Plato. To be sure, there is something of the poor man's Machiavelli in his advice to the youth regarding Tammany Hall—"the most perfect political machine on earth."[4] How does one become politically important? The Platonic answer, of course, is through education, specifically moral education. Plunkitt gives us no such respectable recommendation:

> Some young men think they can learn how to be successful in politics from books, and they cram their heads with all sorts of college rot. They couldn't make a bigger mistake. Now, understand me, I ain't sayin' nothin' against colleges. I guess they'll have to exist as long as there's bookworms, and I suppose they do some good in a certain way, but they don't count in politics. In fact, a young man who has gone through the college course is handicapped at the outset. He may succeed in politics, but the chances are 100 to 1 against him.[5]

Beyond that, the Greek ideal of oration is frowned upon. Plunkitt inveighs against those who speak as having only negative power, while those who are silent have real power. Again, the distinction between small voices and big sticks is not entirely unknown in the annals of American politics, especially in the Teddy Roosevelt "Rough Rider" period during which Plunkitt thrived. As he notes, "The men who rule have practiced keepin' their tongues still, not exercisin' them. So you want to drop the orator idea unless you mean to go into politics just to perform the sky-rocket act."[6]

When Plunkitt addresses himself to issues of ideology, status, and learning, he reduces everything to an assessment of the idea's ability to deliver the vote. American politics is about delivering the vote. The point of view or philosophy underwriting the electorate or the elected does not necessarily characterize American political society, but voting with ballots or bullets does. Reductionism thus becomes a precondition to defining winners and losers. He observes,

> I got a marketable commodity—one vote. Then I went to the district leader and told him I could command two votes on election day, Tommy's and my own. He smiled on me and told me to go ahead. If I had offered him a speech or a bookful of learnin', he would have said, "Oh, forget it!"[7]

Plunkitt does have a notion of changing the political system. A good deal of his energies are dedicated precisely to effecting social change. But unlike the achievement-oriented individual, who in political terms is viewed as the liberal reforming sin by Plunkitt, his own primary concern is the relationship between the politician's practice and the need to be perfectly attuned to what ordinary people want. For Plunkitt, politics as a mechanism for servicing needs replaces attempts to develop systematic theory.

The fact is that a reformer can't last in politics. He can make a show for a while, but he always comes down like a rocket. Politics is as much a regular business as the grocery or the dry-goods or the drug business. You've got to be trained up to it or you're sure to fail. Suppose a man who knew nothing about the grocery trade suddenly went into business and tried to conduct it according to his own ideas. Wouldn't he make a mess of it? He might make a splurge for a while, as long as his money lasted, but his store would soon be empty. It's just the same with a reformer. He hasn't been brought up to the difficult business of politics and he makes a mess of it every time.[8]

Just as Plunkitt distinguishes real change and the rhetoric of change, so too he observes there is a difference between honest graft and dishonest graft. That distinction becomes as useful in the political system as the difference between formal and informal norms is to the social system as a whole. The finely honed distinction between the Philadelphia Republicans and the New York Democrats well illustrates Plunkitt's point:

The difference between a looter and a practical politician is the difference between the Philadelphia Republican gang and Tammany Hall. The Philadelphia crowd runs up against the penal code. Tammany don't. The Philadelphians ain't satisfied with robbin' the bank of all its gold and paper money. They stay to pick up the nickels and pennies and the cop comes and nabs them. Tammany ain't no such fool. . . . It ain't fair . . . to class Tammany men with the Philadelphia gang. Any man who undertakes to write political books should never for a moment lose sight of the distinction between honest graft and dishonest graft.[9]

Plunkitt is not simply distinguishing established judicial norms of thievery from norms of integrity, but indicating that politics is so ingrained a phenomenon in American life that there really is no need for dull-witted thievery. In a sense, one would have to say that Plunkitt's vision of American politics is that the system itself permits such a wide latitude of gains, licit and illicit, that stealing from the political system becomes as unthinkable as stealing from one's family. He draws a precise analogy between the polity and the person.

The politician who steals is worse than a thief. He is a fool. With the grand opportunities all around for the man with a political pull, there's no excuse for stealin' a cent. The point I want to make is that if there is some stealin' in politics, it don't mean that the politicians of 1905 are, as a class, worse than them of 1835. It just means that the old-timers had nothin' to steal, while the politicians now are surrounded by all kinds of temptations and some of them naturally—the fool ones—buck up against the penal code.[10]

Plunkitt underwrites what European (and now even American) critics have said about politics in this nation: that party cleavages are not structural, but operational. They exist only to the degree that they embrace the craft of politics: which is simply making a living in the political world. Political actors share no transcendental visions of the grand old party, no harkening back to Jeffersonian democracy. They simply believe that election day is different from all other days because it alone justifies the existence of ideology or rhetoric, just as judgment day will be the official warranty of theology. For all other days, Plunkitt believed, economy rules and ideology be damned.

Me and the Republicans are enemies just one day in the year—election day. Then we fight tooth and nail. The rest of the time it's live and let live with us. On election day I try to pile up as big a majority as I can against George Wanamaker, the Republican leader of the Fifteenth. Any other day George and I are the best of friends. I can go to him and say: "George, I want you to place this friend of mine." He says: "All right, Senator." Or vice versa. You see, we differ on tariffs and currencies and all them things, but we agree on the main proposition that when a man works in politics, he should get something out of it.[11]

And why, mused Plunkitt, doesn't the intelligent individual go into the political life? Aside from awareness of the rough and tumble of the political world, there is the rise of bureaucratic rationality: the displacement of political bosses by the civil service. Plunkitt believes the substitution of administrative decision making for electoral process and the routinization of political life portend destruction of one of the few joys left in this world.

The civil service gang is always howlin' about candidates and officeholders puttin' money up for campaigns and about corporations chippin' in. They might as well howl about givin' contributions to churches. A political organization has to have money for its business as well as a church, and who has more right to put up than the men who get the good things goin'. Take, for instance, a great political concern like Tammany Hall. It does missionary work like a church, it's got big expenses and it's got to be supported by the faithful. If a corporation sends in a check to help the good work of the Tammany Society, why shouldn't we take it like other missionary societies? Of course, the day may come when we'll reject the money of the rich as tainted, but it hadn't come when I left Tammany Hall at 11:25 A.M. today.[12]

The imagination required to engage in politics is undermined by routinization and bureaucratization. To Plunkitt, the creative imagination is itself submerged by the substitution of policy based on education for politics based on experience. Listening to Plunkitt describe the reason for the Democratic party's failure at the turn of the nineteenth century, one hears not only the faint echoes of the foolishness of arguments concerning graft, but also in its nascent form, the Keynesian proposition that money is for circulation not for hoarding. He contended that

in two Presidential campaigns, the leaders talked themselves red in the face about silver bein' the best money and gold bein' no good, and they tried to prove it out of books. Do you think people cared for all that guff? No. They heartily endorsed what Richard Crocker said at the Hoffman House one day in 1900: 'What's the use of discussin' what's the best kind of money?' said Crocker. 'I'm in favor of all kinds of money—the more the better.' See how a real Tammany statesman can settle in twenty-five words a problem that monopolized two campaigns![13]

Plunkitt delineates the social functions of corruption, its ability to get things done, over and against supposedly rational modes of politics. The administrative-bureaucratic model makes scarce accommodation to Plunkitt's appreciation of politics as a mass activity conducted by people with only a remote sense of the philosophical foundations of behavior. In his own ironic way, Plunkitt illustrates not only the corruption of democracy, which is the customary emphasis of Tammany Hall, but the function of democracy as a means of listening and responding to the whimsies, the follies, as well as the reasonable interests of ordinary people. The purpose of political life is not to resolve ethical problems, but rather to permit people to live in an empirical world in which ethical options are acknowledged but are not necessarily resolved. This quixotic open-endedness typifies the authoritarian political process, in contrast to the doctrinal persuasion of those who write on politics from a totalitarian perspective. Totalitarians are often willing to share the personal risks of politics, but not its "wide open universe" of consequences; which is to say, for people like Plunkitt, politics was the goal of the good life, whereas for the European totalitarian tradition, politics was an instrument to some higher morality.

In his excellent volume on *The Tweed Ring*, Alexander Callow has properly warned against facile dismissal of Plunkitt's type of leadership as superficial and cynical. "For all its exaggerations, no matter how many Tammany's motives for patriotism may be questioned, the super-patriotic appeal was an effective force in cementing the newcomer to the leadership of New York's Democratic Party." He goes on to note that "Tammany's nationalism was not a unique departure from practical politics, but rather a marrying of patriotism and politics to achieve local, practical ends. In effect, Tammany assumed the role of spokesman for American ideals."[14] The party apparatus became a crucial integrating mechanism behind the Americanization process, and the ideology of Americanism in turn served to solidify and unify the party apparatus.

Stalin

It may seem curious in the extreme to link the political fates and fortunes of Plunkitt and Stalin. At the level of style there is Plunkitt's keen sense of humor in contrast to Stalin's humorlessness; whereas at the level of substance Plunkitt was a simple ward heeler and Stalin a complex world figure. Plunkitt's absolute conviction that history means nothing contrasts with Stalin's belief that history means everything. Plunkitt's indifference to how others judged his views is refreshing compared with Stalin's paranoid self-vision of grandeur and demand for ideological loyalty. Nonetheless, beyond questions of form or importance, the two look surprisingly familiar. For both, the problem of winning was not one of many agenda items, but represented the primary, dedicated requirement of the political life.

Stalin's deep concern with victory derived from a long Russian history of defeats.

His determination to seek and maintain power was not so much fueled by personal avarice as a result of such avarice. His obsessional dedication to results emerged early in his rule. Speaking before the first Conference of Russian Industrial Managers, held in 1931, he noted in frightening, prophetic terms the need for preparedness:

> It is sometimes asked whether it is not possible to slow down a bit in tempo, to retard the movement. No. This is impossible. It is impossible to reduce the tempo! On the contrary, it is necessary as far as possible to accelerate it. To slacken the tempo means to fall behind. And the backward are always beaten. But we do not want to be beaten. No, we do not want this! The history of old Russia is the history of defeats due to backwardness. . . . All beat her for her backwardness—for military backwardness, for cultural backwardness, for governmental backwardness, for agricultural backwardness. She was beaten because to beat her was profitable and could be done with impunity.[15]

Stalin's quest for victory and his fear of defeat led to severe paranoia and ultimately to murder. When he assumed complete control of the party apparatus in 1934, he made a speech before the Seventeenth Communist Party Congress (which the Stalinist faction designated as the "Victors' Congress") emphasizing, in euphoric terms, Bolshevik successes in intensifying the class struggle. But as Isaac Deutscher informs us, the victors were also soon to become the vanquished.

> Of nearly 2,000 of those "victors," delegates present at the Congress, about 60 percent were, according to Khrushchev, "arrested on charges of counter-revolutionary crimes (most in 1937–38)." Of the 139 members of the Central Committee then elected "98 persons, i.e., 70 percent, were arrested and shot (mostly in 1937–38)." Thus, in those years alone Stalin annihilated 60 percent to 70 percent of the leading cadres of his own faction; and there were unaccounted victims among the rank and file.[16]

When victory becomes the ultimate goal, the character of leadership itself becomes anomic, estranged from any useful goals beyond personal survival. A number of points characterize this totalitarian thirst for victory. Opposition itself comes to be considered treason in the totalitarian environment. The success of opposition is defined in zero-sum terms as the failure of leadership. Hence those who opposed Stalin were branded defeatists and traitors, and not just losers. Deutscher again is our authority in pointing out that Stalin thought the slaughter of the Old Guard of Bolsheviks had to be done not merely in the name of opposition, and not even in the name of conspiracy against the leadership. Rather, nothing less than treason had to define the nature of opposition. He states that Stalin believed that

> they had to die as traitors, as perpetrators of crimes beyond the reach of reason, as leaders of a monstrous fifth column. Only then could Stalin be assured that their execution would provoke no dangerous revulsion; and that, on the contrary, he himself would be looked upon, especially by the young and uninformed generation, as the saviour of the country. It is not necessary to assume that he acted

from sheer cruelty or lust for power. He may be given the dubious credit for the sincere conviction that what he did served the interests of the revolution and that he alone interpreted those interests aright.[17]

Beyond the impermissibility of opposition was the impossibility of defeat. In his writings, Stalin would only permit a sense of heroism as a sentiment connected with victory. Rewriting history, which Stalin happily encouraged and participated in, ended with the maximum leader writing his own biography. The history of the Communist party had to be rewritten several times to expunge enemies as they were defined moment by moment; the history of World War II had to be rewritten to eliminate the fact that there were obvious miscalculations by the Stalinist leadership with respect to the Nazi invasion of Russia; the constitution itself had to be rewritten to take into account every idiosyncrasy and quirk of the bureaucratic leadership: for example, emphasizing words like democracy and freedom when the purges of the 1930s were at a high point. Even the metaphysics of Marxism had to be adjusted so that Stalin became the philosopher-king in Platonic style. The thirst to win translated into the drive for absolute dominance of the Russian nation, intellectual no less than bureaucratic domination.

The chilling effects of absolutism, nationalism, and a moralism unbridled by a sense of human choice are illustrated by the Great Dictator's abrogation of a free exchange of opinion. In the case of those who question inherited truths, Stalin labels them as "slanderers and falsifiers." Differences of opinion become "rotten liberalisms," and the bare hint of criticism "fraudulent maneuvers." Stalin became the sole source of philosophical wisdom, literary truth, aesthetic judgment.[18] In this, he moved far beyond the pragmatism of a Plunkitt into a moralism which recognizes no authority other than his own sense of history. If the gap between pragmatism and moralism is not easily bridged, it can sometimes, as in the case of the absolute dictator, be encompassed by a single individual leader.

Just as Plunkitt's domain was Manhattan's southern tier, Stalin's was Russia. The limits of the totalitarian commitment were determined only by the turf and terrain governed. This helps to explain the curious acceptance of isolationism throughout much of Soviet history. Under Stalin, many miscalculations, mistakes about the intentions of the German Wehrmacht for example, derived from this absolute certainty that victory for Russia was ideologically ensured, and historically enshrined. Soviet victory was tantamount to victory in the world. Soviet strategies became Third International principles. Stalin as assuredly commanded a nation as Plunkitt did a ward; and the system became the totality of the movement.

Questions of winning and losing, as Stalin saw them, ultimately revolve around issues of good and evil. If there is no victory of one nation over another, one system over another, there can be no triumph of good; if the enemy, whoever that turned out to be, cannot be readily identified that means evil cannot be extirpated. Robert C. Tucker, in his brilliant social psychological study of Stalin, articulates this strong subjective element in the Stalinist concept of winning:

The villain-image of the enemy came to represent everything that Stalin rejected and condemned in himself. All that belonged to the rejected evil Stalin—the er-

rors, flaws, and elements of villainy that had no place in his hero-image of himself—tended to be incorporated into his picture of the enemy, especially the
picture of the internal enemy as villain of past history. Whatever he inwardly cen-
sored from the record of his past deeds and misdeeds was likely to reappear in
characterizations of his enemies. Further, Stalin had a remarkable propensity for
seeing and condemning in enemies the qualities that he condemned *without*
seeing in himself. We can infer from his idealized version of himself as an extremely modest man that one of the qualities he unconsciously rejected in himself
was his monstrously inflated self-esteem, his arrogance.[19]

The task of winning is connected with the problem of historical verification and
personal loyalty. The collapse of the Stalinist empire, the later revelations of Khru-
schev, the painstakingly slow process of legal normalization of the society, the liber-
alization of coercive techniques in favor of persuasive approaches, each helped to
undermine the earlier euphoric sense of victory.[20] Stalinism does not crumble under
Khrushchev as a result of a frontal assault by the new party leadership. Rather he
politely ignored it to make way for new conditions and leaders. Victory is redefined
in somewhat modest terms: the reassessment of the post-Stalin era was made by
Khrushchev in the name of system survival rather than ideological vindication. It
became more important not to risk defeat than to seek moral absolution through
victory. The totalitarian system retreated to authoritarian modalities under the impact of pragmatic requirements of systemic survival. Soviet ideology remained as a
system based upon survival, not principles. In this sense, what first appeared as
sheer oppression under Stalin survives as benign domination by his successors. That
is to say, the Soviet system loosens its control by outright terror in favor of a reward
system that ostracizes and exiles. It imprisons, but rarely kills.

Hutchinson

The radical immoralism of George Washington Plunkitt, based as it was on pure
pragmatism, is not the only type of moral framework for evaluating and confronting
the political process. One must also examine the dilemma of radical moralists: those
for whom morals stand above the historical process, and apart from the political
process. If one can say that Plunkitt is a Tammany Hall boilerplate version of Machiavelli, with equal fairness one can claim that Thomas Hutchinson, last royal governor of the State of Massachusetts, represents an Aristotelian vision in which the
good stands above and beyond the voice of the people, and in which law and order
exceed compassion and human justice in any ordering of political priorities.

One might superficially claim that the problem with Hutchinson is that he cannot
escape from a loser's paradigm; whereas the problem with Plunkitt is that he suffers
from a winner's paradigm, or more simply put, he has an infatuation with "making
it." But this raises a larger, archetypical consideration. Can one lose politically and
win ethically? Do those who survive in the political arena always have moral virtue
on their side? More practically, does any leader ever accept the notion of losing; or
does he simply postpone the date of ultimate victory? This shifting historicity
strikes at the heart of any moral vision of the political process. Beyond that, this

universe of winners indicates a need to move beyond pure historicity in discussing such ideas. If we ask ourselves how long a time span one requires to determine winners and losers, we find that those who are beaten at one point, may emerge victorious at another point. Similarly, those who seem invincible in political affairs sometimes hardly merit a fleeting glance in retrospect. The charisma of office stands above the charisma of personality, and except in the rarest instances, personality is better reserved for use only in maximum crisis situations. Suffice it to say, the force of office tends to endure far beyond the force of personality.

For this reason Thomas Hutchinson, the final governor of the State of Massachusetts under the British Crown, merits deep interest. He not only opposed the American revolutionaries, but did so with a profound belief that his obligations as a British subject were more important than any consideration of rights as a colonist. Bernard Bailyn indicates the reason for studying a loser like Hutchinson in his masterful biography:

> Until we look deliberately at the development from the other side around, we have not understood what the issues really were, what the struggle was all about. It is as clear an example as may be found of what Professor Butterfield described forty years ago: a situation in which it is essential to understand the efforts that had no future if one is to explain the victory of what, in the retrospect of later history, became the forces of progress. Most of the finest human qualities, to which one instinctively responds—the desire to eradicate the cruelties people inflict upon one another; the spirit of hope and enterprise; confidence in the future; above all, the passion to cast off restraints and in some enduring way to release pent-up aspirations—all of this seems to me to have been on the side of the victors. I turn to the losers sympathetically in order to explain the human reality against which the victors struggled and so to help make the story whole and comprehensive. [21]

Hutchinson was well aware that he was on the losing side militarily, if not historically. He knew full well that the price of moralism was his elimination as a political factor in the life of the colonies, ultimately to remain only as a sad footnote to British colonial policy under King George III. As Bailyn notes, the losers were not the British Crown per se, but those loyalist supporters of the empire and the colonies.

> The real losers—those whose lives were disrupted, who suffered violence and vilification, who were driven out of the land and forced to resettle elsewhere in middle life and died grieving for the homes they had lost—these were not the English but the Americans who clung to them, who remained loyal to England and to what had been assumed to be the principles of legitimacy and law and order which the British government embodied. They were the American loyalists, and it is their history that allows us to see the Revolutionary movement from the other side around, and to grasp the wholeness of the struggle and hence in the end to understand more fully than we have before why a revolution took place and why it succeeded. [22]

Hutchinson himself was not, however, interested in simply winning or losing. His principles were precisely those of the English constitutional tradition of Locke. His concerns were not the suppression of contrary opinion, but rather the destruction of what he felt to be political heresy. Indeed, precisely what makes Hutchinson interesting is his adherence to principles of conservatism, rather than practices of pragmatism, and a belief in the ultimate triumph of such precepts. As history would have it, Hutchinson's ideas were vindicated when the constitution of the Commonwealth of Massachusetts was put into effect one month after his death. "[It] exhibited to perfection the ideal balance achieved through the independence and separation of powers which, in an older context, Hutchinson had struggled to retain." [23]

Hutchinson failed in practical sense because he did not understand the moral principles of those who opposed him nearly to the same degree as they appreciated the moral basis of his position. In Hutchinson's dogmatism a certain moralizing style displaced ethical premises. His commitment to personal principle became divorced from other morals, not to mention other practices. Worse, Hutchinson failed to rise to the challenge of oppression that was felt by the colonists. He himself may have understood their concerns, but he could not respond to them because he believed in law and order apart from justice and change. This is the anguish of conservatism, and one faithfully expressed in the following observation by Bailyn:

> For all [Hutchinson's] intelligence, he did not comprehend the nature of the forces that confronted him and that at a critical point he might have controlled, or if not controlled then at least evaded. He was never able to understand the moral basis of the protests that arose against the existing order. Committed to small, prudential gains through an intricate, closely calibrated world of status, deference, and degree . . . he could not respond to the aroused moral passion and the optimistic and idealist impulses that gripped the minds of the Revolutionaries that led them to condemn as corrupt and oppressive the whole system by which their world was governed. [24]

It might well be that Bailyn is right: namely, that Hutchinson, by virtue of his loyalism revealed a lack of imagination, and an excessive quantum of political rigidity that ultimately led to his demise. But I am not entirely certain that Hutchinson's position can be described as myopic or self-serving. Quite the contrary: from Bailyn's own testimony one should have to say that the total disregard of what was in his personal interests, interpreted as utilitarian, ultimately led to his rigidity. In this way, Hutchinson proved himself a moral force of considerable note even though he was of less significance as a political being: a politician eliciting some support although sadly out of step with historical progression.

> Failing to respond to the moral indignation and the meliorist aspirations that lay behind the protests of the Revolutionary leaders, Hutchinson could now only find persistent irrationality in their arguments, and he wrote off their agitations as politically pathological. And in a limited, logical sense he was right. The Revolutionary leaders were not striving to act reasonably or logically. Demanding a re-

sponsiveness in government that exceeded the traditional expectations of the time, groping toward goals and impelled by aspirations that were no recognized part of the world as it was, they drew on convictions more powerful than logic and mobilized sources of political and social energy that burst the boundaries of received political wisdom. Hutchinson could not govern an aroused populace led by politicians manipulating deep-felt ideological symbols. He could not assimilate these new forces into the old world he knew so well, and, attempting uncomprehendingly to do so, lost the advantage of his greatest assets: a deserved reputation for candor, honesty, and a tireless and impartial devotion to the general good. Failing to carry the new politics with him by arguments that were accredited and tactics that were familiar, he was obliged to become devious; inevitably he appeared hypocritical, ultimately conspiratorial, though in fact he was neither. As the pressure mounted, his responses narrowed, his ideas became progressively more rigid, his imagination more limited, until in the end he could only plead for civil order as an absolute end in itself which not only ignored the explosive issues but appeared, unavoidably, to be self-serving. There is no better testimony to the character of the forces that were shaping the Revolutionary movement and that would determine the nature of American politics in the early national period than the failure of so prudent, experienced, and intelligent a man as Thomas Hutchinson to control them.[25]

Hutchinson, in opposition to an overwhelmingly popular cause, shows us that the belief that winning is somehow uniquely connected to the locomotive of history, or is unilinear in character, is foul nonsense. It is true of course that economic class, social groups, and political parties may become obsolete, or may be destroyed. It does not follow, however, that the line of historical change is mapped out in political cosmology equal to that of astronomy in its deterministic proportions. Nor is it the case that historical obsolescence is isomorphic with moral bankruptcy. Winning may more readily unleash the passions than losing. The actual course of events rarely accords with imagined laws of history. As a result, the consequence of winning may not only be postponed in time but abstracted from social space. Hutchinson fell prey to an inability to connect pragmatics to history. This very fact gave his life and work moral meaning quite beyond the ignominious ending to his political career in the colonies.

Trotsky

If the theoretical linkage between Plunkitt and Stalin seems terribly strained, the connection between Thomas Hutchinson and Leon Trotsky may seem equally bizarre, or at least remote. Again, I would suggest that these are at least matters of style, of literary delivery, no less than substance. If Trotsky, unlike Hutchinson, was seriously unaware that he was on the losing side historically, he was certainly aware that he was on the losing side empirically and in immediate terms. Trotsky had no problem with losing his position in the Soviet elite, since the real question for Trotsky at every point was the judgment of history and the ability or inability of the

Soviet system to achieve not only its highest moral purposes, but its proximate political ambitions. If Trotsky could never quite bring himself to denounce the Communist regime, or the system and his personal adversary who caused his expulsion and ultimate extermination, he at least understood the process of political disengagement. His entire life in exile was a testimonial to patience and persistence rather than to victory or nationality. His apologia before the Dewey Commission expressed well not so much any sense of defeat, but rather the ultimate triumph of morality over pragmatics:

> I do not despair. . . . I have patience. Three revolutions made me patient. The experience of my life, in which there has been no lack either of success or of failures, has not only not destroyed my faith in the clear, bright future of mankind, but on the contrary, has given it an indestructible temper. This faith in reason, in truth, in human solidarity, which at the age of eighteen I took with me into the workers' quarters of the provincial Russian town of Nikolayev—this faith I have preserved fully and completely. It has become more mature, but not less ardent.[26]

In his lengthy and tormented period of exile, Trotsky continued to believe in the revolutionary process that brought the Communist party to victory. In this he was quite different from Hutchinson, whose disbelief in the American revolutionary process as such was based on its seeming inability to manufacture a democratic society woven from aristocratic fabric; still Hutchinson too, we are reminded, harbored dreams of his eventual and triumphal return to Massachusetts.

Trotsky's general belief was that the most dangerous psychosis in politics was to fall captive to one's own formula that yesterday was appropriate but inappropriate for the present moment. This same sense of history as infallible—which pushed Stalin to terror—gave Trotsky equal impetus to choose exile. This belief in a deterministic framework stimulated and aroused an acceptance of exile and a willingness to withstand short-term losses and setbacks. Trotsky's opposition to the Stalinist regime ultimately rested on a willingness to accept a circuitous and complex route of democracy, and avoid the short-circuit route of dictatorship, of exacerbating history as it were. If there is a primary difference between Stalin and Trotsky, it resided less in any particular program for Soviet socialism than in the belief that democracy had to be measured apart from, and by different moral criteria than, socialism as a planned economy. Trotsky never ignored the worth or quality of formal democracy as such. Hence his critique of fascism, while like Stalin's, was based on its capitalist character, but had the added dimension of emphasizing its antidemocratic propensities. As he stated:

> There is no epoch in human history so saturated with antagonisms as ours. Under too high a tension of class and international animosities, the "fuses" of democracy "blow out." Hence the short-circuits of dictatorship. Naturally the weakest "interrupters" are the first to give way. But the force of internal and world controversies does not weaken: it grows. It is doubtful if it is destined to calm

down, given that the process has so far only taken hold of the periphery of the capitalist world. Gout begins in the little finger of a hand or in a big toe, but once on the way it goes right to the heart.[27]

What are we to say ultimately, then, about Trotsky and his failure? Like Hutchinson, Trotsky did not understand the moral principles of those who opposed him nearly to the same degree as they appreciated the moral basis of his position. Therein inhered Trotsky's weakness. He was unwilling to take the final step and see the problem of socialism in systematic terms. He responded to Stalin as a false leader of a great event; he continued to maintain that the Soviet system itself, that the Bolshevik revolution itself, was the greatest event in the century. He was willing in short to accept personal loss but unwilling to accept historical responsibility. How a great system generated a degenerate leader was a troublesome problem with which Trotsky grappled but never resolved.

We see that questions of political victory and defeat are by no means simplistic or mutually exclusive categories. In describing these four strange figures we are not simply dealing with two of them who believe in victory at any price, and two others who believe in defeat rather than betrayal of cause; although that comes close to the truth. We certainly are not dealing with people who accept losing at any price. To be sure, the losers—in this case Hutchinson and Trotsky—viewed themselves, and historical forces as well, as having been vindicated as a result of the movements they were intimately involved with. Their analysis of such movements assured them a permanent place in history by virtue of their opposition. It was this opposition which served to flesh out the shortcomings of the systems which each helped bring about in a formative stage.

For Plunkitt and for Stalin, winning meant power; whereas for Hutchinson and Trotsky, winning meant truth—or at least analytic precision. If actual history admits of winning and losing, actual psychology does not. The human capacity to rationalize permits a redefinition of the terms of victory, raising it to a plane of spirituality if need be, and to a level of vindication that carries the full force of moral authority, if not necessarily historical inevitability. The moral limits of politics therefore have to do with whether ethics is to be defined in terms of the politics of power or in terms of the politics of morality. The moral limits of politics are therefore nothing less than the definition of the contest itself, a contest that does not so much admit defeat as support victory, no matter which side assumes temporary control of the reigns of sovereignty.

There is a continuing need to examine losers as well as winners in many dimensions. Those declared to be wrong, as well as those declared to be right, deserve a long view as well as an immediate response in order to get a full-blooded perspective on social change and political processes. Some leaders behave out of personal motives as if there were no political factors; other out of the same motives as if there were no moral forces. Yet, the vocabulary of motives is infinite. Politics in its prosaic sense is an intermediate expression between the private life and the moral goal. In this sense Aristotle properly placed politics as a scale inhabiting a realm between psychology on one side and ethics on the other.

The lives of Plunkitt and Stalin, Hutchinson and Trotsky, tell us about the extraordinary range and variety of political possibilities that must be taken into account far beyond the simple utilitarian impulse to win or lose. The notion of what is politically legitimate is itself subject to a moral process and democratic credos. As a result, the moral bifurcations of political life provide a limiting framework in the pursuit of political tasks. In so doing, one can gain a sense of adventure but not resolve. This brief examination of political leadership seeks to put into perspective the public life of the private citizenry; but it does not necessarily cover the converse: the private life of the public citizen. For such concerns we must still examine the normative bases of human actions.

6. Presenting the Self for Social Immortality

There is a superficial contradiction between sociology and autobiography. The former represents a description of *interactions*, whereas the latter is a self-definition of *actions*. Still, as Florian Znaniecki long ago pointed out, there is a "humanistic coefficient" between actions and interactions that in its own way legitimates the autobiographical performance as an appropriate subject for social science study. "The action of speaking a sentence, writing a poem, making a horseshoe, depositing money, proposing to a girl, electing an official, performing a religious rite, is empirical datum if it is in the experience of the speaker and his listeners, the poet and his readers, the blacksmith and the owner of the horse to be shod, the depositer and the banker, the proposing suitor and the courted girl, the voters and the official whom they elect, the religious believers who participate in the ritual."[1]

Autobiography at its most obvious level is a source of information on people, extraordinary people: deviants, famous, infamous, exaggerated. Autobiography is further a source of role modeling for "ordinary" people seeking a way out of the commonplace—at least vicariously and temporarily, if not more durably. For the purposes of these remarks, I would like to emphasize the strategic components of autobiography, or, more exactly, what performance is being carried forth by the producer of an autobiographic performance.

In this sense, we move from autobiography as a literary event to autobiography as a social injunction: a tactic for making people take seriously the words and deeds of their leaders, an arresting presentation of self, what Erving Goffman properly calls a "performance," for the purpose of giving instruction to others.[2] Autobiography in this way provides a role model for the behavior of others and, at the same time, reveals one either to be an exemplar of moral behavior to be emulated or, the reverse, an exemplar of immoral behavior and hence the pitfalls to be avoided in one's own life.

William I. Thomas, in his underground classic, *The Unadjusted Girl*, appreciated the extent to which there is always rivalry between spontaneous definitions of a situation made by members of organized society and the definitions that that society has provided. The task of the autobiographer, whether consciously or otherwise, is to interpret to society how one should conduct the "good" and avoid the "bad" influences of that society. John Sturrock, in his contribution to *New Literary History* entitled "The New Model Autobiographer," appropriately catches the spirit of this when he notes that biography may become a career, but autobiography is an unrepeatable event.[3] It has an importance greater than its value as a literary artifact. For in the act of providing meaning and unity to a private life, the autobiographer seeks to impart meaning and unity to the social order.

Behind moral injunction and role emulation stand the needs of the autobiographer. That need for transcendence and ultimately for immortality is built into the act of such revelatory writing. Whether such concerns are pathological, existential, or allegorical, the capacity of autobiography to reach beyond the individual and into the state and society also touches each person in a profound manner. Not the exemplary life, but the exemplary society is often at stake. George Herbert Mead pointed out earlier in the century that in the form of the generalized other, the social process influences the behavior of the individuals involved in it and carrying it on. The community exercises control over the conduct of its individual members. But at the same time, the task of autobiography is to point out not only what is common to all but to demonstrate that each person is different from anyone else.[4] Hence, the autobiographical enterprise in some sense demonstrates that we cannot fulfill ourselves unless we are members of a group in which there is a community of attitudes. Parenthetically, we cannot simply be a member of a community without developing a sense of individuation. It is this dialectical lesson turned didactic that autobiography renders meaningful. Louis A. Renza, in his essay entitled "The Veto of the Imagination," captures this double meaning. Although Northrop Frye makes a distinction between imagination and descriptive modes,[5] Renza shows that autobiographical writing entails a dual intention as well. The writer, in the act of becoming privately aware, also must bring that awareness into the public domain through the act of writing. Given his separation from his persona, the autobiographer, to perform his task, must make his language refer to himself allegorically and must invert the public and private elements of discourse so that it will not seem at odds with the residual consciousness of self. This properly illustrates the Meadian paradigm of mind, self, and society.

But the search for immortality is not restricted to an allegorical level. Most twentieth-century cultural and political figures have a highly secular view of immortality. What they are interested in is not so much to affect the course of heavenly events but, like Casanova,[6] to make sure that their impact on worldly events is not easily forgotten. Perhaps this is one reason why not a few autobiographers pretend to speak about themselves as someone else might, that is, by using the third person or inventing a fictional narrator. But this *pacte autobiographique* is not simply one that is restricted to novelists or writers of the past. This ritual of objectifying neurosis did not cease with Jean-Jacques Rousseau. Political figures as wide-ranging as Lyndon B. Johnson[7] and Joseph V. Stalin[8] used such objectifying techniques. In the case of Stalin, the third person was stretched so far that his autobiography was listed simply as a political biography, and the author not as an individual but an institution: in this case, the Marx-Engels-Lenin Institute in Moscow. As it turned out, and as Nikita Khrushchev was later to reveal, this was simply a rubric and device for writing an autobiography in precisely the way the maximum leader felt would be the most appropriate.[9]

The ideological nature of much autobiographical writing is built into the structure of self-justification or self-rationalization. By ideological in this instance I mean little more than rationalization, justification, and eventually exhortation of a specific social vision. It is widely and wisely understood that "talking about one's self is a feast that starves the guest." But amazingly enough, this has not proven to be a sufficient deterrent to the autobiographer. As Guy Davenport later points out: "In the autobiography there is nothing but the author, his aesthetic will, and the grist he needs for his work. As a result, too, every selfish expedient is obeyed in its own explicit exclusion from the feast." [10] The autobiography is a tendentious creation in which the self quarrels, confesses, and admires the world. Since the world in any case is a vacuum, nothing until it is filled, the autobiography serves to fill that void for generalized others as well as for particularized selves.

The Europeans, in this case, Stanislaw Eile and Michal Glowinski, come closest to appreciating the ideological dimensions of the autobiographical performance. Viewing the autobiography as first cousin to the novel, it becomes evident that the autobiography is an act of personal authorization of the narrator, of his or her real life events, and hence presumably different from the personal novel. However, this presumption is hard to maintain in fact since many first novels in particular have exactly such a characteristic. If one tactic of the autobiographer is to refer to himself in the third person singular, another is to create a novel in the first person, depending upon what is going on as written by a presumed third person.

One moves along an almost inexorable path from the autobiography as moral instruction, to personal transcendence, to social ideology, and finally, to divine or historical immortality. Elizabeth W. Bruss does well to introduce the notion of "literary gamesmanship" in this field. [11] The autobiography provides very strong imitations of the confidence racket, of seeking credibility by a highly selective presentation of information. As a result, the game of autobiography becomes one with life itself, rich with moral, aesthetic, and epistemological implications in which the real purpose of autobiography is to construct a meaningful mosaic for others, while subtly insuring a place in the cosmos for one's self. In this sense, perhaps the essay by Christine Brooke-Rose is also the most shocking, for if "biography is always fiction," autobiography is perhaps little else than a special rationalization of biography. [12] But one does not have to view autobiography as either truth or fiction, but more as self-confrontation, and hence, at its very best, as filtered self-awareness, and at its very worst, as unrefined mystification.

For the most part, autobiographies are written by, or ghosted for, those who have a presumed stake in the moral order of a society. It is not necessary that each autobiography presents an exemplary life so much as a successful public life, however filled it may have been with mishap, misfortune, or even misanthropy. Autobiography is thus largely an elite affair involving potential for emulation by the masses. There may be a special problem in the future. For example, how do those who believe in the masses create a legacy of their own good works? Mao Tse-tung did not write a personal autobiography, at least none that has become publicly available. But his wife, Chiang Ch'ing, did provide such a personal statement to an American historian, Roxane Witke. [13] Similarly, Nikita S. Khrushchev employed a comparable device to get his durable image across. [14] How odd. Totalitarian leaders enshrine their immortality by talking to Western commentators, and their works are published in the enemy world! In these cases, autobiography took the form of interview, perhaps the most easily accessible ideologically to those who make and break revolutions.

Another technique is that chosen by Vladimir I. Lenin, whose autobiography in effect was prepared by his wife, Nadezhda Krupskaya, and whose reminiscences are little more than paeans to the great leader.[15] Of course, as I have already pointed out, the simplest and most effective way to write perfect autobiography is to prepare a work about one's own life and then define it as a biography. In that way one has the benefit of objectivity as well as the cloak of anonymity. However, the trouble with this technique is that it is too readily found out.[16]

There is a sociological dimension to autobiography that goes beyond the literary questions; that is, will totalitarian systems, with their special emphasis on mass participation and mass identification, come to find the autobiographical genre intolerable? First, if the autobiography is completely honest, the subject may create such hostile conditions as to invite punishment, exile, or execution. Second, the ideological underpinning of most autobiography must perforce be what makes one life different from another. This, in turn, may imply a level of competition, of the differentiation of self from others, that might be found intolerable in authoritarian regimes. Third, behind all of these rubrics is the fact that ruling elites in totalitarian systems, culturally no less than politically, so identify the course of historical events with their personal lives that there is no longer a need for autobiography. What one has is a series of self-fulfilling prophecies. The autobiographer becomes the engineer of the soul and merely transforms his personal whims into scientific truth. But the dictator, like the showman, can be found out. And at this point, autobiography is transformed into grim comedy.

These kinds of issues exceed the tasks of a strictly formalist set of criteria for understanding autobiography. They certainly have eluded the social scientific literature as well. In fact, while there has been a modest, ongoing sociological interest in biography, from theoretical efforts to fuse biography and history[17] to methodological efforts to reconstruct biography in the creation of research files,[18] there is little corresponding interest in or analysis of the political or strategical aspects of autobiography. There are many reasons for this, starting with the simple feeling that autobiography is not a fit subject for political discourse, implying, understandably if rather conventionally, fear that any sort of professional self-examination is akin to self-celebration. As the case may be, I have been involved, more as an editor than as an author, in stimulating the autobiographical sensibilities.

This started with an attempt to probe the subjective side of social science creativity, to understand what makes some performers outstanding even if they have had common or shared starting points with others in a discipline.[19] In the preface to *Sociological Self-Images*, I noted a genuinely interesting phenomenon: the wide consensus that there is in fact a subjective side to methodology, that the simple egalitarianism of the training process cannot in and of itself either describe or define the limits of intellectual endeavor and creation. Thus what becomes clear is the existence of a set of factors, still less frequently examined, having to do with the behavior of unusual people, and it is these parameters, these factors, that begin to close the gap between the information we have about the world and the knowledge we have about the producers of that information.

In this work, scholars such as George C. Homans, William Foote Whyte, Seymour Martin Lipset, James F. Short, Jr., and Robert A. Nisbet made remarkable contributions. Their work demonstrates that even beyond the subjective aspects of creativity, there is a sense of transcendence that has nothing to do with religious meaning but has to do with the professional life, that is, the transcendence of one's own narrow, parochial frame of reference, the ability to situate one's self in a larger world and to incorporate those experiences into one's intimate world. It was the same lesson that James D. Watson noted in the world of experimental biophysics.[20]

Whatever else autobiography is, it is an act of writing. If the vocabulary of motives for preparing an autobiography is infinite, the capacity to carry it off as a literary device is severely finite. The commentary most frequently heard by those asked to prepare autobiographical vignettes is "painful."[21] The pain derives not simply from the anguish of self-reflection but also from having to come to terms with the requirements of a literary genre unfamiliar to most people outside the area of literature. Yet precisely this infusion will ultimately make possible a transformation of the diverse cultures of science and art into a unified framework and assist in bringing about the humanistic coefficient of which Znaniecki spoke but to which few have paid attention.

American social science, particularly after World War II, doggedly entered the path of professionalization, refusing to acknowledge introspective or autobiographical explorations that strayed too far afield from disciplinary horizons. Whatever else professionalization has produced, it has created a sense of commonality rather than distinct personalities: a focus in the facts rather than on an individual who identified or even manufactured events. The growth of professionalization has thus tended to make the field less individualistic, indeed suspicious of the idiosyncratic potentials of autobiography. Organization men rather than famous figures have emerged as central. In such circumstances, given the impulse to organizational accommodation, the personal, intimate side of scientific creativity has remained largely unchanged. But the most unfortunate by-product of this imbalance between objective facts and personal feelings is a social science lacking in reflective appreciation—either of its achievements or limitations.

7. Alienation and the Social System

Despite the incredible degree of confusion that exists about the term *alienation*— a confusion that has caused many influential people in sociology and psychology to try to do without it[1]—there is a danger in a premature scrapping of the term. There are few enough words in the vocabulary of social science having wide generic implications. In some sense the very confusions about the word *alienation* represent an acute, albeit painful, testimonial to conceptual complications resulting from the autonomous development of the social and behavioral sciences. The heavy freight placed on such words as *anomie, aggression, intuition, instinct*, and now *alienation*, is a burden better met by clarifying the meanings than by urging their premature abandonment on the grounds that any word admitting of multiple different definitions is meaningless, or the equally spurious goal of preserving formal symmetry.

Alienation, like so many other theoretical issues, owes a debt to the philosophical ambiguities of nineteenth-century German realism. Nascent within German philosophical sources were the current schisms and polarization of meanings in the word alienation. Rather than settle upon a questionnaire or survey on meanings of alienation, which ends up invariably in reductionist efforts to chart individual behavior over and against social systems, it might be worthwhile to examine some of the baggage the term alienation is freighted to carry.

Hegel argues that the true meaning of alienation lies in the separation of the object of cognition from the man of consciousness, the philosopher. Hence, for Hegel the chief way of overcoming alienation is through philosophical understanding, an embrace of the rational world; as if to know the world is somehow to be at one with that world, to become identified with it. To be reasonable for Hegel is the same as being at peace. It was in this problem that the equation of reality with rationality was the resolution of the problem of philosophical alienation; just as the reduction of reason to reasonableness was the resolution of the problem of practical alienation.

In the philosophy of Ludwig Feuerbach, alienation comes to be seen as an anthropological problem. The word *anthropology* was being used as a surrogate for *psychology*, since Feuerbach neither knew of nor really appreciated anthropology in any exact, empirical sense. Feuerbach considered the problem of alienation as a separation out, a parceling out, of human consciousness in which one part of man is invested (properly) in the material world, and another in the world of God, the projective ideal world. In effect the dualism in Feuerbach is almost Platonic. The material world being dreary and dismal gives rise to a set of projections about a spiritual world's perfection. As long as these two worlds remain separated there cannot be any resolution of the problem of alienation.

One can say, curiously enough, that the idealist, Hegel, is closer to a sociological view of alienation than the materialist, Feuerbach. The reason is that Hegel conceived of overcoming alienation by means of a set of activities which would connect up the subject of being with the object of the world, whereas in Feuerbach, the resolution of alienation is psychological in that it means an overcoming of the projective neurotic aspects of belief.

It is a disservice to consider Marx's notion of alienation within a strictly philosophical framework, since Marx insisted upon the necessity of a social scientific resolution of what had up to then been viewed as a metaphysical or humanist dilemma. It was Marx himself who made the clear and decisive break with the philosophical tradition of explaining alienation. No longer was alienation a special property of the man of reason. It became a specific property of select classes of men in factory conditions, who were, as a result of oppressive conditions, deprived of their collective rationality; which is a Hegelian way of saying that the labor context of alienation itself represented a scientific break with romanticism, a rupture consecrated in the bedrock of political revolution.

At its source, the word *alienation* implies an intense separation first from objects in a world, second from other people, third from ideas about the world held by other people. It might be said that the synonym of alienation is separation, while the precise antonym of the word alienation is integration. The main difficulty with the philosophical traditions is the assumption that those who are defined as alienated are somehow lacking and that they ought to be integrated. In both Hegel and Feuerbach therapeutic values are assigned to alienation and to integration, to the distinct disadvantage of the former and to the advantage of the latter. That is how we come to the phrasing of the term *alienated from* as somehow opposite to *integrated with*. This mystic faith in organic union invariably found its way into the work of Hegel and Feuerbach, the mystic organic union being for Hegel man as idea, and for Feuerbach idea as man. But to the degree that alienation was seen as a negative concept, to the same degree was the philosophical approach considered abstract, and unreliable in terms of psychological and sociological facts.

The really important break, therefore, which began with Marx, occurred in the modern usage of the concept of alienation, where there is a distinctive concern for distinguishing therapy from description, and separating recommendations from analysis. There is in the dialectical approach a common belief that alienation is no better or no worse than integration, that either concept might serve positive social ends. Alienation is a driveshaft of revolution; and integration is a transitional equilibrium generating new forms of separation from the mainstream, i.e., new forms of alienation. Let us now examine three fundamental categories of the concept of alienation.

In the first place, let us take the psychological meanings of alienation. Perhaps the classic definition is that given by Fromm: "By alienation is meant a mode of experience in which the person experiences himself as alien. He has become, one might say, estranged from himself."[2] It is important to take note of the fact that Fromm severely modifies the Marxian concept. He gives a definition which converts a mode of production into a mode of experience, while the Marxian proletarian laborer is neatly converted back into the Hegelian abstract person. It is evident in the work of Fromm that he is not just concerned with providing a psychological approach to alienation, but he is also giving renewed vigor to the older German romantic categorizations.

Alienation is often used as a psychological surrogate in the literature. Instead of being employed as a phenomenon of separation, it is used as a phenomenon of negation, or even of *lessness*—a suffix prefaced by *power-lessness*, *norm-lessness*, or *meaning-lessness*. In this kind of approach, alienation becomes either part of a larger body of social science literature on anomie or in turn becomes the organizing premise that absorbs anomie. The difficulty is that this definition of alienation as negation does not connect up various forms of negation. Further, alienation as anomie tends to describe the social system in terms of an assumed rationality: that which has the power, norms, and meanings is contrasted with the personality system or that which is not a condition of rationality.[3]

At its most elevated form, the psychological definition of alienation is linked to the notion of ideology by a hidden set of assumptions about the unnatural condition that alienation represents to the human spirit. This in turn is fused with the notion of how intellectuals view their roles in a social world. "A great deal of contemporary thought finds a state of alienation precisely in those ideologies which profess to predict with high confidence the outcome of people's behavior. Intellectuals especially find themselves alienated in a world of social determinism; they wish for a world in which the degree of social predictability would be low."[4] In Feuer's concept of alienation, the notion turns out to be much more positive in its potential effects than in almost any other theory. With Feuer it is almost as if one has to overcome integration rather than alienation to arrive at scientific truth. Integration is held to yield precisely the kind of normlessness which is characteristic of an identification with rootlessness and machinelike behavior in general. Feuerbach thus offers a prototype of what in the literary tradition of Zamyatin, Huxley, and Orwell is the alienated man as an anti-utopian—a social realist.

The main contribution of the psychological school of alienation has been to demonstrate the universality of the concept, its connection to the personality structure as well as the social structure, and therefore its existence in socialist societies no less than in capitalist societies.[5] The psychological school holds that the foundation, the reservoir of nonparticipation in the social system (or even refusal to participate in that system) may be constructive as well as destructive. In this sense alienation is more akin to defiance than it is to disorganization. It is not a synonym for neurosis or psychosis so much as it is a notion of marginality, which is consciously or unconsciously held. The problem of alienation stems from a lack of accurate perception of social norms rather than from an active defiance of these norms; that is to say, alienation is a condition of ignorance even more than it is of exploitation.

The sociological tradition is perhaps a consequence of this distinction between psychic disorganization and social disorganization. A whole new set of variables is called into force. In this Marx himself set the tone, since alienation was viewed as the particular response of the working man to the externality of his product. It was, in effect, a class dysfunction between the producer of goods and their ownership.

What, then, constitutes the alienation of labor? First, the fact that labor is *external* to the worker, i.e., it does not belong to his essential being; that in his work, therefore, he does not affirm himself but denies himself, does not feel content but unhappy, does not develop freely his physical and mental energy but mortifies his body and ruins his mind. The worker therefore only feels outside himself. He is at home when he is not working, and when he is working he is not at home. His labor is therefore not voluntary, but coerced; it is *forced labor*. It is therefore not the satisfaction of a need; it is merely a *means* to satisfy needs external to it. Its alien character emerges clearly in the fact that as soon as no physical or other compulsion exists, labor is shunned like the plague. External labor, labor in which man alienates himself, is a labor of self-sacrifice, or mortification. The external character of labor for the worker appears in the fact that it is not his own, but someone else's, that it does not belong to him, that in it he belongs, not to himself, but to another. Just as in religion the spontaneous activity of the human imagination, of the human brain and the human heart, operates independently of the individual—that is, operates on him as an alien, divine or diabolical activity—in the same way the worker's activity is not his spontaneous activity. It belongs to another. It is the loss of his self.[6]

Once Marx opened this Pandora's box of the social and cross-cultural locale of alienation, it was just a matter of time before others would see alienation of different social sectors from those Marx had dealt with. Thus, for example, in a modern view of bourgeois society, that held by C. Wright Mills, alienation becomes a lower-middle-class phenomenon, something which debases salesgirls, technicians, and even intellectuals in a similar way. In this, Mills provided not only a bridge from one class to another, but even more important, a way of viewing alienation as a problem for all nonruling classes, and not just the factory-anchored urban proletariat. "In the normal course of her work, because her personality becomes the instrument of an alien purpose, the salesgirl becomes self-alienated. Men are estranged from one another as each secretly tries to make an instrument of the other, and in time a full circle is made: one makes an instrument of himself and is estranged from it also."[7]

Most recently we have had the example of alienation as a specific artistic problem, as a problem connected to the marketing of ideas rather than to the production of goods. In this sense alienation is seen to have different functional prerequisites. The new work of Alberto Moravia contains a clear delineation of the alienation of the worker from the alienation of the artist. He offers a clearly defined expression of qualitatively different notions of alienation that are involved in different social sectors. In this approach there is an attempt to link alienation to specific types of work done, and hence to a fragmentation of the notion of alienation rather than fragmentation of the notion of stratification.

The standard sociological perspective is to see alienation as a phenomenon of a unitary type, with differences being attributed to the stratification system. In Moravia, quite to the contrary, we have the unique case of a stratification system giving rise to different forms of alienation. In this we have a more advanced sociological notion of alienation than any thus far given.

There is no relationship between the alienation of the worker and the alienation of the artist. The worker is alienated because, in the economy of the market, he is a piece of goods like any other and as such he is defrauded of his surplus value, or of what represents his value as a man, whereas the artist creates an object that has no market (or, if it has, it is not that of necessities that always have a market) and no real price in money or kind. In other words, when he hands his book over to the publisher, his music to the conductor, or his painting to the art dealer, the artist has already been paid and whatever he receives after that is a bonus. Hence, the alienation of the artist consists in the total or partial prevention of his expression, or of his true relationship with society.[8]

The third general variety of alienation theory is based on considering it as part of a general cultural milieu. Within this framework, we find alienation spoken of in national or state terms, for example, the American ideology or the Soviet ideology. Marx, for instance, in dealing with the German ideology, dealt with that ideology as if it was a reflection of the ruling class diffused throughout the general society of the times. The newer cultural pluralistic approach emphasizes the mass cultural approach. Boorstin offers a particularly interesting variety of this approach.

We expect anything and everything. We expect the contradicting and the impossible. We expect compact cars which are spacious; luxurious cars which are economical. We expect to be rich and charitable, powerful and merciful, active and reflective, kind and competitive. We expect to be inspired by mediocre appeals for "excellence," to be made literate by illiterate appeals for literacy. We expect to eat and stay thin, to be constantly on the move and ever more neighborly, to go to a "church of our choice" and yet feel its guiding power over us, to revere God and to be God. Never have a people felt more deceived and disappointed. For never have a people expected so much more than the world could offer.[9]

The culturalist approach is no less critical of alienation as a status than any of the other approaches. Even from the quotation just read one can see their criticism is severe. What is new and particularly interesting is the assumption of the national character from which the concept of alienation flows. The mass cultural school at its peak, with men like Dwight MacDonald and David Riesman, represents an interesting fusion of the psychological and sociological approaches. Alienation comes to be seen as a discrepancy, a measurable discrepancy, of achievements and expectations. At the general sociocultural level, it is a discrepancy between national demands or national purposes and individual demands for an extension of autonomy and pluralism.[10]

One final expression of this cultural style is the tradition of alienation as a religious phenomenon, specifically, alienation as characteristic of marginal religious groupings. This view of alienation held by men like Karl Barth, Paul Tillich, and Martin Buber has strong ties to Feuerbach. Commentary on the current status of Jews in America is illustrative. As Isaac Rosenfeld once said, "Jews are specialists in alienation." They are alienated from a diaspora, alienated from a redemptive God, and alienated from nationalism as such.[11] Of course, alienation as an authentic religious expression has become a major theme for all Western religions.

This view of alienation as marginal has a great deal in common with the psychological view, just as the mass cultural view has a great deal in common with the sociological view. One can begin to detect a synthesis taking place in present-day expectations of alienation: a systematic linkage of psychological states, sociological classes, and cultural forms.

The location of the problem has now decisively shifted. The problem is no longer a fusion of psychological or sociological cultural techniques. The study of aliena-tion is now confronted with a distinction between two modalities of analyses, one normative and the other descriptive. The normative approach tends to emphasize root categories, such as those provided by Seeman and Nettler in their respective works emphasizing operational definitions capable of survey designs.[12] Descriptive analysis tends to emphasize the weaknesses in the psychological approach by point-ing out that the formal modes of analysis are invariably ad hoc. While operational approaches disaggregate alienation into its psychological components, they provide little indication of how the types of alienation or the models built are related to a larger social structure or why they should be restricted to three, four, or five in num-ber. Descriptive approaches tend to see alienation in a problem-solving context. While they have difficulty in settling upon the relation of alienation to deviance, marginality, creativity, etc., they do have the value of linking analysis to empirical, rather than formalistic modalities.[13]

It might well be that this is simply a social scientific reflex of the ongoing debate concerning the analytical and synthetic modes of argument. Whatever the case may be, it is clear that the literature on alienation has tapped into something extremely meaningful in the emergence of modern social science. Once the various meanings and levels at which the term alienation is employed can be properly understood, then social scientists will be better able to employ alienation as a central variable in discussing other features of social structure and process. The task of philosophy in this area might be a clarifying one, to show how various usages of alienation are either synonymous, overlapping, or entirely different from one another. The phi-losopher might develop some kind of logical or periodic table of alienation. This is what modern philosophy of science is all about.

The concept of alienation has become a sociological fixture because it points to a series of distinctive psychological conditions brought about by a variety of causes: from a sense of insignificance in a world of power to the intensification of private experience at the expense of the public commonweal. Organizing concepts like alienation are usually pegged at a level of generalization that is sufficiently ambigu-ous to serve the cause of narcissism at one end of the scale to revolution at another. From my own perspective, alienation is the generalized expression of loss—of per-sonality, power, prestige, or what have you. When loss becomes intense it is experi-enced as a style of life (which accounts for Feuer's positive alienation); when win-ning is seen as an unattainable goal, alienation serves to express both the longing and the unavailability of success in social life. If such a broad-ranging definition is accurate we can expect to have the concept of alienation with us long after the em-bers of any personal relocation or political revolution have died down.

8. Futurology and Millenarian Visions

One of the pleasant fictions of orthodox sociologists is that science is modern, in contrast to journalism, which is backward. I suspect, however, that in this respect sociology, like all other persuasions touching upon the life and death of human beings, falls prey to its worst examples and conventions. The cult of futurism, not only in its sophisticated sociological expressions but also in its pedestrian ideological forms, exhibits many of these tendencies. We have Norman Vincent Peale desperately urging us into the future by demanding an end to social problems in the name of personal resolution.

> As a nation we have a future, a real future. And one reason I believe this is that increasingly people everywhere are hearing a fresh, new, vital question. It is not that old helpless query, "Why doesn't somebody do something about things?" That is passé, a bygone question. Instead, lots of people nowadays are resolutely asking, "What can I do?"[1]

Then we have Lowell Thomas revising the Panglossian Doctrine by locating the best of all worlds in the United States.

> After roaming the world for more than six decades, I am more convinced than ever that ours is the grandest country on earth, and so far as I know this is the best of all worlds. Why they are even getting ready to reopen the gold mines high in the Colorado Rockies. . . . Let's get ready for the best year we have ever had.[2]

With such universal pomp and circumstance, it is little wonder that the sociological response to demands for a better future has been quick in coming.

The Rise of Oracular Sociology

A curious role sociologists play in contemporary America is that of oracle. It is understandable, if not entirely laudable, that in a secular society a group of professionals should perform ministerial functions. Sociologists have assumed this role not only because of the decline of faith in organized religion but also because a need continues to be felt for some kind of generalized wisdom about salvation as collective, terrestrial, imminent, total, and miraculous.[3] By default, or because of the modesty of others, sociologists become new theologians in a universe in which God has presumably been killed—sometimes by social scientists themselves.

The recently published papers of Daniel Bell,[4] Leo Cherne,[5] George Harris,[6] and the decennial thoughts of Daniel Patrick Moynihan[7] are impressive in that they suggest the persistence of an oracular tradition, even among empirical social scientists. What might have formerly been an uncomfortable role becomes all of a sudden quite gratifying. Social scientists appear untroubled by the clerical role despite the fact that few claim theological license (although the American sociological ancestry is very much wrapped up with theology). They respond to a need for realistic yet comforting answers during a period in history in which theological tradition does not offer the kinds of answers that are desired by a highly industrialized and modernized society.

Unlike the theologian, futurologists tend to exaggerate differences with the past; they have an apparently insatiable need to distinguish our times from all others. For them, we live only in the present moment in time and only in that moment in space. Therefore, it is little wonder that the futurologists want to see the present moment in special terms, even if those terms are cast in the dismal language of crisis and convulsion. Perhaps theologians, who deal in larger time spans, have greater wisdom than social scientists, for they suggest a continuity of present needs with past performances. An essay by Barbara W. Tuchman[8] makes this same point most succinctly. She describes a "typical" century, the fourteenth century, and implies that the twentieth century might be very much like that century. After all, idiot kings and corrupt dynasties have much in common with corrupt executives and idiot advisors. The fourteenth century, she observes, was violent, bewildered, disintegrating, and calamitous; in brief, exciting but not especially distinguished.

Some sociologists share with futurologists that extraordinary enthusiasm for the present, an assumption that the period they are living through is somehow more fragile than any other, filled with tragedies not before felt, and accomplishments not before realized. One way we do this is by spurious arguments, by centennial analogies, by comparing ourselves with great epochs like the thirteenth-century City of God and the eighteenth-century City of Man. Tuchman well understands that our age may be a much more ordinary and prosaic period than we admit to ourselves. Indeed, our centennial accomplishments to date are more in the nature of destruction than construction. The fourteenth century had its black plagues, in which nature violated man; but what prior century could boast of three holocausts costing millions of lives: Nazi concentration camps, the atomic bombings of Japan by the United States, and the Gulag Archipelago in the Soviet Union? The plagues of our age are visited by people upon other people. Certainly, such criminal immolation has no comparison in any previous century.

This sense of the ordinariness of the past might well be consoling and instructive, especially in the face of our own civil disarray. Reflections on ourselves from the perspective of six hundred years might provide a more revealing, albeit more modest, image than the clutter of immediacies does. For that matter, simple comparison with a great era like that of ancient Athens or thirteenth-century Paris is gratuitous. Certain ways of behavior, certain reactions against fate, throw mutual light upon other epochs. Tuchman shrewdly notes that the fourteenth century was nondescript in terms of actual world historic achievement. Yet to the people who lived in the fourteenth century, like those of our twentieth century, it was a moment of truth. It is intriguing that, when we compare two epochs—any two epochs—we rarely treat an ordinary century like the fourteenth century in comparative terms because of our temporal self-centeredness. If one is Roman Catholic, the choice is usually the thirteenth-century City of God; if one is secularist, the choice is usually the eighteenth-century City of Man. Academics are not interested in dull centuries. We do not want to believe that our particular century is dull, that we are living through one hundred years of relative uncreativity. Yet it is entirely possible that our century is not quite as exciting and not quite as precisely delineated an era as we should like to believe.

We are now going through a period that is somewhat different from former great epochs, but more like the dull fourteenth century: an antihistorical, superstitious era. In the past, the passion for truth was historical; the feeling throughout the nineteenth century, in the tradition of Michelet, Hegel, and Marx, was that to know history was somehow to know truth. In the twentieth century, with the decline of historiography and with the decline of faith in the veracity and accuracy of historical judgment, we have turned our passions upside down. We are now much more consumed by a presumed knowledge of the future. Futurology is as important in Eastern Europe as in the United States and Western Europe. Intellectuals now demand, not so much *past* confirmation of the present, but *future* confirmation of the present.

One cannot push the analogy with past centuries too far. There are specific characteristics of the twentieth century that distinguish it—unfortunately not so much in its creativity as in its crematoria. Ours is the century of total destruction. Hiroshima, Nagasaki, Auschwitz, and Belsen all have as their common denominator the capacity for technological totalitarianism: specifically, the genocidal destruction of select, sample populations. The existence of a psychological threshold, not a military or technological threshold, with respect to the use of atomic weapons and gas chambers illustrates the enormous differences between the potential for total annihilation in our century and that of any previous epoch, much less the fourteenth century. The black plagues may have taken an equivalent number of lives, but they did so through ignorance of unseen germs, natural causes, in short through (presumably) providential anger and not political willfulness.

The tentativeness of present-day social life has led to a veritable celebration of what past centuries thought of as negative personality traits: alienation, privatization, anomie, and so on. Beyond that, the huge concentration of destructive power in the hands of the very few has properly infused a feeling of powerlessness as well as aimlessness in the very many. Thus the very scientific discoveries that should have encouraged feelings of greatness and even grandeur have to the contrary encouraged the deepest feelings of collective and individual doubt about science, technology, and knowledge as such. In other words, every paradigm that defines the modern order of things now conjures up the deepest feelings of pessimism and returns us to the millenarianism and salvationism that are likely to adopt the rhetoric and mannerisms of this supreme age of analysis and science.

Both sociology and futurology are a consequence of the same problem: namely, our own discomfort and disquiet with the present moment. What we really want to know about is ourselves; and what we want to elucidate under any criteria is how to live in this twenty-four-hour period, followed by the next twenty-four-hour period.

From this point of view, futurology, or the "science" of looking into the future, is in fact based upon the same psychic feelings and needs as those of intellectuals who insist upon looking into the past to cope with the present.

Plunging into Oracular Sociology: Decennial Tendencies

Despite these lengthy prolegomena on the risks and dangers of oracular sociology, I shall tread the same murky waters. Knowledge of past errors scarcely prevents us from making similar mistakes in the present. My immodest goal is to characterize the 1970s in contrast to the 1960s; and I hope, at the same time, to elucidate the enduring features of this century in contrast to past, and in all likelihood, more humane centuries.

An American paradox is that today's outrage may well turn into tomorrow's commonplace, while nearly every commonplace statement can with equal impunity become intensely suspect. This is a nation built upon polarities: brutality and sentimentality, nobility and infamy, philanthropy and high thievery. But these are not the sort of dialectical interactions that lead to regeneration and transformation; rather they are unyielding bifurcations that characterize American society. The forms of such polarizations constantly change, yet reconciliation remains as distant as ever. Perhaps this is why after two hundred years Americans are still in nervous search for that elusive higher ground and remain as fascinated with their own past and future as any nation in Africa or Asia, while being no more confident of the future than these new nations.

The first major transformation that distinguishes the 1970s from the 1960s is what might be called the decline of racial politics and the sublimation, although less pronouncedly because of its later start, of sexual politics. Despite the endless stream of outpourings, ravings, and mouthings about problems connected with race and sex in America, the fact of the matter is that the steam has gone out of many ascriptive sentiments. One need only note that the only potent organizational forces in American black life date from the 1950s and earlier: the NAACP, the Urban League, and the black churches. With the marginal exception of the Black Muslims, or Nation of Islam, practically every organizational form of the sixties has either been dissolved or has receded into obscure oblivion. The struggles that now take place are largely between the black bourgeois and the black proletariat, between blacks in the suburbs and blacks who remain behind in the hard-core poor areas of the city. These are as intense as, and even more intimate than, relations between blacks and whites. Issues dividing the races remain real enough, but the very selective and partial nature of their resolution has only highlighted intraracial strife between those who are making it and those who are not.

This same sort of fragmentation, although taking profoundly different shape, is now evident in the movements of sex and generation against being confined and defined by an ascribed status. Since the women's movement was largely amorphous to begin with, it has not suffered from a loss of what it never possessed: a coherent organizational form. Still, one senses a genuine polarization along class lines between demands of women for economic equality and others for sexual freedom. Organizational priorities remain unsettled. While these demands need not be polarized, given the different constituencies involved at each end of the ideological stick, economic and sexual needs tend to become disaggregated. It would seem that the higher the economic status of women, the greater the demand for cultural forms to follow suit. Such demands, very often against the constraints of parenthood and household chores, share much in common with the general middle-class drives toward psychologism, privatization, and intensely personalistic explanations of worldly events.

In the 1970s there was a decline particularly in the confrontational aspects of politics and a pendulum swing back to what might best be termed achievement politics—i.e., "getting ahead of the system." "Getting ahead" politics can mean anything from policy making in a corporate context, to rising within a trade union hierarchy, to participating in working-class politics. The return of an achievement orientation to the economic and political life of America was a central reality of the 1970s, and this factor was highlighted by the renewed vigor of industrial unionism in that period.

A great deal of American history makes sense in terms of this dichotomy between achievement and ascription. It explains the forms of mobility, not just the facts of mobility. Sociologists are much too cavalier about the words *class*, *sex*, and *race*, not realizing the difference between possibilities of income mobility and the relative immobility of items such as race, religion, and sex. Certainly the deepest fear of the black community is that even with class mobility, and even with the possibility of socialism, they might still be confronted by profound racial bias in American society. Indeed, if the patterns of the socialist world are to be taken remotely seriously, one would have to say that such nationalist fears are considerably supported by the evidence. Socialists, like sociologists, have much to explain for their inability to take account of huge gaps between class mobility and relative racial immobility within advanced industrial nations.

The emergence of black consciousness was greatly enhanced by anti-establishment black organizations that emerged from the civil rights movement of the 1960s. Even as catalysts, such organizations as the Congress of Racial Equality and the National Welfare Rights Organization served an immense purpose in the sustained drive for increased black participation, representation, and equity. But it was an equity within the system rather than against the system. Likewise, the organizational expression for women's rights, from the National Organization of Women to the various splinter groups urging everything from lesbianism to abstinence, also served to redress major grievances within American society. And as long as high production and profitability were maintained, such demands by women could be met. The generational or student movement was simpler yet to accommodate, since for the most part its basic demands were for greater educational participation rather than any increased portion of the American pie.

The specific organizational forms that emerged in the 1960s quickly fulfilled their norms and ceased to exist. In place of these organizations, more broad-gauged and

even conservative forms emerged that better suited the scope and magnitude of racial, sexual, and generational needs. It is a melancholic truth that radical expressions of protest, when anchored to real needs, find these same demands articulated—often in a diluted form, to be sure—by mainline social and political agencies.
As a result, radicalism finds itself subverted as often by its successes as by its
failures. This certainly seems to be the case for the 1960s, during which forms of
repression, while real enough, were not nearly at the force commensurate with the
destruction of these new organizations. Such destruction came about as a result of the
inner contradictions of a left with a series of programs, but without the support of a
mass base to carry them out. The price of ideological purity came high: insulation
from working-class economic realities and isolation from mainline political reforms.

In the wake of the disintegration of sixties' organizations a new aspect arose, one I
refer to as the Hobbesian condition of working-class sentiments in contrast to their
often presumed Marxian condition. The working class, especially its vanguard trade
union quartile, became the bulwark of the established order, rather than its enemy.
The tensions that emerged in the 1970s were much more heavily weighted on the
side of class politics, rather than race, generational, or sexual politics. Perhaps it is
a tribute to the wisdom of traditionalists in the trade union movement that they saw
this coming more clearly than did most spokesmen for the new left, who deprecated
class economics in the name of a raucous, often nonexistent mass politics.

The resurrection of trade-union movements came about in a politically conservative climate, in contrast to the racial, sexual, and generational politics of the sixties
that took place (ostensibly at least) in a more radical antiwar environment. This is a
crucial difference between the 1970s and the 1960s, because this geist helps to
shape the character of class struggle and of something even more basic: how the
social system and the political order are to be run, how they are to be altered, and by
whom. The question of class once again became a central consideration, whereas
the question of ascription or caste was reshelved. The consequences of this change
are not easy to ascertain. But as long as there is serious, growing doubt in the public's mind that the American economic system may not be able to deliver high levels
of goods and services to its citizenry, the pendulum will remain firmly on the side of
achievement considerations. It is only when goods turn into goodies that the clamor
for greater equity among contending ascriptive groups becomes central.

One serious consequence of this return to achievement considerations in both
politics and economics is polarization between the haves and the have-nots. This
gap increased markedly even in the first few years of the 1970s. Haves and have-
nots are defined not simply in terms of racial, generational, or sexual criteria, but in
terms of clear economic criteria. Class polarization results from inflationary economics; it is a consequence of less housing, less money for mortgages, fewer available mortgages for existing housing, shortages and price increases in food, gasoline, and other goods. Those who continue to have a substantial stake in the system
have the wherewithal to live in very high style.

In contrast to the earlier decades of the twentieth century, a distinct class polarization took place in the 1970s as a result of an economic situation much different

from the Depression years, but one that had nonetheless similar consequences: a widening gap between wealthy and poor, between opulence and impoverishment. There was a selection of haves and have-nots, as there always has been. But curiously, there was also polarization even within black life: a slender majority of the black community could be classified (and from their own point of view had to be classified) as middle class rather than lower class or working class. This was an enormous shift, not only in black life, but in the character, in the tenor, of the 1970s. It was no longer quite so easy for everyone to fit the old category of middle American.[9]

Along with this polarizing element was the depolitization of the young. Economic polarization, the resurgence of an achievement orientation, and the plain fear of working-class conservative power reduced generational consciousness. Beyond that, the collapse of generational power was a response to something that is inevitable in almost every generation, but is extremely painful when it occurs: *la trahison des clercs*, the treason of intellectuals.

The leadership of the political generation of the young in the 1960s became either quiescent or self-liquidating by the 1970s. Rennie Davis formerly urged the young to participate in civil disobedience; in the seventies he wanted his dwindling constituency to crawl, if necessary, to serve the One Perfect Master. Others, like Jerry Rubin, have become prophets of a hi-tech capitalism, including the wonders of investment in the stock market. Others claimed leadership in nonexistent communist and radical organizations before fading into oblivion; still others have turned to new cults or returned to the true and perfect church; and finally, some became jet set radicals. Such tendencies within the leadership of the youth generation of the 1960s generated a disorientation that contributed enormously to quiescence.

In past generations, conservative, liberal, and radical organizational life shared a democratic code turned into fact: leadership emanated from the rank and file. In any organization, leadership was a function, in part of quality, of chance, of virtue, of opportunity, and of being in the right place. One way or another, leadership depended on membership. But the radical movement that emerged in the sixties had no membership. The leadership, if you could call it that, was appointed by the United States government. When they indicted the Chicago Eight, they endowed, or perhaps bestowed, leadership status on people who were not leaders in any sense of the word—except perhaps in the McLuhan sense of being media celebrities, i.e., leaders in terms of knowing how to get television and press coverage.

What emerged in the 1960s, in retrospect, was a leadership fabricated by the United States government through a series of political trials. As a result of this singling out, ordinary people became self-appointed and self-anointed leaders. The strange leadership of the young, not being subject to normal organizational constraints, behaved without a sense of organization and discipline except that imposed by courtroom regimen and trial procedures. Their rampant individualism was an important factor in the demise of generational politics. McLuhanism rather than Marxism prevailed. Cultural heroes emerged who were infrequently, if ever, tied to organizational requisites. Hence a high level of idiosyncratic behavior prevailed in dwindling left-wing politics.[10] Personal style tied to media participation replaced impersonal, organizational methods of politics.

One notices the unmistakable linkage between leisure life, the private life, and the intense psychologism of that life. The public consequences of all this are the dissolution of the family as the essential unit, the breakup of marriages (though not the idea of marriage), and the breakup of community life. In general, psychologism as an ideology reflects the intense personalism in current living. The result is not so much the rugged individualism of past efforts at social mobility as it is a not-so-rugged isolationism from mainstream society. Even people who in previous generations rarely had much concern or much use for this kind of psychologism now find themselves entwined in this perspective whether they like it or not, through wives and children or through relatives of one kind or another who have chosen alternative ways of living. The world of leisure and the polarization of opulence and impoverishment are also linked to the return of class, because only class permits the life of leisure, which in turn makes possible a psychologistic point of view. The poor always live in terms of economic realities. But for the affluent, the satisfaction of material needs has led to a lessened interest in greater wealth and a concerted effort to convert affluence into immediate gratification.

This polarization between work and leisure, hand work and head work, is just as evident in the Soviet Union as it is in the United States. The gap between working for the state and having fun is even deeper, broader, and more alienating in the so-called socialist world than it is in the capitalist world. Perhaps the problem is industrialization per se, rather than production in relation to capitalism. In any event, an essential task of the twentieth century has been to overcome this dichotomy in an effort to make work a genuinely creative activity and leisure a real contribution to the work life of society. In this respect the size of a society may turn out to be as significant as its structure; and hence, I would argue that small societies or small nations have a better opportunity to solve big problems than enormous nation-states whose priorities are most often transhuman, if not categorically antihuman.[11]

Some Further Extrapolations: Centennial Tendencies

American society (in the past) has been remarkably stable at both its economic and political levels. One cannot help but admire Alexis de Tocqueville's *Democracy in America*, not only for its historical perspicacity, but also because it still seems to be such a clear and adequate description of the social psychology of Americans nearly 150 years after it was written. Likewise, one can hardly read Karl Marx's writings on the *Civil War in the United States* without feeling a similar sense of the unresolved nature of this country: North versus South, industrial versus agrarian, internationalist versus isolationist, and a host of issues raised but not necessarily resolved by the American Civil War. I am not suggesting that American life is static—far from it. Rather, the fundamental thrust of this country, its guiding value scheme, has remained remarkably vibrant throughout its two-hundred-year history. This fact has been the bane of reformers and revolutionaries; for the very ability of the nation to absorb and co-opt new industries and ideologies alike depends on this valuational underwriting of the system by the people as an entity. It may well be that things are now falling apart or that huge transformations are in the works. From my point of view again, rather than emphasizing how dramatic and apocalyptic the year 2001 will be in contrast to the year 1984, I find it much more feasible and sociologically interesting to take into account the dialectic of discontinuities and continuities within American life that have made possible the expression and subsequent absorption by the society of radical options without those radicals expressing them emerging victorious.

If one were to extrapolate further, the entire twentieth century embodies a remarkable turning away from the nineteenth-century focus on controlling modes of production to a more subtle struggle to dominate the mass media. Daniel Bell properly refers to a new scarcity, not of goods, but of information and coordination of time. He points out that the time becomes in the end an economic calculus. This calculus, however, is not entirely cultural or superstructural; in part, it is a political calculus. But Bell misses the point of his own observations: information is a consequence of control and domination and not simply orchestration and coordination. The United States could not have had the kind of political movements that emerged in the 1960s without television and the entire spectrum of the media. Likewise, one could not envision the kind of national political scene that existed in the 1970s in relation to Watergate without the existence of a well-established apparatus to allow for the instantaneous dissemination of news. In fact, the Watergate television hearings have been referred to as "Sesame Street for adults." With the exception of the devastating Army-McCarthy hearings, this is the first time in which the citizenry actually participated in senatorial hearings. The opportunity to participate, even symbolically, in the communication of ideas becomes even more important than the productive capability of the society. The struggle to dominate the informational system becomes itself a major source of social struggle often involving a major cleavage within political life. Nonetheless, while the confidence in politics eroded, there was no corresponding decline in faith in the legitimacy of the system as a whole.

In previous epochs the political subsystems in America were sufficiently separated from society as a whole to operate undisturbed, no matter what the immediate condition of the larger society might have been at any particular moment. Thus, in the past, those things that most closely affected ordinary people—transportation, communication, energy, power, commodities, foodstuffs—operated despite momentary and even endemic political crises or national tragedies. Indeed, the autonomous characteristics of the economy in past time is attested to by what used to be the relative imperviousness of the gross national product to political pressures. In the latter part of the twentieth century, this seems far less true. In the past, radical demands for greater equity were made and could be met with relative tranquility as a result of the ever-expanding profitability of the economy. Thus the sixties were superior in economic terms to the fifties, and radical politics took place more as a response to affluence than to poverty.

In the seventies, at a time of intense political crisis at both the presidential and congressional levels, we experienced a serious failure of the economic subsystem to maintain its past level of peak efficiency. Not only has a strong undertow of economic inflation wiped out personal savings and the idea of saving itself, but we have also experienced a series of minor calamities that approximate wartime conditions: fuel shortages, an energy crisis, food shortages, paper shortages. Whether such shortages are real or induced, their consequences are real enough. If life in the United States is not quite crisis-ridden, it is at least much more tentative; and the assumption that the good things will be abundantly available has gone by the boards. The automatic American faith that every need would be fulfilled and that every expectation would be realized was severely jolted in the 1970s. What might be called the ordinary activities that go on at the subsystemic level became problematic. Since this occurred precisely when the rest of the system was being shaken to its foundations, the character of the seventies can be referred to as a crisis period, however terribly overworked and overburdened that word and the suggestion of apocalyptic change it evokes may be. The 1970s, unlike the 1960s, made plainer than ever before the necessity to choose or, more exactly, the necessity to articulate, the underlying premises of the political system as a whole, if there is to be any sense of direction in resolving the keenly felt problems in the social and economic subsystems.

In an international context, a clear point of departure from the 1960s was the conviviality, if not necessarily convergence, of the United States and the Soviet Union. This political and economic situation was, worldwide, the most decisive aspect of the 1970s. Why it came about is much less a matter of presidential initiative than of fundamental strategy. On the one hand, multinational corporate structures must maintain every sort of hegemony; on the other hand, multinationalism needs an international realignment to avoid adventurism between the small powers and confrontations between the major powers at an international level. Big-power doctrines of peaceful coexistence have been reduced to a rundown of brutal, hard, ungenerous, and unyielding variables.[12] A largely hospitable climate is common to both the United States and the Soviet Union. The peoples of both nations are basically the same racial stock. Both peoples have nominally Christian traditions. Both are major industrial powers, sharing a faith in commodity affluence. Finally, both peoples have a powerful armed force and have in the twentieth century been militarily victorious, for the most part. Under the circumstances, the showdown politics of the Cold War have yielded to the accommodation politics of multinationalism. The realignment was almost inevitable on the basis of these combinations and permutations of socioeconomic factors. This rapprochement has been disastrous to the pretensions of parity by the Third World. It presents an uninviting framework for the needs of the backward nations, for whom the struggle between the United States and the Soviet Union has provided the basic wedge, a basic foot into the development-aid door during the Cold War period of 1948–71. Now that wedge has vanished and with it the edge that derived from the big-power confrontation and competition.

A shattering aspect of the twentieth century is the severe limit to any fundamental structural changes in a century that was declared to have shaken the world. Take as an example the Hobson and Lenin theories of imperialism in relation to both the first and eighth decade of the century. One finds at the beginning of this century that the United States, Russia, Japan, Western Europe, and England, the big five of imperialism, dominated the world. Now, as we draw to the close of the century, after two world wars, countless numbers of miniwars, endless social confrontations, international realignments, and permanent cold wars, whatever changes may have taken place in "systemic" terms, the list of major powers is the same: the United States, Russia, Japan, Western Europe, and England.

Every major imperialist power at the end of the twentieth century remains in the forefront of both industrial production and mass consumption. But this is less disturbing than the continuing peripheral character of the Third World to both production and consumption. Admittedly, socialist nations like China and capitalist nations like Canada, Brazil, and Australia in all likelihood will emerge as major powers of the twenty-first century. It would be foolhardy to ignore such a probability. However, progress can be very slow. Even seventy-five years and two-and-a-half world wars later, the shift of real power and industry has barely begun to take place. My point here is not only an economic one concerning the relative stability of the dominant powers over time, but also a social-psychological one: futurologists have often promulgated exaggerated notions that somehow things are changing much more rapidly than in fact they are. My point is that fundamental economic controls exercised by political elites have been enhanced rather than destroyed by technology and invention in the twentieth century. Labels have changed with breathtaking suddenness, but systems have changed much more slowly. To be sure, even where systems have changed, mechanisms of domination and repression have remained intact and, at times, even been enlarged and enhanced in the name of revolution.

One has to ask finally whether war ever really settles the question of power. The presumption, whatever the political persuasion, has almost always been that warfare in fact determines and defines national and international realignments as well as determining the winners and losers in the larger rational sense. But Germany and Japan, who presumably were losers in the classical game of imperialism, are now emerging as the most powerful nations in the world. Such a situation is hard to understand and even harder to respond to emotionally and intellectually. It is difficult to define enemies and friends when they change on a decennial basis. China was a friendly nation during World War II, an enemy in the 1950s and 1960s, and became a friend in the 1970s. Similarly, Japan was the enemy in the 1940s and has been a friend since the 1950s. Russia was a friend in the 1940s, an enemy in the 1950s, a not-so-good friend in the 1960s and 1970s, and an enemy in the 1980s.

The psychological feeling of the present period is the breakdown of parochialism and the rise of cosmopolitanism; a rise in a generic "goodwill" approach for people, for nations; a kind of pluralism in attitude; a breakdown of the idea of the church triumphant or the nation triumphant. National and other chauvinisms are collapsing not because of any new enlightenment or because people have become instantaneously virtuous, but because the world has become smaller. The tactics and strategies of the moment have changed so profoundly that no one believes in the intrinsic superiority or inferiority of anybody; or if they retain such beliefs, they can no longer put them into use on a grand scale. The result is what one might call democratization through strategy and tactics.

Another phenomenon, and one that obviously is of great concern and consequence, is the militarization of political life in the Third World. There are, in fact, few nations with civilian leadership in any part of Asia, Africa, or Latin America. Even in the poorest parts of Europe, such as Spain, Portugal, and Greece, the military has allied itself with elitism and expertise. The military as a political force (in contrast to its functions as a professional force) is typified by nondemocratic politics or by politics by expertise rather than by mass persuasion. In the 1970s, the military pressure on civilian forms of political rule became precipitous, even in the United States and Western Europe. Whether or not the kind of democratic politics that we have known and that we are presently dedicated to preserving can withstand the impact of bureaucratic expertise and administrative collectivism will become a major test for democratic rule in the coming years. The impact of elitism, the impact of decision making behind the scenes, keeping not history but a mass public in ignorance, is a problem that can no longer be dismissed. We have already seen the cracks in the democratic mirror in the United States and certainly in Europe. Thus one would have to say that a deep-rooted phenomenon of the 1970s was not simply the militarization of political life, but perhaps the change in the very style of governance, even in the industrial nations of the West. Whether or not the democratic style and the democratic system can be maintained in the face of the ongoing drive toward industrialism and the kind of nationalism that requires a military organization (if nothing else than as a symbol of relative power) is a moot point. The collapse of civilian leadership in many parts of the world has now spread to the more developed nations—with consequences yet to be understood.

Many American intellectuals tend to evaluate American realities in terms of Marxist categories, i.e., to see events in terms of class and revolution. Yet in America, the Hobbesian war of all against all, and the demand on the part of all contending groups, is not for revolution but for law and order: meaning, very concretely, a demand on the part of the masses that their elites rule—the Hobbesian paradigm. The working class has mounted an attack on effetism and privatization; it displays an anger and animosity toward a world of leisure and opulence that it fails to share. In previous decades, in previous centuries, we conceptualized the social sources of change as emanating from below. Now the impulse for change comes from the top, from political and economic elites. Innovative programming comes from a professional intelligentsia, the so-called new class. As a result, from an unrequited fear that the bourgeois emphasis on innovation is risky, poorer people demand order, structure, and survival of the system. In the early 1980s this certainly was a factor in the strategy and tactics of Republican party politics, no less than that of the conservative wing of Democratic party politics. We are witnessing a shifting phenomenon that in general overrides classical European Marxist notions of class interest: the middle Americans want the system to survive, while the so-called ruling classes are much less certain about the matter. This is true in terms of the uneducated vis-à-vis the educated; the rank and file vis-à-vis the avant-garde; ordinary parishoners in contrast to church reformers and radicals. At every level one finds a similar three-step structure to class values, with a small ruling class and a shrinking welfare class far less certain of an American ideology than a large middle stratum.

This view has little in common with the fashionable concept of working-class authoritarianism. The insistence on legitimacy and law is a far cry from a demand for restoration and reaction. Indeed, what we are increasingly confronted with is a three-tier system: a working class concerned with legitimacy; a middle class with intense reforming instincts concerned with social change, and when it cannot achieve that, a change in rhetoric and ideology; and finally, a ruling class made irresolute by competing and nearly balanced claims of the lower classes and the middle classes. What appears to be a wavering, unsteady characteristic of the ruling class is indeed a quality of American and Western life in general. This sense of political and moral ambiguity is a result of attempts by the ruling class to lean simultaneously in two directions: toward the political needs of a mass constituency and toward the sociological needs of a class constituency. This tension between mass and class in American life reflects itself in a ruling elite not nearly as sure of its goals as it was earlier in the century, but not quite as puttylike and amorphous as those who deny the existence of a ruling class entirely would have it.

As long as this three-tiered class system exists as an unresolved triadic dilemma, one is in the grips of a Hobbesian world. The conservative poor and the liberal rich may be transitory aspects of an economy in stagnation rather than symptomatic of a long-range revision in economic reality. Yet to start from Hobbes is to take seriously the autonomy of political analysis. The very preeminence of political sociology rather than political economy is the essential touchstone of our age and a key reason why so much inherited wisdom has failed us when we need it most.

The last part of the twentieth century is an age of political sociology rather than political economy. Problems of policy making, fiscal distribution, energy allocation, and the like are determined by the political system. To be sure, this political system must operate within the parameters and limitations of the economic system. But the economic classes have become limited partners in this preserving process. The survival of the market economy depends on the strength of the American state. And it is hardly a casual afterthought to note that the survival of the planned economy depends largely on the strength of the Soviet state. The present century has been a world of structural reversals, no less than role reversals: of political bases and economic superstructures. This has been the shattering lesson of twentieth-century capitalism, socialism, and fascism alike. To forsake this century morally for a utopian future that might be better or for a grandiose past that surely was better is a reasonable enough posture. But to falsify essential, overriding facts of this century is a risky proposition. Overcoming the two sides of false consciousness—ideology and utopia—is, after all, what the social sciences are pledged to perform.

Part II. Polity

9. Interest Groups and Political Partisans

The emergence of political action groups from a diverse set of vantage points—from big business to big labor, from pro-life to pro-choice, from gun control to gun toting, ad infinitum—has raised anew some fundamental issues in American society. Specifically, the key question posed is the relationship of national systems to personal interests. With only a slight variation in language, from scholarly journals through popular weeklies, the theme being widely echoed is similar: the decline of American national commitment and a corresponding increase of single-issue groups.

What is so remarkable about the assault of interest-group politics on the political process is its currency across ideological divides. One can hear echoes of complaint from left no less than right. It turns out, on inspection, that most critics are not nearly as disturbed by interest groups as they are by advocates of interests in opposition and contrast to their own. This hardly astonishing finding does not, however, obviate the need for probing this phenomenon of political action committees; it does compel an appreciation of their actual role in American society.

Robert J. Pranger, in an impressive essay on the decline of the American national government, views the source of interest-group politics on "the crowding of preemptory demands at the national level." This crowding could well become even more congested by more refined interest groups. The rapid decline of any belief in the public good has been associated with the national government's fall from its legitimate constitutional position.[1] A similar attack on interest-group or single-issue politics was launched by Kevin Phillips when he described the situation as "nothing short of the Balkanization of America." Indeed, for Phillips, the only alternative way of describing the situation is the tribalism of America. He prefers the notion of Balkanization because of its "cloudy, geographic character." In essence, Phillips believes that,

> as the politics of natural-gas pipelines resemble the plots and counterplots of Zagreb and Sofia, so also can one find just as much social Balkanization in the rise of feminism or "gay rights," or in "Red Power" demands of American Indians—for tribal sovereignty and the return of former Indian lands—from Maine to California. For the past several years the symptoms of decomposition have appeared throughout the body politic—in the economic, geographic, ethnic, religious, cultural, biological sectors of society. Small loyalties are replacing larger ones. Small outlooks are also replacing larger ones.[2]

The range of people striking the theme of America the splintered extends from Henry Fairlie on the right to David Broder on the left. For Fairlie, this fragmentation is not simply reflected in interest-group politics, but in the breakdown of American ideology. He bemoans the loss of an American national religion. Fairlie contrasts the great sermons of the past which united the preacher with his audience

with the tired political rhetoric of the present, which only breeds suspicion and contempt for either side. Fairlie's position, because it is so nicely articulated, deserves
citation:

> When our politicians now reach to tired images, like the 'war' on poverty or the
> 'war' for energy, it is because there is no sense of community for them to arouse.
> There is no eloquence to move us, because they can find no community to move.
> Images and parables and allusions—the stock of every good sermon in the past—
> were drawn from a communal life that was strong and immediate. You cannot
> address a sermon to an individual; you can address it only to a communion. If we
> find it difficult today to use the big words—Loyalty-Patriotism-Comradeship-
> Duty—it is because we try to give them a meaning for the individual only,
> whereas they have meaning only in the individual's ties with his fellow beings. It
> is this that we lack, and it is why we lack the eloquence of sermons.[3]

David Broder sees the solution to interest groups in much more secular terms, not
as a restoration of faith or political ideology, but rather as a reinvigorated party process. The alternative is dim indeed: interest-group extortion.

> Eventually, the candidates may conclude that adherence to their party offers them
> their only real protection against the extortionate demands of the single-interest
> groups. Eventually, the American voters may rediscover the truth that, without
> strong political parties, Congress and the president will be unable to come to
> grips responsibly with serious national problems.[4]

In Broder's view, the single-interest constituency is the only option, and not a
terribly attractive one to party politics. The political process becomes frustrated by
the mobilization of opposites: right-to-lifers vs. abortion-rights-supporters; gun
owners on one side and gun registration advocates on the other; farmers who demand 100 percent parity and others who want a return to a free grain market worldwide; those who advocate unrestricted industrial growth in contrast to those who
advocate environmental protection. The proverbial middle-of-the-roader is torn
apart by these extremes. According to Broder, not only the existence of interest
groups, but their uncompromising nature, destroys the potential for mass politics in
America.

Leading major news weeklies have dedicated special features to the subject. *Time*,
in a patrician philosophical mood, views America as having "entered a period of
ascendant factionalism, a time when the larger desires of society can scarcely be
heard for the insistent clamor of its numberless segments." These larger national
desires remain unspoken and can only be guessed at by the citizen. But *Time* also
adds its own dimension, at least to the rhetoric of this discussion, when it speaks of
"group pushing."

> These groups tend, in a time of fading political parties, to dominate the debate of
> all problems and often prevail in the resolution. They have become the under-
> takers for the professional politician's career and the manipulators of legislative
> bodies. What they cannot achieve by law they are often willing to achieve by

defiance. They have, most of them, an aversion to cooperation, conciliation and compromise.

The author of this essay, Frank Trippet, goes on to raise an interesting point that is at the emotional heart of much criticism of political action groups: the general decline of American sensibility.

> The rise of factionalism has occurred right along with some general diminishing of the traditional American respect for the sensibilities of others. Under the reign of permissiveness (made possible by the acquiescence of a majority of Americans), a handful of pornographers flaunt their wares heedless of the public incidentally offended, and pimps herd their whores along city streets with the same tyrannical disregard for those they might offend.[5]

This rebellion against single-issue politics, often identified with neoconservative ideologists, has been taken over by liberal politicians. Internalizing this charge and claim, Senator Gary Hart of Colorado, in an interview with *Newsweek*, explained:

> I hate to get on the plane for Denver. For three hours, the lobbyists just line up in the aisle to get a word with me. Most of them are special pleaders for business, and they generally have two messages. The first is that there is too much government, too much taxation and spending—and that they want something specific from the Federal government.

Former Senator Dick Clark of Iowa, in the same interview, attributed his defeat in a bid for reelection to the Senate to this same lobbying instinct. When an official from the Machinists and Aerospace Workers Union urged Clark to change his mind about how he would vote on a specific measure, he went on to register the following conversation:

> He said to me, "OK, if that's the case, we won't support you." I responded, "Look at my voting record as a whole. Don't make a decision like this based on a single vote." His reply was "We don't give a damn about your overall voting record. We're interested in this bill—period."[6]

Even Senator Edward Kennedy has cryptically remarked that representative government is "in the worst shape I have seen it." And given the personal assaults on his integrity, it is small wonder that he should feel this way.

Local and state political issues, such as the Jarvis-Gann Proposition 13 in California, rapidly go national. Pollsters examine states and constituencies responsive to tax relief issues, and then work up lists to generate new support from these special constituencies. Politicians in anticipation of new constituencies developing around issues respond to such interest politics. As a consequence, it is implied that intermediate layers of the political system are bypassed. Real grass-roots organizing around issues is surrendered in favor of media organization.

Part of the problem is the paralyzing effect on politics of mass media. Because its representatives are unwilling to make decisions that adherence to the special-interest point of view implies, committed voters increasingly seek relief in amendments, propositions, and initiatives. These are exactly the kinds of electoral mechanisms that are vulnerable to single-issue groups. They enable such groups to make direct appeals to national government rather than deal with the complex infrastructure of local and state government. Such devices further enable interest groups to avoid a political environment in which the issue which is of overriding importance to them is compromised. Such direct appeals, precisely to the extent that they are successful, subject legislative members and government executives to forms of pressure that they avoided in the past. They increasingly must respond to specific decisions in the context of an overriding discontent. The response that this discontent requires, whether it be equal rights amendments, right to life proposals, or homeowner tax relief, may anger other constituencies which represent other special-interest groups. These are crosscutting pressures with which politicians have heretofore not had to deal, at least not en masse.

Most of these new mail-order pressure organizations—from the National Federation of Independent Business to ERAmerica—direct their efforts toward Congress. They are not above arbitrarily taking credit for electoral victories of those they support, or claiming a hand in the defeat of those whom they oppose, even though such claims may be tenuous and not infrequently a press agent device to generate higher dollar returns on mail-order promotionals. Often these groups are led by former elected officials, for whom Washington, D.C. has become a way of life not easily surrendered. Proximity to power magically issues into a metaphysical presumption of power. These groups enhance their strength by claiming broad-based support from a wide array of organizations—both real and chimerical. The pyramid-building effect of single-issue pressure groups provides a thin veil of groundswell politics where no real force of numbers exists. Frequently, mailing-list memberships are simply arranged to attract the same people, functioning like solicitations in the magazine or mass bookclub fields and multiplying memberships rather than enlarging constituencies.

The continuing appeal of most politicized single-issue forums to the national political parties is of great significance. While some groups make a thinly disguised appeal to bipartisan support, many others have both strong and direct ties to each of the parties. In this way, interest groups, far from undermining traditional political parties, serve only to underwrite their efforts. New interest groups' appeal to popular support for funding provides more ammunition for those who believe in the ongoing strength of party life in America than the converse. There is scant doubt that groups on the liberal side still show affinity to the Democratic party, whereas those groups on the conservative side of issues reveal an equal sense of allegiance to the Republican party. Often such linkages are mediated and even muddled by token individual supporters drawn from the opposite camp. However, this very sensitivity to opposition parties tends to confirm, rather than disconfirm, continuing belief in the two-party system and government by legislative decision making.

There can be little doubt that the current wave of interest-group politics has had serious impact on the executive branch of government no less than on the legislative or electoral processes. In a recent series of articles on "Governing America" John

Hebers reports that "The United States is becoming increasingly difficult to govern because of a fragmented, inefficient system of authority and procedures that has developed over the last decade." Right, left, and center often concur in this judgment. Representative Philip M. Crane, Illinois Republican and chairman of the Conservative Union, views such failure as the "natural result of 50 years of big government." Tom Hayden, a major political voice of the left and now a California figure of some note, reports "You can take any issue you want, and the system isn't delivering. There is no glue holding the country together." And former President Carter's chief advisor for domestic affairs speaks of the United States as "an increasingly fragmented society."[7]

Perhaps the best way to illustrate the practical concerns which underlie these cries and alarms is a canceled 1980 White House Conference on Families. The conference was canceled because a decision could not be reached on whether a "white Catholic male" stemming from an "intact family" should be appointed as assistant director to offset the fact that the director was a "divorced black woman." Quite apart from the subject matter that the conference was to discuss were the panoply of organizations—American Home Economic Association, U.S. Catholic Conference, the National Association of Social Workers, the Italian American Foundation, among others—all of whom were determined to register their claims and hence effect policy through its findings and recommendations. Rather than permit this "potential land mine," as one participant called the conference, the meetings themselves were jettisoned.[8] It remains a moot point whether any serious, operational policies could have been pursued at such a conference given the depth of preexisting interest-group rivalries. What is not moot is the power of such groups to determine not only political goals, but the structure of American policy making as a whole.

There are in fact large numbers of lobbying activities: five hundred corporate lobbies, fifty-three lobbies for minority groups, thirty-four for social welfare agencies, and six for population control. Add to this overseas lobbies such as the sixty-one pushing Japanese business interests and the ten arguing for Israeli political interests—to name only two—and interest-group forces appear to be at a magnitude far greater than anything known in the past. The interest group has become the political action arm of many social organizations formerly seen as strictly voluntary associations.

Considerable numbers of people can be mobilized on an issue-by-issue basis. John Gardiner's Common Cause to Ralph Nader's Congress Watch exist to make sure that their interests are properly represented and monitored. Conservative groups are no less adroit than their liberal counterparts. Thus a group like Robert Kephart's National Taxpayers Legal Fund seeks to offer nothing short of personal freedom from the "powerful bureaucracy itself" in exchange for a modest monetary contribution. Ordinary citizens, nearly half of whom absent themselves from national, presidential elections, clearly prefer to vote with their dollars than their feet. Many political action committees which now litter the national landscape serve to enlarge considerably the actual base of decision making in this country.

In a world of political oversimplification, in which sophistication becomes the enemy of the slogan, it is little wonder that a cry for national patriotic revival is heard. As Charles Peters puts the case:

> For most of the twentieth century, patriotism has been strong in America. Large numbers of people from all classes volunteered for service in World Wars I and II. As one who worked on the staff of the Peace Corps in the early sixties, I know many of our volunteers who were motivated by patriotism—they were ashamed of the Ugly American and wanted to show the good side of their country to the world. But Vietnam changed all of that. First it killed the patriotism of the educated youth who resisted the war from the beginning. Then even more viciously it destroyed the patriotism of the poor who went to Vietnam and realized they had been suckers.[9]

This dilemma and disunity of government, defined as a ceaseless round of conflict and interest groups, has reached sufficiently high proportions to elicit a one million dollar program on conflict resolution sponsored by the Ford Foundation. In the administrative prose of McGeorge Bundy, interest groups in America are the centerpiece of issue-related conflicts, and must therefore be addressed directly.

> America in recent years has been swarming with conflicts and disputes of all sorts. The issues range across the entire social spectrum—for example, racial equality, energy allocation, environmental protection, consumer rights, and equal educational opportunity. Conflicts over these matters arise among interest groups, between interest groups and government, between levels of government, and between individuals. Thousands of administrative agencies, and other decision-making bodies have had great difficulty in attempting to resolve such large numbers of conflicts efficiently and fairly. And, the quantitative problem is compounded by the growing complexity, technological sophistication, and interdependence of society's problems.[10]

The objectives of this new foundation effort are to strengthen the capacity of existing formal institutions, to find better ways of handling disputes outside the formal political apparatus, and to identify reforms that may help either to avoid or simplify conflicts in the future. But no funds are seemingly allocated to discuss the possibility that conflict resolving mechanisms already in place are the problem, whereas conflict situations may be the essence of democratic procedures. It is one of the weaknesses of opponents of interest groups that they see the groups as such as corrosive and even corrupt, and see a return to a simpler national model as not only desirable but necessary for the survival of democracy itself.

The nub of the argument is in the first place empirical: what alternatives are there? Second, ethical: what are the implications of the present situation? On the analytic side, there seems to be a considerable association of the growth of special interest politics with a decline of national politics or national consensus. In point of fact, at the very time interest-group politics grow larger, so too has the resistance to the national government. Many claims of special interest groups are intended to redress national power in favor of a new federalism. What actually has precipitously declined in postwar America are intermediary forms of political structure: the collapse of local politics, the weakening of voluntary political associations, the decline of mass participation in the political process. The political party system itself has failed to represent these interests. The intermediary structures have not declined in the national system. Hence the chief imagery of the conservative arsenal, the description of the way in which interest groups sap national goals, is profoundly inaccurate. What has been sapped are intermediary forms of mass participation, not the political system of promotions and elections.

A critical factor has been the rise of the mass communications media, as a device for expressing public opinion. Television in particular, by virtue of its special qualities, has focused solely on issues, promoting focus on people rather than ideas. Television generally has had an easier time focusing on specific issues than providing a context of general political concerns. Interest-group politics is the handmaiden of the mass media. The mass media do little to weaken a sense of national allegiance or national loyalty. They do weaken a sense of local and community participation.

A critical element that has not been addressed is the crosscutting impact of special interest groups. Because the *political* process and the political system remain too powerful, the need for *social* compromise and coalition becomes greater rather than smaller in the current situation. Coalitions are continually made between advocates of civil rights and gay activists, or between feminists and environmentalists. For the most part, the power of interest-group politics has been the defeat of a candidate rather than his election. It is true that mobilization around a special interest or single issue can defeat Representative Don Fraser or Senator Dick Clark. It is not true that the groups that mobilized against them have the capacity to elect representatives and senators of their own choice. Thus, the power of interest groups to dislodge is much greater than the power to promote.

The lobbying efforts of industrialists have always been recognized as a legitimate part of American politics, from *Mr. Smith Goes to Washington* to *Advise and Consent*. Thus, what the PAC's offer is a more sophisticated extension of a well-entrenched theme in American society, and not a new phenomenon. A staple theme in American letters has been the honest politician versus the grafting lobbyist. What tends to be new is not the lobbying effort, or even the single-interest group, but the social sources of those groups: the phenomenon of black power, red power, or gay power. In fact, these new movements, measured by overall corporate expenditures, tend to be pathetically weak and not nearly as effective as the older lobbying effort. Much of the current rebellion against interest-group thinking seems in part a reaction to these new types of groups. With the exception of Matthew Josephson, Ida Tarbell, and some early muckrakers, it was rarely perceived that business lobbyists splinter America or that commercial activities deserve close civic scrutiny. What minority group lobbyists perform is thus to turn our attention to this hidden aspect of criminality. Unless one assumes the utter naturalness of business lobbying in a business civilization and the deviance of all other forms of registered political claims, such scrutiny, whether of product lines or corporate managers, has now become natural.

It has become increasingly difficult to ascertain the quality of these single-issue groups. Their strength often derives from living in an age of mass marketing and mass mailings. The possibility of having an organizational base of 30,000, 40,000, or 50,000 people is simply a function of dollars invested. Very low returns of only 1 or 2 percent on selected mailing lists can generate such numbers with relative ease. However, thus far there are no empirical studies that show these mailing-list respondents can actually be mobilized for political ends beyond giving an occasional donation. The numbers involved in interest-group politics, while initially appearing frighteningly large, are in fact relatively modest. By negative inference, such groups provide indicators that the party apparatus, not to mention the political process, remains intact. Such single-issue groups provide sensitizing elements to political networks compelling attention to issues of broad public concern that the party apparatus tends to respond to more slowly.

The assumption that single-issue politics contribute to the breakdown of the two-party system is subject to serious critical examination. Political parties still carry within themselves, slightly lower voting participation notwithstanding, the base of political continuity in America. Further, many interest groups have in fact become absorbed by one or another party. For example, one finds the Democratic party a stronger supporter of gun control legislation and the Republican party a stronger supporter of the National Rifle Association. Political parties continue to express a wide variety of interests, both in their platforms and in bloc-voting patterns. This is not a uniform condition; Congressional crossings often take place. But that precisely is the legitimate role of an interest group: to influence individuals within each party to break ranks on the basis of an issue important enough to do so, whether on matters of environment, energy, or taxation.

Interest groups themselves vary considerably. Sometimes they take the form of a specific organization, such as the National Association of Evangelicals, the National Rifle Association, or Common Cause. Other times, interest groups are identified amorphously, as the Sunbelt versus the Snowbelt. But whether one should use such broad demographic characteristics as examples of single-issue politics, or simply as a transformation in national demographic or urban patterns, is difficult to pinpoint. The Sunbelt as a social-organizing premise is deeply limited by differences in state boundaries, state political systems, and local needs. There is slender correlation between voting patterns and select political variables in the Sunbelt, or in the Snowbelt for that matter. There are precious few ideological signs to distinguish the two except the high cost of petroleum in the Snowbelt and the relatively easy access to petroleum in the Sunbelt. A secondary differentiation might be the power of trade unions. But even this varies considerably from state to state, locality to locality. Whether geography, theology, or any single organizational pivot, constitutes a constellation of new political forces is even more doubtful.

There is another confusion between interest groups and the process of communication. American society is undergoing not so much fragmentation as professionalization. The growth of specialized fields and the division of labor mean that it is not enough to be identified as a member of a middle class. New layers of interest arise in terms of being doctors, lawyers, dentists, union organizers, and writers. Dentists themselves fragment into specialized areas as do lawyers and accountants, and others as well. This is not necessarily a consequence of interest groups' politics but of the specialization of knowledge as a social activity, and the transference of that knowledge to an audience that must find it useful in the public domain. The empirical distinction of single-issue politics, or the rise of fanatic factions, or Balkanization, thus comes upon some extremely difficult factual issues. Rather than prove beyond a doubt that democracy is ailing, such views tend to prove the contrary: the continuation of a vibrant political life in American society.

What then of the values that are being inculcated by this collective assault upon interest groups as such? There can be no doubt of the authenticity, the sense of anguish, about special interests. There also can be no question that there is a growing concern not only as to whether this nation can adhere or endure, but what the quality of this nation will be in a world of special-interest groups. We now inhabit a society in which even the basic language of the nation is subject to challenge, and the forms of our political, cultural, and economic life are also subject to polarizing tendencies. However, the risk involved in the assault on interest groups is that it spills over into a possible repudiation of the right to voluntary association. And the United States as the center of such voluntarism is thus subject to an assault on a cornerstone of democratic practice in the name of preserving democratic theory.

The attack on single-interest politics is all too often reduced to the pure and simple. Political moralism has tended to get the United States into trouble in the postwar world. The exaggerated sense of manifest destiny and national purpose made the Vietnam War a programmed monstrosity. The imposition of political monism in place of pluralism is the elemental goal of those who consider democracy some sort of medical disaster. The sensibility voiced by this attack on single-issue politics is a sensibility of an older age in which presumably everyone knew their place and everyone was willing to accept the predestined leadership role of America in world affairs. It strikes me that the high correlation between the proliferation of interest groups and the decline of confidence in American political institutions is far from spurious or accidental.

The situation in representative government has been transformed over time. When representation meant one legislative figure standing for every two hundred fifty or every twenty-five hundred persons, the relationship of the governed to the governor was well known and easily identified. When two senators represented states of less than one-half million people, the sense of responsibility to the constituency was high. When those same two senators represent twenty million, there is a corresponding weakening of that sense of identification with the public. The rise of interest-group politics in America may then be viewed, not as a function of decay, but of growth. The demographic transformation of a colonial nation to a major world power brought in its wake new varieties for expressing discontent, even rebellion. The interest group of today is oftentimes closer to the town hall of yesterday than the political apparatus it supposedly has superseded. It is responsive to pressure from below in ways that are more natively American than the current electoral climate often permits. The relationship of dollars to demagogues, of honors to recipients, is much clearer in single-issue organizations and group associations than in the political party structure as it currently exists. In short, the current frontal assault on single-interest politics and special-interest groups is part of the Madisonian belief that liberty is to factionalism what air is to fire. It is part of the federalist inheritance over and against the democratic persuasion. The Jeffersonian persuasion organizes the polity in favor of the diffusion and division of authority as the source of national strength.

In the long pull of more than two hundred years of American history, what we are witnessing is the struggle between Jeffersonian and Madisonian claims, only in more complicated and complex sociological conditions. The Jeffersonian position, while silent in theory and having few overt adherents, continues to gain strength at the expense of the more sophisticated Madisonian viewpoint, not by virtue of any theoretical genius, but rather by virtue of the fact that America has become a mass democratic nation, hence the forms for expressing that democracy have changed and have become less a matter of elites who have time for the party life and more a matter of participating interest-group life. One thing has become evident in this debate over interest groups: individuals must organize if they are to gain any measure of strength or security, and political action committees are an authentic response to this urging. The argument of parties versus groups is therefore a discussion over what kind of organizational life America is to have, not a needless choice to be made between them. Seen in this way the current emphasis on group life is by no means a categorical evil and, quite the contrary, may yet turn out to be the basis of an expanded, more inclusive twenty-first-century democratic society.

10. Bureaucracy, Administration, and State Power

The world today contains many societies, at different levels of development, that have different kinds of responsive and influential administrative networks. Although the term preindustrial society has no recognizable denotive content, it has become virtually unavoidable and, if meaningfully defined, has its uses. The character of mechanization has shifted, and the role of policy making has enlarged, but these changes suggest not a postindustrial society but simply an evolution of the industrial order. We still inhabit a universe largely defined by preindustrial characteristics. The industrial sector remains far from dominant in social systems.

The phrase postindustrial society is infelicitous because it identifies an inherently transitional movement from something called industrial. The phrase is also ambiguous, referring as it does to cultural norms in the most advanced nations. It is subject to a variety of interpretations, of which few reflect reality and even fewer are mutually compatible. Societies do not emerge full blown. We are still trying to ascertain meanings to ascribe to industrialization. Much has happened since the end of World War II—above all, the ability of mankind to destroy totally and practice genocide. Authoritarianism, no longer confined to a single state apparatus, expands to the global decimation of peoples.

The term postindustrial is often employed as a hygienic way of saying authoritarian in an age of the dominance of public sector or at least the ascendance of policy over politics. The postindustrial vision admits only of a deeply pessimistic view of society and conjures up for its creators an image of engineering totalitarianism. Whether such a series of postulates adds up to postindustrial society or a technocratic state with authoritarian tendencies is a choice of language and an amplification of different pessimisms. But the contours of social structure and social stratification have undoubtedly shifted dramatically.

The principal characteristics of Western society are evident: private property, private control of investment decisions, and an industrial base that primarily demands technological efficiency. Along the axis of technology we may identify developmental sequences: preindustrial, industrial, postindustrial. There is an inherent contradiction between the principle of bureaucratization, based on hierarchy and role segmentation, and the principle of equality, based on participation. The social tensions in Western democracy have been framed by the contrary logics of bureaucratization and participation, supported by a change in institutional scale that leads to a pronounced shift in functions. The major principle of postindustrial society is the codification of theoretical knowledge, specifically new technological-scientific activities based on computers, telecommunication, optics, polymers, and electronics. Control of the means of information augments struggle over the means of production, and hence the character of work alters significantly. Work becomes struggle among persons rather than against nature. In a postindustrial utopia, living in society becomes a free choice by free people, rather than a banding together against nature or an involuntary banding in routinized labor relations imposed from outside.[1]

The theory of public administration emerged as a justification and celebration of developing practice. It has an inevitable bias toward the practical, toward getting things done, and an impatience with frustrating questions that in their breadth and scope may prove incapacitating.[2] The private woe of public administrators has been theory writ large. They have preferred middle-range theories, and, if those are unavailable, no theory at all. This is not the first time that practical people have lived a full and useful life without knowing what they were doing.

The relationship of public administration to economics, sociology, political science, and psychology bespeaks an insecure search for a theoretical anchor. As administration becomes distinguished from its parts, it no longer can make do with makeshift definitions. How does one train a public administrator for the Department of Commerce rather than for the Department of Health and Human Services? How does one train city administrators in contradistinction to national administrators? Determining entry-level skills becomes more exacting in an era of affirmative action. There are questions of the relationship between politically appointed administrators and the civil service administrators.

If public administration is not a science, what is its art? Here the giant assumption, central to understanding government per se, is that administration is a function of state authority or authorities. One administrates things, peoples, and ideologies on behalf of an employer called the state. Administrator and state directly connect with administration and policies. The conventional nineteenth-century image of social classes that manipulate bureaucracies to gain advantage is not accurate. Rather, a big administrative machinery that manipulates other sectors becomes decisive: Labor forces decrease in size and increase in power.

Public administration takes place in a context of policy inversion: a transformation of power from the economy to the polity, mediated by the monopoly of allocation and distribution of public funds. Public administration services not one class or sector but the state. The class interest of the middle administrators is the class interest of top administrators to the extent that they are directly linked to forms of state power. Public administration is therefore inextricably linked to state power. To say that administrators are politically neutral is naive. To be neutral with respect to a party or an interest group is perfectly reasonable, even a prerequisite of sound administrative procedures. But for the administrator to be neutral about state power as such is a contradiction in terms. For the essential politics of the administrator is the survival, prolongation, and strengthening of the apparatus. This is administrative politics writ large, whatever the disclaimers about political participation writ small—i.e., party loyalty or partisan activity.

The essential contest in class terms shapes up as one between elites and masses or, expressed ideologically, between statism and populism. Those with suspicious, antistate populist activities and those with populist concerns can no longer rest easy with old-fashioned formulations about class. Today, classes, sexes, races, and ethnic groups directly confront state authority. The legal mechanisms and financial systems make possible broad layers of social change in attitudes and behavior precisely by reinforcing the ascribed features of the status system.

Administrators do not oppose change. They demand that changes occur through a legal enlargement and acceptance of the administrative apparatus. To the extent that the system as a whole can manage a framework of rewards and punishments which appeals to the state, state power becomes enhanced and public administration enlarged. To the extent that the state cannot manage rational rewards and punishments or cannot orchestrate and mobilize the economy to do its bidding, it invites popular opposition and rebellion.

The postindustrial world resembles the postfeudal, monarchical world of Machiavelli and Hobbes more than it does that of entrepreneurial capitalism. Again, the relationship of ruled to ruler has become simplified. Mediating institutions such as parties and pressure groups are reduced to fundamental conflict and competition. In the dialectic of postindustrial conflict the manipulation of funds and forces rather than the administration of people becomes a rallying cry within administrative work, much as it did for the nineteenth-century utopians who argued for the withering away of state power.

The rationalization process compels the state to confront new leviathans, from multinational corporations to NASA-type space programs that require budgets equal to conventional government expenditures. Public administration turns to the state as a tool for monitoring and evaluating potential threats to the commonwealth. The emergence of regional trade and national associations also requires a tighter framework for state decision making. Everything from arranging sales to supervising contracts demands administrative servicing. While mediating agencies within a nation lose some of their potency, the need for state power grows as a response to external agencies.[3] The state must negotiate with a wide variety of foreign and domestic agencies and interest groups; public administration does not lack for new areas to conquer.

Much is taken for granted in public administration; even its size and scope remain obscure. As late as the mid-1930s, recruits for public administration came from among a wide variety of professions and disciplines. But by the postwar period public service had become a field unto itself. Administrative personnel operate in the executive and legislative branches of government; serve interest groups that range from veterans and homebuilders to the handicapped and police chiefs; work in regulatory and monitoring agencies; manage the roughly five hundred separate congressionally sanctioned grants-in-aid programs; and deal with lobbyists. The size of the federal administration has increased dramatically.

The increasing commitment to administrative expertise stands in inverse proportion to the electorate's sense of diminishing returns. These considerations pertain only to the federal bureaucracy in Washington, D.C., in which administration is the central occupation. Recent demographic estimates of state and local government administrators—exclusive of salaried managers and those who work in private ad-

ministration—count nearly 5 million people working as public administrators, na-
tionwide. Between 1950 and 1979 public administration trebled.[4] The 1980 census
will undoubtedly show further growth. Public administration represents a large segment of the labor force: well educated, increasingly specialized, and willing to interpret and execute the will of the state.

The postindustrial concept is organically related to public administration and its
enlarged role in changing class relationships. Weber's trepidations about the growth
of bureaucracy were well grounded.[5] The public sector has grown at a pace and in
power far beyond older classes. The proletariat has declined as capital-intensive industry has replaced manual labor; family farms have shriveled in size and number as
technology has improved food and agricultural production; the bourgeoisie as an
owning group has been allowed to remain constant in numbers, but its decision
making has been reduced by the need for public-sector support.

Middle management in industry has grown apace with the public sector. The in-
comparable decision-making functions of administrators permit one to think of industry, no less than government, as a set of bureaucratic institutions or leaders with
divergent ideas.[6] But if neither government nor industry offers a single rational
actor, both offer a picture of two central facets of advanced industrial society that
operate with profoundly different models of economic well-being. The contrast in
economic philosophies between the public and private sector is well known. The
critical contradictions between these two sectors prevent any new class of administrative workers from emerging despite functional similarities.[7]

Public administrators function as a subclass of the public sector, and industrial
managers function as a subclass of the private sector. The character of class competition also changes dramatically in the postindustrial world. The familiar competition within the private sector between bourgeois and proletariat yields to the less
familiar but more potent struggle between the administrative vanguards of each sector. Older forms of class competition remain intact, but even these are mediated by
new administrators and their authorities, interests, and regulations.

The Sherman Antitrust Act of the late nineteenth century introduced a tension
between public and private sector that has not yet abated. It is precisely the tilt toward the public that permits one to characterize our epoch as postindustrial. Implicit is a shift not only from goods to services, or commodities to ideas, but more
exactly, a shift in locus of power and the force of numbers.[8] Public administration is
properly perceived as a subclass that functions as an independent social force and
represents the public sector in its great struggle to enlist the private sector in the
goals of equity and opportunity. The public administrators function in the classic
bureaucratic mold as representatives of the national interest against the industrial
managers. Whether public administration can do so without undermining the innovation and initiative of an advanced society becomes the challenge during the next
decade.[9]

The power of the American style emerged with raw pragmatism that rests on
problem solving. Public administration in particular grew with only a barely disguised animus for theorists—those for whom a rational comprehensive model has

had meaning. Public administration was celebrated as the science of muddling through. As Charles Lindblom pointed out, the only widely acknowledged problem was the swiftness of technological innovation, so that there was an "absence of enough persons who [were] knowledgeable in computer use." The solution was better functional division of technology and more extensive training.[10]

To look back even a short decade is to observe a brave new world of public administration, in which technological breakthroughs came rapidly and solutions to thorny problems were registered through improved data control. Governance through data control reached its crescendo in the United States with the Vietnam War, the Watergate scandals, and a series of uncovered legislative deceptions. As the mechanics of administration became unmanageable, the science of muddling through led to a series of overseas defeats and domestic miscalculations. As a result, there was a dramatic disaffection from centralized government as a source of acceptable authority. The left searched for "community," the right sought after "order," while the liberal consensus snapped.

The major theses of the 1960s articulated in advanced texts by major theorists have remained unresolved. Little more could be expected when even the most advanced researchers proposed that public administration overcome its "crisis of identity by trying to act as a profession without actually being one."[11] The implications were clear: Concern for the social conditions of administration yielded to the professional status of administration. As a review essay of the ten leading public administration texts points out: "Only one author devotes much space to posing the question of which groups and social classes are best served by the administrative structure of the state."[12] As the emphasis has inexorably shifted from broad social issues to narrow professional issues, micromethodology has replaced theory: problems of measurement, evaluation, and even monitoring of programs and plans have rapidly displaced more fundamental concerns. Under such circumstances the source of new inspiration in public administration inevitably shifted from public service to the citizenry to methods for increasing efficiency and reducing costs.

The cutting edge of public administration theory shifted to France in the 1970s. During the 1960s, those who saw government in functional categories confronted those who saw government as a total system, i.e., in structural terms. The debate raged between ideologists who preferred the language of bureaucracy because it reflected the actual hierarchy of government and technocrats who preferred public administration precisely because of its nonhierarchical or functional characteristics. Those who urged system perspective were denounced by those who insisted on a partial theory. Some saw bureaucracy as generic, others saw administration, with public administration as one facet. Finally, the educators argued about whether public administration should be considered a separate discipline akin to business administration or part of the social and political sciences.

In France, after the collapse of the May 1968 student rebellion, the higher functionaries, disturbed by the anarchism on the left and the fascist potential on the right, began to examine the premises of postindustrialism as a question of elitism versus populism, rather than of social classes or even of social functions. In the hands of public administrators the state became the guardian of public against private interest. Two schools of thought emerged. Michael Crozier led one school, arguing that the administrative apparatus had as its unique charge the supersession of social stagnation by institutional investment to render habits, negotiations, and systems of rules more comprehensive, more open, more complicated, and more efficient.[13] The constraint on investment was not lack of finances or political will, but the need for serious analysis of change and a deeper personal involvement in institutions. In contrast, Nicos Poulantzas, in his seminal work, announced that the decline of legislative power, the strengthening of the executive, and the political role currently assumed by the state administration now constitute the tripartite leitmotiv of political studies.[14] The economic role of the state, not the need for efficiency or innovation, undergirds the expansion of public administration. Ernest Mandel elaborated on this theme by noting the heavy increase in the service sector and hence the expansion of administrative state power. Unlike Poulantzas, he argued that such a shift does not "lower the average organic composition of capital."[15] Rather, this expansion only deepens the contradictions of capitalism by increasing the fiscal burdens of the state. For the French intellectual left, bureaucracy should mainly be viewed not as an impediment to inefficiency but as a response to structural deformities within the private and entrepreneurial sectors. For Poulantzas, administration becomes the terrain on which an "unstable equilibrium of compromises" between the power elites and the popular masses takes place and is elaborated.[16] His view is a far cry from the earlier Marxist characterization of bureaucracy as serving class interests.

Non-Marxists like Crozier entered the discussion to argue that the central role of administration lies in adjudicating the claims of interest groups and in bringing about innovations that cannot be made by the private sector alone.[17] Poulantzas, deeply antitotalitarian, centered his attack on the giganticism of state power. He concluded his last work with a full and vigorous critique of Stalinism as an extension of Leninism.[18] But the 1970s ended with the same intellectual indecisiveness as the 1960s. Resolution of the issues on the basis of dependence versus the autonomy of public administration emerges as merely a more advanced form of the same theoretical bind that characterized American thinking in the 1960s. The reason is not difficult to locate. Researchers like Crozier are essentially policy oriented meliorists, interested in getting society going again, whereas theorists like Poulantzas and Mandel hold no hope for moving forward through administrative efficiency so long as a market economy remains the essential motor for economic development.

The debate between social scientific and historical materialist approaches partially arises from the reification of administration itself. It makes little sense to argue an anticapitalist premise when state power grows with equal force in planned as well as market economies. As Jean-Jacques Servan-Schreiber shrewdly notes, the ability of the Soviet Union and East Europe to insure a minimal living wage to their entire population depends on this maintenance of a high degree of coercion.[19]

Today the specific politics of administration concern only its own expansion, but more generally, its specific political aims are circumscribed by the larger forces of state and economy. The concentration of administrative power occurs in all socioeconomic systems designated as postindustrial. One reason for employing the term postindustrial is that it avoids the reductionism of identifying the concentration or curtailment of power with any one kind of economic environment or party apparatus. Differences between social systems and nations have not evaporated. They remain potent cultural forces. In any democratic culture, control is in the hands of the popular sectors, which struggle against bureaucratic regimentalism. Personal leadership is common to all types of economic systems. Public administration, with its impersonal norms, comes up against the political apparatus it presumably serves, with its continuing norms of personalism and charismatic authority.

The administrative apparatus, however close it might appear to the state apparatus, must remain responsive to the people led no less than to the leaders—to the broad stratum of taxpayers outside the decision-making process. Public administration cannot be characterized as part of the state any more than it can be viewed as a buffer against it. They must both try to mediate between the machinery of power and the interests of the public while trying to control the budget. This sort of conflict becomes an essential proprietary consideration in postindustrial environments in which older forms of conflict have collapsed. Polarization remains deeply embedded in advanced social structures but takes the form of efforts to dominate the allocation of funds rather than the supervision of classes. In consequence, postindustrial society is in some respects close to postfeudal society: social relations become rationalized by the bureaucracy just when technological forms of negotiating those relations become ever more complex.

The relationship between the planners and the financiers (middle-management bureaucrats or public administrators) in advanced states becomes especially intriguing.[20] It can either generate severe friction between those who make policy and set the nation on its long-range course, and those who carry out policy and hence do not easily tolerate interference or sudden shifts of direction; or it can become a symbiotic relationship in which forces are joined to preserve and extend state power. Since those at the top of decision making have natural antipathies toward those in middle management, one might well expect antagonism. Increasingly, these antipathies are held in check by decision making, which has itself become postindustrial in the special sense that data determine decisions. In this evolution decision making has increasingly been removed from the political arena.

Certain characteristics of bureaucracy prevail over policy-making concerns. The growing professionalization of government work, whatever the type or level, moves to counter politization. As a result, one should not expect the end of public ideologies so much as the decline of party politics. The essential danger is closure on political participation. The main issue is not how administrators function in postindustrial societies but how government administration—local, state, regional, and federal—begins with a theory of negotiation between policy makers and political officials but ends with the assumption of the reins of state power.

Politics becomes identified with the national interest. The defense of those presumed interests against overseas transgressions becomes central. Hegel overwhelms

Marx: the state, not the class, becomes the main organizing premise. Public administration is uniquely situated to take full advantage of the new conditions. Reared in a tradition of professionalization before politization, organized to serve the needs of the state directly and not any one subset of special interests, and directly tied to governance without the encumbrances of elections, it becomes the basic sponsor of the national interest, the guardian of the state, and the arbiter of its specific survival capacities.

Hence, there is a growing conservatism within the public administration sector, not as an ideologically traditional quest for community and order, but as a determination to preserve the state and its interests against military incursion from abroad and fiscal disintegration from within. Public administration creates a solid phalanx because the power of mass politics has long since been drugged by the narcotic of the communications media. The steady expansion of public administration binds the administrative apparatus to large-scale programs and plans, while further inhibiting the emergence of any grass roots, local, state, or regional opposition. A certain equilibrium, longed for by federal administrators, becomes the norm, resisting even the most determined efforts to establish a "new federalism."

The attempt to distinguish administration from politics is understandable, but it ultimately remains an exercise in futility. The bifurcated vision derives from a Western democratic belief that professionalism is somehow uniquely antipolitical or, better, purely instrumental.[21] As Gordon Tullock puts it:

> There is no way this sort of ultimate policy formation by low ranking personnel can be avoided; it will arise on occasion in all organizations, no matter how efficiently these are organized. . . . Not only in initial decisions, but all subsequent decisions, may be made by men operating at the lower reaches of the hierarchy. The sovereign neither ratifies nor disapproves of these decisions either because the chain of command is so clogged that he does not hear of the issues at all, or because he is lazy, or because he fears that any decision on his part will, in turn, annoy his own superior in the hierarchy. In such an organization as this, the lower ranks, after perhaps vainly trying to get the higher officials to take action, may be forced to make decisions. Out of a series of such events, a sort of organized policy may develop by precedent, and the higher officials may never have to make any choices of significance at all.[22]

In a period of computer technology, administrative decisions by fiat become frequent. The equation of expertise and administration leaves the people out of the reckoning. But since the people are the ultimate repository of power, elected officials are compelled to take responsibility for decision making. Opposition to this enlarged federal apparatus will come from a revived populism—from an opposition to government and its services that will undoubtedly cut across traditional left and right lines. The Jarvis-Gann amendment in California provides one indication. It is impossible to convert this populism into a left or right impulse, any more than one can identify government administrative actions as left or right. The shape of things to come is already plain: a struggle between the state, with its organized participants, and the people with its interest groups, tax resistance, and, ultimately, sheer numerical force.

Violence, including sabotage and terror, is more likely in a depoliticized context than in a political one. Politics is an essential cement of moral authority, for it alone guarantees a sense of participation and control over state power. But in the antiseptic climate of top-down rules and regulations, in which party identification is low and political allegiance shaky, the legitimacy of the state can be severely threatened. The administrative machinery of government appears to be the government itself. Popular actions will become less symbolic and increasingly oriented toward direct action. Things get done by threatening bureaucrats with the dire consequences of a given interest group. Hence, the web of government—that delicately laced network of authority and legitimacy—can easily become unhinged in a brave new world of bureaucratic determinism.

Postindustrial technology has been unevenly absorbed. Line managers have been afraid of the new technology, while those staff members who procure it have emphasized the efficiency of machines rather than the effectiveness of programs. As one recent report indicates: "The impact of computers on the federal government's operations and procedures is pervasive; and federal expenditures for computer-based information systems exceeded 10 billion in fiscal year 1977."[23] In the immediate future much more effort will be devoted to developing symbiosis between electronic information systems and administrative tasks; it will be necessary to model complex systems, as well as to process routine data. Forecasting and assessment of technology are linked to greater use of advanced computer systems. Until now public administrators have focused on short-term uses of advanced technology. In the next round long-term planning is likely to prevail. The danger is that complex decision making will become the responsibility of machines rather than human political actors. Here is an area of maximum potential danger for public-sector policy making.

However moot the good or evil potential of technology, public administrators not only react to a postindustrial technology but have long helped guide it. The military and nuclear sectors are particularly vulnerable. Directing technology involves two kinds of apparently contradictory activities which are also opposites of the same coin. These activities are the encouragement of technology and regulation.[24] Because of the enormous costs in research and development and the consequent impact on profitability, technology has become an organic part of public administration and decision making.

Administration is a service as well as a system. Advanced societies evolved toward increases in this service sector. But against this inexorable tidal wave of paper work over hardware production, allocation over innovation, and decision making over mass politics, stands the specter of a new public managerialism—of a new class that loses intimate contact with ordinary events and plain people and so jeopardizes the political system as a whole. Even if bureaucratic administration is impervious to internal assault, its removal from the taproots of incentive and innovation makes any society susceptible to destruction from without.[25] The need to consider public administration as a servant or at least an agent for developing incentive, and not a master of government, is the alpha and omega of democratic life, and also insures the future of public administration as an entity apart from special or private interests.

It is dangerous to conceive of postindustrial technology as necessarily feeding the fires of administrative domination. Mindless slogans and irrational specializations tend to thwart any sense of citizen participation. But certain developments, like cybernetic systems design, can facilitate radical, technological, and social decentralization. The distinction drawn by Manfred Stanley between technology as a social tool and technicism as a bureaucratic ideology is worth pursuing. The aims of education, whether administrative or political, are serviced by redesign of social research methods, the institutionalization of linguistic accountability, and the critique of irrational specialization.[26] The pace of technological innovation and the size of bureaucratic administration growth have both quickened. On the assumption that historical clocks cannot be turned back, the need to harness the former and counterbalance the latter becomes a major task of democratic culture, which must itself be made sensitive to new patterns of administration.

Conflict between branches of government will remain in a technological context. The executive branch will still mobilize its bureaucrats to disprove the claims of legislatively appointed bureaucrats. But such conflict among administrators should become less significant as the tasks of governance become more complex. The entire arsenal of populist politics will be required to offset the advantages of bureaucracy. Electoral politics are episodic, sporadic, and ideological. Administration is continuous, fluid, and rationalistic. If the two sides need each other, in a more proximate sense, such a need is tempered by recognition of different constituencies, functional prerequisites, and, ultimately, different visions of law and order. Holding this dialectical chain intact, maintaining unity through opposition, becomes an essential task for constitutional law and a pivotal function of the modern judiciary. Democracy has been and will continue to be affected by the rise of public administration in a postindustrial society in which state power grows and in which the relationship between politics and economics is inverted, with politics becoming the base and economics the superstructure.[27] Democracy will also be attacked for its inefficiencies. That is the essential meaning of totalitarian postindustrialism. The adjudication of the innate tensions of mass demands and organizational rules becomes the essential role of public administration in a democratic community.

Democracy is decreasingly defined as a system and increasingly as a process of the mutual articulation of interests that can be adjudicated and negotiated in an orderly and maximally noninjurious way.[28] Conflicts between public administration and mass politics should be viewed only as a late twentieth-, possibly a twenty-first-century possibility. As old conflicts between judicial, legislative, and executive branches of government decrease in importance through increase in the technology of scientific decision making, a clustering effect may occur in which a government that takes lives is pitted against one that leaves people alone. The private sector will come to mean those areas of individual performance left intact, without special interest incursions, rather than a portion of the economy left under entrepreneurial control.

A new system of checks and balances might evolve in accord with the emerging characteristics of the political process as a whole. The basis for such programmed differentiation of tasks and distinction in goals may not be spelled out constitutionally except as a series of mandates that permit administrative functions in a pluralistic context. The specific functions of various branches of government will appear more rational in a context of opposition or at least of functional differentiation of administrative-bureaucratic tasks. At one level this is the politics of the last word: The executive head who spends twenty hours on the budget has the final say, not the administrators who spend thousands of hours in preparing it. The congressman or originator, purveyor, or mediator of preferences must vote on legislation even though bureaucrats and managers may inundate him with evidence that a bill is too costly or not operational.

Major movements of our time revolve around the size and strength of the administrative bureaucracy. It becomes necessary to make it responsible, increase its efficiency, and decrease its power. To the extent that the obstacle to further political development is administration itself, either through tax pressure or through withholding of political legitimacy—to the extent that the obstacle is the individualistic propensity of the popular will—one can expect political elites to prevail over popular forces.

Whatever the nature of the economic system, our epoch bears witness to a constant expansion in state power, bureaucratic norms, and administrative domination and disposition of people. The economic system a nation lives under has become less important than the fact of state growth and its allocative mechanisms. New forms of popular rebellion have little to do with class membership and cross traditional social boundaries. Advanced technology helps insure a simplified society more direct in its conflicts of choice and interests. The new technology offers potentials for both dictatorship and democracy. The outcomes are in doubt, not because of the feebleness of social research, but because of the willfulness of human actors. Before the torrent of populism the wall of every known elitism threatens to crumble. But populism itself comes to provide a new form of irrational solidarity—a tactical option to elitism that still leaves undisturbed the essential structural inequalities of advanced postindustrial societies, East and West.

11. Political Bases of Equity Goals

Evaluation methods are strongly correlated to strategies employed in equity programming and research. Without attempting to settle the issue of specific advantages that might accrue to any particular approach, this essay nonetheless aims to demonstrate that ends desired often determine choices in methods selected. A series of such broad-gauged methods are examined: evaluation research, cost-benefit analysis, quality of life measures, substitution strategies, and microanalytic simulation. In each instance evidence is adduced that the methods and procedures of research adopted—sometimes through scholarly initiatives, other times through government directives—serve quite specific epistemological and valuational premises of the researchers and agencies involved. The basic purpose of this exploratory study is to link problems in social policy to the style of analysis pioneered by the sociology of knowledge.

The assumption that methodology occupies a realm unto itself is belied by various efforts to eliminate or at least obviate the problem of inequality in American society. Methods, each of which coexist in the behavioral science matrix, are viewed sequentially and discretely in real world contexts. Hence, the selection of appropriate methods itself provides a strong pretesting of the strategies selected to deal with the issues involved in social inequality. In considering evaluative research, cost-benefit analysis, quality of life measures, substitution strategies, and new simulation techniques, there is no wish to claim the technical superiority of one method over another, or even to assert their mutual exclusiveness. Rather, each in its own way indicates how the research frontiers in the study of inequality telegraph outcomes by the choice of methods and strategies employed.

The simplest way to define evaluative research is to say that it is a method to measure whether a program is achieving its goal. In this sense, the object of the program is decided upon prior to the evaluation which takes place. There are basically six questions that must be answered before an evaluation can take place: (1) What is the nature of the content of the objective? (2) Who is the target of the program? (3) When is the desired change to take place? (4) Are the objectives unitary or multiple? (5) What is the desired magnitude in effect? (6) How is the objective to be attained? These questions play a major role in the selection of methods to be used in evaluating equity programs. Objectives are presumed to be a direct outcome of the social consensus. What in fact is evaluated are methods used by the program or agencies to achieve the goal. What is open to evaluation are the procedures and aims of the programs. Throughout his work, Suchman emphasizes that the goals of social programs being evaluated are formed by social values, not scientific research:

> In our approach, we will make a distinction between "evaluation" and "evaluative research." The former will be used in a general way as referring to the social

process of making judgments. This process is basic to almost all forms of social behavior, whether that of a single individual or a complex organization. While it implies some logical or rational basis for making such judgments, it does not require any systematic procedures for marshaling and presenting objective evidence to support the judgment. Thus, we retain the term "evaluation" in its more commonsense usage as referring to the general process of assessment or appraisal of value.[1]

Suchman continues his discussion by stating that evaluative research is the scientific method of proving the worth of a "social activity." Again, it should be noted that evaluative research is primarily interested in assessing the worth or effectiveness of the program being advocated. If we were to use a means-end continuum, evaluative research has a declared interest only with the means and with measuring whether or not the ends are being achieved by the means employed.

This is made clear by Suchman's discussion of experimental design and methodology. Nonetheless, a large segment of evaluative research is concerned with the goals of the programs. This is done, as shown in the six questions stated above, so one can measure the effects intended. Experimental designs and methods are intended to show how one can control for variables outside the program that may affect its actions and the results for the target population. Again, the designs take the form of a cause and effect relationship. All are meant to show whether a given effect (goal) is achieved by a given cause (program). The goal or effect itself is not evaluated by the research since this type of social science research requires a set of assumptions that may well be a feature of a period when equity demands were high and the economic growth pattern was equal to those demands.

The economic cost of the goals to be achieved or the availability of resources is not brought into question, despite a foreknowledge of the impracticalities of the ends sought.

We are currently in the midst of a "War on Poverty" which has as its ultimate goal nothing less than the elimination of economic, educational, medical, and social deprivation. Granting the rather difficult and even impractical nature of this goal, not to say its logical inconsistency, there is no denying the surge of activity in these areas and the initiation of domestic and international programs costing billions of dollars. One has only to look at the daily newspaper to find new developments in education, public health, medical care, urban redevelopment, and social welfare. Legislation in all these areas attests to the willingness of Congress to support, even if on occasion with hesitation, these social "reforms." Their public popularity has given rise to increasing citizen pressure for even "bigger and better" programs.[2]

There was a large political consensus in the Johnson presidency, for example, that the government should make use of its great resources to achieve equity goals. The goals themselves were conceived in terms of distributive justice, and not in terms of economic costs or even the potential for achieving such legally mandated goals.

This type of paradigm is currently defended by the work of Levitan and Taggart. Their stated goal in *The Promise of Greatness* is clearly put forward:

> The case against the Great Society's social welfare effects is based on selective use of the facts and a set of biased standards. This analysis has tried to demonstrate the effectiveness of the Great Society's initiatives, as well as to counter the arguments of its critics. Negative judgments have been rebutted by analysis of their limitations, contradictions and biases. Reasonable achievement has been demonstrated relative to realistic goals, without the supposition of failure.[3]

Although admittedly partisan, Levitan and Taggart's work provides examples of several key assumptions of evaluative research in social science. The first segment of their book sets forth the goal of the Great Society and its programs. This is done by discounting the public pronouncements of the period and substituting more realistic program goals. Much evaluative research represents a program-by-program approach. In Levitan's work there is a review of the program, the goal of the program, and a listing of target populations for each program. In turn, each program is evaluated as to its effect upon the target population. The programs dealt with include income support, health care, low-income housing, compensatory education, manpower programs, civil rights, and community organizations. There are only limited attempts to move from programs and targeted population frameworks to a societal level framework in the evaluation. Most of the discussion of the macrosocial level is in the form of a brief polemic for continued expansion of government programs. The goals are not themselves questioned.

Evaluative research came upon the problem of differential targeting of rewards and payments to support goal-oriented efforts to increase social equality. Hence, the special emphasis on the needs of the poor, minorities, and the racially oppressed was perceived to exclude rather than include large chunks of the industrial working class. And as programs of welfare, child care, medicaid, food and family assistance were hatched, without regard for the cost factor by evaluative research teams, the wrath or backlash of the organized working class grew, matched only by the innate conservatism of the propertied and monied classes.

At the risk of a digression, but also to indicate that policies forged by leaders must remain sensitive and responsive to the public interest, we should look more closely at the momentous backlash of the proletarian sectors of society against the welfare poor and the wealthy elites alike. Both of these latter groups presumably forged equity goals that only weakened the relative gains made by the working class. This class has come to realize that the relative distribution of wealth in the United States has not accrued proportionately to itself. It is simply a matter of the top elites retaining their privileges, but they have done so by buying off a politically volatile but economically unproductive bottom of the class hierarchy. A great many people in the working class feel that they have not benefited from public spending any more than from private accumulation. They have not partaken of the general income surge of the 20 million people who own stock in private corporations, or the 10 million people in the academic profession, or of all the people in the white-collar and upper-income white-collar realm. The organized working classes, through their union leadership at every level, have stated that they did not partake equally, proportionately, to the general rise in public-sector spending for the welfare of the marginal classes below in rank during the War on Poverty.

When the working classes look up they perceive groups with rapid upward mobility beyond their own ability to move likewise. When they look down at the marginal underclasses they see a similar movement based on threat rather than talent. All kinds of lower-income people are moving to a point where they are close to the income possibilities achievable by the working classes. Rewards for not working approach those available to people who work. Once taxes are accounted for, the actual take-home pay of many blue-collar workers is not much higher than the funds received by those who receive food stamps, welfare benefits, social services, or protracted unemployment payments.

Whether this situation is a response to a myth generated by the political establishment or mystification generated by professors is less significant than the near-universal consensus that working-class discontent is real. There is nothing psychological about the rebellion against public policy toward social welfare. There is enough reality in the charges against welfare and tax dodge systems to make working-class resentment against both the top and bottom a potent factor in populist politics. The formation of public policy has too often been addressed to people in the underclass by those in the ruling class, without adequate regard for people in the working classes.

There is a new triclass structure in American life. Yet we do not have either a policy or a theoretical framework that takes account of this underclass/working-class/ruling-class tracking system. The organized working class has, through its voting preferences, revealed demands for law, order, and conservation. It perceives corruption and deception as essential ingredients of both a squeamish ruling class and a ravaged underclass. When working-class demands are not met by their rulers, a breakdown in confidence presents itself. When vast portions of society are unprepared or unwilling to work, decadent conditions obtain. This pattern is not a matter of professional conspiracy or political stupidity, but of unequal distribution of wealth, and the inability of limited new resources to meet ever-expanding demands.

Before turning to current strategies for coping with problems of inequality, it is advisable to summarize briefly the inconsistencies and inefficiencies of earlier programs and policies. Probably the master dilemma was that earlier programs were predicated on eliminating income poverty rather than dealing with economic inequality. As a result, a series of programs were devised of a stopgap nature that failed to account for new problems such quick-order measures invited. Robert Havemann has outlined the nature of these problems bluntly but accurately.

> The structure of this set of programs has major weaknesses: (1) It is built around specific categories of people, eliminating some poor families completely; (2) A number of programs have state-determined eligibility requirements and benefit

levels and, as a result, equally poor families of the same structure may be treated quite differently depending on where they live; (3) Because of this variance in the treatment of families, some families with able-bodied nonworking heads may end up with more disposable income than other families with full-time working heads; (4) Taken together these programs contain incentives that discourage the work effort on the part of the recipients, encouraging family break-up, and promoting migration from low to high benefit regions; (5) Because of the patchwork nature of the programs, there are serious administrative inefficiencies, and equally serious inefficiencies in the targeting of benefits toward the needy family units.[4]

This clearly represents a basic compendium of complaints about public policy, not only toward family maintenance programs, but the larger issues of work versus welfare implied in such a concert of criticisms. Rather than review the social policy legacy of the past in a jaundiced light, it is more profitable to examine a series of measures and strategies intended to overcome past problems, and hopefully move the policy-making apparatus to a new and higher ground.

The rise of cost-benefit analysis in the 1970s represents not only a new method for evaluating social programs, but a new set of domain assumptions and priorities that account for class sensibilities formerly left out of the reckoning. The awareness of class sensitivities toward programs went from evaluative to cost-benefit analysis, and marked a return to economics and away from sociology and social welfare as an essential mechanism of analysis.

Cost-benefit analysis is not necessarily conservative; however, it is correct to note that such an approach shifts attention from the goals to the contents of programs. An interesting example of this political crosscutting effect is a recent study by Robert Dorfman which indicates that a much greater proportion of environmental costs accrue to the lowest income sector, while conversely, those who stand to gain the most from environmental and political control programs are often located in high income groups. Dorfman makes a strong case that the redistribution of income is not a proper function for the EPA. His data suggest strongly that the "environmental protection programs entail a redistribution of income, perhaps of substantial magnitude. But redistributing income is not a proper function for the Environmental Protection Agency. Some people object vigorously to redistributing income as an incident to government programs enacted for other purposes."[5] The purpose of cost-benefit analysis is broadly to measure the degree of asymmetry in the allocation and distribution of goods and services. Clearly, it focuses on those aspects of public policy which draw attention to how much the public pays, whereas evaluative research techniques focused on how much the public gets.

At the auditing level, cost-benefit analysis is a method of subtracting the cost of an activity from the benefits to be derived from the activity, a standard procedure for most industrial firms and organizations. Cost-benefit analysis of whole social programs, however, differs from this method in that the level of analysis is not merely the firm or organization, but the social system as a whole. Cost and benefit are not calculated on the profit and loss ledger of any single special interest, but the cost and benefit to the entire society. This differs from evaluative research by bringing under analysis not only the targeted population but the entire society. It also differs from evaluative research in that cost-benefit analysis brings into question the goals of a program as well as the contents and commitments of a program. The benefit or goal of a program is assigned a value other than a purely moral one, or one already agreed upon by the political consensus as worth achieving. In a work on this subject, Ezra Mishan states the following:

> The general question that a cost-benefit analysis sets out to answer is whether a number of investment projects, A, B, C, etc., should be undertaken and, if investible funds are limited, which one, two, or more, among those specified projects that would otherwise qualify for admission, should be selected. But why bother with cost-benefit analysis at all? What is wrong with deciding whether or not to undertake any specific investment, or to choose among a number of specific investment opportunities, guided simply by proper accounting practices and therefore, guided ultimately by reference to profitability. The answer is provided by a familiar thesis that what counts as a benefit or a loss to one part of the economy— to one or more persons or groups—does not necessarily count as a benefit or loss to the economy as a whole. And in cost-benefit analysis we are concerned with the economy as a whole, with the welfare of a defined society, and not any smaller part of it.[6]

Most cost-benefit analyses are spent in ways of calculating the cost of a given project. In Mishan's major work, for instance, of sixty-seven chapters, only four deal with determining the benefits of income distribution, while the remainder are centered upon cost factors. Benefits are to be measured in terms of consumer surpluses. Consumer surpluses are "the maximum sum of money a consumer would be willing to pay for a given amount of the good, less the amount he actually pays."[7] Benefits are to be calculated by the increase in consumer surplus. An increase in consumer surplus means that the price of a good declines and money is freed for other goods. By far the major concern of cost-benefit analysis is the calculation of costs for a particular project. The cost of a policy includes not only the immediate cost of producing given goods or services such as labor and resources, but also start-up costs and research and development costs. These two additional concepts of cost give insight into the domain assumptions of cost-benefit analysis.

Let us examine the concept of start-up or opportunity cost. This is a measure of the cost of using the resources for this project and not other projects. This implies that resources are finite and using them on one project means other projects cannot be undertaken. These resources include both fiscal strength and natural resources. This is far removed from evaluative research in which resources were largely excluded from calculations of the costs of innovative policies. This implies that resources were thought to be unlimited and hence not a factor that needed evaluation.

A related area of cost is that of external diseconomies. These are spillovers from normal production of goods and services that are conventionally not included in cost-benefit analysis limited to a single firm or project. These costs include such items as air and water pollution and similar dysfunctions of economic activities, to the larger society. The domain assumptions of these two types of cost are better presented in an earlier work of Mishan, *The Cost of Economic Growth*, where cost-benefit analysis is applied to economic growth. Mishan states his goal to be the improvement of resource allocation.[8] Throughout the work, Mishan cites the external diseconomies of growth in terms either of depletion of limited resources or the increase of pollution.

Cost-benefit analysis includes a criticism of transfer payments as well as economic growth. Mishan argues that transfer payments have little effect as a cost or benefit on a whole society scale.[9] They do not increase consumer surplus, i.e., benefit, but may result in an opportunity cost at worst. This view again should be contrasted to evaluative programs which were composed mostly of transfer payments. As we have already noted, this tilt toward a consideration of program and policy costs has a corrective dimension—reducing equity-oriented programs—and a radical element—increasing demands for the preservation and protection of the natural environment.

Many flaws in the cost-benefit model emerge as it is examined more closely. The first problem of cost-benefit analysis, despite elaborate charts and methods to measure benefits to the contrary, is whether there really is such an entity as benefit to the society as a whole. If what counts as a benefit or a loss to a party or the economy may not be transferred to the society as a whole, how can one arrive at a benefit for the whole? The second problem is an overemphasis upon external diseconomies while drastically understating possible external economies. Mishan falls into this pattern. Although he does not mention external economies, most of his discussion deals with diseconomies or costs. There are also some problems of method in cost-benefit analysis, particularly in predicting future costs and benefits of actions. These problems have been pointed out in recent economic policy research.[10] But in the main, one can see from different approaches which arose in the past decades that they are differentially used by those who continue to advocate such goals as full employment and equal access to job opportunities; in contrast are those who see absolute equality as resulting in a breakdown of economic rationality.

In this comparison of evaluative research and cost-benefit analysis we have shown some differences in domain assumptions of the two paradigms and two decades. Unlike evaluative research, cost-benefit analysis brings into question not only the goals of the program but also the contents of that program. It places its level of analysis not only in terms of target groups but also effects upon the society as a whole. It tends to emphasize such problems as economic and environmental spillovers of unmanaged growth from the programs and limited resources in any given period.

Recent trends calling for new and more complex measures and indicators of the quality of life have major ramifications for equity demands. These measures form the basis for a redefinition of equity and new demands not previously part of the policy agenda. It is a change exemplified by demands to satisfy quantitative criteria at the peril of ignoring the qualitative aspects of spreading forth new goods and services. Along with the policy redefinition of equity to mean sharing quantities, new minorities and old groups have emerged demanding a greater participation in the wealth of the nation. A far different and largely unanticipated consequence of changing the quality of life indicators is the erection of new barriers, the drawing of attention to costs of equity, and the splintering of coalitions formerly working for equity as quantitative in nature.

Older definitions of equity, associated with evaluative programs, can be characterized as seeking to create minimum standards of living centering around the concept of income. In the period 1960–70, most definitions of poverty were concerned with setting proper income levels that would remove one from poverty. This is made clear in a brief prepared by an official of the Social Security Administration which discusses setting the correct income level.

> There is not, and indeed in a rapidly changing pluralistic society there cannot be, one standard universally accepted and uniformly applicable by which it can be decided who is poor. Almost inevitably a single criterion applied across the board must either leave out of the count some who should be there or include some who, all things considered, ought not to be classed as indigent. There can be, however, agreement on some of the considerations to be taken into account in arriving at a standard. And if it is not possible to state unequivocably "how much is enough," it should be possible to assert with confidence how much, on an average, is too little. Whatever the level at which we peg the concept of "too little," the measure of income used should reflect at least roughly, an equivalent level of living for individuals and families of different size and composition.[11]

Given this definition of poverty in terms of income and minimum standards of living, demands for equity and programs to fulfill those demands were presented in terms of achieving those minimum levels. Examples of these programs and their domain assumptions abound in the area of transfer payments, job programs, and housing for the urban poor.

Transfer payment programs exemplify this quantitative concept of equity. These transfer payments were intended to lift people above the income level of poverty and hence provide the basic standards of living that were considered to be the minimum. Under the social programs of the Johnson era "cash benefits for maintenance of incomes in 1968 [were] estimated at $14.6 billion, or 57 percent of all aid to the poor."[12] The symmetry between the concept of equity and goals of transfer payment programs is illustrated by Ginzberg's discussion of their success.

> On balance, the Great Society programs were not failures. What were the major programs? In Robert Lampman's view a solution was found for income poverty. We obviously did not make structural changes that fundamentally altered the lives of all poor people. But we took care of much of their problem of deficient income via food stamps and other subsidy and cash programs. During the Great Depression poor people lived out of garbage cans. That situation happened repeatedly in our large cities. Fortunately, we are not at that level any more.[13]

In the area of job programs, the emphasis was again upon quantity of jobs and not the quality. The programs were concerned with decreasing unemployment, increasing the labor force, and again, increasing the income levels of lower income groups and the unemployed. Little thought was given to the nature of the work to be done or the satisfaction of those doing the work. The evaluation process tends to become circular. The costs of evaluation inhibit any but the determined estimates.[14] The government is only concerned with overcoming obstacles to employment, not its quality. Ginzberg quotes a former secretary of labor to show that the domain assumptions concerning equity rarely understood the quality of life issues.

> He said, "What are you talking about? In good periods when the labor market is tight and you have a job you cannot stand, you find yourself another job. When the labor market is weak and there is much unemployment, you feel lucky if you have a job, even one that leaves something to be desired. I do not know any frustrated workers.[15]

This same quantitative approach to equity and its related programs can also be shown in the area of federal and local housing programs. The goal of most governmental programs was to increase the amount of standard housing available to low-income groups. The criteria for housing were set mostly in terms of health and safety. A quick review of the Baltimore City Housing Code, considered one of the best in the nation, shows that the bulk of the code is concerned with such health factors as plumbing and ventilation and safety factors such as fireproofing and fire escapes. The only interest in more aesthetic factors is that walls be clean and smooth (not necessarily painted or papered) and that all repairs had to be done in a workmanlike manner. The older concept of equity can be defined as an incremental concern with maintaining a basic level of keeping people alive. The major area of attack was income levels. The government sought to achieve equity by raising incomes above the poverty level.

Social indicators and measures of the quality of life have been a part of American social science since the early days of the social pathologists and their attempts to measure the disorganization of urban areas. The Presidential Committee on Social Trends, formed in 1929, attempted for the first time to measure comprehensively the quality of American life and to construct a set of social indicators. This proved to be a false start, and social indicators did not receive their real push until the 1960s. The push within the government for social indicators came from two areas: first, from the Department of Health, Education, and Welfare in connection with social programs of the period, and second, from environmental protection agencies' attempts to enlarge the definition of environment to include not only the physical or biological, but also the social. In turn, the environment to be protected became not only the physical but also the social one.

Despite huge gains in social science methodology since the 1920s and the Hoover Commission, there is still little consensus as to what composes the proper quality of life, and how it is measured. Recent studies of the quality of life range from measures of purely objective studies of economic and social conditions to the more subjective and psychological measures of happiness of the populations. The Department of Health, Education, and Welfare defines social indicators as:

> a statistic of direct normative interest which facilitates concise, comprehensive, and balanced judgment about the condition of major aspects of a society. It is in all cases a direct measure of welfare and is subject to the interpretation that, if it changes in the "right" direction, while other things remain equal, things have gotten better or people are "better off."[16]

Illustrating this step toward sharpening the entire system of gathering social indicators, the United States census will now take place every five years rather than every ten. The first such mid-decade census will occur in 1985. Several developments are responsible for the necessity felt by Congress and the president to double the census frequency. Among these is the large number of special surveys for public policy planning the Bureau of Census has been asked to undertake as a consequence of the social indicators movement. Special surveys have investigated everything from whether families think their neighborhoods are decent places to live to screening populations to determine how many people have been victims of crime. Such qualitative measures, thought to be statistically sophisticated, still take as their data base the national census; and as the American populations become increasingly mobile, that base becomes obsolete in much less time than in the past.

A growing number of government financial aid programs, such as revenue sharing and educational assistance programs, allocate funds to states and localities on the basis of population. In fiscal year 1976, $39 billion of federal funds was allocated according to formulas based at least in part on population statistics. And population mobility quickly renders qualitative measures out of date. For example, in distributing federal educational funds to children from poverty level families in individual school districts, only an actual person-by-person count can provide accurate data. Such social indicators of poverty as whether a family unit has a flush toilet and a bathtub or, if available, whether it has exclusive use of such facilities or shares them with others are now commonplace measurements of the quality of the nation's housing. But the main point is that qualitative social indicators have a direct and profound effect on quantitative economic measures.

Social indicators have a strong normative component. Social indicators are a social accounting system that would yield a good rough approximation of optimal and minimal standards for American community life.[17] There is only a slender consensus concerning what elements comprise the quality of life and what is to be included in any such measure. Liu summarizes three models:

> 1. Precise definitions of what constitutes quality of life, e.g., happiness, satisfaction, wealth, lifestyle, etc.; 2. Definitions through the employment of a specific type of subjective or objective social indicator, e.g., GNP, NEW, health or welfare indicators, environmental, etc.; 3. Indirect definition by specification of variables or factors affecting the quality of life, e.g., a group of social, economic, political, and environmental indicators represented by different types of composite indexes.[18]

It can easily be seen how social indicators can have ramifications for equity demands, particularly with their emphasis upon normative interests. The ramifications affect not only existing areas of equity, but the opening of new areas to equity as well. The ultimate purpose of social accounting is expected by its advocates to issue into social opportunity. It is postulated that legislation should allow all sectors of society to dip into a common pool of knowledge so that the present esoteric-exoteric dualism, which is in reality a split between the more and the less affluent sectors of society, can be finally dissolved. S. M. Miller realized the effects of using social indicators to achieve equity as early as 1967 when he criticized existing economic definitions of poverty.

> In the last third of this century we need new approaches to the quality of life in every country. We suggest that a minimum approach by government in any society with significant inequalities must provide for rising minimum levels not only of incomes, assets and basic services, but also of self-respect and opportunities for social mobility and participation in many forms of decisionmaking. The approach which we suggest broadens the economic perspective from a narrow concern with "income." [19]

A rapid view of some of the items included in measuring the quality of life will show how the older definition of equity and its related programs could not handle the problems raised by social indicators. Liu uses such items as percent of owner-occupied housing units, air, water, visual, and noise pollution, parks, numbers of doctors, dentists, and hospitals, numbers of cars and motorcycles, and population density.[20] It appears obvious from just these few indicators that minimum income equity cannot account for all these areas; and beyond that, and none too subtly, qualitative measures are themselves transformed into quantitative indicators. The examples of work and housing illustrate how dramatically standards change when qualitative indicators are used in conjunction with quantitative ones.

In the area of work, the concept of equity changes from just having a job to having a job that is rewarding and satisfying. The Campbell, Converse, and Rodgers study shows a high degree of relationship between satisfaction with the quality of life and work satisfaction. Those groups most discontent with their jobs are in lower income groups. They respond not only in terms of wages, but in terms of relations with co-workers, job comfort, and creative challenges of a job. The presumption is that Americans are no longer satisfied with the economics of job or income parity, but must have emotionally satisfying activities related to the experience of work. In the area of housing, Campbell notes that:

> The social setting, including interpersonal relations and the type of housing (i.e., whether or not one is living in single-family housing) are salient factors influencing an individual's level of satisfaction with the community. Other important factors related to general satisfaction include the physical conditions of the residential environment, the convenience of having nearby public and private facilities and services, the size of one's dwelling, and the presence of conditions such as spacious, quiet, and safe surroundings.[21]

Again, these conditions are not included in existing definitions of standard housing equity.

The framework developed by Campbell places work satisfaction and the quality of life into a larger pattern of aspirations and expectations. The creation of measures of quality of life and public dissemination of these results will possibly increase expectations and even heighten anxieties of many groups currently considered satisfied. Urban white ethnics, for example, could become dissatisfied with their housing. Although this group in current housing terms lives in standard or superior housing, its members continue to live in dense population areas lacking many services and amenities registered in these quality of life indicators. Campbell calls for social indicators research on *all* minorities, leaving the definition of who constitute the minorities open-ended.[22]

Social indicators and measures of the quality of life carry within themselves not only new equity demands but also new potential barriers to equity. These barriers come in two research areas. The first is that equity in one area such as jobs and housing may affect other areas such as environmental and ecological quality. The second factor is the breakup of existing groups working for equity by virtue of the highly refined nature of new qualitative indicators.

The first area involves the cost of growth and the constraint of limited resources. These problems play a minor role in social indicators. Expansion to meet new housing demands, new cars, and new services also carry with them increased costs in terms of pollution and energy. At the same time, equity demands in the physical and biological environment carry costs in terms of social and economic equity. In Liu's study of metropolitan areas it is the older industrial cities that score low in both social and environmental indices. Attempts to solve one problem impede and frustrate efforts to solve the other. Solving the social problems creates more pollution, while fighting pollution increases social problems. Dorfman[23] and Baumol[24] have shown that environmental protection costs more for the poor and has a greater effect upon their standard of living than for the rich.

A second barrier to equity is a change in political forces dealing with equity concerns. A study by Springer and Constantini shows that those concerned with the environment are generally liberal and support other equity demands.[25] This presents the possibility that a schism may occur in which people will be compelled to withdraw their support for equity demands in favor of environmental concerns, or vice versa. This could signify a union of environmental groups with conservative economic sectors, or failing that development, a decline in those favoring equity for the lower classes if it meant higher levels of pollution.

Environmentalists' action is filled with illustrations of higher costs and hurdles to alternatives to oil and natural gas. Environmental action has hindered the use of alternative resources in several ways. The first and most direct is their opposition to strip mining. Although the federal strip mining bill was vetoed by President Ford many states have passed similar laws. An additional hurdle is air pollution control laws which require low sulfur oil and high grade coal. This limits the demands for a large amount of coal that would be inexpensive. A second area of conflict is in the exploration for new oil resources. Examples of this are the battle over the Alaskan pipeline and opposition to exploration off the Atlantic coast once the petroleum "crisis" passed. The third area of confrontation is nuclear energy. The environmentalist groups are pushing an all-out assault upon nuclear generators, even if this means higher use of conventional fuels.

A major tenet of present-day economic analysis which plays an important role in policy formation concerning energy and pollution is the concept of substitution. The concept of substitution means that a rise in the price of goods or services results in consumers switching to lower-priced but equivalent goods or services. The classic example of substitution has been consumers' demands for meat. A rise in the cost of beef results in consumers replacing beef in their diets with a lower-priced meat. The process results in a lower demand for the scarce foodstuff and in turn, a normal price schedule is once again established.

The concept of substitution has been used to attempt a lower demand and conserve limited supplies of energy. It derives from the classical free market notion of supply and demand. In many areas this has met with considerable success, while in other areas it has been a limited success or outright failure. One area of success has been in the substitution of easily available alloys for copper, while a major failure has been in transportation and attempts to force substitution of automotive use. By comparing these two areas of substitution, one a success and one a failure, we can better understand how social factors as well as economic factors affect the forced substitution of one good or service for another.

In the area of copper "a sharp increase in copper prices always leads to substitution." [26] The substitution is made so easily that it becomes an economic threat to the Third World nations whose economies depend on the export of copper. A review of the uses of copper and its substitutes will show that there is little social effect, at least for consumers, in its substitution. Copper is used in construction and electrics for plumbing and wiring. In both of these uses it is easily replaced with plastic and steel pipes and aluminum wiring. In both cases substitution has little effect upon the final product, except lowered cost. Most homeowners would be hard pressed to tell whether their house wiring is copper, steel, or aluminum. This is much the same with other uses of copper. For the consumer, it is of little importance if the wiring in one's stereo or television is aluminum or copper, or if "chrome" plating for automobiles is metal or plastic. (It should be noted that copper is itself a substitute for gold and silver which are better conductors.) In sum, there is little social barrier to raw material substitutes as long as such substitution does not alter the final product or alter the consumer's social costs.

Attempts at forced substitutions in modes of transportation either to save on petroleum consumption or to control pollution have met with either limited success or failure. A change in modes of transportation, unlike substitution for copper, carries with it great consequences for social and individual behavior. To conserve fuel, curbing the use of private automobiles is central. They account for nearly 40 percent of petroleum consumption in the United States. They also have become less efficient converters of gasoline into vehicle-miles. Most programs to curb the use of cars have centered around the increase in the purchase cost of automobiles, or lowering the cost of using public transportation. A third way is the more efficient use of transportation by increasing numbers of passengers per vehicle. This forced substitution of energy-saving modes of transportation for automobiles works best when connected to private-sector, free-market requirements.[27] One recent review of these programs states that "behavioral changes (with respect to personal travel) are quite difficult to effect: people are extremely resistant to purely economic forces that seek to change their travel modes and extent of travel."[28]

Programs in California which attempted to create legal and physical barriers to continued use of cars, or distinctions between slow private lanes and fast public lanes, met with civil disobedience and destruction of barriers. In Los Angeles, laws to reserve "diamond lanes" or the faster lanes on freeways for car pools and buses have resulted in persons carrying dummies in their cars to look like car pools. In Berkeley, physical barriers to discourage the use of cars resulted in the following acts by drivers: "The shock of not being able to drive down streets in a straight line so enraged some citizens that in the first weeks 30 stop signs were stolen, and thousands of dollars worth of damage occurred in 200 attacks on the barriers."[29] Several criticisms suggest themselves. The first and most obvious is that in the use of the automobile, criteria apart from cost, such as time and comfort, are involved. This has already been widely demonstrated, although the way to take other factors into account is certainly not yet clear. It is difficult to know whether the reason why econometricians confine themselves to relatively few factors is that they think they represent the most important behavioral relations or simply that they are the only ones that can be measured simply and satisfactorily.[30]

The automobile driver does not perceive his car merely as a means of transportation, but as central to a life that he has developed as a result of, and maintained by, automobiles. Residential patterns have changed as a result of the car, and call for continued use of a car. This places jobs, services, and shopping outside of the range of public transportation. An example of this is the beltway phenomenon of car-oriented shopping centers and services. One need only list the number of nouns that have become modified by the adjective *drive-in*. One may encourage smaller or safer autos. But the substitution of public transportation introduces a whole new area of controls.

Central to this car life-style is time saved beyond any concept of leisure. A. J. Harrison states that this plays a major role in transportation use.[31] The car allows for shorter travel time and longer range. It provides door-to-door service from home to job. It also is central in leisure activities; the short weekend trips, the drives in the country, and the nights out are all by cars. Researchers have found that drivers prefer the freedom of the car over the control of timetables.

A major factor that prevents the substitution of alternate modes of travel, such as subways, is the social meaning of the auto beyond just transportation. Cars have become a status symbol in America. Every introductory class in sociology stresses this point. The car, and which car you own, becomes the symbol of your position in society. Increases in cost of owning and operating may only serve to increase the status of the owner. Switching to a smaller car (or for some groups a larger car) causes a loss (or gain) in status. Substitution always involves tradeoffs. To gain high average speed, rail systems have fewer stations. To serve mainline systems means to limit the ability to serve subareas of a region. Regional long-haul design may reduce local trip-taking capability.[32]

Substituting modes of transportation, unlike substituting for copper, requires changing not only methods of travel but also large areas of social behavior from resident patterns and leisure activities to status system. Any calculus of relative costs of transportation modes must take into account the social factors associated with that mode of transportation. This holds true for other products such as food, which imply social and cultural complexes quite beyond the considerations of cost and supply. Indeed, the cultural and religious factors involved in the consuming of food have resisted even famine and starvation conditions.

A serious problem with substitution strategies is that they involve the manipulation of large numbers of people, admittedly for worthy environmental goals, but nonetheless manipulations at a broad level. Automobile patterns are only the beginning. Forcing new ways of living on individuals is a necessary concomitant of energy reduction and saving devices. This is not to say that some forms of substitution are not both necessary and even inevitable. It is to point out that efforts thus far have been thwarted precisely because of the high premiums Americans place on libertarian values, even at the risk of equity goals. Hence, such strategies as car pooling, special bus lanes to encourage fewer automobile drivers at peak and rush hours, rail service in place of automobile use for work, high utilization of apartments by large numbers of people, all of these have met stiff and usually successful resistance.

It might well be that the breaking point has not yet been reached. That is to say, there remains surplus in the American economic structure to permit successful resistance to substitution techniques. Quite apart from the cost-benefit level is whether in fact any agency mandated to protect the environment also has the right to manipulate public opinion and human behavior on a grand scale. These are but some of the deep structural issues which have manifested themselves in the latest efforts to foster an egalitarian society.

A new social science tool designed to predict lifelong patterns of human behavior in response to certain government income programs has been introduced by the Urban Institute in Polity Exploration Through Microanalytic Simulation. This work describes the advent of new economic forecasting models developed over seven years at the institute and successfully refined into a working version by the end of 1975.

Unlike older modeling approaches, newer simulation techniques use data about individuals, families, and households to create a representative population and thereby avoid the uncertainties in using cruder measurements of economic performance—the macroanalytic data of national averages and aggregates. Previously, because policy makers have been unable to imagine the specific impacts of a federal program on various subgroups of the American population, billion dollar programs such as Medicare, welfare, and Social Security produced unexpected and unwanted results. Spokesmen for this approach argue that:

To select prudent governmental policies affecting unemployment, social services, income distribution, national output, inflation, education-health, and the like requires the capability of predicting what the results will be, based on a realistic model of the economy. If policymakers are considering one tax law as compared to some other tax law, or one spending policy as compared to some other spending policy, they should know what the consequences of all the laws and policies under consideration are likely to be. One way to find out is to try out the policies and see what happens. This has often been done, but it can be a costly and painful way of smoking out errors, not very satisfactory from the standpoint of the affected citizens or the economy. Policies should be selected on the basis of their fruit; but it would be preferable to sample the fruit before applying policies to the real world. If a sufficiently accurate model of the economy were available, it would make such sampling possible.[33]

The newer forecasting techniques return economic and social modeling to the mainstream of small group theory where the focus is given to individual, family, or corporate behavior. This newer simulation effort seeks to develop a model population that could age year by year and continue to yield highly detailed and reliable profiles of individuals and special groups: acquiring added years of education, entering the work force, getting married, having children, undergoing divorce, reentering the work force, obtaining income from earnings or wealth or welfare or retirement programs, migrating, taxation, and death.[34]

A distinguishing feature of newer forecasting techniques is that these changes are not allowed to occur in isolation but are explored in the many different ways they would be experienced by individuals. A person's age, race, sex, educational experience, and family status, for example, all affect earning capacity, longevity, and family status stability. With microanalytic simulation, policy makers can hope to answer with some accuracy questions like: How much will a new proposed program cost in the next decade? How will the benefits be shared twenty years from now by low-, middle-, or upper-income groups? By women versus men? By urban versus rural households? By the elderly versus the young?

One application of such forecasting is to project the costs of the country's largest welfare program, Aid to Families with Dependent Children (AFDC). One experiment with the model compared the consequences for the number of AFDC caseloads if: (1) the divorce rate over the next decade remained roughly at the 1974 level, or if (2) the divorce rate accelerated at the annual rate of 5 percent experienced in the early 1970s. It was found that the higher divorce rate, by conservative estimate, would generate an increase of about half a million AFDC cases by 1982, representing an annual budget increase of $611 million.[35]

As in previous attempts at simulation, whether micro or macro, problems occur in translating simulations into actualities, particularly extrapolating from past data to future conditions. Thus, in carefully reasoned illustrations of the new forecasting techniques, the Urban Institute project reports growth rates in earnings of women which are higher in their simulated versions than in the actual empirical data over the past several years. A similar experimental conclusion indicates that increasing women's participation in the labor market to the point where they work for as many hours as comparable men yields its greatest benefits to husband-wife families and much less benefit to female-headed families. But this does not account for such extrinsic items as qualitatively higher taxation or net amount of income over and against gross earnings. Another great difficulty with microanalytic simulation is its virtual inability to forecast changes in trends and tendencies. As long as similar conditions prevail in the future as obtained in the past, then simulation technique does serve as a sophisticated corrective to simply aggregating data. It is precisely the change in trends that accounts for most difficulties in policy making.[36] Hence, these newer approaches must be viewed in a more modest light than those who put forth these claims have been willing to acknowledge. Even methodologists most dedicated to these new sampling techniques are compelled to acknowledge that breakthrough phenomena cannot really be accounted for in projecting into the future.

12. From the New Deal to the New Federalism

The phrase New Federalism has generated intense public debate—unequaled since the formation of the New Deal fifty years earlier. Other administration-inspired concepts such as the War on Poverty and the New Frontier did not so much announce a policy departure as enshrine an ongoing commitment to domestic change. Many of the socioeconomic groups who were in the forefront of the New Deal viewed their interests as threatened by this New Federalism; labor leaders, sectional interests, and minority groups seriously mistrusted the contents and thrust of its policies, and from more conservative groups representing the national defense, pro-life, and religious interests, the critical crescendo was no less fierce. Any serious analysis of the Reagan administration must appreciate the centrality of the New Federalism to its long-term aims: the reduction of inflation, the control of federal spending, incentives to further growth, and finally, an increase in private sector employment that supposedly would ensue from such policies.

The New Federalism was new only to the extent that its "turnback" and "swap" aspects involve specific exchanges of services between national and state government. The fifty states would manage activities connected with public assistance, whereas medicaid services would be assumed by the national government. The assumption was that the savings in bureaucratic costs would compensate for the reduced dollar amount in certain areas, further that state and city management of key programs would eliminate the sort of nightmarish government mismanagement remote from the actual sources of problems. In this way, the "hidden hand" of the free market would assert its claims against bureaucracy, presumably bringing about a new equilibrium through revitalized allocation devices.

Administrations live and die in four-year cycles. If the first two years of the Reagan administration could be said to represent putting the New Federalism in place, the following two-year phase could be said to be the empirical test for the efficacy of such programmatic shifts. The time frame is closer to three rather than four years in duration, since appeals to the electorate in any final year of office depend heavily on the efficacy of the policies enacted in the first three years. Still, it must be noted that the impulse toward state-managed programs had already begun in earnest during the final two years of the Carter administration, and with some notable successes.[1]

Negative reaction to the New Federalism was especially severe at the exchange level, i.e., the assignment to the states of the two major welfare programs (Aid to Families with Dependent Children and Food Stamps) with the federal government assuming complete control of Medicaid (the program of medical aid to the poor). The assumption behind the proposed swap was that the movement toward socialized medicine was largely realistic, and control of such funds relatively easy to monitor, whereas welfare packages differed so dramatically from state to state as to affect negatively everything from state taxation to regional demographic flows. The statement adopted by the AFL-CIO executive council well expressed the negative sentiments of organized labor on the New Federalism.

> The President's proposal is an ill-conceived scheme to reduce anticipated huge federal budget deficits while neglecting the nation's most fundamental needs. It would shift huge costs to state and local governments. It does not address the real and most pressing problems the nation faces—massive unemployment, a huge tax giveaway to the rich, runaway interest rates and a depressed, stagnant and inflation-prone economy.[2]

Nor did sharp criticism come only from labor sources. Management-oriented analysts have also entered the fray. They too charged that the tax burden on the states would increase enormously, and at the expense of the federal portion of support. In terms of dollar amounts it might well be that the northern states would suffer the most losses, but in many program areas, it is the South and West that would find themselves cut back most severely. Advocates of a modified Sunbelt ideology like Bernard L. Weinstein shrewdly pointed out that the proposed trust fund, in making no distinction between rich and poor states, would exacerbate interstate disparities in fiscal resources, to the disfavor of the southern tier of the nation.

> Though interregional differences in fiscal capacity—and income—are not nearly so great today as they were twenty years ago, a wide gap still separates the "rich" states from the "poor" states. To a large extent, the gains of recent decades can be attributed to increased federal involvement in a wide range of human and social service programs. In particular, grants-in-aid have recognized the special problems of low-income communities by compensating for inadequate fiscal capacity at the local level. If the federal government withdraws from the intergovernmental grant business entirely, interregional disparities in income and wealth may widen once again.[3]

What is unclear in this sort of analysis is whether the maintenance of government subsidies in welfare and food programs is really intended as support for the poor or to make sure that the stalled Sunbelt miracle continues unabated at the expense of the rest of the country, with the government bureaucracy picking up additional costs which southern states, with their lower fiscal supports for the unemployed and the welfare needy, have traditionally passed along.

The administration predicated its New Federalism proposals on a set of three assumptions: (1) tax levels at the time it entered office were so high as to discourage investment and growth, making reductions in federal tax burdens the key to future economic expansion; (2) the private sector was more' effective in responding to the needs of the poor by providing employment and training; (3) too many past social programs of a top-down nature failed; thus the legitimate needs of the poor were best addressed and administered at state and local levels. A significant architect of the Johnson administration's Great Society program, Sar Levitan, however, pointed out that governmental expenditures were not a waste or a failure, but essentially a huge success. In providing basic income maintenance, equal opportunity laws, support for women and minority job opportunities, educational opportunities for young people, and social security for the aged, the record of achievement far outstripped its supposed weaknesses. Levitan calls attention to the distinction between the pluses of a decentralized administration and the minuses of a decentralized responsibility. In failing to distinguish the two, and in not making clear the huge role of state management in everything from unemployment insurance to social security, the New Federalism has a states' rights quality that is notoriously unworkable and reactive.

> We live in one nation. In an era when so many of our economic and social problems take on global proportions, the return to an outmoded concept of states' rights may not be in our collective best interests. The real meaning of federalism is a form of government where powers are shared among all levels of government, not one in which the federal government abdicates its responsibility to address social problems.[4]

What we have is a series of highly critical responses, across the ideological divide, one that takes a hard look at the New Federalism and finds it wanting in terms of vision no less than practice.[5]

Neither the conceptual framework nor policy implications of the New Federalism are about to vanish. Quite apart from the specifics, there remains a general sentiment that big government, high taxation, and economic stagnation hang together, and threaten libertarian aspects of American society. And the impulse of the New Federalism was as clearly libertarian as those behind the New Society were egalitarian. The huge differential between the domain assumptions of a free people living unimpeded lives versus those mired in class, sex, and race differences doomed by exploitation and prejudice may be played out on a canvas called the New Federalism or the Great Society. Each reflects ongoing tensions and strains of a nation which has yet to resolve differences stemming from its origins. In this sense, arguments over the New Federalism are a continuation of American ideological war by other slogans. They differ only in that the dominant rhetoric of the past fifty years—extending from the New Deal to the Great Society—is now a set of outsider claims, bruised but hardly beaten.

There is a commonsensical view that difficult times tend to produce a leftward swing in the electorate. Perhaps the ultimate evidence for this supposition was the New Deal era and the election of Franklin Delano Roosevelt. The United States was two full years into a depression at the time of the Roosevelt 1932 landslide, and without arguing labels or their meanings, we can agree that it did represent a leftward trend, at least as measured by support for strong federal intervention to produce equity in business and reduce imbalances in wealth. Franklin Delano Roosevelt also had to contend with the overriding problem of high unemployment (rather than inflation). He was also the last president elected for whom large-scale economic factors were central and interest-group politics still largely underdeveloped. The election of Ronald Reagan followed years of double-digit inflation, relatively modest levels of unemployment (except among racial, age, and ethnic cohorts, which experienced high unemployment), and a mushrooming public sector more adroit at bailing out the weak in the private sector than taking care to run the public's business both efficiently and equitably.

The depression economy which brought Franklin Delano Roosevelt and the New Deal to office was especially severe on the working class; the relatively tough economic conditions which brought about Ronald Reagan's presidency affected most directly a much expanded middle class. Middle America felt left out of the deliberations between rich and poor. The number of industrial workers belonging to a union has been relatively frozen since the New Deal. Between 1935 and 1980, the trade union sector grew from seventeen to twenty million, whereas levels of participation in the overall work force went from twenty-five to one hundred million. Even if this growth in the labor force cannot be attributed solely to the middle sectors or white-collar workers, it is clear that the broad middle classes, as specifically defined and objectively internalized, have become the bastion of the American dream—and its attendant frustration.

What precipitated the Republican victory of 1980, no less than the Democratic congressional victory in 1982, were not demands either for a leftward or rightward movement, but rather demands for social change and righting of the wrongs brought about by an enlarged bureaucratic rather than social net. Demands for change tend to have a negative impact on the party in power and decision-making elites. Rather than a left/right phenomenon, we have an insider/outsider phenomenon in which the party out of power benefits to the extent that dissatisfactions exist, either with the level of inflation or the level of unemployment. Obviously this holds only when a crisis is not sufficiently deep as to affect the legitimacy of the system. It is clear by the constancy of voter turnout and electoral participation, not to mention the national climate and rhetoric, that the legitimacy of the American system if anything has been enhanced in a post-Vietnam and post-Watergate environment that wants a greater dispersal of power.

Electoral outcomes should not be interpreted as an automatic ideological swing. Concerns for social policy areas remained high. Recent elections signal a concern for higher performance of projects and programs funded by the federal government, rather than demands for their total dismemberment. The watchword has become accountability through local and state control, not the simple elimination of programs and policies.

> The evidence is overwhelming that the public wants an extension or maintenance of most government programs on all levels, even if they cost more money. Of course, people also feel that the government is inefficient, that the tax system is unfair. All of this suggests a mood of dissatisfaction, not only with government operations but with other institutions, usually expressed in abstract terms. The majority of Americans are, in one way or another, upset that the American promise is not being realized; they also feel that they have a right to all the expected payoffs.[6]

Reagan administration policies attempted to address these concerns in dramatic new ways; the slogan of the New Federalism has provided a convenient framework to organize the essentially political no less than economic sources of decentralization. But to what extent are the subjective concerns about the unrealized payoffs of the economic system objectively rooted?

Reagan is at once the president of the United States and a spokesman for an American social movement. Even if his party falters at the polls in any given election, the Reagan constituency has achieved a dynamism of its own. Recent conservative attacks and defections only highlight these social movement aspects. Reagan moves in terms of political interests rather than social stratification, but the interchangeability of the two under the New Federalism is manifest.

> Reagan's constituency is not simply a collection of disparate interests—every candidacy faces that problem—but rather an authentic social movement around which particular interests have coalesced. The life and heart of the campaign are not to be found in elite concerns with economic and foreign policy, but in mass concerns with social and moral issues.[7]

This approach encounters troubles, however, when it considers how such social and moral issues are to be implemented. While exhibiting an appreciation for the connection between public governance and private morality, conservatives are often unclear what the government can do about these matters. What the executive branch can influence is the power of economic leveraging of moral goals. By a wide variety of measures—tax reductions, special advantages instead of disadvantages to married couples, income retirement accounts, all-savers certificates, self-employment, retirement, and pension funds—the Reagan administration succeeded in dramatically increasing the advantages of work over welfare. That these new devices are unequally distributed, that these quick-fix promotions carry the risk of deep social fissures along racial and cultural lines, and that measures of expanding work opportunities remain cloudy, while entirely true, do not detract from the middle-class aspects of Reaganism as a social movement whose moral concerns are addressed through economic levers. Middle sectors have traditionally contained a streak of strong biases against races and groups perceived as outside the mainstream; and this is certainly no less the case with the New Federalism.

Taking an opposing position, John Kenneth Galbraith sees the Reagan administration in its formative period as a "simplistic attack on the social consensus." He sees real harmony as based on the maintenance of public services, full employment, and market regulation. While one might argue with this framework, the more substantial issue he claims is over taxation, or that specific mechanism of reallocation whose aim it is to insure the social consensus.

> Taxes on the affluent . . . reduce that freedom of those so taxed to spend their own money. . . . The differential effect of taxes and public services on people of different income is something we must not disguise. Taxes in industrial countries are intended to be moderately progressive; in any case, they are paid in greatest absolute amounts by people of middle income and above. Public services, in contrast, are most used by the poor. The affluent have access to private schools, the poor must rely on public education. The rich have private golf courses and swimming pools; the poor depend on public parks and public recreation.[8]

This distinction between public and private, and growth and taxation as a means of leveraging social distinctions would be acceptable rhetoric in normal times. But these are not normal times.

There is a short-run possibility that economic stagnation may serve to bolster Reagan's support, not undermine it. Too many people who once shipped their children off to boarding and private schools are now forced to depend on public education; these same people must now turn to hospitals or clinics rather than private physicians for their health care. Keynesian mechanisms work best when there is sufficient growth in the economy for a portion of any surplus to go to public sector concerns. However, when growth rates dwindle from 5 percent to 1 percent or less, and the penetration of the middle sector into the higher occupational strata is blocked, then the notion of increased taxes confronts widespread citizen opposition. The social welfare consensus likewise dissolves. The helping hand becomes the harmful hand.

Testifying before the Committee on Ways and Means of the House of Representatives, Felix G. Rohatyn was of two minds on imposing an economic policy and philosophy inconsistent with the will of the people. Still, he registered strong disagreement "with the philosophy expressed by the president's statement that tax policy should not be used for social change." He believes just the opposite: "that this country was built on the notion that *all* its public policies should be aimed at social improvement and not at maintaining the status quo." [9] The trouble with this approach is a vagueness as to what constitutes the status quo, let alone social improvement. The maintenance of experimental programs, whatever their rationale, in times of economic growth is one thing; the advocacy of these same programs in a stagnant economy is quite another. If the tilt from emphasis on social benefits to concern about economic costs has become self-evident, the source of that tilt, the profound stagnation in the wealth of the American nation, has apparently not permeated the critical consciousness. The status quo no longer exists, or better, has become a status quo ante. Concerns for fiscal balance are intended to stimulate social change, not of the sort we have been accustomed to in the recent past, but changes of a profound sort nonetheless. The social consensus has shifted from a 10 percent unemployed to a 90 percent employed. Federal monetary policies are still being used to change the status quo by the monetarists of the New Federalism, but in ways that are anathema to those for whom regulatory mechanisms remain the essential cement of social peace in advanced industrial nations.

Pursuing a similar high ground, although with a different ideological approach, Robert L. Heilbroner sees supply-side economic theory as just dangerous generalization, an argument disguising a demand for a return to a more hierarchical and inegalitarian vision of the world. When push comes to shove, Heilbroner sees little innovation in the Reagan years. Far from considering Reaganism as a social movement, Heilbroner views it as an ideological posture disguising the paucity of innovation.

What is likely to happen over the next decade? Nothing. I say so from a profound skepticism about the efficacy of supply-side stimuli. But from a more history-laden point of view, I mean something different by "nothing." I mean that the slow, almost invisible trends of the past will continue to have their way, not because these trends have a life of their own but because they express the inner motions, the self-created dynamic of the system. I will mention only two of these trends: (1) State-owned or state-dependent organizations will emerge as the leading agents of accumulation. (2) As part of this statist movement, I would expect to see the emergence of an ever more explicit reliance on national planning.[10]

Arguing that such trends are irreversible under a Republican administration, or rather that they express an inner logic of the capitalist system, Heilbroner omits consideration of the things which have happened to produce a crisis in the political economy to start with. The long-run trend of statism (which is at least as endemic to socialist as to capitalist systems) is not mentioned by Heilbroner. However, the short-run trends of reducing the size and impact of the federal bureaucracy seem significant. The irony of liberalism is that statism has come to sustain, through a variety of legislative and judicial decisions, present levels of the welfare budget. If statist trends are not reversed, this is less likely to be due to conservative demands for maintaining failing industries intact than to maintaining social equilibrium between the class system (including a full panoply of 100 million working people at all levels) and a mass system (including 30 million who do not work at all, or remain in the twilight zone of the economy).

The libertarian element in the New Federalism, the assault on bureaucracy as such, derives from a transvaluation of state power: far from being the vanguard of bourgeois power, it has become the central appeals board of locating and limiting welfare power. This change in the character of the state, more than any change in the ideology of the New Federalism, helps to explain why important social changes can be expected in the next decade. Only if one holds to a belief in the state as the armed oppressor of the working class, or some variation on the Marxian theme, can one believe that nothing will happen in the next decade. The great fear of the conservative forces is not that nothing will happen but that too much will happen; that the dismantling of the federal-state apparatus will decentralize authority and open up a series of Hobbesian valves in which warfare of all against all will take place unmediated and uncontrolled by the federal apparatus. The key features seem to be shaping up as a struggle between the working class and the underclass, or between those for whom work is central and those for whom other forms of identification— race, sex, and age—are central. Not the self-regulation of the work force so much as the self-regulation of these interest groups will in all likelihood militate and even cancel out plans to dismantle even a fraction of federal bureaucracy and frustrate attempts at New Federalism in which local control displaces centralized administration.

If for Galbraith the tax abatement program has gone entirely too far, for a critical supporter such as Jude Wanniski, the Republican program has not gone nearly far enough. He is particularly disturbed by Reagan's early support, reinforced by the Cancun Conference, of efforts to continue underwriting Third World debt by artificial bailouts followed by "interlocking connections in the Eastern Establishment."

Reagan increasingly is viewed as encouraging the sort of high taxation and physical capital that is diametrically opposed to a supply-side view of United States development. In this Wanniski articulates a line of opposition also being put forth by Jack Kemp. Wanniski believes that in the Third World

> entrepreneurial activity was smothered by confiscatory tax rates. And, because the infrastructure did not foster growth, tax revenues did not increase. The revenues that were received had to be applied to debt service, while costs of financing general government were taken care of by the printing press and inflation further discouraging indigenous initiative. This, of course, was not the developmental path the United States or other industrial nations followed. The classical formula focused on human capital, on people not things. Policy did not focus on consumer demands for things, but on individuals to supply their talents and energies to greater production.[11]

The position of the United States at a variety of international conferences does resemble supply-side prescriptions. But even if the notion that "high tax rates defeat their own purpose" can be taken seriously in a Third World context, it must be recognized that the problems which most of these developing areas face have precious little to do with high taxation. These societies are often unable to collect even minimal taxes, and thus incapable of providing necessary social and welfare services. The president's reticence to apply internationally what he advocates nationally, far from representing a policy of inconsistency, shows an appreciation of the sharp differences between advanced and developing nations, between societies which do and do not have adequate growth-making infrastructures.

Too often the appeal to a New Federalism has been carved in bureaucratic stone. Emphasis has been focused on the need to reduce the size of the federal budget, and the consequent need to change fiscal priorities at the top and permit state and local municipalities a larger share in the management of tax funds. The reverse side of that appeal is not so much bureaucratic inflation as the potential for economic stagnation. The announcement of no-growth as a policy by the Club of Rome was somewhat tardy, postdating by several years the actual absence of growth in the economy. More than proclamations about federal spending, stagnation provided the fuel for a New Federalism. This translates into continuing personal loyalties, despite mixed signals in which federal deficit spending increased despite strong prohibitions and prescriptions to the contrary.

There is significant longitudinal data that has been largely overlooked in recent political discussions in order to explain how the New Federalism gained momentum, despite or because of the existence of economic stagnation as a long-term secular trend in the United States. If the data does not necessarily speak for itself, it does not require too much interpretation or interpolation to explain the meaning of the Republican presidential landslide.

The watershed year was 1973: the year of the OPEC boycott and oil embargo. Even though these events took place under the Republican administration of Richard M. Nixon and were dealt with in a rather cavalier fashion over the next several years by another Republican, Gerald R. Ford, the deepening of the crisis did not actually take place until the election of a Democrat, Jimmy Carter. The ills which befell America in the postboycott environment came home to roost during that administration. If we compare the years 1976 and 1980 and measure the resources spent in billions of dollars on new automobile purchases with respect to gas and oil for transportation purposes, we will find a near-perfect inversion: new automobile sales rose by 21 percent or from 38 to 46 billion; whereas gasoline and oil consumption rose from 44 to 90 billion or twice that of automobile sales and double that of previous gasoline and oil sales. This 102.7 percent increase in energy expenditures represented not simply a shift from one industry to another, but a huge export of capital rather than the circulation of capital represented by automobile sales.[12] Even with energy costs leveling off, this pattern represents a major change in the structure of Western economies.

The growth rate in the case of petroleum has been significant, but in the period between 1976 and 1980 there was virtual stagnation in actual dollar terms in automobile purchases, while the level of expenditures in gasoline and oil purchases more than doubled. Rarely in American peacetime history has there been such an intense export of capital. Long-run tendencies do not indicate a decline and fall of capitalism, but rather a diminution in the distinction between American and other varieties of capitalism. There has been a corresponding rise of the free market system through the redistribution of what was formerly viewed as strictly American wealth.[13]

Understanding this pendulum darkly, all recent administrations have sought to mesh domestic and foreign policy. There could no longer be a foreign policy that did not take into account the huge shift in resources, in capital expenditures, and in the distribution of the means by which an industrial civilization had the capacity to survive. American power drained of economic vitality stared down any policy initiatives in the final years of the 1970s. The hostage crisis represented the symbolic fruition of a stagnant situation well appreciated by the world community in economic terms long before the Iranian crisis materialized.

The New Federalism is viewed by the current administration as the first fundamental doctrinal change since the Roosevelt administration. It is probably more so in ideological than structural terms, since economic tendencies operate quite apart from political rhetoric. If we take the growth in median family income, measuring not only actual dollar growth but constant dollar growth, it is again clear that 1973 was a watershed year, and that the level of stagnation reached absolute proportions after that year. This is a nation which witnessed nearly a doubling in median family income between 1950 and 1970. When there is high growth, there is a greater capacity to absorb social welfare programs and social costs. Where there is no growth or exceedingly low levels of growth, the willingness to absorb social welfare programs is sharply reduced. Between 1950 and 1970 American society emphasized the benefits of social programs; in the following decade we emphasized the costs of such programs, or put in even starker terms, America shifted its values from sociology to economy—from a search for ways to achieve equity to a recognition and acceptance of economic inequalities.

The most dramatic shift to the American consumer and producer alike has been from growth to stagnation. Between 1950 and 1960 the average householder income rose from $11,361 to $15,637, a percentile and actual dollar improvement of over 50 percent. Between 1960 and 1970, using the same data base household income rose from $15,637 to $20,939, an equally sharp increase in actual consumer dollars constant to the Consumer Price Index. Now when we move from 1970 to 1980 in constant dollar terms, the shift is from $20,939 to $21,023, a stagnant situation in constant dollar terms, and an erosion of nearly 70 percent in consumer purchasing power over that decade. Thus, while actual dollar amounts rose, real income remained stagnant and this meant for the working person in particular the revolution of rising expectations came to a crashing halt in the last decade. There had to be a sharp falloff in what money could buy during the past decade or a sharp falloff in the same sort of expenditures in order to maintain the previous so-called quality of life.[14]

The shift in American society on a wide set of measures proceeded in lockstep fashion with changes in real income gain between 1950 and 1970 in constant dollars. Gains in real income were considerable both in dollar and percentile terms. Keynesian mechanisms of social welfare programs and refertilizing the economy by flooding the market with soft dollars seemed an easy price to pay in a world of growth. But as we look at the years from 1970 through 1980, these enormous levels of growth shriveled virtually to zero in real industrial growth. The following indicates how dramatic the turnaround has been first in the expansion and then the retrenchment of real income of Americans, a shift sufficiently potent to void previous generosities and equities toward those less fortunate. In statistical terms, the gains in real income from 1950 to 1960 were 37.6 percent; from 1960 to 1970, 33.9 percent; and from 1970 to 1980, 0.2 percent, or virtual and complete stagnation.[15] The middle class itself stagnated, viewing itself as economically unfortunate and politically disenfranchised during the Carter era. They seemed puzzled as to the way in which social growth was taking place in America.

It is scarcely accidental that there were taxpayer revolts and homeowner resistance to social programs from California to New Jersey. Even social welfare programs manifestly not benefiting particular minorities or the poor received declining support. Taxpayer revolts reflect the collapse of any gain in real income over the past decade and not any noticeable shift to the right in social attitudes. Indeed, when economic growth is registered, voters turn to a more generous spirit of sharing. This is evidenced by many past statewide legislative referendums receiving surprisingly strong voter support.

Turning to what has happened to upper-income families in the United States we again note that 1973 functions as a watershed year. Here too the patterns of stagnation, even decline, from 1973 to 1980 become apparent, with an absolute stagnation in the number of people with incomes of $25,000 and over, $50,000 and over, and a relative decline in the percentage of such people in the overall population vis-à-vis the work force as a whole. While stagnation has been the norm in working- and middle-class family life, upper-income families have fared much better. For example, families with incomes of $25,000 and over in constant 1980 dollar terms went from $45,539 in 1960 or 18.9 percent growth, to $55,054 or 41.9 percent growth in 1973, and finally to $60,309 or 39.3 percent. Figures of family income of $50,000 and over again reveal a constant growth in real dollar terms from 7.3 percent between 1960 and 1973, to 6.7 percent between 1973 and 1980.[16] In other words, upper-income families and the upper class generally were able either to pass along the costs of inflation or absorb such costs through savings, annuities, or interest. In political terms, thus, the upper class was the least negatively affected by the energy crisis or by the Keynesian policies of the Nixon, Ford, and Carter administrations.

Let us translate these economic data into social-class terms. First, the United States has a work force that expends increasing amounts of money on energy sources and raw materials with decreasing potential for saving or investment. Second, the United States has a middle class exhibiting absolute stagnation in constant dollar terms. Third, this country has an upper class that has become impermeable, closed rather than open to large numbers of new recruits, even those who may strongly identify with the American mobility dream.

Turning to the political rather than the economic aspects of the New Federalism, one notes that both Republican and Democratic administrations held essentially to the Keynesian mechanism of economic problem solving: greater federal expenditures, higher taxation, larger amounts for public assistance, and above all a technique of pass along and pass through which spared the lower classes the worst kinds of suffering and moreover spared the upper classes any costs incurred in this new federal technique. The data confirm an uneven distribution of costs borne by the middle sectors, and they also confirm a largely marginal, even nonexistent cost to the very rich. The data further show exactly what everybody knows: that working and middle classes paid inordinately for past policy mistakes. But it must be added that supply-side formulas, while easing inflationary pressures on the middle sectors, only increased employment pressures on the working classes.

The class system itself became part and parcel of a highly volatile interest-group network which operated at cross-purposes to specifically occupational or industrial aims. Class factors expanded to create a temporary Republican majority, and to create a pattern of political realignment which shifted those social classes with a stake in society to a conservative direction, over and against the racial, gender, ethnic, and even age factors that move in more radical directions. The class phenomenon, insofar as it expanded support for a Reagan victory, eroded interest-group politics based on more volatile and more parochial factors.

One of the frequent mistakes made in most analyses of the New Federalism is to identify it with either a conservative revolt of the very wealthy or a revolt of the working class to create a sort of right-wing populism. What more nearly took place and what postelectoral statistical analysis tends to support is that Republicanism had a large, broad-gauged impact, for different reasons, on the class system as a whole. Not supply-side economics as a general theory of society, but the realities of a no-growth economy with soaring costs of regulation and declining labor productivity helped to underwrite the 1980 electoral outcomes.[17] The presumed right-wing turn of the population thus represents a technical rather than an ideological adjustment.

It was bred of disillusionment with a broad pattern of stagnation that threatened to result in absolute decline in standards of living by people who have long been accustomed to responding to wants rather than to needs along both the social and economic axes.

To the extent that the Reagan administration has reduced levels of inflation and prevented patterns of recession for a reasonable amount of time the New Federalism also contains the prospects for continuing unemployment at 10 percent. The Republican party can expect to solidify its base on a broad range of the American class system. To the extent that the Republican party can solidify this turnaround of economic fortunes of the working, middle, and upper classes, class factors will themselves diminish in importance, and people will once more turn toward more specialized forms of association in terms of race, sex, and age, as mechanisms for bringing about a better distribution of fortunes.

There is a serious economic transformation taking place in American society. What began with the New Deal as a broad-based rebellion against privilege has now concluded as a class-based rebellion against a different set of privileges accruing to the welfare underclass. It represents a return to a Hobbesian world in which a class is measured by what it contributes and not by what it destroys. The fabric of American society for the present is predicated on a class consensus rather than a class struggle. And if this makes for strange bedfellows within the political party system, it makes for equally strange allies among interest groups seeking a better life for their specialized clientele.

While the verdict may be out on the efficacy of the New Federalism, it is already apparent that some very important changes have taken place: collective addressing of the major issues of social system, economic system, state power, administrative domination, indeed the domain assumptions of capitalism and communism as competing systems are all under scrutiny. The flabbiness of past analysis rested on a confrontation of the political values of democratic liberalism versus the despotism of totalitarian communism. But that has readily become an exercise in rhetoric, too costly in real-world terms. Current levels of debate relate to systemic values as such: to capitalism, communism, and varieties of societal forms based on neither. It is exhilarating intellectually as well as politically that the intellectual class—new and old—is able to debate the great questions of the century without suspicion or denigration.

The dark foreboding of the New Federalism as a precursor to fascism has clearly not come to pass. Quite the contrary, rarely in the postwar environment has such a high level of dialogue involving such a wide variety of officials and nonofficials taken place. To the extent that a major international crisis can be averted, and to the equal extent that the reduction in government supports does not result in open or disguised warfare between classes and masses, will this administration have indeed become a watershed. The measure of openness in the political system is dialogue about the nature of society itself. One can take any signs of political repression as a valid measure of the end of the experiment. The economic report card is clearly mixed: the Reagan administration must be judged successful in terms of reducing inflation, bringing interest rates down to manageable proportions, and creating a climate in which investment priorities can be defined. This administration has been much less successful in stimulating higher employment, better retraining techniques, or in satisfying the needs of the least privileged social sectors.

There are many further challenges facing the Reagan administration if it hopes to make the New Federalism viable: shrinking the 16-million-member bureaucracy without causing a paralysis in the 100-million-member work force; reducing federal expenditures on basic goods and services in the forlorn hope of increasing private sector support by an equal amount; reducing tax burdens on individuals and corporations (with some sense of equity), while increasing revenues through greater sales and productivity. It would be fatuous to assume that these central goals will be achieved, but it would be foolish to denounce the effort as either worthless or preposterous. Far from being a reflection of a purely conservative ideology, these efforts represent a major response to an endemic crisis in the American economy that requires political surgery, no matter who occupies the executive office. The current administration has gambled its commitment to capitalism by placing the wealthy, owning classes of America on public display as rarely before in the last half century. It has given the wealthy special tax privileges, but also placed the burden of societal growth squarely on their shoulders. It is the vice of so many of Reagan's supporters and even advisers that they either disbelieve or do not take seriously public displays of moral concern and fiscal rectitude. This opens the way to yet a new round of cynicism which has become the dominant psychic motif of our political process.

Many critics of the current administration have emphasized that the policies are unlikely to succeed. It is my contention that the New Federalism is likely to be successful, not as a political ideology so much as an economic necessity.[18] Stability or improvement in inflation rates, in productivity levels, in the international balance of payments, and in many of the economic indicators measuring success may also be achieved. It might be wiser if concerns were to shift and focus upon the social costs of such success. For example, it may involve a resigned acceptance of higher unemployment than the New Federalism can accept; declining support for the aged, needy, and handicapped; and a breakdown of equity supports for large numbers of minorities, which can only result in a hardening of the stratification hierarchy within American society with little corresponding impact on redistribution.

To recognize that social stratification is an inevitable byproduct of economic and occupational differentiation is one thing; but it is quite another to accept as fiat differences among classes, ethnics, and races in the name of some higher principle of competitive society. The latter tendency seems to characterize the thrust of the New Federalism, a course of action which can only intensify the conflict of values in America between those of competition and rewards for achievement, associated with commerce, and the broader values associated with democracy and equity, which have characterized America's civilization. Marketplace values have been basic to American society. But so too have egalitarian values, which have maximized participation in the benefits of the commonwealth as a whole. This conflict between values sets the stage for fundamental political debates over the course of the next several decades.

Alarms and misgivings notwithstanding, federalism has to do with a retention of individual liberties and a safeguarding of community values. The worldwide sweep of increasing community power at the expense of bureaucratic authority is not restricted to any one kind of social system. It extends from Tito's earlier experiments in worker management and norm-setting in factories, to Mitterand's present stunning decentralization of authority and increase in rural self-control. Indeed the decentralization of national life is a cornerstone of Miguel de la Madrid's plans for Mexico between 1983 and 1988. Seen in this light, the New Federalism, discounting the sloganeering aspects and search for presidential uniqueness, is part of the revolt against bureaucratic authority, one which cuts across inherited class and regional interests. Decentralization represents a frontal assault against political corruption at the top and federal intervention and mismanagement of programs and funds at municipal levels. It is not a cry for dismantling government. There has been no numerical reduction in the United States federal bureaucracy. It is simply an acknowledgement that bigness is not goodness any more than smallness is beauty.

Clearly, this essay offers more by way of problems with the New Federalism than it does solutions. Although this is an essay on the New Federalism, its concerns are with social formations and ideological proclivities. Only now, when some implementation has taken place are we in a better position to raise the core policy questions desperately in need of resolution. I shall leave for another occasion an attempt to resolve these policy dilemmas of the New Federalism. For now it suffices to state these issues clearly and concisely. Only thus can we all move from history to policy.

The first question is whether a shift in such items as block grants to the states creates a corresponding rise in bureaucratic and administrative costs. As a rule, decentralization, whether of municipalities or universities, is highly cost inefficient. And while there may be some excellent sociopolitical reasons for deregulation or decentralization, doing so flies in the face of other administrative imperatives, such as budgetary constraints and fiscal management. This contradiction in the New Federalism needs to be faced.

Second, while it is prima facie the case that states compete with one another for federal resources, and one should add, contribute unevenly to the central administration, it remains a question whether any given state can properly and vigorously argue its need for supports before a federal administration, even one of reduced size and potency. At the same time, it must be inquired whether or not the states can more appropriately work with each other in this new federalist climate. It would seem that, for now at least, the goals of working together, while highly laudable, exhibit no corresponding mechanisms for increasing the networks between the states. Annual conferences of governors or mayors tend to address, even lecture, the federal government on further needs and spend precious little time evolving new mechanisms for interactions—state to state.

Given the history of state administration and state legal agencies, the third question must be raised whether this intermediate form of government can serve to maximize citizen needs and requirements. After all, a good deal of the federal legislation on labor, minorities, and discriminated-against majorities, from Roosevelt to the Nixon and Carter administrations, came about precisely because of inaction, ineptitude, or just plain special-interest actions on the part of states. Clearly not all states are the same in their historical response to equity issues—Wisconsin is not Texas and Minnesota is not Mississippi. However, that is precisely the point at which federal funding becomes equity leveraging. The present administration has simply not made clear how the process of decentralization would prevent an erosion of recent gains by the public interests, or for that matter, how a return to the defects of the old federalism are to be withstood.

Fourth, the pass along from federal to state levels may serve to obstruct and inhibit further "trickle-down" to cities and communities. While in theory accountability will be higher in state-administered block grants than in federal agency grants, in practice states may use this very proximity to cities and communities to thwart and frustrate such requests. If American politics already reveals wide fissures between state and local governments in fund allocations and priorities, what assurance is there under the New Federalism that further imbalances will not be created even as old imbalances are presumably removed?

Fifth and finally, is there an appropriate talent pool at the state level to monitor, evaluate, and implement the New Federalist guidelines? After all, it has been reasonably argued that the federal administration is low on expertise, that many of the most talented policy personnel have gone into private sector activities. If there is a limited talent pool at the power center, how much is this the case at the state peripheries? The juridical and executive decrees may shift program obligations and even fiscal responsibilities, but in so doing, one might expect greater and not lesser sorts of administrative problems.

These five points by no means exhaust problems with the New Federalism. They may indeed each be addressed and overcome during the implementation phase. Enthusiasts might also charge that taking intellectual potshots at this massive program and policy shift serves only to thwart the political will, and uses present economic difficulties to negate any sort of long-term reforms. Still, these cautionary remarks may serve to remind the policy sector that the New Federalism, while a large-scale effort to implement small-scale controls, does not address the structural foundations of American society—which if sound can withstand some social experimentation, but if weakened beyond redemption will be little affected by administrative palliatives.

13. Transnational Terrorism, Civil Liberties, and the Social Fabric

The polarization of political behavior and the fragmentation of political belief are well illustrated in the rhetoric concerning terrorism and what to do about it. Attitudes towards the uses of terror and the functions of terrorists range from a gratuitous belief in terror as the only possible means to bring about social change to a view of terror and terrorists as the last refuge of scoundrels. The range of views extends from terrorists as the only authentic heroes in a notably unheroic age to their demotion as petty criminals who coat their venal acts with an ideological gloss.

In such a climate of opinion, the attempt to introduce gradations and shadings of meaning into the problem of terror invites instant rebuke from an impatient left and retaliation from an outraged right. Only "reformists" and "bleeding hearts" apparently are willing to challenge the common rhetoric. Despite the rhetoric, communist dictatorships, no less than democracies, no less than capitalist systems, must face the problem of terrorism. Skyjackings, assassinations, bombings, extortions, and sabotage do not stop at any national or regional borders.

The definition of terrorism employed here is the selective use of fear, subjugation, and intimidation to disrupt the normal operations of a society. All social systems seek ethical and legal norms that satisfy the conditions for continued human survival without giving offense to the major ideological premises on which these respective societies have come to rest. Consequently, while different social systems react differently to terror in accordance with their vision of self-interest, no surviving society can be indifferent to the problems raised by terrorism.

Special problems in the analysis of terrorism and civil liberties exist for the analysts themselves. Research social scientists, often responsive to a governmental or semi-official agency whose prime concern is political or industrial tranquillity, can easily tailor their models to suit the needs of clients, thereby overlooking many alternative possibilities for analyzing terrorism. As the collective repository of empirical, even normative wisdom on the subjects of both terror and liberty, they are charged with the task of arriving at satisfactory formulations of the problem, if not meaningful solutions, while operating within a paradigmatic framework unexamined or uncritically imbibed.

Social scientists who accept a civil libertarian viewpoint must decide how to respond to an attack on civil liberties by those presumably acting in the name of terror. Even more damaging may be the response to terror by the organized society itself. Before we settle the question of what to do about terrorists, we might also try to ask what are the consequences of action and then determine a scale of levels of response in terms of levels of assault on the system. Our efforts reflect a pragmatic Deweyan viewpoint. Living in democracy is living experientially; living experientially is living dangerously. To prevent social change in the name of democracy is already to have lost the battle.

An alternative approach of social science to the study of terrorism would be to disaggregate the types of violence perpetrated and thereby defuse the emotionalism surrounding the issue of terror. At this time, the emphasis among researchers is to aggregate information on letter-bombings, hijackings, and assassinations, which consequently blurs essential distinctions between random terrorist movements and foreign-controlled movements. The need for legal sanctions against the random murder and incarceration of innocent "third-party" people is manifest. We also need to emphasize that a place for legitimate dissent remains a steady need if the world community of nations is not to become frozen into its present political positions, along with the economic and social inequities such a freezing of policies entails.

Social science must first determine whether terrorism is a function of larger ambitions and aims, thereby making it a dependent variable. Second, social science needs to distinguish types of violence and injury perpetrated against persons and places in order to help establish some qualitative measures of terrorism and counterterrorism. Third, social science should provide empirical assistance to the legal efforts involved in developing international measures to combat the terror of guerrillas and counterterror of the state. These three interrelated tasks will help restore a feeling of the independent and objective role of social science in combating terror and safeguarding civil liberties.

This essay is restricted to one part of this widespread discussion of terror: the question of safeguarding civil liberties when the state invokes counterterror or force to quell disturbances. My aim is to describe the costs and benefits of the control of terror, showing how and why terrorism arises, who the terrorists are, and what the impact is on civil rights and liberties. Only then can appropriate policies and postures be set forth.

We are in a high-risk situation, not simply with respect to those who are labeled terrorists but perhaps more pointedly with respect to what occurs in the social system as a result of measures to contravene terrorist activities. It would be sheer sophistry to deny the existence of terrorism by the dubious method of asserting that either its complexities or ambiguities somehow eliminate the problem. We must therefore first outline how terrorism affects the civil liberties of all citizens. Then we can turn our attention to how counterterror works and what it all means for our civil liberties.[1]

The first point is that the power to inflict injury is a bargaining power that in its very nature bypasses the due process of law and seeks an outcome by means other than the democratic or consensus problem-solving formula. Within its very nature, the act of terror—whoever performs it—in some sense violates civil liberties. All the cries about redressing injustices cannot disguise this violation.

A second point is that terrorism presumes not simply what is socially valued but what victims can tolerate; that is, a kind of threshold of pain replaces a sense of shared values and of the rationality that comes with consensus politics. As a result, the act of terrorism, without regard to who performs it, involves a substitution of pain or punishment for reason in the adjudication of political and social ends.

The third point is ubiquitous but nonetheless important. A policy of terror assumes the social system to be inherently law-abiding, not only as a rational goal but as an ongoing functional prerequisite. It also presumes that the desire to return to the rationality of the maintenance of a system and its goals helps those engaged in terror reach their ends. Again, civil liberties are confronted here as an ongoing mechanism to which one wants to return, considering the state of terror as a temporary aberration.

The fourth point is that terrorism as a policy is antidemocratic and violates a sense of civil liberties as democratic liberties because the terrorists' requests, demands, or ultimatums are addressed to a leadership structure rather than to the people. Terrorism demands instantaneous decision making and consequently places a very great strain on the conventional legal mechanisms, which require due process and a strong evidentiary base to take action. As a result, terrorism is an appeal to elites.

A fifth point, which is both most disturbing and yet difficult to define analytically, is that terror generally involves a violation of the civil liberties of those who are nonparticipants or noncombatants. Terrorists usually have as a foil those people who are innocent of any crime. Whatever else civil libertarians believe, they do mean to hold people responsible for having committed no specific criminal acts. To them terrorist acts are clear and evident violations of civil freedoms of both individuals and collectivities.

The increase in the amount of terrorism, spontaneous or organized, inevitably invites countermeasures. These extend from increased security checks, greater police surveillance, and improved search-and-seizure measures to changes in the legal code like the restoration of capital punishment. At the same time, organizational and ideological forms also change. In place of criminology, there emerges a new emphasis on victimology; in place of national organizations dedicated to civil liberties, there arise organizations dedicated to maintaining civil order. Consequently, the costliest aspect of the increased resort to terrorist solutions to political problems is not the destruction of physical property; it is the decimation of the social and political fabric—the complex series of norms and laws upon which conflict resolution ultimately rests.

The seeming procrastination and reticence of national and international legislative bodies to curb terrorism seem to derive from some inchoate appreciation of the political costs involved. To be sure, when particular societies are attacked by terrorists, caution often is discarded. Yugoslavs highly resistant to formal condemnations of Palestinian terrorists are outraged by American passivity in the face of Croatian nationalist hijackings. Soviet officials, even more resistant to the idea of a United Nations ban on skyjackings, can hardly contain their sense of outrage at Jews who confiscate planes to escape to Israel. Syrians who are quite willing to see citizens of Tel Aviv randomly blown up hang the representatives of the Palestine Liberation Organization (PLO) when they perform similar acts in Damascus. However, when all is said and done, it is easier to stretch the notion of tolerable limits within civil society than to establish inelastic legislation that would do more to escalate the levels and perhaps amounts of terrorism than lead to international pacification and tranquillity. The idea of legislation as a magical cure-all, or even a limiting element on terrorist actions, is itself of dubious worth—a conceptual palliative more than a pragmatic solution. To address the consequences of terrorism and leave untouched its causes is not only to insure higher levels of punishment but also increased sophistication in terrorist crimes.

In 1968 President Lyndon Johnson established a major task force, the National Commission on the Causes and Prevention of Violence. Analyses of historical and social causation proceeded smoothly enough, but the commission encountered problems mainly at the policy level: What could be done to prevent violence in the future? In form if not in substance, the problem of violence then was similar to the issue raised by terrorism now. At a meeting of this commission in 1968, I said:

> The destruction of the anti-war movement, whether in its abstract universalist or pacifist form, or in its nasty, brutish, or opportunistic form would represent a far greater loss to the integrity of American democracy than any silence in the streets of our major cities or quiescence in the hubs of our major universities. Obedience is not tranquility. Seething heavily is not the same as breathing easily. The anti-war movement has caused destruction in government operations, increased the cost of domestic military preparedness, stimulated disaffiliation from major parties, and has been a general nuisance for an already burdened police force. But these are costs that can be borne by a society still capable of distinguishing between national concern and national celebration. Those who want law and order, of whom there are many, as well as those who want lawlessness and disorder, of whom there are a few, must weigh carefully the premium price to be paid in a punitive state in which a rage for order displaces a rationality of innovation. That price would be nothing short of a total militarization of the nation.[2]

A society without terrorism is quite possible to achieve. Fascist systems manage quite adequately to reduce terrorism by a series of devices: mass organizations in which membership is compulsory; block-by-block spying networks; mandatory police identification certificates; clear delineations of "friends" and "enemies" of the regime. With the increased sophistication of computerization techniques, such mechanisms for social and personal control are increasingly available. The question remains: Does a citizenry wish to pay such a premium price for social tranquillity? One might consider the quantum of violence within a society as a crucial indicator of genuine social health.

Beyond serving as a potential beacon light on social maladies, the potential for terror also is a lively reminder that state force has its counter. There is no need to try to settle the question of causation, that is, whether the state force precedes the violence of its opponents. The hardware in the hands of the state is almost always greater, more pervasive, and more devastating than the disruptive possibilities available to terrorists. One need only consider the activities of the CIA and the FBI to see how damaging to the body politic state force can become and how ineffectual those efforts to forestall terrorism were.

American intelligence operations involve hundreds of thousands of individuals and require the expenditure of billions of dollars. They are carried out by a complex community of organizations among which functions interact and overlap. As the Senate committee investigating activities of the CIA and FBI noted: "The task of democratic government is to reconcile conflicting values."[3] The fundamental question faced by a democratic society is how to reconcile the clash between secrecy and democratic government itself. Secrecy is an essential part of intelligence activities. However, secrecy undermines the capacity of the United States to deal effectively with the principal issues of American intelligence addressed by a select Senate subcommittee on intelligence activities. In its final report, the committee states that "the very effort to deal with problems of terror, violence, and domestic intranquility has led to this kind of incredible malaise within the legal system, whereby the entire country has been rendered under the control of a paralegal system, a paramilitary system, in terms of dealing effectively with threats of violence."[4] The question of civil liberties is not simply examined from the point of view of the terrorists but from that of the counterterrorist as well. One need only remember Watergate to see how counterterrorist activities can erode our civil liberties.

To make sense of the subject of terrorism, one must introduce a concept based upon qualitative micropolitics or the large-scale examinations of specific issues to balance the current emphasis on quantitative macropolitics, or the small-scale analysis of large-scale issues. Social researchers are obligated to discuss large-scale political events not only in aggregate numerical terms but in impact terms. We are obligated to demonstrate the discreet nature of terrorism as it affects particular and specific actors in any political dramaturgy. Only through a linkage of the qualitative to the quantitative, of micropolitics to macropolitics, can a holistic sense of terrorism be framed.

If we discuss terrorism in terms of the number of people killed by design or by accident, there clearly is no comparison to the genocidal behavior of Stalin in Russia or Hitler in Germany. The state has nearly unlimited power to terrorize entire communities, ethnic or racial groups, and, of course, religious networks. If terrorism is mentioned simply in terms of lives dispatched, the holocaust in Nazi Germany, the genocidal benchmark of our century, certainly far outstrips and outranks the desultory and random performances engaged in by contemporary terrorists functioning beyond the influence of the major political systems.

If by terrorism we mean disruption of entire political systems or social organizations, then the determined but relatively impotent acts of those defined as terrorists can hardly be compared to the disruption caused by a major automobile accident on a superhighway in a densely populated area. Rarely does organized terrorism create the kinds of massive temporary breakdowns in social systems that might be occasioned by a power failure in a big city. I have always been surprised how impotent any transitory disruption of modern society is. What is really involved in a definition of terrorism is the symbolic meaning of terrorism and its support systems.

When a person or group is assassinated or kidnapped because of its national origins or religious affiliations, the action speaks to the entire fabric of attitudes of one group toward another. Consequently, although the numbers involved in terrorism are usually quite limited, the calibrations are unusually large. Moreover, terrorism involves death and destruction by design, and it is clearly different from the random character of highway accidents or technological breakdowns.

If one argues that terrorism is a special method for hastening historical change, does anyone really know what scheme historical timetables follow? The conventional Marxist rhetoric about speeding up or slowing down history presumes a normal rate of historical change that has eluded almost any kind of empirical test. It is therefore perfectly appropriate for terrorists or anybody else to argue that they help to shape the course of historical events. On the other hand, the question of measurements is just as much a problem for terrorists as it is for pacifists. Ultimately, both must appeal to the same muse of history, rarely with telling or convincing effect.

Some people insist dogmatically and in the face of experience that Marx said that one cannot make a successful revolution without realizing the full potential for growth of the old social system. They are wrong to persist in believing that Marx's statement constitutes a revolutionary prohibition to social action. The problem remains empirical: What constitutes the full realization of a past social order? To employ Marxism as a determinism is to ignore those elements in radical doctrine that are based on the will of the human actor to shape the outcome of social and political drama. In this sense, terrorists score very low on a determinism scale and very high on a voluntarism scale. They are not, however, deprived of either ideology or doctrine. They uniquely believe that individual acts, sometimes with collective sponsorship, can alter the course of history in ways defined exclusively by their own revolutionary wills. Those more concerned with "scientific" socialism assume a high level of social determinism, of history acting behind the backs of human actors, and therefore of events moving in a certain inexorable pattern, whatever an individual wills. This determinism can also be viewed as a strategic option. As a result, the difference between terrorist and pacifist visions of the revolutionary process represents a philosophical option or series of options; neither provides anything resembling empirically verifiable propositions about the world. The great danger of those who claim that terrorism is simply a form of either political or psychological madness is that each psychologism will end up as a metaphysical denial, if not a metaphysical pathos, of the value of political action. Ultimately, the role of action in changing the course of human events, not any single strategic set of positions, must be examined. Those who argue against terrorism simply because of its promulgation of acts or deeds are at least in as difficult a bind empirically as those who argue that every act performed changes the course of historical events.

What is required is a kind of qualitative micropolitics, an empirical test for measuring the continuity between the Anarch at one end and the Behemoth at the other. To properly understand terrorism, it is necessary to measure the quantum of force utilized by any given society, or state within such a society, as a social indicator and characterization of that society. The amount of violence engaged in by individuals to effect their desired ends is one such measurement. The amount of violence engaged in by the armed forces and police units of the state to prevent social change from occurring represents the opposite pole on the same measurement of change. In addition, we must measure the types of violence, for example, skyjacking and assassination at one end, letter-bombs and demonstrations at intermediary levels, and the tossing of rotten eggs and oranges at the lower end of the scale.

The weakness in the Anarchist position inheres in its imbalance. Taking a life in the name of social justice carries no corresponding recognition of the rights of a state to take a life in the name of social order. At the same time, the state invariably has chosen to exercise a monopoly on life-taking activities, decreeing as illegal all other forms of life taking by individuals. The state decries in the name of social order any uncontrolled or spontaneous forms of terrorism. At the extremes, we have a mutual definition that life taking is a monopoly of the individual Anarch or of the collective Behemoth, but from an operational point of view, there is little to choose between them. We have a problem of social accounting at one level and moral constraint at another. For the most part, our researches have focused too exclusively on who is taking a life and far too lightly on the life that has been taken. Perhaps a shift in emphasis would lessen the quantum of violence, but such speculative assumptions are for a different essay and a different time.

The problem is not so much terrorism as who has the monopoly on the use of force. The tendency has been to seek mechanisms to obstruct terror and remove it from its sources either in state authority or antistate power. As a result, we are left with a self-defeating concept that narrows and distorts scientific analysis. Let us take as one illustration a problem that arises in some forms of quantitative macropolitical approaches. One might speak of the basically unsuccessful results of the use of terror to overthrow state authority. Suppose we measure success not by the coup d'etat but by the temporary disruption of the normal administrative activities of political systems. Would the same results obtain? The question is rhetorical. The question of success and failure rates of terror becomes far more sobering, although the numbers involved may be infinitesimally small. For example, can one really deny that the assassination of John F. Kennedy, followed by the assassinations of Robert Kennedy and Martin Luther King, Jr., and then by the attempted assassination of Governor George Wallace, changed the structure, and not just the style, of American presidential politics in the past decade? One might well argue that the series of legitimacy crises that led up to Watergate were a direct, traceable consequence of these single acts of assassination and terrorism.

Although assassination attempts represent only a small number of assaults upon political leaders, they are clearly consequential acts in macropolitical terms.[5] The very nature of the political process was profoundly interfered with, if not interrupted, by these largely successful assassination efforts. One runs a severe risk of becoming politically blasé by adopting a computerlike approach to terrorism and by assuming that numerically small aggregates are not really significant, without at the same time defining who is subject to terrorism and assassination. If we connect aggregate data to flesh and blood and take seriously the qualitative traumas involved in terrorist assassinations of a president, a candidate for the presidency, and a leading figure within the black liberation movement espousing nonviolence, as well as an attempt on the life of a major figure in Southern conservative political thought, then the essentials of American political history can be seen to be inextricably connected with terrorism. As a result, it seems premature to label terrorist activities "unsuccessful" simply because of the limited numbers involved. They have involved the elimination of one man in Dallas, another in Memphis, and another in Los Angeles.

In questions of terrorism, the measurement of success cannot simply be its ability to topple the social order but rather its ability to loosen that order symbolically by weakening the legitimating capacities of elected officials, by casting doubt on our concept of the rights of a society and the obligations of a state. In traveling, for example, the act of boarding an airplane involves an acceptance of commonplace procedures that only a few short years ago would have been deemed a direct violation of civil liberties. To board an airplane one has to have all luggage examined and one's own person scanned or frisked. A separate section in the airport is designated only for passengers who have boarding passes. The ordinary pattern of greetings on departure or arrival by loved ones is no longer permitted. When arriving at a destination, one can no longer place luggage in a locker in most airports, bus stations, and rail terminals. Restrictions on locker storage are a consequence of a solitary bomb left in a locker at LaGuardia Airport in 1975. Contrary to what many have spoken of as exhibitionist tendencies of terrorists, no one has ever claimed responsibility for the LaGuardia bombing or for many other similar incidents. The self-celebration or self-attribution on the part of terrorists is not itself an axiomatic property of terrorists but is subject to great variation. Anonymity, like publicity, may have real and symbolic consequences. Most people probably accept frisking and new baggage procedures as a necessary and acceptable cost of safe flight. Nevertheless, one has a perfect right, even a duty, to raise questions about these new social costs of travel; certainly one has the right to inquire about the permanence or transitory nature of these new surveillance procedures.

In any evaluation, one has to locate the consequences of terrorism if one wants to use the rhetoric of terrorism; one cannot simply reduce the problem of violence to one of how many people are killed in a given time or place. The paucity of numbers involved in terrorism, although important, is not necessarily or invariably crucial. The failure to distinguish what is important symbolically from what at the same time may be trivial numerically casts serious doubt on a purely quantitative analytic framework. The social impact of terrorism rather than the aggregate levels of terror should become the central focus in any system of analytic measurement.

Too many people oversimplify by presuming that terrorism serves to demoralize and demobilize populations and to distinguish societies generally. Terrorism in many instances may serve as an integrative mechanism binding people together in a common cause. The Israeli raid on the Uganda airport, in which 103 people hijacked from an Air France flight in June 1976 were liberated, was widely thought to have galvanized and unified Israeli society as no other event had since the Six-Day War in 1967. As a result, sporadic acts of terror like the raid mobilized sentiments in such a way as to guarantee the very survival of the system that the terrorists had aimed to destroy. The ubiquity of terrorism extends beyond definitions. The word has failed to generate a scientific or legal consensus because the results of terror have proven so contradictory.

There are several important considerations having special meaning for those in the social science community who work in political science, sociology, economics, or psychology. The central issue is what might be called anticipatory socialization. Social scientists need to work within intellectual parameters that presuppose not only the existence of terrorism but a structure of the world in anticipation of heightened terrorism, involving consequently a heightened response to terrorism. Under the prompting of special bureaus like the Atomic Energy Commission and the National Aeronautics and Space Administration, many proposals have been made by sophisticated groups of social scientists dealing with the potential in America in the nuclear age. Research was conducted on events that have never happened and perhaps cannot happen, that is, the ability of small bands of terrorists to steal atomic weapons or fissionable materials in order to hold the country for "ransom." Serious doubts exist that terrorists, even if successful in obtaining fissionable material, would have either the scientific or technological capability to produce atomic weapons. Without presuming expertise on the commercial nuclear industry as an attractive target for terrorist designs, anticipatory research on nuclear terrorism may invite a tightening of counterterrorist techniques that, if fully enacted, would end democratic safeguards to individual rights.

It seems reasonable that social scientists might engage in anticipatory research of potential terrorism, but a problem exists in the word "potential." A high risk is implicit in the research on the prevention of events that have not happened. Such research does not plumb events that have not happened, but researchers can develop structures of analysis that are self-fulfilling. What results from anticipatory research is an antiterrorist industry that will directly impinge on civil rights and that presumably deals with charges against crimes that may or may not be committed. If the social science community lends itself and its analytic capacities to the study of the potential dangers of terrorism, merging its rage with futurology and with the needs of administrative bodies, the threat to civil liberties is menacing.

Risk is the nature of the democratic system because the range of permissible acts is itself an operational guideline to democracy. It is in the nature of the system to permit modes of uncontrolled and experimental behavior. To insist that mechanisms must be created to prevent acts of terror omits the role of political marginality in constructive social change. It is in the nature of a pluralistic society to indicate when an attack on terror is more risky than the randomization of the terrorism itself. There may be little else than an algebraic equation involved: At what point is the threshold of terror so high as to involve immediate response by authorities? On the other hand, we have been drastically confused by the difference between events and a general theory or system of response. It is certainly legitimate for a society to respond to the threat of immediate and dangerous situations. It is not fair, within the context of civil liberties, to have a systemic, built-in structure to anticipate every form of terrorist behavior. That structure will inevitably destroy the stability of pluralism and critical thinking.

One fear invited by the current emphasis in research on terrorism is that the social sciences may become a servant of policy and policy-making groups without having a check against those groups. Rather than having a dialogue, social scientists may not be heard or consulted by policy makers. On the other hand, social scientists must be careful not to assume that social science means futurology and nothing but futurology. We have, for example, some serious methodological problems that require attention.

Good social science must not begin with the assumption of the correctness of one's own clientele and the incorrectness of others'. We must consider that we do not know who our friends or our adversaries are at any given moment. The vagaries of history being what they are, today's battlefield companions may be tomorrow's antagonists. Moreover, we are not entirely certain about the correctness or incorrectness of goals and values, even if we do agree on instrumentalities or the lack of instrumentalities. We always have to assume in good social research that we are dealing with an interaction process. So much of what is called social science assumes an asymmetry of analysis that occurs because of the purchased character of much social research. When research is purchased, bought, and sponsored, we must remain cautious about the problem of moral as well as methodological asymmetry. American social scientists, in particular since the Project Camelot days of counterinsurgency and civic action programs, should be extremely conscious and cognizant of this problem and must not repeat the errors of only a generation ago.

Terrorism may not be an analyzable concept unto itself. Terror is often a tactical function of situational frameworks. Terrorism may be part of an instrumental network based on proximate ends and may denote nothing over and above that instrumentality. We have no assurance, despite the size and scope of the literature on terror, that we really have an independent variable. A great deal of evidence indicates that terror is a dependent variable. The simple rotating of factors involving violent behavior is not going to determine a fruitful line of scientific inquiry. Factor rotation will only cloud the question of independence and dependence in terms of levels of explained variances. One has to measure strength of factors, not merely list and compute them.

American civilization has an innate capacity to convert everything into an industry. Beyond the question of whether we are creating a terrorism industry is a problem in the algebra and bookkeeping of terrorism. At what point does a viable, open society assume the potential for deviance? Historically, deviant behavior, marginal behavior, and even terrorist behavior are highly consonant and congruent with rapid degrees of industrialization and modernization. If we completely succeed in eliminating what we are now calling terror, what are the consequences for the potential overall economic growth of the society itself, and what are the consequences for the liberties of individuals in that society? Both of these questions seem to be questions of ethics and accounting. Until these questions are addressed empirically as well as valuationally, one has to decide to maximize security or to maximize liberty.

Rather than search for avenues of definitional precision (a search legal theorists have done without notably reducing the actual quantum of terror), the social scientist might pay close attention to the role of terrorism as a strategy and tactic rather than as a principle and premise. A terrorist does not represent a systematic analyst, nor does a terrorist necessarily represent terrorism as a world view unto itself. Terrorism becomes a method to establish claims to justice, to seek new societies, and to release frustrations that cannot be meliorated through normal political channels. Consequently, the solution to the problem of terror is invariably beyond the framework of counterterror and discussions of it. Responses to terror must be accompanied by a strengthening of the social fabric as a whole and specifically of the economic order. That strengthening cannot be reduced to increased surveillance; it clearly entails real changes in the social system like new weightings in the distribution of wealth, power, and status.

If we extrapolate terrorism from the social fabric in which it is found, terrorism loses its specific meaning, and efforts to predict "the next round of terror" or the "next contagion" remain a formal exercise largely devoid of content. We require a qualitative micropolitical analysis to complement a quantitative macropolitical analysis. Without such complementary analyses, we will remain immersed in a one-sided picture. By remaining limited in our analyses, we do a profound injustice to the herculean research that has been done on those who dispense terrorism as well as those who are its recipients. We need information on terrorism, but what we also need is a theoretical framework in which terrorism does not elicit the fears, doubts, and recriminations that the word itself clearly invites.

14. Routinized Terrorism and Its Unanticipated Consequences

A subtle and far-ranging shift has occurred in the grammar of politics. In the 1970s congressional committees studied "alleged assassination plots involving foreign leaders"; indeed, Senator Frank Church's Select Committee to Study Government Operations bluntly accused the executive branch of the United States of "institutionalizing assassination" through CIA actions.[1] In the 1980s congressional committees emphasize problems of "security and terrorism," and Senator Jeremiah Denton's equally select Subcommittee on Security and Terrorism of the Committee on the Judiciary takes up issues ranging from the origin, direction, and support of terrorism to the Turkish experience with terrorism.[2] Undergirding this shift in the rhetoric of committee reports is a profound transformation in the public sense of where the main danger to American society resides—not in internal police power but in external guerrilla power. The question of terrorism, far from being a simple academic exercise, is front and center on the political stage. A review of current policy with respect to terrorism is clearly in order.

In the last decade terrorism has become routine. The number of incidents of international terrorism, which has the support of a foreign government or organization or is directed against foreign persons or interests, almost doubled in the decade 1970–1980. Deaths resulting from international terrorism in the same period increased from 131 to 642; terrorist attacks causing casualties (especially bombings and assassinations) have risen dramatically.[3] Once extraordinary and unusual phenomena have become a major activity for an enlarged intelligence industry. Nevertheless, we have not thought much about the social and political consequences of the routinization of terror. Social scientists and historians have made exhaustive analyses of everything from the causes of terrorism, to the nature of the terrorist, to the relationship of terrorism to ideology. But what are the consequences of terrorism—unanticipated or otherwise?

The literature on the causes of terrorism is rich.[4] If the causes of terrorism can be established and eradicated, then study of its consequences becomes moot. But we are no closer to determining terrorism's roots and eradicating them than we were ten years ago. If terrorism is to remain very much a living presence in our midst, we had best be more deeply appreciative of its limitations as well as its potentials.

Those who have examined the consequences of terrorism can be grouped into two general camps. In one are scholars such as Walter Laqueur,[5] who believes that in historical context terrorism has hardly ever had a lasting effect. Ted Robert Gurr[6] shares Laqueur's conclusions, if not his intellectual disposition, and sees terrorism as an epiphenomenon of short-lived duration that has rarely been particularly effective. In the other camp are writers such as Albert Parry,[7] who sees terrorism as increasingly effective as it ceases to be a remote spectacle and becomes an immediate peril. Others, such as Brian Crozier, emphasize contagion effect,[8] likening terrorism to smallpox and global epidemics. Those who believe terrorism to be effective come from all ideological quarters; there is no apparent correlation between those who see terrorism as effective and any special political viewpoint.

What if we disaggregated the issue of the consequences of terrorism and examined which goals have been achieved and which have been frustrated by terrorism? I define terrorism as the fusion of three properties in an indefinite mix: (1) a type of unconventional warfare engaged in by a group, usually against civilian targets, (2) in which violence or threat of violence is employed to induce fear for the purpose of (3) changing the bases of law and authority affecting attitudes, emotions, and opinions through a culturally unacceptable form. If we accept as a given that the major purpose of terrorism is to change a government or an established authority and not simply to increase fear or hysteria, then we can assess how successful terrorists are in achieving their goals. For we can certainly establish if terror has brought about the downfall of governments.

Terrorism has emerged partly in relation to the decline in mass political participation. The concentration of power in the hands of a small clique or an elite serves a double-edged purpose: it permits the leader of a nation to employ terrorism as an overseas tactic, as in Libya, and it makes rulers and ruling groups that are less politically integrated vulnerable, as has been the leadership of Egypt. The potential for disrupting the ordinary processes of governance is greatest where mass participation in the political process is lowest. At the same time, terrorist acts are more disruptive to a dictatorship than to a democracy, precisely for the same reason: a dictatorship lacks a broad, mobilized popular support base. Who can doubt that the assassination of Fidel Castro in Cuba would produce more far-reaching consequences than the elimination of José López Portillo in Mexico?

Although terrorism is most damaging to totalitarian regimes, such regimes are much less vulnerable to terrorism. Precisely because they consider techniques of surveillance and control so important, dictatorships offer better military and police protection than do democracies. Dictators like Muammar Qadaffi or Castro or Alfredo Stroessner are virtually impervious to random assaults, unlike, say, American presidents or Catholic pontiffs. Unless a palace guard revolts or is infiltrated, a Caesar's death is unlikely or uncommon. Yet when such deaths do occur, they have enormous political impact. There is an evident paradox: dictatorships use terrorist methods but can suffer mortal injury from terrorism; and democracies use terrorist methods much less frequently but can easily be permeated and wounded by terrorism.[9] This remains a core problem for those who would define terrorism as a technique of rotating power (as in parts of the Third World) or as a style of overthrowing systems (as in parts of Western Europe).

It is important to distinguish social from political costs of terrorism. At the social level, terrorism has had a dramatic effect on life-style: it has supported a surveillance-equipment industry, greatly increased investigation and interference with private individuals, and encouraged a preference for low-profile (anonymity) rather than high-profile (ostentatious) life-styles. There have been social costs: increasing privatization and decreasing public participation by elite groups and a corresponding reduction of civil liberties.

Except for regicide (the assassination of senior leaders), terrorist acts have tended to have little impact on political systems. Terrorism has led to better police protection, increased military armaments, and a general popular revulsion against the terrorist. Sometimes the results are politically counterproductive. The decline in electoral strength of Western European Communist parties is largely a result of the terrorist phenomenon. The electoral victories of socialist parties in France and Greece, coupled with a decline in Communist party strength and beliefs in both countries, tend to support this.

Terrorism has been successful under the following conditions. First, terrorism has succeeded when tied to nationalism, as in Northern Ireland or the Basque country of Spain. Undisputed claim to territory is the single most important element determining the success or failure of terrorist actions or movements. Even a well-organized and well-financed group such as the Palestine Liberation Organization has felt the absence of a staging area. The PLO's displacement from Syria, then Jordan, and its unsteady relationship with Lebanon have tended to limit its successful use of terrorism against the target population, Israel.

Second, terrorism tends to be successful when linked to specific forms of regicide and unsuccessful when randomly directed. The bombing of a bus or the destruction of physical property, if unattached to clear political objectives, can be counterproductive. In this sense, the level of a terrorist organization's sophistication can largely be defined by its targets. In general, the more focused the target, the more advanced the terrorism; the more random the target, the less effective the terrorism.

The most successful terrorism is linked to the foreign policy of installed regimes. In present-day Libya, the regime sponsors terror and legitimates certain overseas operations. Its ratio of success in these operations can be related to the regime's support—an advantage over the low-intensity adversarial relationships that often exist between governments and terrorist organizations.

Terrorism has been least successful under the following social conditions. When the terrorist group is not connected to a class, race, ethnic group, or other institutionalized form of human association, its achievements tend to be desultory and purely ideological. In countries such as Italy, which has had a highly refined terrorist network, the self-segregation of the terrorist organization from the general political process has led to its deep isolation, what the terrorists themselves refer to as "infantilization." Terrorism fails when it is connected to random assassinations, destruction of untargeted property, and unspecified dismemberment of either people or property without regard to who they are or what they represent. Random terror, which has been characteristic of urban terrorism, creates a backlash effect. Finally, when a terrorist organization ceases to exist as a legitimate force that can grow in numbers of recruits, the state police apparatus usually can overwhelm the terrorist organization and all but destroy its effectiveness within the political process.

Admittedly, this brief statement of the conditions under which terrorism is effective is subject to empirical scrutinies of all sorts and from all quarters. One might argue that the assassination of Martin Luther King failed of its purpose in that black mobilization was much higher and federal legislation more vigorous after King's martyrdom than before his death. Still, in the most fundamental sense that the sole unifying leader of black political and religious life had been felled, and with him came the end of the sorts of coalitions with other groups that brought the black communities of America into the political mainstream, one must say on balance that his murder in 1968, no less than the assassination of Robert Kennedy a month later, was highly successful. Both deaths killed off any prospects of a center-left administration of the United States in the period 1968–76.

It might also be argued that Libya's international influence derives less from its use of state terrorism than from an accidental advantage of oil riches coupled with United States policies that have permitted Qadaffi to pose as an Arab David against a Western Goliath. It can be further argued that Libya's influence waned considerably with the setbacks it suffered in Uganda and later Chad. But on balance, one would have to say that Libya, in its role as key funding agent of terrorists from the IRA (Irish Republican Army) to the PLO, and as resting place and watering hole for terrorist leaders and would-be usurpers of that leadership, was a key factor in the rejectionist front that inspired the assassination of Anwar Sadat and has prevented the Camp David process from reaching maturity.

But whether history-writ-large assesses current forms of terrorism as winners or losers, it is clear enough that terrorism as a tactic has had a dramatic effect on the course of many nations previously thought impregnable to such assaults. When a tactic reaches massive proportions, it can be dismissed as something belonging to the backwaters of politics; for all of its distasteful aspects, terrorism has become a mode of doing politics—a tactic raised to a principle, as it were.

The impact of terrorism is measured on a worldwide basis rather than on local or regional bases. The killing of Sadat in Cairo, Egypt, set off a wide array of worldwide consequences; a similar assassination a century ago would have had only a local impact. Earlier "anarchist" assaults only rarely had an international impact, as when the assassination of Archduke Ferdinand precipitated World War I. Usually such assassinations may have far-ranging impact but do not even cause a break in diplomatic relations. The wider awareness of terrorist activities is partially a result of improved worldwide data-gathering processes and communication rather than any inherent change in the magnitude of terrorism's impact.

Terrorism is perceived as a multinational dilemma and often as an assault on the legitimacy of the world order. The world seems riskier as a result of terrorism, but terrorism has had the unanticipated consequence of facilitating interdependence between nations, who find they can set aside differences in political orientations in order to preserve and protect the world community of nations. Nationalist and separatist impulses have never been more robust, but the search for world law and for mechanisms for communication across boundaries of political or systemic differences is higher than ever on the agenda of nations.

One way to evaluate the consequences of terrorism is to assess its impact on a society. In this regard the lack of impact of the PLO upon Israeli society is most instructive. Shlomo Gazit, former head of Israeli military intelligence, has said:

> The success and effectiveness of our [Israeli] security services and measures and the very low standard of the Palestinian terrorist's professional achievements make the overall impact of this activity on Israel rather limited. Just to give you an idea—during the last fifteen months, beginning April 1978, we had twenty-eight Israelis killed (civilian and military) by that kind of PLA [Palestine Liberation Activity]. This should be compared to about seven hundred persons killed in road accidents during the same period.[10]

Gazit is discussing the premier terrorist organization in the world, one with a maximum of manpower, weaponry, and funding. Thus, without in any way diminishing the considerable global influence of the PLO, its capacity to inflict direct injury upon Israel and even to threaten the survival of the state remains minimal. Its strength derives from its ability to reinforce and undergird organized opposition to Israel in other nations and world bodies, not to inflict a mortal blow on its opponent.

In evaluating the PLO claim that it is a guerrilla movement rather than a terrorist cluster of disparate organizations, it is worth remembering that a particular territory (the West Bank and Gaza Strip) has been the sole factor enabling Palestinians to claim self-determination within an intra-Arab context and that this geographical focus has been the foundation that made support for the PLO possible. Indeed, this geographical claim about the boundaries of Palestine provides the common denominator among the some twenty organizations that constitute the PLO. Destroying PLO claims of legitimacy thus becomes Israel's primary target in upsetting the present narrow band of PLO consensus. Whatever the merits or demerits in the PLO approach or the Israeli assault on its geographic claims, it is clear that the thread between land and legitimacy ultimately determines whether this or any other group is defined, in world opinion, as nationalist guerrillas or terrorist outcasts.

Terrorist groups ultimately are engaged in a search for legitimation, an attempt to move up the ladder from terrorism to militarization to insurgency through the destruction of their opponents by any means short of self-immolation. Increased terrorism also increases demands by authorities for total mobilization of society and the expansion of a national security force. In this sense, terrorism inadvertently tests the health of a state, its ability to survive threat, bluster, and a variety of assaults.

Walter Laqueur's recent assessment of terrorist activities not only demonstrates the limited consequences of terrorism but argues the need for a more ample analytic framework:

> A realistic assessment of the terrorist activities over the last ten years would have shown that there has not been much change: in some countries terrorism has been in decline, in others there has been an upsurge. Overall, despite some striking attacks which attracted a great deal of publicity, such as the shooting of the Pope,

terrorist groups have been less in the limelight than was the case ten years ago. This is true of Turkey as well as of the Middle East generally, of Latin America, and even of Northern Ireland where the number of victims has declined. Italy is an exception, and there may be one or two others, partly due to the reemergence of extreme right-wing terrorism. All this does not mean that there will not be another rise in such operations in the future, but there is less justification today for treating terrorism as practically the world's most pressing problem.[11]

One may not accept Laqueur's judgments about the difficulties democratic societies have in combating terrorism or the special role of the Soviet "contractor" in respect to clientelist "subcontractors." However, we need to develop a means to assess the impact of politically sponsored violence. Such a calculus would take into account that terrorism can strengthen rather than weaken organized social and political opposition by the state. Of course every effort to suppress terrorism perforce involves techniques of investigation and intrusion on the privacy of citizens that ultimately weaken the bases of democracy. Israeli commitment to democracy has been weakened by the perceived necessity to respond instantly and massively to PLO terrorism. But high levels of democratic participation still remain. This itself may be an achievement, given the duration and severity of terrorist threats to Israeli survival and sovereignty.

It has been argued that diminished commitment to democracy is a major goal of terrorist organizations; even those with little potential for success are content to destroy democratic institutions and do not really expect that the society or state being opposed will easily crumble. The formulation presumes that terrorists seek to prove a political point rather than gain a military edge. It is true that democratic societies have been forced to curb some marginal rights, but totalitarian societies have not come about as a result of terrorism assaults. To be sure, totalitarian societies preserve power by eliminating opposition political parties, destroying voluntary associations that do not serve the state's interests, and preventing spontaneous, individual expressions of difference. Totalitarian societies are unlikely to be toppled by terrorism, which thrives best in the fertile soil of democratic systems. But it does not follow that terrorism necessarily represents a form of class or racial rebellion against oppressive conditions. Terrorism does weaken democracies, but it does not necessarily lessen exploitation or repression. And contrariwise, the absence of terrorism by no means signifies a tranquil or consensually grounded society.

International legislation on issues ranging from controlling air hijackings to strengthening INTERPOL has resulted from a perceived threat to world order. Far from eating away at the vitals of the world political economies, terrorism has reinforced a powerful backlash by legitimate societies. The negative side is that political change has become identified with the illicit methods of achieving it. Terrorism operating in the name of radicalism often generates conservative consequences. But the multinationalization of terrorism is linked more by efforts to sabotage existing regimes than by any common core ideology.[12] If one looks at results, the differences among members of the network become obvious.

This does not mean that it makes sense to try to distinguish between "left" terrorism and "right" terrorism.[13] Terrorism is a unitary phenomenon in practice and in theory. Groups such as Baader Meinhof can and do fuse a variety of jumbled symbols from national liberation to anti-Semitism and work with political systems and regimes extending from the Soviet Union to Libya. To speak of "radicalism" as a revival of participatory democracy and "terrorism" as a simple resort to violence[14] is to miss the essential multinational mix. Believing that neo-Nazi activity is directed from Moscow may comfort those who would like to place terrorism in one corner of the political spectrum, but it misses the essential character of terrorism as such, its antistatist characteristics, its categorical eschewal of democratic and legal norms for changing regimes and polities. Abstractions such as "the international Zionist conspiracy" provide a blanket ideology for terrorists on the left and the right, from Europe to Africa, an ideology that permits a wide latitude of meanings and hence participants.

Political systems, like people, compete with each other, and they sometimes exceed the boundaries of peaceful competition. Because terrorism is a twentieth-century plague infecting all social systems, the resulting development of mechanisms to ensure the political survival of systems as such can create new forms of international association. For example, except for the PLO, relationships between Israeli and Lebanese border communities could scarcely have developed. The routinization of terrorism as a multinational problem cannot be denied, but political organisms have shown an increased capacity to unite and create a new basis for legitimacy. Routinized terror makes political risks higher, but it also increases the rewards of political legitimacy.

Terrorism does weaken democracy, the structural victim of terrorism. The cycle may begin with a terrorist kidnapping or killing, followed by the enactment, enforcement, or strengthening of antiterrorist laws and a corresponding suspension of constitutional safeguards. The third stage is the acceleration of terrorist activities in the name of overturning despotic rule. Legislation that restricts human freedoms sometimes precedes rather than follows terrorist assaults, but the same cycle ensues —only with a different causal starting point. Whatever the personal victims of terrorism assaults, the collective victims are the citizenry and constitutional safeguards.

As a tactic, terrorism has failed to reach its primary objective, changing the foundations of state power, and for that reason it has earned the scorn of revolutionaries no less than the wrath of conservatives. It has had mixed success in achieving its secondary objectives: being taken seriously by established authority, obtaining high media coverage, and insinuating itself as a factor in negotiations concerning critical geopolitical areas. In its tertiary goals terrorism has been especially effective: it has reduced the operational range of democratic societies and has compelled them to curb essential freedoms in the name of survival; in so doing it has provided support to its prophecy that democracy is vulnerable and democratic societies are hypocritical with respect to their claims of political superiority.

One might well argue for a system at some midpoint between democracy and dictatorship that could measure and monitor terrorist acts. Policy proposals are not lacking: stronger weapons controls, computerized surveillance systems, juridical limits on civil compliance with illegal demands, censorship of mass media to prevent undue publicity for terrorist activities, and so on. Such midway systems would in fact erode the democratic process. Policy-oriented safety devices against terror are too easily extended to tools for institutional constraints upon the body politic. Informal constraints become normative limits to democratic decision making.

Those who would support general policies countering terror with paramilitary structures must be willing to bear the consequences of a world without democracy; just as those who would countenance a purely Hobbesian world of anarchic competition and lawless individuals must bear the burdens of a world lacking in organization or coherence. Those who would exaggerate tactics, either as laissez-faire approaches toward terror or as heavy-handed regimentation to prevent terror, must equally come to terms with the imperfections of democracy and the infections of dictatorship.

Seen in this way, the consequences of terrorism have little to do with the rise and fall of societies and a great deal to do with limits each society imposes on the civil liberties of its citizenry in order to secure its survival. Nondemocratic societies are more brittle and more vulnerable to destruction than democratic societies. But the attempt to meet the challenge of terrorism by a heightened defense posture and increased security measures converts democratic societies into garrison states or into a new feudalism in which security firms usurp public police power, often widening rather than limiting the scope of lawless operations.[15] This vicious dialectic can be broken down in two ways: by the absolute crushing of opposition, as in totalitarian systems, or by accepting the risks of terror as a permanent feature of developed, mobile, and liberal societies, as necessary evils along with prostitution, gambling, drugs, and other forms of deviance. Policy options take on meaning only in the context of what elements of its political soul a society is willing to risk. It is important to understand the successes and failures of terrorism so that we can assess policy options—and risks—in a real world context. We may decide that terrorism is but one of the many continuing curses that must be borne if the democratic balance wheel is to endure.

Even if we reach a consensus about the sources of terrorism, that it reflects elite rather than mass discontent, personal dislocations rather than deep social cleavages, we cannot move directly to a policy designed to eliminate terrorism without a much clearer notion of the likely social consequences. For example, how much militarism is the American public likely to accept in efforts to curb domestic terrorism?[16] Just as benign tumors sometimes look like critical cancers, varieties of terrorism may also "look alike" but function differentially in a variety of social contexts. One must pay careful attention to such distinctions, not just to satisfy bad academic habits of nitpicking but to justify a continuing quest for democracy in a political universe of expanding social uncertainty.

15. Revolution, Retribution, and Redemption

The Gulag Archipelago[1] is a classic statement of social reality. It will rank as a foremost contribution to the literature on power and powerlessness long after the biography of the author ceases to be a point of contention or argumentation. A sure measure of a classic is that any one specialist is unable either to encapsulate or to emasculate its contents. From this flows a second measure of high quality: the desire it arouses in specialists of every field to interpret the book's contents from a particular professional vantage point. In a work such as this, ubiquity and grandeur go together.

Since *The Gulag Archipelago* is a work of autobiography as well as of biography, sociology, and history, it is impossible not to comment on Solzhenitsyn, although the efforts to lionize as well as dismiss this extraordinary man are really quite independent of this latest publication. Yet *The Gulag Archipelago* also stands apart from the personal career of a single individual, even its author. Indeed, the work is more than the sum of the 277 other contributions, many made by persons Solzhenitsyn has kept anonymous. While it can be considered as all one piece with his other works, specifically, *One Day in the Life of Ivan Denisovich*, and his more recent novels, *The Cancer Ward* and *The First Circle*, this book is singular. *The Gulag Archipelago* is an experiment in literary investigation. Thus, those who would argue that the book has exaggerations or mistakes must be cautioned. This is not the work of an empirical social researcher, but its achievements as a study in systematic state imprisonment are remarkable.

Solzhenitsyn is a writer. It would be a mistake to call him a sociologist, or for that matter, a novelist. He conveys experiences, he recites the truths of an entire society. He captures the essence of civilization in the behavioral degeneration of one individual toward another. On the other hand, in the tradition of literary realism, his individuals typify and represent an archetype within society as a whole. Beyond that, Solzhenitsyn is entirely a product of Soviet society and of the Russian literary tradition. His intellectual vision is fused with a sense of politics characteristic of Soviet Marxism as a whole and with a capacity for irony characteristic of Russian literature, particularly its nineteenth-century classic period. He knows nothing of formal social science techniques, could probably care less about ethnographic safeguards, and is not interested in characterizing a society from the point of view of a general theory of political systems. Yet, few works have ever told us more about the political system of the Soviet Union, the history of an organization called the Communist party, or the fate of individuals within the penological system known as the USSR. Solzhenitsyn takes for granted that the Soviet Union itself is a total institution, a network of integrated agencies of coercion dedicated to the survival and promulgation of maximum state power over minimum human beings. Few have been privy to write from inside the whale, yet even those who have suffered similar outrages have been unable to create such a compendium of horrors.

The Gulag Archipelago should be viewed as a series of experiences, a set of lessons in fear and courage, in being oppressed and in doing the bidding of the oppressor, in working the system and in being ground down by the system. Whatever polarities come to the human mind appear in *The Gulag Archipelago*. In this sense, Solzhenitsyn has written the great Soviet dialectic, the supreme work of literary and social analysis that finally, after fifty-five years, has put the Soviet experience into a perspective that can at least be theoretically tested. Vague, didactic Leninist tracts on the withering away of the state, outrageous Stalinist equations of Soviet life with the principle of happiness, the Brezhnev-Kosygin reduction of détente into a series of statements about mutual stagnation: these mythological politics give way, crack apart, in this documentary history of Russian suffering before, during, and after the Russian Revolution. We now have an experiential work that, if tested, may resolve questions about the nature of Soviet society or at least permit a huge step forward in the development of political theory.

This book brings to mind, with its documentary evidence of the slaying and imprisonment of tens of millions of Russians, comparison with the Japanese experience at Hiroshima and Nagasaki as recited in Robert Jay Lifton's *Death in Life* and the Jewish experience of the holocaust as recounted by Raul Hilberg in *The Destruction of the European Jews*. But the Soviet experience is unique, precisely because terror was self-inflicted, because Russians killed and maimed Russians. In this sense, the banality of evil spoken of by Hannah Arendt in her *Eichmann in Jerusalem* is carried one step further, for the terror is not American airplanes over defenseless Japanese cities, or the destruction of European Jews at the hands of the Nazi Gestapo. However awful these other holocausts might be, the enemy was external.

The Gulag Archipelago offers a special sort of Dostoevskian nightmare in which Russian spies upon Russian, Communist betrays Communist, Red Army officers destroy other members of the Red Army. All of this national self-immolation, in Solzhenitsyn's words, "cauterized the wound so that scar tissue would form more quickly." But as Solzhenitsyn hints, there is more involved; the Marxist principle of criticism and self-criticism is raised to a pathological new high, in which ideological purification is a consequence of purgation, in which intraparty struggle replaces in principle all party democracy, in which the notion of scientific evidence is overwhelmed by the notion of organization-inspired rumor. For these reasons, *The Gulag Archipelago* has a fascination and a horror beyond even the literature of concentration camps. To die at the hands of a foreign tormentor or of a powerful adversary may be awful, but at least it is understandable. To suffer the same fate at the hands of one's own is a form of barbarism which permits Solzhenitsyn to consider Soviet Bolshevism as almost in a class with German Nazism. This point has thoroughly outraged Soviet commentators on the book who have grown up with the belief that the fascist hordes were history's worst example of cruelty. Solzhenitsyn's comparison of the Soviet system to fascism must itself be ranked an act of extraordinary criticism and condemnation. He has stepped over a psychological threshold of commentary few others have dared cross.

The essence of *The Gulag Archipelago* is the equation of Soviet political sociology with criminology and penology; that is, Soviet-Marxist praxis turns out to be the theory and practice of penology, of imprisonment. In Solzhenitsyn's paradigm of imprisonment every aspect of the Soviet system is converted into a science. There is a science of arrest, involving a structured system of questioning according to various criteria: nighttime and daytime, at home and at work, for initial arrests and recidivists, independent versus group arrests. Then there is the science of searches: how to conduct body searches, how to check out houses, even urinals; in short, how to flush out people. Then there is the science of purge: how to isolate the victim from his own party apparatus, which Solzhenitsyn calls a grandiose game of solitaire whose rules are entirely incomprehensible to its players. The enormous impact of Communist cadres on the Russian masses does not derive from their presumed vanguard position but from their unique ignorance of the real nature of Soviet history. The ordinary Russian peasant, spared the patina of Marxism-Leninism, was better prepared for the terror than the party cadre who bought the package labeled "dictatorship of the proletariat"; hence these peasants were not caught unaware of the Stalinist terror—as were the intellectuals. All of these various and sundry facts of the twentieth-century history of the Soviet science of the destruction of personality had very little to do with the lofty claims of Lenin or Stalin. It is as if the Archipelago is a nation apart, as if the Archipelago alone had the right, ironically, to experience social science as social engineering while the rest of the society paraded forth under the mythical banner of Marxism.

We have the amazing experience of social science emerging in the Soviet Union as a function of the rise of a prison system involving tens of millions of people. Pavlovian behaviorism, stripped of its humane ambitions, found its fulfillment in the Soviet state. This transition from Marxism to Pavlovianism was made possible because the Gulag Archipelago was more than a geographic sector. The prison system of the Soviet Union was far-flung but it was connected psychologically, as Solzhenitsyn said, fused into a context, and almost invisibly, imperceptibly, carried forward as a nation of the damned.

In this sense, Solzhenitsyn's *The Gulag Archipelago*, while reminiscent of the writings of Raul Hilberg and Robert Lifton, also makes one think of the writings of Erving Goffman in *Asylums*. He combines both macroanalysis and microanalysis. It is a study in working within a system, surviving it and operating so as to make the system collapse under the weight of its self-imposed lunacy and limitless bureaucracy. A great deal of the book's social psychology has to do with the counterscience of prisoner life, the grim humor of survival in which a mistake means a life, and hence a science that has to be equal or better than the various sciences of arrest, search, seizure, and imprisonment inflicted by the state.

One of Solzhenitsyn's major contributions is to note how terrorism functions as a structural feature of Soviet society, rather than as an episodic moment in Russian time. That is to say, Solzhenitsyn does not simply speak about the Stalin era, or special quixotic moments in that era where terror was high, but of the entire period of 1918–56. The Gulag Archipelago existed because the need for terror replaced the practice of liberty within Russian life. Indeed, there was not very much liberty to begin with, since the czarist era was hardly concerned with the distribution of justice. However, the revolution of mass democracy never took place, at least for Solzhenitsyn, and terrorism immediately became institutionalized. Within this structural framework there were special eras, for example, 1929–30, when 15 million peasants were either slaughtered, uprooted, or imprisoned; 1937–38, when party personnel and intellectuals and cadres of the military were entirely wiped out; and again in 1944–46 when armed forces personnel, prisoners of war, and all persons having contact with the West were similarly destroyed. Only the purges of 1937–38 were remembered because intellectuals and party personnel were able to articulate their mortification. Millions perished in this Yagoda epoch, but still more perished in the other two high-purge periods.

Solzhenitsyn indicates that a fourth huge round of purges was being prepared in 1952–53, this time against Jews and other national minorities. This "final solution" has since been verified by many journalists and researchers. However, the costs were considered so high that even the other members of the Stalin-appointed Politboro withdrew at the thought of another round of purges. These strictly internal purges were apart from Soviet military acquisitions after World War II, which carried their own severe punishment of native populations. The occupation of the Baltic countries was ruthless, but it cannot be placed in the same category as mass waves of terror. One would have to offer the same cautionary note with respect to the Civil War period between 1918 and 1922. By minimizing the gap between peaks and troughs in the exercise of terror, the need for analysis is thus lessened.

The most fundamental issue of social theory raised by *The Gulag Archipelago* is whether terror is intrinsic to the Soviet system or whether it is confined to the Stalinist epoch covered by the book. Solzhenitsyn's viewpoint is that terrorism is endemic to the Leninist definition of Bolshevism and continues to plague the Soviet landscape. The viewpoint of a rather wide-ranging group of Soviet scholars and observers is that terrorism was a special technique of Stalinism employed to stimulate development and industrialization in a uniquely backward set of social and cultural circumstances. Solzhenitsyn's position is that Stalinist terrorism was a technique employed by the czarist secret police with equally telling (but limited) effects, and hence cut from the same cloth. Terrorism is not solely endemic to the secret police under Bolshevism but is part of the history of modern Russia dating back to the czarist *Okhrama* (secret police). The terror of wartime conditions is finite and determined by military considerations rather than party idiosyncrasies. This might better serve to distinguish the exercise of violence in the Leninist phase from the resort to terror characteristic of the post-1929 Stalinist consolidation. Nonetheless, the continuation of terrorism argues in favor of Solzhenitsyn's structuralist explanation. The turn away from terrorism (and toward benign authoritarian rule) in the post-1956 Khrushchev era was not a function of Socialist evolution but rather of strains and stresses within Soviet rule.

While Lenin in practice preferred norms of "socialist legality," nothing in the Leninist corpus would or could limit terrorism as a strategy and tactic of development. Stalinism is thus a direct theoretical consequence of Leninism, not its diabolical corruption. Ivan Stadnyuk, the figure in the Soviet Writers Union identified by Solzhenitsyn as the man responsible for his expulsion, published an assessment of Stalin as a man who adapted rapidly to the Nazi attack and pulled Soviet war efforts together in contrast to Khrushchev's characterization of him as a man "paralyzed by his fear of Hitler like a rabbit in front of a boa constrictor." In short, Stalinism remains a viable, if risky, option should "democratization" get out of control.

My own view, as expressed in *Three Worlds of Development*, is that Soviet society has been transformed from totalitarian to authoritarian modalities. The rise of middle sectors, bureaucrats, teachers, party officials, technicians, skilled craftsmen, and so on, has created the seeds of a consumer society without a conflict society, a mass society without mass democracy. This authoritarianism permits the continuation of Bolshevik legends and myths but does not permit the reinstitutionalization of the kind of terrorism that existed under Stalin. History, at least Soviet history, moves in a peculiar way: not one step backward to generate two steps forward, as Lenin suggested, but rather, nineteen steps backward to permit twenty steps forward, as Max Nomad has suggested. To think in purely communist terms, empirically at least, has meant a betrayal of the socialist ideals of mass democracy in favor of a codebook of party control of society by a narrow band of elites. The connection between the freedom of individuals and the necessity of development is not an easy issue to resolve, especially in the light of foreign assaults upon the Soviet Union. Rather than speak the unspeakable about the limits of democracy it is simpler for Solzhenitsyn to retreat into religious self-actualization. But the foreknowledge that history rarely moves lockstep in place with justice may help us appreciate better the Soviet horror without that collapse of moral nerve always entailed in a categorical denial that the future contains the possibility of improving upon the present.

At the theoretical level, Solzhenitsyn is saying that Russia was not ready for socialism, indeed was unfit for it because of its backward economy and political and social conditions. The Leninists attempted to speed up, even defy history, flying in the face of Marxian assumptions that each social system must run its full course before there can be a normal transformation of capitalism into socialism. But according to Solzhenitsyn, the very backwardness of Russian society overwhelmed the Bolshevik Revolution, and instead of breaking the back of feudalism, the Bolsheviks wound up breaking the backs of their own followers and supporters. The very attempt to speed up the historical process of economic development in the face of lethargy and backwardness boomeranged, and lethargy and backwardness became the hallmark of Soviet development.

Along with others, I would argue that coercion is a necessary component of development, that the sacrifice needed for high development would be impossible without a mythic sense of purpose. In point of fact, the Soviet state constantly spilled over, failing to distinguish coercion from terrorism, failing to distinguish the forms of state self-protection from the rights of citizens. Within such a system the Soviet Union achieved a level of development which, even today, is lower than that of its capitalist adversaries. The outcome was not simply political betrayal but economic stagnation and a dangerous kind of frustration, not so much within the Gulag Archipelago but among those who might point to the Archipelago as a possible source, indeed a major source, of the central problem of Soviet life—the problem of legitimacy.

Another central theme in Solzhenitsyn's work is the differential forms of punishment meted out to common criminals vis-à-vis political prisoners. The constant denial of the existence of political prisoners by Soviets becomes a charade to mask the criminal nature of the state itself. Thus, legislation is created to distinguish forms of criminality. "For him [the thief] to have a knife was mere misbehavior, tradition, he didn't know any better. But for you [the political prisoner] to have one was 'terrorism.'" Thus, we have the master dialectic between crime and punishment, the individual and the state, the rights of the person and the limits of authority, and perhaps more painfully, the obligations of the citizen and the rights of the state. *The Gulag Archipelago* is compelling not simply as an exposé of Soviet party history or its penal system but as an introduction to the entire gamut of normative issues that have plagued Western civilization since its inception. Of course, Marx and Engels recognized these issues and dealt with them by fiat, declaring in principle that socialism would witness the withering away of the state. But in Stalinist practice such a diminution of authority never occurred: circumstances always blocked the path of true historical necessity; and in the vise of this cruel hoax, tens of millions of Russians were squeezed to death.

In some sense, Solzhenitsyn's volume suffers the defects of its virtues. Like the American prison literature of Malcolm X or George Jackson, it has a searing intimacy that at times disguises a paucity of theory. No large-scale explanation of the Soviet experience, no cost-benefit analysis, is forthcoming. One is left with the feeling that no meaningful mass involvement in Soviet society was registered in the past fifty-five years, a point of view which is clearly unrealistic, first given the Soviet Civil War experience, and above all, the large-scale popular support for the state generated during the war against fascism. It may very well be that the Russian people were fighting the enduring features of Russian civilization rather than the Bolshevik system. Exactly such a pan-Slavic appeal was made by the Nazis (with mixed results as the archives of Smolensk indicate), an appeal which seems to have left at least a small mark on Solzhenitsyn himself. One must wonder whether the slavophile in Solzhenitsyn explains why little is said of repression and terror under czarism, and why he offers so little in the study of continuities in Russian terrorism.

Ironically, the theory offered to explain Soviet terrorism comes close to a conspiratorial view of history, as if the devil were masterminding the takeover of the Soviet world and the explusion of God: "It was essential to clean out, conscientiously, socialists of every other stripe from Moscow, Petrograd, the ports, the industrial centers, and later on, the outlying provinces as well. This was a grandiose silent game of solitaire, whose rules were totally incomprehensible to its contemporaries, and whose outlines we can appreciate only now. Someone's far-seeing mind, someone's neat hands, planned it all, without letting one wasted minute go by." This is not to deny that real conspiracy existed. Wherever democracy is absent, the potential for conspiracy is present. But to explain such a gigantic event as the death and imprisonment of tens of millions of people as a conspiracy, it seems to me, falls badly short of what is required at the macro level of explanation. The answer is right at hand: the fundamental impulse of both Stalinism and Leninism was rapid development. Industrial development can sacrifice consumer modernization along with the people it involves in the developmental process. One might argue that the amount of terror was not commensurate with the tasks at hand, that less terror and more benign forms of coercion might have achieved the same results; but the denial of the results is what weakens Solzhenitsyn's analysis. His myopia concerning Soviet achievements also denies him the possibility of a real theory explaining Soviet terrorism and returns him to a primitive Christian view of good and evil that even later Christianity has abandoned. Goethe once explained that the trouble with Christianity was its impulse to cast problems in terms of good and evil when, in fact, the real ethical problems people face are choices between good and good. This choice of goods, or perhaps of evils, breathes real-life tension into social systems. And it is the absence of this awareness of the struggle between developmentalism and terrorism, between the creative life-giving forces no less than the death-making forces, that makes Solzhenitsyn's work an unrelieved horror, or better, a series of horrors relieved by the author's personal genius as a writer.

The Gulag Archipelago has given us what few believed would ever be possible: a case history of the Communist party of the USSR, not a series of party visions and revisions, not a series of myths and illusions consecrated to the initial holders of power, but a study in state authority untrammeled and unfettered by popular will. The history of the Communist party of the Soviet Union is ultimately the history of crime and punishment in the Soviet Union: the ultimate fusion of politics and deviance.

As a result, it really matters little that this is not a balanced or fair-minded work, that it fails to recite properly and fairly the heroic events of Soviet development and of Soviet people in the face of all sorts of foreign military adversity. Were this a work balancing the worth of the Soviet system on a cost-benefit scale, we would simply have a volume in economic theory, or, even worse, a bookkeeping, double-entry system, that fails to measure in qualitative terms the monumental architectonics that made possible the Gulag Archipelago. What is so awful about this book is that one realizes no one remained untouched by the Gulag Archipelago. In fact, the dirty little secret of the society as a whole was that the Soviet Union *is* the Gulag Archipelago, and that the description of prison life *is* a description of Soviet life. It serves little use to recite the joys of industrial achievement in the face of this awful truth. The Soviet Union became, at least between 1918 and 1956, a total institution. What has happened since then to change the parameters of the game, to limit and curb the prison-house atmosphere of the USSR? Solzhenitsyn does not tell us whether the Archipelago ended in 1956 or whether he simply stopped his story at a point beyond which he had no firsthand evidence. We are left not so much with a conclusion as with a giant ambiguity. Perhaps the issues will be resolved in the next five parts of *The Gulag Archipelago*. Or perhaps there will be no other parts and we will have to reexamine, in the light of this work, the nature of state power, the workings of an economic system, and the consequences as well as benefits of making a revolution.

The leitmotif of this book is the painful and shameful absence of mass resistance. "Today those who have continued to live in comfort scold those who suffered." Solzhenitsyn adds rhetorically: "Yes, resistance should have begun right there, at the moment of the arrest itself." This sense of moral turpitude, not unknown to a generation of Israelis reflecting on the European holocaust, is all-pervasive, not the least because Solzhenitsyn survived his own shame of silence. But he learned his lesson well. *The Gulag Archipelago* can be viewed as a lesson in courage, a statement of personal survival through conditions of imprisonment, intimidation, and indignities. In the fusion of biography with history this masterpiece comes to fruition, and the dedication "to all those who did not live to tell it" is redeemed.

"I am finishing it (*The Gulag Archipelago*) in the year of a double anniversary (and the two anniversaries are connected): it is fifty years since the revolution which created Gulag, and a hundred since the invention of barbed wire (1867). This second anniversary will no doubt pass unnoticed." In this way a herculean project began as a testament in 1958 and, completed in 1967, came into the world. But now that additional decades have passed it is quite evident that, although pageantry of the fiftieth anniversary of the Soviet Revolution has long passed and the invention of barbed wire did indeed pass unheralded, we have been given as a gift of suffering a twentieth-century masterwork.

The *Gulag* is classic because it makes plain the essence of the century, not simply because it was written in our times. The dialectic of the century emerges on countless pages and in endless details: in the guise of socialism we receive bureaucracy; in the place of popular control we are provided with elite management; instead of the liquidation of state power there emerges an augmentation of such power; in place of abundance through industrial development we get deprivation as the price of such development. And ultimately, in place of justice we get the law. If before Solzhenitsyn we were unable to recite conventional platitudes about this century being the best of times and the worst of times, we are forced to the grim realization that these have become simply the worst of times. Even in comparison to other troublesome ages such as the fourteenth century, one must recognize as a redeeming virtue the unconscious force of nature wreaking havoc with humanity. The conscious force of repression (sometimes called racial destiny and other times historical necessity) destroys so many people that the concept of humanity itself assumes a tenuous dimension.

It shall come to pass that the literate population of the future, if there is to be a future, will be divided between those who have read and understood the lessons of the Gulag, and those who have not read—or even worse, read and not understood—the broad implications of this "experiment in literary investigation." Already, the cloudy voices of cynicism, fused with the fatuous voices of childlike optimism, have begun to assert the exaggerated political manners of Solzhenitsyn. Using as a pretext his Harvard commencement address on "The Exhausted West" (it is far simpler to make statements and render judgments on excerpts from a speech than work through the experience in three volumes of the *Gulag*), intellectual scribblers and political hags are assuring one and all that Solzhenitsyn not only does not understand American society but has already lost touch with Soviet realities. In the meantime, like a phoenix the *Gulag* remains: beyond contest, beyond dispute, and as is that rare characteristic of a masterwork, beyond good and evil—doomed to repetition in Democratic Kampuchea (Cambodia) and only God knows where else.

The major accusation launched against Solzhenitsyn concerns his emotivism and presumed mysticism. Underlying this charge is the more serious charge that he lacks adequate analytic categories, hence that his critique is one-sided, that it fails to take into consideration the positive achievements of Soviet industrialization. While it is doubtlessly correct that emotional language is used, it is simply nonsense to claim that mysticism is preached. Irony makes the sufferings described and the outrages committed bearable. The catalogue of evils presented never—*not on a single page in three volumes*—involves any mystical commitment to blind faith or self-destructive acts. To be sure, in so far as any act of heroism, courage, and self-sacrifice involves a transcendent belief in the human condition, Solzhenitsyn stands accused; but to the extent that mysticism is adaptation or surrender to antihuman behavior or acceptance of a man's fate, he is entirely innocent. This is, after all, a special variety of prison literature; and prisoners who write books seek freedom, not immolation. Indeed, the burden of the final volume is a testimony to rebellion, resistance, and retaliation. For Solzhenitsyn, it became an effort to answer the question: "Can a man's urge to stop being a slave and an animal ever be reactionary?"

Solzhenitsyn's *Gulag* has an implicit analytic scheme which deserves to be dealt with seriously, even profoundly. For in this towering statement of prison life in Soviet society there are lessons about twentieth-century social systems as a whole. The political sociology of Soviet society illumines the contours of a future that indeed works. Herein lies its terror for us all. And if that political sociology spills over into a political theology, it is nothing less than a consequence of universal ideologies confronting each other in mortal, perhaps eternal, combat. And if this creates an aura of Manicheanism, of the substitution of good for right and evil for wrong, reification in itself must be viewed as a consequence of political systems, of state power reaching out for an ultimate domination of individual life. The evils of capitalism which spawned its goods was an impersonal dialectic necessity for Marx in the nineteenth century; but the goods of communism which spawned its evils was a draconian choice made by Bolsheviks old and new and then advertised as a necessity.

Stalin enjoyed posing issues in a pseudojesuitical manner. Every phenomenon became a rhetorical question. "Is such the case? Yes (or No) such is (or is not) the case." Hence, he gave us the political question, the national question, the women question, ad infinitum. Solzhenitsyn's *Gulag* can be read as a parody of Stalinism. He takes these macroscopic questions and shows how they work in microscopic concentration camp circumstances. The marriage of Marxist theory and Russian realities was stress-laden from the outset. The bitter rivalries and factions within the revolutionary movement attest to this strain. Stalin's great achievement was to have consolidated the Leninist pivot and created a new orthodoxy. But to do so meant an end to rivalries, factions, and debate itself. The doctrine was saved while the intelligentsia was wasted.

The depolitization of Soviet society is an underlying reality with which every dissident and deviant must contend. The ordinary Soviet citizen goes about his business not unlike the ordinary Nazi citizen: learnedly ignorant of events and myopically closed to the human consequences of the Gulag. Rebellion is such an unusual event that its recording by Solzhenitsyn becomes a major aspect of the third volume. While not quite reaching the epic proportions of the Warsaw ghetto uprising, the record of resistance from Kengir to Novocherkassk—personal and political— forms the essential core of the third volume. But such uprisings remain sporadic and isolated. They are handled bureaucratically, involving scant potential for resistance. It is therefore not the character of rebellion that becomes startling, but the simple fact that resistance is even possible. Leviathan emerges as a total way of life, cut off from popular limits.

The Stalinist decision to emphasize economic development and industrialization muted any efforts at personal liberty. Only when work norms were not met or when political confusion arose from a series of crises of succession were any displays of resistance tolerated. What Solzhenitsyn depicts is the first society in which economics is completely sundered from politics, or better, in which bureaucratic systems management becomes the norm. The USSR becomes a country without a polity; and without a people who determine the nature of justice there can be no morality. Only political participants acting in complete freedom can determine the nature of goodness. The USSR is not only the antithesis of the Aristotelian paradigm; it doesn't even measure up to Platonic communism since the dialectic of the best and the brightest is reduced to the dynamics of the mediocre and the mindless.

The Christian persuasion notwithstanding, Solzhenitsyn, quite like other exiles who preceded him, continues to be the conscience of a socialism gone awry. Like every Russian of the modern age, he grew up with a belief in the national question as resolved by the socialist system. Lenin and Stalin, in their wisdom, appreciated the fact that no revolution could be successful only in class terms. The ethnic and national variable was the crucial linchpin to the successful conclusion of the revolutionary phase.

> Only when the twentieth century—on which all civilized mankind has put its hopes—arrived, only when the National Question had reached the summit of its development thanks to the One and Only True Doctrine, could the supreme authority on that Question patent the whole extirpation of peoples by banishment within forty-eight hours, within twenty-four hours, or even within an hour and a half.

In fact, the nations of Russia which did not fit plans for unification were extirpated singly and collectively: Chechens, Ingush, Karachai, Balkars, Kalmyks, Kurds, Tatars, Caucasian Greeks, Germans, Balts, Estonians, Karelo-Finns, and, as Solzhenitsyn reminds us, the Jews were being readied when Stalin came to his end in 1953. The numbers of peoples totally liquidated read like an anthropological who's who of European peoples. When one asks who inhabited the Gulag it becomes evident that these millions of minority people were declared the chosen ones.

> Neatness and uniformity! That is the advantage of exiling whole nations at once! No special cases! No exception, no individual protests! They all go quietly, because . . . they are all in it together. All ages and both sexes go, and that still leaves something to be said. Those still in the womb go, too, and are exiled unborn, by the same decree.

One might argue that this is the necessary price of national unification. But if that be the situation, it is a price extracted with a gigantic political myth, with the promissory note of the rights of all peoples and nations to self-determination. Ideology and reality were never further apart. What the West did with a melting pot the Soviets did with melting people: a system of hard labor, penal servitude, exile, and death. This has become the style of Soviet subsistence. Perhaps the end of ethnic groups is an anthropological and historical fact, but the end of people as individuals is a political and military policy. And the Bolshevik authorities saw fit to make no fine, hairsplitting distinctions.

Solzhenitsyn offers a traditional romantic vision of women. If they are not elevated in their nature, they are at least deserving of very special concern. But instead of this being an irritant, one realizes that this is not only a sincere sentiment frankly expressed, but a shrewd antithesis to the Marxist equation of women's liberation with socialism. Indeed, the special pains Solzhenitsyn takes with their camp treatment, the abuse they endure as women, would indicate that the Soviet Revolution has transformed society uniformly: with the treatment of women no better or worse than the treatment of peasants, intellectuals, and ethnic minorities. But what makes matters worse is the special vulnerability of women: the unique torments of an unwanted pregnancy, gang rapes by violent criminals as a reward for their abuse of political prisoners, types of work that are brutal and serve as a special form of demoralization for women.

> The body becomes worn out at that kind of work, and everything that is feminine in a woman, whether it be constant or whether it be monthly, ceases to be. If she manages to last to the next "commissioning," the person who undresses before the physicians will not be at all like the one whom the trustees smacked their lips over in the corridor: she has become ageless; her shoulders stick out at sharp angles, her breasts hang down in little dried-out sacs; superfluous folds of skin form wrinkles on her flat buttocks; there is so little flesh above her knees that a big enough gap has opened up for a sheep's head to stick through or even a soccer ball; her voice has become hoarse and rough and her face is tanned by pellagra.

But the women came to the Gulag sharing with the men the same illusions, and later, the same slow emergence of consciousness. Among the early women prisoners were those hauled off into the Gulag driven naked between formations of jailors singing to their tormentors: "I know no other country/Where a person breathes so freely." But by the fifties, these same women became the ferocious defenders of their fellow inmates, fused into solidarity by long sentences and desperate lives.

Events outsoared the casual contempt which the thieves feel for *females*. When shots rang out in the service yard, those who had broken into the women's camp ceased to be greedy predators and became comrades in misfortune. The women hid them. Unarmed soldiers came in to catch them, then others with guns. The women got in the way of the searchers, and resisted attempts to move them. The soldiers punched the women and struck them with their gun butts, dragged some of them off to jail (thanks to someone's foresight, there was a jailhouse in the women's camp area) and shot at some of the men.

When the prisoners rebelled at the penal colony and won forty days of self-determination, that represented the first real breath of freedom these women had known.

The runaway escapes to enjoy just one day of freedom! In just the same way, these eight thousand men had not so much raised a rebellion as *escaped to free-dom*, though not for long! Eight thousand men, from being slaves, had suddenly become free, and now was their chance to . . . live! Faces usually grim softened into kind smiles. Women looked at men, and men took them by the hand. Some who had corresponded by ingenious secret ways, without even seeing each other, met at last! Lithuanian girls whose weddings had been solemnized by priests on the other side of the wall now saw their lawful wedded husbands for the first time—the Lord had sent down to earth the marriages made in heaven! For the first time in their lives, no one tried to prevent the sectarians and believers from meeting for prayer. Foreigners, scattered about the Camp Divisions, now found each other and talked about this strange Asiatic revolution in their own languages. The camp's food supply was in the hands of the prisoners. No one drove them out to work line-up and even an eleven hour working day.

For the Gulag does not offer a confrontation of traditionalism with modernity, but convention against barbarism. And in the Gulag everyone knew barbarism would win out in the end. Hence "newlyweds . . . observed each day as their last, and retribution delayed was a gift from heaven each morning." Irony of ironies: prisoners knew a freedom denied to citizens of Soviet society as a whole.

The tension of the first two volumes of the Gulag largely derived from the loggerheads at which criminals were juxtaposed over and against politicals. Repeatedly, Solzhenitsyn shows how the regime utilizes criminals to intimidate and even assassinate political prisoners. The reviled *lumpenproletariat* of Marx is eliminated under Stalin. The *lumpen* become the prisoner class. These vast strata perform the same tasks on behalf of the state, from strike breaking to organized mayhem. The cynicism of this is displayed by the offering of women to the criminals, by moving them into camps where political trouble is brewing. Solzhenitsyn rises above the cheap claptrap of jailhouse lawyers who try to interpret every act of imprisonment as a political torment. He uses language exactly and precisely, in short, scientifically.

Their commune, more precisely their world, was a separate world within our world, and the strict laws which for centuries had existed in it for strengthening that world did not in any degree depend on our "suckers" legislation or even on the Party Congresses. They had their own laws of seniority, by which their ring-leaders were not elected at all, yet when they entered a cell or a camp compound already wore their crown of power and were immediately recognized as chiefs. These ringleaders might have strong intellectual capacities, and always had a clear comprehension of the thieves' philosophy, as well as a sufficient number of murders and robberies behind them. And what did their word "frayersky"—"of the suckers"—mean? It meant what was universally human, what pertained to all normal people. And it was precisely this universally human world, *our* world, with its morals, customs, and mutual relationships, which was most hateful to the thieves, most subject to their ridicule, counterposed most sharply to their own antisocial, anti-public *kluba*—or clan.

Hence, for two volumes these miserable, incarcerated creatures play out a living class struggle while the Soviet authorities offer dialectical enthusiasms about the achievements of the Gulag: "A collective organism, living, working, eating, sleeping, and suffering together in pitiless and forced symbiosis."

The tension of the third volume shifts. Prisoners who are ordinary criminals learn, albeit slowly and painfully, the manipulative nature, the essence of the regime, while the abused politicals learn to adopt the cutthroat ethic of the criminals—in a kind of Darwinian trade-off. But it is one that worked for a short time at least.

By 1954, so we are told, it was noticeable in transit prisoners that *the thieves came to respect the politicals*. If this is so—what prevented us from gaining their respect earlier? All through the twenties, thirties, and forties, we blinkered philistines, preoccupied as we were with our own importance to the world, with the contents of our duffel bags, with the shoes or trousers we had been allowed to retain, had conducted ourselves in the eyes of the thieves like characters on the comic stage: when they plundered our neighbors, intellectuals of world importance like ourselves, we shyly looked the other way and huddled together in our corners; and when the submen crossed the room to give us the treatment, we expected, of course, no help from neighbors, but obligingly surrendered all we had to these ugly customers in case they bit our heads off.

It turns out that a third category of prisoner exists in Soviet labor camps, distinct and distinctive: the religious prisoner. This well-represented group is extremely important. They bear witness to tragedy; but they do so in a way which confronts the vacuum of Soviet ideology with the force of some higher belief. In their nonviolent commitments, they are the touchstone of conditions for all prisoners. When religious prisoners are tormented, maimed, or shot, that becomes a cue that all hope is lost. Resistance is the only recourse—futile and folly-laden though it may appear.

The Jews are represented in all three categories. Solzhenitsyn doesn't make much of it; he doesn't have to. The surnames of Gulag residents reveal this fact. Hence, Jews suffer a sort of triple risk: if they engage in entrepreneurial acts they are reviled as bourgeois remnants; if they engage in human rights activities they are condemned as Zionist plotters; and if they assert their religious commitment to Judaism they are obscurantists and fossils substituting ancient dogma for the science of Marxism-Leninism. This threefold persecution makes the Jewish condition especially poignant and dangerous. The liquidation of the Jewish population of the Soviet Union is just as much an agenda item as their liquidation by Nazi Germany. The Nazis were cruel: they wanted dead bodies as well as dead souls. The Soviet authorities are willing to settle for dead souls only, hoping, like the Inquisition, that the living bodies will convert to communism, becoming in the process productive workers of the state.

One perplexing, even haunting, question that remains is why Solzhenitsyn's *Gulag* has the continuing capacity to shock and disturb. Surely it is not for lack of a literature on the subject of Soviet state terror. The archives are filled with scholarly treatises and personal testaments alike. Such early efforts as Vladimir Tchernavin's *I Speak for the Silent*, Pitirim Sorokin's *Leaves from a Russian Diary*, and Ivan Solonevich's *Russia in Chains* have the capacity to evoke similar powerful moods and sentiments. To be sure, Solzhenitsyn exhibits an exactitude as well as a collective judgment rarely before assembled in such force. And there can be no question that his fame as a great writer, not to mention the circumstances of his exile from the Soviet Union, also played a part in making the *Gulag* special. But I think another element is present, one with ominous consequences. Our analysis of Soviet society is, like our analysis of nuclear conflict, too easily based on a spurious exchange theory, on a trade-off between industrial growth or postwar survival and the number of deaths involved. Hence, we are inclined to accept certain levels of death or even mass annihilation if the ends in view can be achieved. Thus, if it takes 30 million lives to create the beatification of Soviet man, then so be it. But which 30 million? And why one number and not another? Could the same results be achieved with fewer deaths or less suffering? What in past centuries was a sense of historical cost, even necessary cost, for social change and economic expansion, in our century has become a willing, and even an enthusiastic endorsement, of the idea of costs to achieve not infrequently spurious benefits. I submit that the special nature of Solzhenitsyn's impact derives from his keen awareness of the substitution of engineering for ethical criteria in evaluating the human soul. He does not speak against development, but rather for those countless millions who paid the price for development. And in compelling a fresh review of the actual costs paid and the dubious benefits received, he has restored the balance between political realities and moral possibilities.

Even a masterpiece has flaws. Indeed, Solzhenitsyn's single-mindedness would make that inevitable. The major problem in *The Gulag Archipelago* is a rather weak empirics of concentration camp life between 1957 and the present. The transition from totalitarianism to authoritarianism in Soviet life is left unexamined in favor of a vaguely stated premise that only a total overhaul in the Soviet system, indeed a counterrevolution, would change the internal dynamics of Russian life. And yet, even Solzhenitsyn despairs about a present generation of Russian youth who walk about with their portable radios and shaggy girls under their arms, and who couldn't care less about the Gulag system. But is that system the same? Is it merely a shell of its former self? Is this a work of history or social life?

In terms of values and norms Solzhenitsyn answers in the affirmative: that Gulag lives. And we have every reason to believe this is the case. Predetermined prison sentences of dissidents continue unabated. Soviet persecution of the politicals has few rivals in the world. The dried-out Leninist rhetoric continues unrivaled. Still, there does seem to be growth in the middle sector, and the concomitant demands for observing legal norms that did not formerly obtain. The sheer reduction in numbers within the Gulag requires some sort of explanation that Solzhenitsyn is seemingly unable to provide. In this sense, the depolitization, the absence of even a vague memory of oppositional politics in Soviet society, has been so thoroughgoing that the need for an immense Gulag has been reduced. Perhaps this is more frightening than the Gulag itself, implying as it does a society which has itself become a willing penal colony, where good people are given time off for good behavior as long as they strictly observe one rule: do not question the political regime and its bureaucratic processes.

By the time this extraordinary work was completed, a work the author never once saw in its entirety prior to publication, Solzhenitsyn realized its literary imperfections: repetition and jerkiness, what he calls the mark of a persecuted literature. But such repetitions, far from being superfluous, appear essential. The apostles each repeated the story of Christ's crucifixion and redemption. The magnitude of human suffering is not an easy lesson absorbed at one sitting. The Afterword to this monumental offering is one of those rare moments when the hyphen between Judeo-Christian heritage is breached: the Father of historical redemption fuses with the Son who bears special witness to human suffering. Solzhenitsyn concludes: "I want to cry aloud: When the time and opportunity come, gather together, all you friends who have survived and know the story well, write your own commentaries to go with my book, correct and add to it where necessary. Only then will the book be definitive. God bless the work!" When the *Gulag* is published inside the Soviet Union, in one of those huge editions Soviet publishing has become famous for trumpeting, then we shall have an operational test of Russian freedom. Until that blessed event this towering set of volumes will stand between us and go gently and blindly into the totalitarian temptation.

16. Marginality, Originality, and Rootless Cosmopolitanism

At first appearance it might appear to be stretching relationships between an American sociologist (Daniel Bell), an Israeli historian (Jacob Talmon), and a European political jurist (Hannah Arendt). But for those who have read the chapter entitled "Left-wing Fascism," the connections are clear: these three figures are essentially left-wing antifascists, although antitotalitarians might be a better phrase since the specific form of repression and the exact style of oppression are less important to these towering figures and their contents.

They also have in common what the Soviets like to refer to as "rootless cosmopolitans"—people whose connection to nationalist impulses is (blessedly) weak or at least cast in terms of other considerations, such as religion, class, and race. But the "rootless" part is clearly subject to modification. True enough, both Arendt and Talmon are uprooted people, wrenched from the ashes of war-torn Europe. And Bell is from an immigrant family only one generation removed from the European holocaust. If they did not directly address the issue of winning and losing, although arguably all three did just that in considering issues of historical and philosophical import, they most certainly sensitized a generation into an appreciation of the dubious nature of victory and the transitory nature of defeat. Any considerations of fascism and communism, democracy and autocracy, market economies and planned economies, courage and treason—issues each of them dealt with at length—must perforce give us a deeper appreciation.

Bell

Montaigne long ago established the criteria for style and substance in the essay form: it must be well written, precise, with a focused theme and moral purpose directed to the question: *Que sais-je?* Daniel Bell's essays in *The Winding Passage: Essays and Sociological Journeys, 1960–1980* live up to Montaigne's highest standards. Bell brings to his work not only the twenty years of sociology herein covered but a previous twenty years of journalism that obviously contribute to the pungent, targeted nature of his enterprise. *The Winding Passage*[1] represents the best work of a highly civilized urban *freischwebende Intelligenz* in the best sense of that much-abused phrase. It is the sifted excellence of a sociologist in midpassage. We should all read these papers not only to be in the presence of a vital intellectual force but also to evaluate what that force stands for in specifically professional terms. I am not certain whether Bell claims too much or too little for his sociology, for its significance lies less in the relationships between goods and information than between the good and the knowable. This formulation may sound a trifle soft methodologically, but it has the merit of drawing attention to Bell's special skill at infusing social life with deeply philosophical meaning.

We enter Bell's world only when we make a commitment to close encounters of a philosophic kind. I do not mean ideological postures or metaphysical abstractions but the constancy of asking the Aristotelian question: What are the causes and consequences of bringing about change in the realms of being? And how are those realms carved up in our age along social, economic, and cultural dimensions? What keeps these large issues in manageable proportion is Bell's unswerving journalistic dedication to the concrete. The play of abstract ideas in concrete settings is what sets this man's work apart from that of his fellow sociologists.

The Winding Passage is divided into five parts and seventeen chapters; each of them represents areas of research in which Bell has become well known. In fact, not a few of the essays are distilled versions or microcosms of those larger works. Many themes in "Prophets of Utopia" are taken up in the *End of Ideology*. "Techne and Themis" extends positions mapped out in *The Coming of Post-Industrial Society*. And the final section on "Culture and Beliefs" echoes many of the statements expressed in *The Cultural Contradictions of Capitalism*. This is not to suggest that these essays are somehow less valuable or valid for having antecedents or descendants; quite the contrary, a knowledge of Bell's larger works will make reading these essays a double treat: first, they illuminate his sociological sense of the world; and second, they amplify the larger works by Bell on similar subjects.

I have no quarrel at all with the first section on technology. Indeed, these two essays contain some of the best thinking by a sociologist on the relationship of technology to society since Ernest Burgess in the 1930s and Fred Cottrell in the 1950s. But I am somewhat less certain that he has resolved the problem of relationships of the new technology to the social system any more than his sociological forebears. Even if we accept the Greek distinction between a material culture in progress and a moral culture in eternal recurrent cycle, we still cannot seem to open the windows on the monads. That is to say, although modernity bursts the walls of technology in the early essays, it turns out that in the later essays modernity itself seems to be bankrupt. For Bell, the new code word of the age is not so much "progress" as "limits." But then, we might well ask, what is the connection between the technological and the sacral? There are many teasing indicators of new combinations and permutations, but slender connective tissue on the dialectic. The monads remain sealed atomic parts, shrouded by the mystery of being transformed into culture.

It may be too burdensome to expect a series of linkages to a retrospective volume. It is better to read each essay as a separate analytic framework with a moral charge behind it. Read in such a way, each essay is breathtaking in the range of information and the quality of imagination. "The End of American Exceptionalism" is an especially stunning example of Bell's quintessential liberalism and probably his lingering socialism. Starting with the problem of why socialism has not come to American shores, a myriad of prophecies notwithstanding, he emphasizes the qualities of the legal and constitutional system in the New World, rather than emphasizing economic well-being, as have earlier explanations by Leon Samson and Seymour Martin Lipset. If Bell is correct that American exceptionalism has passed away, world capitalism has clearly not dissolved. If anything, the weakening of American capitalism, the wider distribution of world resources and wealth, has been strengthened by the addition of new players on the world scene, often at the expense of the American dominion. That the Eurodollar replaces the American dollar or that natural resources replace consumer goods as major commodities of value may reduce American exceptionalism or increase moral anguish, but neither necessarily impinges on the character of socioeconomic arrangements on a worldwide basis. A peculiar variety of national myopia prevents Bell from developing an appropriate international frame of reference in which to assess the present-day United States.

It is in the nature of such a volume that each reader engages the author in private dialogue. It is perhaps best to permit each reader to argue with *The Winding Passage* in his or her own way, without excessive intrusion by a reviewer. However, it is important to draw out the essential sociology with which he operates, for while Bell is frank enough to state that there is no unifying or singular architectonic to his work, the variety of themes addressed do add up to a genuine, if not entirely original, sociological framework. One of his major points, with which I am in full concurrence, is that we should worry less about the originality of a mind using theory to interpret and penetrate the social world.

There is in Bell a strong attack against holism, against viewing the world as a series of parts adding up to a teleologically determined whole. He argues instead that society is best understood as composed of diverse realms, each obedient to and situated within an axis, which in turn becomes the regulatory or normative principle that legitimates action in that field. Bell situates these realms in the economy, within the principle of functional efficiency; in the polity, with its principle of equality before the law; and in the principle of culture, or the enhancement and fulfillment of self. It is a special aspect of Bell's thought that he tends to be committed to personal fulfillment rather than social order. This identification with Marx rather than Durkheim on so fundamental an issue also separates him from the conservative mood with which he has so often and, in my view, so wrongly been identified by his critics. His emphasis on the cultural has another element, a disenchantment with much that passes for mainline sociology, a movement away from problems of the middle range into analysis that connects such issues as crime and deviance to larger patterns. It is interesting to note that these essays become longer and more complex as they move from concrete subjects, such as national character or national guilt, to the larger issues of the present period.

The final essays on the exhaustion of modernism might well stand as Bell's statement about the exhaustion of sociology. Bell's present pursuits are characterized by his groping for a new vocabulary. This search for new key words and trends, for new ways to gain a sense of the sacral, indicates his dissatisfaction with an earlier trinitarian model of economy, society, and culture. Although Bell does point the way toward an understanding of the problems in each realm, he has yet to explain how a new integration or, for that matter, a present disintegration of social scientific paradigms provides help in the pursuit of a new vocabulary. The groping and the lurching are brilliantly etched, but if they lead to a new theology rather than a new sociology, then I am not sure that I share the sense of purpose and challenge captured in this intellectual odyssey.

Bell's attack on C. Wright Mills in "Vulgar Sociology" is painfully on target. But unlike almost every other essay, it is pugnacious and ungenerous; it seems more a pique with another variety of essayist and moralist than a key statement of his paradigm. In an age of bubbling optimism and touching faith in the American century, Mills articulated a new pluralistic basis for leftist thought, a pragmatic vision, part of the debates on the left from which the excitement of the 1960s seemed to flow. (How strange it is that the excitement generated by intellectual debate is now taking place on the right.) Despite Mills's failure to appreciate the heterogeneity of government, the military, and business, and despite a line of analysis often flawed by amateurish emulators, this does not deprive Mills himself of moral sophistication in the midst of prevailing sociological orthodoxies. In the former he was unique, in the latter, alas, in a large company. Bell would have been better advised to sustain the pitch of grace and elegance captured in his other essays, rather than remind his readers of an earlier age, when bellicosity and anger toward one's opponents were more commonplace.

"Reflections on Jewish Identity" is the second essay that I had difficulty reconciling with the volume as a whole. Bell reflects the sorts of problems characteristic of many Jews who came from socialist and radical backgrounds; namely, an inability to appreciate that Judaism is not simply a religious supplement to an already rich ideological diet but itself a total perspective and framework for action. An embarrassing autobiographical excess ends up creating problems rather than explaining them, by emphasizing the moral travails of the author rather than actual conflicts within Judaism. We are rhetorically asked if we must accept a Jewish God, a jealous God: "Do I have to accept the sins of my fathers, and my children those of mine? This is not an academic question, for it confronts us everywhere." This is indeed an academic question. Jews are not expected to accept the sins of fathers or bequeath their sins to children. Accepted is the culture of the fathers, and bequeathed is the commitment of that culture. There is more of Sombart's Calvin than Scholem's Moses in Bell's sense of the Jewish. The "community [of Jews] woven by the thinning strands of memory" reflects more on Bell's weakening sense of community and his own reliance upon memory than the actual condition of Judaism. Bell missed a golden opportunity to move to a higher ground of synthesis by failing to explore in his own Judaism an analytic structure rather than a memory trace.

Bell is so widely regarded as a political figure in sociology, if not as a political sociologist, that it is surprising how little of the book treats political themes on either a national or international scale. His abilities with technological literature are unsurpassed, and his sense of the economic context of culture and the cultural texture of stratification is again flawless. But whether he is discussing utopian or ideological themes, the level of discourse is often twice, sometimes thrice, removed. Even when Bell examines prospects for mobilization of politics in the United States, it is within a context of the dissolution of "insulated space" as represented by "the contemporary revolutions of communication and transportation." Unlike Seymour Martin Lipset or Reinhard Bendix, on whom political science has had a profound impact, Bell has a deep commitment to the sociological paradigm in a pure and older fashion. Even his heroes (Veblen and Fourier) tend to reveal this. Bell is simply not taken with Machiavelli or Hobbes. It is how politics is affected by the economic and cultural realms, rather than the workings of the political process, that captures his attention. In this respect he is perhaps a purer variety of sociologist than his detractors have appreciated. Even in discussing the decline of authority, where political analysis would seem inevitable, categories remain distinctly Weberian: the status system of society, organizational life, institutional life, professional life, and cultural life. The political life as such is simply not much of a factor in this collection.

The strongest difference I have with Bell's essays is with his mood rather than content. The dark picture of a series of unresolved dialectical tugs may properly suit our epoch and certainly may explain the decline of the secular and the triumphal return of the sacral. Just as assuredly, within sociology few have better captured this sort of imagery. Only the essays of Edward Shils and Robert Nisbet come close. And perhaps dialectics seen as marginality is the proper posture and academic stance. My own preference is not to overidentify the pessimistic with the profound but to be more concerned with the character of the next synthesis than the structure of the present contradiction. In an ideal world of social theory, both tasks can and will be performed simultaneously; if a choice of strategies must be made, the search for new combinations, new ways of overcoming old dilemmas, the smashing of dialectical icons seems more appropriate to the tasks of our discipline. However, in the likely event that this optative mood may be little more than intellectual whistling in the dark, one can scarcely be better equipped to appreciate the cultural contradictions of the structures of ideologies that we live with than by reading and digesting these masterful essays.

When we move from Bell to Arendt we remove ourselves from primary concerns with ideology to basic interest in value. The American assault on holism yields to a European defense of holism. There is no doubt that Bell and Arendt represent quintessential types. Still, the linkages, although obscured by an ocean of language, are much greater and more profound than the disparities. Both shared a postfascist and postcommunist concern with the survival of democratic society. Both understood the moral bases of social action. Both returned to classical sources for a sense of personality survival in a world of technological no less than political dominations. Hence, to move from *The Winding Passage* to *The Life of the Mind* is much less jarring than might be anticipated. Indeed, it is the sense of common problems bequeathed by a century of war and a half century of extremisms that links two premier figures in contemporary social and political theory. They provide the organizing framework in a world grown weary of bloodless systems and lifeless formulas.

Arendt

The Life of the Mind[2] represents a culminating philosophic effort, alas not quite complete, but something less than one-third to be guessed at. Even stating the obvious is bound to create some misunderstanding, since Arendt disclaims being a philosopher or professional thinker. Indeed, publication of a large part of the first volume on *Thinking* in *The New Yorker* magazine, not to mention that the two volumes were issued by a widely respected but thoroughly commercial publisher, might lend some weight to such a disclaimer. But in fact, the work is thoroughly philosophical in the German classical tradition of Kant, Hegel, Nietzsche, and Heidegger. It is a measure of Hannah Arendt's justifiable fame as the author of such works as *The Origins of Totalitarianism, The Human Condition, On Revolution*, and *Eichmann in Jerusalem*, among others, that a work so demanding, so requiring intimacy with major figures of philosophical history, would receive wide hearing. Under the circumstances, one might well have anticipated commercial drivel from editor (Mary McCarthy) or publisher (William Jovanovich). It is to their lasting credit that no such posthumous exploitation is attempted. McCarthy's postface is entirely professional and pellucid. Everyone connected with this project exhibited at least one central element of good judgment ("judging" was to have constituted the final volume of this trilogy). That element is good taste.

The Life of the Mind picks up on themes first expressed two decades earlier in *The Human Condition*. The first two parts of the new work, offered as the Gifford Lectures for 1973 and 1974 respectively, seem to express polar opposites. The earlier work emphasized the active life, comprising what we do: labor, work, action. The new work involves the contemplative life: thinking, willing, and judging. But this triad is only superficially antithetical to the earlier one. Labor, work, and action are interconnected as biosocial activities, whereas thinking, willing, and judging occupy far more autonomous realms in the contemplative life. The triads remain, the polarities remain. But the special nature of philosophical activities is in asking unanswerable questions and hence establishing human beings as question-asking beings. In this way, Arendt sought to get beyond the atomism that afflicts the social sciences in particular—the search for the magical keys to the kingdom: *society* for sociology, *culture* for anthropology, *polity* for political science, *money* for economics, and *personality* for psychology. The magic key is less in the artifact, as stated in *The Human Condition*, than in the demystification of all artifacts, as in *The Life of the Mind*.

The temptation to examine this work as if it were flawed by virtue of being incomplete is not simple to resist. But there are so many broad hints, fragments from lectures, and outright statements on judgment, that the work can be examined as a complete effort. The relationships between thinking, willing, and judging are set forth early in the first volume. And like a profoundly risky move in chess, the disallowance of any intertranslation among the three categories drastically weakens the work. For instead of searching out areas of analytic linkages, that is, ways in which the act of thinking involves willing and judging, considering each of these aspects of a naturalistic theory of mind—perhaps along the lines of G. H. Mead or Y. H. Krikorian—we are required to see each aspect as a windowless monad. It is curious that this should be so, since Arendt was so familiar with Aristotle and the remarkable way a sense of emergence created linkages: biological issues into social, social into political, and political into ethical. Indeed, these basic categories have survived two thousand years, and if the contents of modern science are no longer Aristotelian, the twentieth-century impulse toward the unity of science remains inspired by the Greeks. This major dilemma notwithstanding, Arendt's work is such a mighty penetration into basic concepts that it transcends its own checkmate. She can at least claim a draw between the idealistic and naturalistic traditions that propel her work.

These volumes consecrate Hannah Arendt's lifework, even if they do not effect a synthesis of epistemology and ontology. For the essential statement in *Thinking*, made many times over as variation on the theme of mind, is the quintessential point about twentieth-century existence: that it is not the struggle between theory and action that is central but the struggle between theory and theory. Thinking is the hallmark of a free person living in a free society. To reduce action to behavior and then interpret behavior as if it were thought is for Arendt the shared fallacy of dialectical materialism on one hand and behavioral psychology on the other. For both, whether in the language of revolutionary act or operant conditioning, fail to understand that reducing thinking to doing is the end of the process of thought and the beginning of thought control and behavior modification.

In place of the casual slogan about theory and its issuance into practice, Arendt poses the question early on: "What are we 'doing' when we do nothing but think?" For the totalitarian temptation is to assume that those not engaged in the collective will, in the process of bringing about progress, are doing nothing. This is the metaphysical equivalent to the theological fear that idle hands make idle minds. The reduction of metaphysics to a form of poetry by the positivist tradition is in fact a call for the repudiation of speculation as a human activity in itself. Arendt shrewdly notes that the crisis in philosophy, ontology, theology, and social theory comes into being as a result of pronouncements by the intelligentsia itself. But what makes such premature "deaths" of disciplines so risky is that what begins as a disputation among intellectual elites concludes with popular disbelief in the worthiness of thinking as such.

> These modern "deaths"—of God, metaphysics, philosophy, and, by implication, positivism—have become events of considerable historical consequence, since, with the beginning of our century, they have ceased to be the exclusive concern of an intellectual elite and instead are not so much the concern as the common unexamined assumption of nearly everybody. With this political aspect of the matter we are not concerned here. In our context, it may even be better to leave the issue, which actually is one of political authority, outside our considerations, and to insist, rather, on the simple fact, however seriously our ways of thinking may be involved in this crisis, our *ability* to think is not at stake; we are what man has always been—thinking beings. . . . Men have an inclination, perhaps a need, to

think beyond the limitations of knowledge, to do more with this ability than use it as an instrument for knowing and doing. (2:109–10)

Bridling the will is no small matter. Its subjugation to reason is more than an indication that in the hierarchy of thinking, willing, and judging, willing comes in a distant third. That this portion of *The Life of the Mind* was completed, while only fragments of the portion on judging were done, should not confuse the reader into thinking that the will somehow mediates the claims of thought and taste. Arendt was forever the political philosopher par excellence; and unlike Kant, her sense of philosophic categories was filtered through twentieth-century awareness of totalitarianism. She saw will as clashing constantly with thinking. In her words, "the will always wills to do something and thus implicitly holds in contempt sheer thinking" (1:11–12). But more, this impulse to will translates itself into a constant search for the *novus ordo seclorum*. The will remains the final resting place of men of action. Such activists constantly demand new foundations, constantly destroy what was and is, in the name of the new and the yet to be. Perhaps in this Arendt's strong conservatism emerges; certainly her critique of the men of action would indicate such a predilection.

> There is something puzzling in the fact that men of action, whose sole intent and purpose was to change the whole structure of the future world and create a *novus ordo seclorum*, should have to go to that distant past of antiquity, for they did not "deliberately" [reverse] the time-axis and [bid] the young "walk back into the pure radiance of the past." . . . They looked for a paradigm for a new form of government in their own "enlightened" age and were hardly aware of the fact that they were looking backward. More puzzling, I think, than their actual ransacking of the archives of antiquity is that they did not rebel against antiquity when they discovered that the final and certainly profoundly Roman answer of "ancient prudence" was that salvation always comes from the past, that the ancestors were maiores, the "greater ones" by definition. (2:215)

But I suspect that more than conservatism is at stake. For theorists of the act, of freedom, always have a way of terminating their freedom with their own visions of society. Since for Arendt the capacity of beginning is rooted in the human capacity for renewal, it requires no end point. Terminus is not freedom but death, and in this sense freedom as system is a doomsday called utopia. That is why judgment becomes so important for her. For judgment makes transcendence of will possible, without a denial of reason. The aesthetic sense is not an accoutrement but a necessary faculty that tells people that what is perfect to one person or one ruler may be imperfect to another person or ruler and downright ugly to yet a third person and a third ruler. She locates the source of democratic survival in the pluralism of judgment.

What has consistently infuriated Neoplatonists and Marxists alike about the Kantian view of aesthetic judgment is its distinction between beauty or taste on one hand and applicability and moral purpose on the other. Arendt states the Kantian argument quite bluntly:

> If you say, What a beautiful rose! you don't arrive at this judgment by first saying, all roses are beautiful, this flower is a rose, hence it is beautiful. The other kind, dealt with in the *second part*, is the impossibility to derive any particular product of nature from general causes. . . . Mechanical in Kant's terminology means natural causes; its opposite is "technical" by which he means artificial. (2:256)

Judgment thus is concerned with that "enlargement of mind" that derives from evaluating "something fabricated with a purpose." But far from supporting an elitist vision of aesthetics or culture, Arendt drew precisely the opposite, namely a populist, conclusion. Taste is a community sense (*gemeinschaftlicher Sinn*), and hence while not all people are geniuses, all people are capable of rendering judgment. What is so terribly important about this populist vision of judgment as both autonomous from thinking and willing is that it provides the solution to the problem of democracy and also that basis of unity among the polis.

But Arendt still leaves us with a problem: the contradiction between the idea of progress as the law of the human species and the idea of human dignity as an inalienable, unchanging, normative aspect of individual human beings. This presumably would have formed the nexus of the third volume on judgment. For those to whom limitations on knowledge constitute a fact to be overcome rather than celebrated, the problem bequeathed by Kant, and now Arendt, is a challenge of no small magnitude or light consequence.

Arendt suffered a dialectical passion, or at least a commitment to the reality of reification: the warfare between thought and common sense, the Greek question and the Roman answer, the gap between the past and the future; thinking and doing; the active life and the contemplative life; the impotence of will versus the omnipotence of the will. This gives her writings a tremendous tension, a dramaturgical sensibility that has virtually disappeared in the empirical tradition. Perhaps that is why she can so readily and categorically dismiss Hume's dictum on reason being the slave of the passions as "simple minded," while Locke does only a trifle better as a believer in "the old tacit assumption of an identity of soul and mind." Indeed, the British empiricists fare less well at Arendt's hands than at those of her master, Kant.

It is to Kant that the work is really consecrated. For her divisions of thinking, willing, and judging derive in great measure from Kant's great works: *Critique of Practical Reason*, *Foundations of the Metaphysics of Morals*, and *Critique of Judgment*. And from the "Transcendental Dialectic" of the *Critique of Pure Reason* she drew the cardinal lesson: the insolubility of the nature of providence, freedom, and immortality by speculative thought. But what Arendt does, what is so unusual about her work, is that Kant's deadly logical purpose is infused with the excitement of Hegel's dialectical scaffold. Whether by intent or accident—and to know Hannah Arendt and her work is to know that scarcely a word, much less a concept, happens randomly—Kant is given the ultimate victory in the classical philosophical struggle. This is no cheap victory, but a victory over titans like Plato and Hegel. For Arendt, it is Kant who gives us conscience as a realm of freedom unto itself; it is Kant who understands that judgment is something that can be practiced but not taught; and it is Kant who sat astride of the will, uniquely understanding will as neither freedom of choice nor sheer spontaneity of activity. Kant's will becomes Arendt's will, "delegated by reason to be its executive organ in all matters of conduct" (2:84–85). Karl Popper's proponents of the closed society (Plato and Hegel) now meet their match in Arendt's proponent of the open society (Kant).

Arendt points to a great divide in modern scientific quests: on the one hand it is the positivist quest for truth; and on the other it is the rationalist quest for meaning. For her, it is a basic fallacy to confound the two, a fallacy that even figures like Heidegger fall prey to. The distinction between the urgent need to think and the desire to know is an operational way of distinguishing thinking from doing. And here, although the Greeks are called upon to bear witness to this distinction, I daresay it is Arendt's Jewishness that provides the missing link. For it is the historical role of the Jews to search and not find redemption and the redeemer, in contrast to the truth announced by Christianity of redemption through the son of God, that really distinguishes Arendt's claims for thinking as the ultimate act.

Here one must confess to a strange myopia in Arendt, an all-too-conventional vision of the history of philosophy as a movement from the Greeks to the Romans to the Christians to the medieval Schoolmen, and finally to the Germans. But such a mechanical rendition of the history of philosophy fails to explain why Heidegger the existentialist falls prey to the same error as Carnap the positivist. Why does the metaphysical impulse to certainty take precedence over epistemological distinctions? Is not the answer at least in part located in the shared scientific vision of the age, in which the quest for meaning is seen as less urgent than the delivery of truth, even the imposition of truth on nonbelievers, infidels, and heathens? Perhaps in the third volume on judgment such matters would have been addressed. I suspect otherwise. Having rejected the philosophic dialogue as written by opponents of the open society as the life of the mind, she was left powerless to cope with the betrayal of that life in its post-Kantian phase. The elementary forms of democratic expression are put forth as being in mortal combat with the evolutionary Nazi and historical Bolshevik forms of antidemocracy. The allies of the demos are left disarmed, so to speak, wrecked by intellectuals announcing the death of intellect.

There was a time when one would have had to shuffle in embarrassment for considering a metaphysical work in a volume of essays on sociology. But these are not such times. With figures such as Marx, Mead, and Husserl anchoring major tendencies in current sociology, no apologetics for reading such a masterful treatise is required, nor need it be hidden under sociological pillows. To be sure, those who represent phenomenological, symbolic interactionist, and humanistic varieties of sociology will probably be far more attracted to this pair of volumes than advocates of behavioral, functional, or physicalist sociologies. But to disentangle a potential audience for such an undertaking is aptly evocative of what Professor Arendt understands as the topsy-turvy world of action and theory.

The Marxian and existentialist notions, which play such a great role in twentieth-century thought and pretend that man is his own producer and maker, rest on these experiences, even though it is clear that nobody has "made" himself or "produced" his existence; this, I think, is the last of the metaphysical fallacies, corresponding to the modern age's emphasis on willing as a substitute for thinking. . . . And this is of some relevance to a whole set of problems of theory and practice and to all attempts to arrive at a halfway plausible theory of ethics. Since Hegel and Marx, these questions have been treated in the perspective of History and on the assumption that there is such a thing as Progress of the human race. Finally we shall be left with the only alternative there is in these matters—we either can say with Hegel: *Die Weltgeschichte ist das Weltgericht*, leaving the ultimate judgment to Success, or we can maintain with Kant the autonomy of the minds of men and their possible independence of things as they are or as they have come into being. (1:215–16)

As long as thinking, willing, and judging are viewed as three basic mental activities that "cannot be derived from each other" and that "cannot be reduced to a common denominator," the very edifice Arendt attempts is subject to the same criticisms as any other absolutism. In twentieth-century terms, her work consecrates the collapse of acceptable paradigms in social science and philosophy. Hence the trinity of thinking, willing, and judging can do no more than confront each other in field after field, discipline after discipline. But if Arendt did not effect the grand synthesis (nor does she claim at any point to be after such a holy grail), she sheds a great light on what is ailing our social and behavioral disciplines. We at least know what the sources of division are with a precision and a clarity that make possible new creativity. And that is ultimately what the life of the free mind is all about.

It is ironic that the author of *Eichmann in Jerusalem* should also be a supreme devotee of German high culture. For there can be no mistaking that in philosophy, law, and politics, Hannah Arendt was a complete product of the German Enlightenment. The century has been rolled back with these volumes: as if Hitler and nazism had not happened, as if German liberal thought were an unbroken chain of continuities. But this is not the case. And Arendt in her towering works has been a prime mover in enabling us to understand the essence of the totalitarian persuasion. But at the last, she remained true to the tradition of German liberalism. The French language that she loved counted for little more than a Cartesian footnote; the English constitutional tradition, which surely nourished her faith in compassionate justice over and against impassioned (nonrational) vengeance, counted for little. Russian democratic thought from Herzen to Solzhenitsyn scarcely existed for her. And perhaps most shattering to those who saw her primarily as a Jewish writer, the Hebrew tradition is reduced to several hyphenated footnotes to Christian theology. In the end, in the long pull, this remarkable woman, scholar, critic, exile, and teacher turns out to be not an avenging angel remorselessly pursuing her totalitarian quarry but the last loving product of German Enlightenment: the keeper of a flame she herself had helped resurrect from the charnel house of postwar Europe. The dialectical process is indeed mysterious and insoluble, as Kant insisted. It brought forth, fifty years late, in a foreign language, by an exile from Nazi repression, the last hurrah of the Weimar Republic and Central Europe.

Talmon

A special group of Central European Jewish intellectuals has helped define the nature of twentieth-century social and political life, giving shape to destructive potentials of our age only dimly understood by those who worshiped at the altar of absolute progress. Central to neither class enthusiasms below nor national hubris above, these people—actually outsiders—possessed a keen insight into the driving forces of the times, notably the unitary character of the totalitarian threat, the tragic gap between promise and performance in the revolutionary process, and the failure of internationalist rhetoric to resolve national realities.

These émigrés from Berlin, Vienna, Warsaw, Budapest, and their environs were, for the most part, not speaking and writing from a conservative bias or defending constitutional tradition; there was little to defend in the world of crumbling empires in Central Europe. They were not concerned with restitution or restoration of an old order, for they knew old orders to be a threat to their own survival as Jews, intellectuals, and cosmopolitans. They often discussed socialism and left-wing democracy. They were motivated by a passion for economic justice and elementary forms of democratic rule. Their involvement with the socialist dream, minus the maddening character of socialist practice, gave these people a special rhetoric. Among this group were such persons as Hannah Arendt, Hans J. Morgenthau, Hans Kohn, Franz Neumann, George Lichtheim, Walter Laqueur, Henry Pachter—and Jacob L. Talmon.

Jacob Talmon (who died in 1981) was the author of many works. *The Myth of the Nation and the Vision of Revolution*[3] is a key one. It is the final volume of a trilogy on two hundred years of modern political life begun a quarter of a century ago with *The Origins of Totalitarian Democracy* and followed a decade later with *Political Messianism*. This, in my judgment, is the best of the three volumes. In fact, it is nothing less than a masterpiece. Here Talmon brings us to the twentieth century and ideological polarization, its central feature. In its eclecticism, it seems less a "thesis book" than the previous volumes, less concerned with establishing a tension based on dialectical opposites that were not quite as polarized as Talmon imagined—such as democracy and totalitarianism or empirical politics and messianic relations. The complex nature of the political fabric sometimes got lost in earlier volumes of the trilogy. In *The Myth of the Nation*, Talmon displays a much greater sensitivity to the wide disparities that exist within the same thinkers, the same nations, and the same classes.

Talmon did not write in any conventional sense; strictly speaking, he transcended dynastic history and social history. His is a special kind of intellectual history: history as written by political ideologists who were either politicians or close enough to the political marrow to inform practicing politicians. *The Origins of Totalitarian Democracy* was peopled with figures of the Enlightenment such as Rousseau, Helvétius, and Diderot, and with great political actors such as Robespierre, Danton, and Saint-Just. *Political Messianism* ranged from technocrats to theocrats, from

Saint-Simon to Blanqui, who were in and of themselves both political actors and intellectual leaders. *The Myth of the Nation* continues in this tradition; major figures include Marx and Engels, Lenin and Trotsky, and, in Western Europe, Mussolini and Hitler and their intellectual progenitors. Talmon weaves a tight interchange among social, political, and intellectual events, breaking down conventional distinctions that usually impede rather than enhance a sense of history.

Few genuinely heroic figures appear in Talmon's work, and those who continually announce a utopian future are dealt with severely. That is true for Marx, Engels, and Lenin in the current volume no less than for Saint-Simon, Babeuf, and Fourier in the previous volumes. But there does emerge in *The Myth of the Nation* a sense of the political leader as intellectual but not ideologist—and this offers insight into Talmon and his notion of who constitute the political prophets of peace and war. In the figure of Jean Jaurès, the nineteenth-century French socialist, one can sense Talmon's archetype. He describes Jaurès as having had a passion for fairness, an extraordinary poetic capacity for empathy, a marvelous quickness of sympathy and imaginative insight, combined with an unmatched gift for words. Talmon had those qualities. Those who knew him realized that his concerns were those of Jaurès: a life of intellect and politics tempered by a survivalist attitude toward society. Talmon also read into Jaurès what was true of himself: that these very characteristics made him yield easily to inferior men with narrower horizons or limited understanding but greater self-assurance. Fanaticism and dogmatism, and not just democratic dogma, were the true enemies of both Jaurès and Talmon.

The Myth of the Nation is divided into nine parts, which I shall summarize briefly here. The work begins with the growing dichotomization of class or nation that took place after the revolutions of 1848. Talmon gives particular emphasis to the dilemmas involved in postutopian socialist thinking on the role of the nation in the development of a revolutionary strategy based on pure class assumptions. The work then moves dramatically to the world of Germany under Wilhelm I in the late nineteenth century, in which the question of the emancipation of the proletariat is dwarfed by the issue of national destiny. Europe between 1848 and 1914 was driven by national cohesion more than class emancipation. Whether in Germany or Russia, Talmon saw revolutionary internationalism as the tenuous thread in the face of an overpowering demand for national separatism and survival. The third section of the book, which discusses Austria, is another case study of the issue of class or nation. The Austrian experience, while limited in global terms, was in fact prototypical with respect to what took place in Europe in the rest of the twentieth century. The fourth part takes up the special role of the Jewish dimension. Talmon tells us that although the Jewish role in European history was hardly new, Jews did become dramatically significant during the early part of the twentieth century. And, he says, the encounter between Jew and gentile, even more than the encounter of the gentile with the Jew, was first as a bourgeois adversary and second as a communist enemy. The Jew appeared as the extreme example, an unstable element in the nationalist equation. The inability of large portions of European society to handle situations in which the Jew became a spokesman for both the forces contesting each other led to a breakdown of Enlightenment and Romantic rhetoric. As Jews became archetypes, animosities against them crystallized from both the left and the right. Consequently, they became "the enemy" for national and class ideologies and interests, a source of tension rather than resolution. And as extremism became the order of the day, Jewish centrism, along with gentile liberalism, became identified as the main foe.

The fifth and sixth parts analyze how the dilemma between class and nation was finally resolved in pre- and post-revolutionary Russian practice. The seventh deals with how the general will of the proletariat was translated by Lenin and Stalin into a particular Russian national will. The last two sections point to the alternative fascist-Nazi resolution of class and nation, which emphasized the national question beyond that of class. The fascists spotted the weakness in classical Marxism, its denial and denigration of nationalism, and their ideologists proved pivotal in developing a theory of socialism based on ultranationalist considerations. Nationalism, according to Talmon, permitted and even encouraged alliances between communists and fascists. It was also the factor that made the clash within Europe inevitable. Finally, Talmon takes up the hard questions of the nature of post–World War II problems in a spirit of tentativeness. But the themes of Third World development and modernization are clearly beyond the ken of his world view. He does not ask: What is the role of Western democratic forms with respect to Third World demands for political equality? What is the place of the Soviet Union as midwife to national liberation movements and new totalitarian systems? What military formations are taking place in the Third World? What are the inner tensions within energy-rich and food-poor developing areas? The strictly European context of his thought offers few clues, much less firm answers.

Talmon's last work projects a feeling that the new world is unfolding, a world unfamiliar to him and his European colleagues. In that sense, *The Myth of the Nation and the Vision of Revolution*, his final book, is a fitting conclusion not only to a personal career of outstanding brilliance but also to the end of a social epoch, one in which the European sensibility could still impose cultural order upon social chaos. Talmon understood that his epoch began with the demands of the French Revolution for both a revolutionary process and democratic goals implemented from above. In his world, Europe became a center of political, social, and economic experimentation. A rising tide of new social classes tested Europe's commitment to transnational economic involvements in contrast to strictly national political goals. Finally, in Talmon's own century, nations destroyed all visions of class solidarity, much less of human brotherhood, and in so doing deprived Europe of the opportunity to fulfill its highest and noblest dreams.

Talmon's work deserves careful scrutiny. Whatever one thinks about his treatment of particular themes, he provides remarkable insight into an era of European preeminence that no longer exists and that can no longer determine the fate of worlds. Yet though the old conflicts may not have much bite, there may still be lessons to be learned in the development of a strange and bland pan-Europeanism: lessons about the value of pluralism and survival in the face of struggles that seem insuperable and unending. That the price of the pacification of Europe proved so terribly high, taking a toll in so many millions of lives, can only be reflected upon with a deep sense of tragedy. Still, a sense of triumph emerges from the rubble. Talmon's trilogy informs us of the high risks and improbable outcome of all forms of fanaticism. Perhaps the non-European world will profit by these lessons, but the chances of this happening, as Talmon himself makes perfectly clear, seem slim given the imperviousness of new nations to the history of older nations. It is on a note of sorrow that the present volume (and the trilogy) is concluded. The passing of a great man is heralded by the passing of an entire historical era.

What we are left with is not a consensus on policy or even a unified field theory of society. Rather, Bell, Arendt, and Talmon provide us with a series of sensitizing concepts best expressed by the word *conscience*. Their shared appreciation of the rise and fall of societies, of the normative characteristics of individuals and their need to remain intact during these societal undulations and upheavals, and of the moral bases of judgment if not of behavior forms a chain of sensibilities no less than analyticities. But the more subtle point of it all is that nothing comes easy: moral probity may carry with it psychological obtuseness, whereas historical relativity may carry with it personal paralysis.

The dialectic of life is a felt tension, not a set of silly formulas about quantity and quality, about negations of negation. The life worth living is built upon conscience because conscience alone permits an appreciation of experienced dilemmas and their excruciating nuances, survivalist victories in the face of widespread annihilations, comedies built upon the quicksand of tragedies, bitter personal defeats snatched from the jaws of apparent victory. The universe alive contains possibilities for all things save its own destruction and annihilation. And it is the lesson bequeathed to us by Bell, Arendt, and Talmon (and others like Aron, Lichtheim, and Halevy) that personal conscience, untrammeled by imposed authority and tradition, is the ultimate guarantor of human survival. Conscience makes possible living in a world of victories and defeats because it alone permits an understanding of their ontological permanence. Beyond individual conscience is not social practice but only collective death: the end of conscience is the end of history, and the end of history is the end of the world as we know it. Guard conscience and the possibilities of survival, even growth, remain firmly intact. This then is the message of rootless cosmopolitanism, against which the thundering hordes of rooted nationalism are pitted in remorseless struggle. And as long as the struggle continues, we all have a chance.

Part III. Ideology

17. Left-wing Fascism

Vladimir Lenin issued in 1920 a stunning pamphlet on left-wing communism. Several decades later, a left-wing fascism has materialized, and the concerns of this essay are how, like its predecessor, it deserves to be characterized as "an infantile disorder." It was easy for Lenin to recombine elements in political society to forge new theories, yet it seems terribly painful for his followers to do likewise. For Lenin, the Bolshevik struggle was two-sided, chiefly against opportunism and social chauvinism, but also against petty bourgeois revolutionaries operating on anarchist premises. Lenin's own words, in *"Left-Wing" Communism: An Infantile Disorder*, are equally appropriate to the conditions of the 1980s:

> The petty bourgeois, "driven to frenzy" by the horrors of capitalism, is a social phenomenon which is characteristic of all capitalist countries. The instability of such revolutionariness, its barrenness, its liability to become swiftly transformed into submission, apathy, fantasy, and even a frenzied infatuation with one or another bourgeois "fad"—all this is a matter of common knowledge. But a theoretical, abstract recognition of these truths does not at all free revolutionary parties from old mistakes, which always crop up at unexpected moments, in a somewhat new form, in hitherto unknown vestments or surroundings, in peculiar—more or less peculiar—circumstances.[1]

My statement will discuss a similar infantile disorder in the context of United States political life in the 1980s, a disorder so profound that it is properly characterized in post-Leninist terms as left-wing fascism.

Fascism is not simply a political condition but is brought about by rooted psychological dislocations; these, linked to larger concerns, exercise an independent dynamic. The very term *infantile disorder* sharply focuses on the subjective qualities of fascism. Even a politically oriented analyst such as Leon Trotsky speaks, in *The Struggle against Fascism in Germany*, of the cycle of fascism as "yearning for change . . . extreme confusion . . . exhaustion of the proletariat . . . growing confusion and indifference . . . despair . . . collective neurosis . . . readiness to believe in miracles . . . readiness for violent measures."[2] While these characteristics are invariably linked to a social class, a constant fusion-fission effect characterizes the momentum toward fascism. These terms also describe religious-political movements like Sun Myung Moon's Unification church and political-religious movements like Lyndon LaRouche's National Caucus of Labor Committees (NCLC), whose name was changed to the United States Labor party (USLP).

It would be foolish, even dangerous, to suppose that a set of psychological variables or political positions determines disposition toward fascism. However, appeals to authority, tradition, or the mystique of nation, blood, or race are necessary preconditions. Ideological denunciation of appeals to evidence, discourse, rationality, individual conscience, decision reversals, or consensus for specific policies are also characteristic. Rejection of these elements of psychic or intellectual conditioning is a key factor in determining a propensity toward fascism. If the success or failure rate of fascism has to do with economic dysfunctions and political systems, preconditions for fascism have to do with social psychology, the mass psychology of a people. Inroads of cults into American life provide somber evidence of a propensity toward fascism.

We have so taken for granted distinctions among left, right, and center that it has become difficult to perceive new combinations of these categories. New practical political integrations disquieting to the liberal imagination are hard to absorb. If Lenin was correct in his criticism of left-wing European communism for its exaggerated emphasis on purity at the expense of victory and on vanguard putschism at the expense of mass participation, similar phenomena of a different ideological persuasion are taking place in America. The purpose of this essay is to suggest the character of this recombination of political categories: how it functions in American life not simply to alter the nature of marginal politics but also to affect mainline political decision making.

While my analysis is largely confined to United States conditions, the state of affairs I call left-wing fascism is an international phenomenon. The following examples are illustrative. Massimiliano Fanchini was arrested in connection with the Bologna bombing. He first drew attention as part of a Palestine Solidarity committee, which he helped organize with another fascist, Franco Fredo, who was jailed for killing sixteen people in Milan in 1969. Claudio Mutti, known as the "Nazi academic" because of his post at the University of Parma, founded the Italian-Libyan Friendship Society and helped publish speeches by the Ayatollah Khomeini in Italian. The supposedly leftist Baader-Meinhof gang, which earlier only lectured the Palestine Liberation Organization on the need for armed struggle, bought its first load of small arms from the neo-Nazi Bavarian underground. Christopher Hitchens, foreign editor of the *New Statesman*, noted in a recent article: "There is a small and squalid area in which nihilists of left and right meet and intersect. There is a cross-fertilization, especially in Italy. Fascists often borrow demagogic leftist titles. One of the agreements facilitating this incest is a hatred of Israel; the other one is a hatred of democracy and a mutual conviction that Fascist/Communist takeover will only hasten a Fascist/Communist victory."[3]

Chaotic Ancestry

Like all movements, left-wing fascism has a somewhat chaotic ancestry. Foremost is what might be called the later Frankfurt school, which emphasized in an uneasy mix the early Marx and the late Hegel and which was most frequently, if not necessarily properly, identified with the works of Adorno. The characteristics of the Frankfurt school derive from Adorno's strong differentiation between mass culture and elite culture, and his concern with the massification of society in general. For the first time in the history of Marxism, Adorno addressed a strong attack on mass culture. The obscurantist-elitist aspects of Adorno's *later*, post–World War II work does not refer to the democratic socialist analysis of the Frankfurt school offered by Franz Neumann, Max Horkheimer, and Herbert Marcuse, among others. Nor does it even refer to Adorno's efforts at developing a political psychology while he was working in America on the "Authoritarian Personality" project. But to deny the antipopular and teutonic characteristics of Adorno's later works, worshipfully introduced in English by British and American scholars who should have known better, is to deny the obvious—and the dangerous.

Whether it be popular music or popular art, there is a clear notion in Adorno's work that mass culture is tasteless, banal, and regressive. His assumption is that such culture evolves in some abstract sense through commercialization of social classes and the existence of a worthless society. This critique is pointless since the emotional assault is on the masses for having such a culture. In many respects, Adorno thus sets the stage for a culture of left-wing fascism, which represents an attack on the popular organs of society for being what they are and a corresponding elitist demand that they be otherwise, that is, purified.

The Adorno line of reasoning, its critical negativism, assumes that what people believe is wrong and that what they ought to believe, as designed by some narrow elite stratum of the cultural apparatus, is essentially right. With Adorno, the theory of vanguard politics is carried over into the theory of vanguard culture. The cultural apparatus is blamed for the elevation of mass culture into high culture. Attention given the so-called Frankfurt school in present radical circles derives not from its origins in antitotalitarian and anti-Nazi activities but rather from its elitist outcomes: attacks and assaults on masses and their culture. The prewar Frankfurt school, with its emphasis on rationality as the basis of revolution, was corrupted in the hands of Adorno. It became a doctrine of rationality as cultural traditionalism. In this way, Adorno became central to the thinking of the avant-garde of left-wing fascism.

A second element of this belief characteristic of left-wing fascism is Marxism as praxis—or without Marx, and sometimes without Lenin. This results in what might be called praxis theory or action theory. It does away with the need for either an economic base to revolution, essential for Marx, or the political base of organization held essential by Lenin. What remains is a residual sentiment favoring revolutionary mysticism. The vaguely anarchical assumption is that the sum total of what one really needs is an action group, some kind of organized group or *foco*, usually clandestine, to create sufficient chaos or destruction of the state and society in selected periods of the capitalist economy. The combination of economic chaos and political protest will in itself somehow produce revolutionary action. Multinational terrorism will move into a breach, presumably magically offsetting the multinational economy.

This is often called the Cuban model of revolution, inspired by the works of Régis Debray. The transposition of a model from a small island like Cuba, with its special conditions of single-crop socialism, is quite difficult. What was originally a theory for social change in Cuba becomes enlarged into a universal theory of change; one is left with a "theory" of the vital force. The theory of the putsch, the clandestine conspiratorial small group capable of seizing power at the proper moment, is common to fascism and until recently was not associated with Marxism. The theory of the *foco*, or revolutionary focus, first reduces Marxism by stripping away its sense of economic forces of oppression, then by stripping away its emphasis on the political sources of organization, and finally by stripping away its mass base. One is left with a theory of small group conspiracy, or terrorism in the name of Marxism, rather than a theory of Marxism as a source of social change and revolutionary action involving broad masses.

A third vital pivot is nationalism, in which the demand for revolutionary change is lodged in patriotic claims of the total system, a demand for the moment, having nothing to do with history and antecedents. Such a nationalist approach insists on spontaneity and is not necessarily linked with historical forces or recurring patterns. At this level left-wing fascism is fused to a theory of anarcho-syndicalism. The nationalist pivot involves not so much a doctrine of liberation as a doctrine of activity uninhibited by the need for social analysis. It is predicated on a notion of will and action at the correct moment to preserve the nation against its real or presumed enemies.

Other elements in the nationalist tradition fit into this left-wing fascist model: that every ordinary individual craves order over chaos; that one does not need a special theory of society to achieve revolutionary action; that individual economic origins are less important than social roles. These elements from Pareto, Sorel, and Mosca are incorporated into a left-wing fascist interpretation of the world, in which psychological mass contagion replaces social history as the interpretation of human events.

The sources of left-wing fascism are not abstract. Those who are enamored with appraisals of American society that seek immediate gratification and relief from ailments have become innovative in organizational form no less than ideological norms. Seeking ways to effect social change regardless of scientific or social base is the key to left-wing fascism. The effort to enlarge the cult into a state religion, the attempt to impose order and leadership on a society that seems purposively leaderless and fragmented, is characteristic of fascism—right or left, religious or secular.

In left-wing fascism we are dealing not so much with the notions of traditional political involvement or traditional minor political parties but with the notion of the act as the primary determinant of both political means and ends. This involves inspiring others while servicing the needs of the actors, whether one is talking about special groups of nationalists or extreme self-styled radical groups seeking direct confrontation with other radical groups. The very act of confronting the enemy replaces any sense of organization or systems analysis. Action determines and defines one's place in the hierarchy of a political movement. In left-wing fascism the guerrilla movement replaces the clandestine bund as the organizational vehicle. But its impact is not simply to be dismissed because of its barricade orientation. The latter provides the basis for the militarization of politics, its decivilianization, a central precondition to the fascist seizure of power.

Elitism and Populism

The main political source of left-wing fascism is its strange denial of America and the democratic system, together with the assertion of socialism as an abstraction. Left-wing fascists have the unique capacity to examine socialism without comment on the activities of the Soviet Union. They talk about the United States rather than about the loss of democracy. There is an inversion: the search for socialism becomes close to an abstract utopian ideal, but when it comes to a discussion of democracy, discourse is critically and severely linked to the United States as a nation-state. The rhetoric constantly shifts. So-called enemies are unambiguously identified as the United States and its allies. When dealing with its own allies, however, left-wing fascism turns socialism into a generalized hypothesis rather than concrete forms of socialism as they are expressed throughout the world. What Adorno appropriately called the "collectivization and institutionalization of the spell" becomes the new fascist norm.[4]

Left-wing fascism accepts socialism as an abstraction but rejects socialist practice and reality, and hence critique as a source of democratic renewal. The history of fascism in the United States mirrors that of Europe. Socialism, far from being dropped, becomes incorporated into the national dream, into a dramaturgy for redemption, for a higher civilization that will link nationhood and socialism in a move forward. This combination of words, *national* and *social*, generates a new volatility. These two words together can arouse stronger and more active participation than either of the concepts taken separately.

The weakness of traditional right-wing organizations is that they asserted the primacy and value of Americanism as nationalism apart from socialist values. The weakness of traditional forms of leftism is that they have asserted socialism over and against American or national values. The potential strength of left-wing fascism, such as that practiced by the NCLC, is its unique combination, its ability to see how these concepts of Americanism and socialism can operate together as a mobilizing device in the development of a new fascist social order. The unique characteristic of left-wing fascism is its capacity, like its European antecedent, to combine very different ideological strains, traditional right-wing and traditional left-wing behavior, and come up with a political formula that, if it has not yet generated a mass base, has at least the potential for mass appeal.

The contents of left-wing fascism are heavily based on an elitist vision of the world. At every level of society it juxtaposes its minoritarianism against majoritarianism. It may take libertarian or authoritarian forms, but it always defends its leadership vision over any populist vision. Some examples are the hip versus the square, the gay versus the straight, the individualistic free soul versus the family-oriented slave, those who believe in the cult of direct action versus the fools who participate in the political process, those who practice nonviolence over those who assert willfulness and violence as measures of human strength and courage, those who have strong affiliations with cults and cultism over and against the traditional nonbeliever (a marked departure from the antitheological vision of most forms of leftist and socialist behavior), those who argue the case for deviance over and against mainline participation in the working class or in segments of class society, those who choose underground organizations in preference to established voluntary organizations, and ultimately, those who choose some type of deracinated behavior over and against class behavior and participation.

Historically, communists, like fascists, have had an uncomfortable attraction to both elitism and populism. The theory of vanguards acting in the name of the true interests of the masses presupposes a higher science of society (or in the case of fascism, a biology of society) than that susceptible to being reached by ordinary citizens. The superstructure of science, like culture generally, becomes a realm in which elites act in the name of the public. What happens to the notion of the people determining their own history in their own way? Here populism, or pseudopopulism, steps in to fuse formerly antagonistic trends. In some mysterious, inexplicable manner, these mass forces must be shaped or molded. Under communism, in sharp contrast to fascism, the stratification elements in the national culture are deemed unique or uniquely worth salvaging. But in the anti-ideological climate of the "new world," people (class) and folk (race) blend, becoming the raw materials for fashioning the new society.

Left-wing fascism does not so much overcome this dilemma of elitism and populism as it seeks to harness both under the rubric of a movement. Having its roots in the 1960s, left-wing fascism views the loose movement, the focus, the force, as expanding upon the fascist élan and the communist vanguard. It permits a theory of politics without the encumbrance of parties. It allows, even encourages, a culture of elitism and crackpot technocism, as in the LaRouche emphasis on computer technology as a general ideology, while extolling the virtues of a presumed inarticulate mass suffering under inscrutable false consciousness.[5] The mystification and debasement of language displaces the search for clarity of expression and analysis, enabling a miniscule elite to harness the everyday discontent of ordinary living into a grand mission. Left-wing fascism becomes a theory of fault, locating the question of personal failure everywhere and always in an imperial conspiracy of wealth, power, or status.[6]

Fascism requires a focal point of hatred to unify behind. Thus, when fascists advocate anti-Semitism, they are simply using a tactic. It becomes not simply a tactic of fascism, nor is it opposed by communism. It becomes a modality of affixing blame, of finally locating the enemy. As a consequence, left-wing fascism operates in the climate of a post-Nazi holocaust, a post-Stalinist Gulag, and a monopoly of petroleum wealth by forces historically antagonistic to Jewish ambitions. The new left-wing fascist segments, weak within the nation, can draw great strength from "world forces" deemed favorable to its cause. The unitary character of anti-Semitism draws fascist and communist elements together in a new social climate. Anti-Semitism is the essential motor of left-wing fascism. The grand illusion of seeing communism and fascism as polarized opposites, the latter being evil with a few redeeming virtues, the former being good with a few historical blemishes, is the sort of liberal collapse that reduces analysis to nostalgia—an abiding faith in the unique mission of a communist left that has long lost its universal claims to a higher society. This catalog of polarities, this litany of beliefs, adds up to a life-style of left-wing fascism. Isolating any of these reified frameworks may lead to the conclusion that the dangers are less than catastrophic. But in this panoply of beliefs and practices, one finds the social sources of left-wing fascist participation and belief.

Even in the formation of the new left in the 1960s, the roots of a left-wing fascist formulation were in evidence. Now, in a more pronounced form, what has evolved is a strong shift from a class, party, or movement concept characteristic of the sixties and the cries of cultism.[7] We have cults not only in the strictly religious sense but in the political sense as well—marginal movements gaining small numbers of adherents but having a profound impact on the edges of society. Like the Nazi movement in the early 1920s, these left-wing fascist movements of the 1980s, such as the LaRouche organization and various socialist parties, are considered too small and inconsequential to have any impact on the body politic. But the danger to the society as a whole is that as the active element in the political process shrinks, this fringe becomes increasingly important. They do have sufficient numbers for a seizure of power once one takes into account that they do rely for victory on technology and not numbers. They rely on organization, swift movement, willfulness, and the ability to seize the critical moment. In this sense, left-wing fascist movements are not unlike the Nazi movement of the early twenties; although weak, marginal, and leaderless, they are in fact very much part of a social scene marked by powerful economic dislocations and putschist tendencies in segmented political processes.[8]

Once left-wing fascism is seen as an authoritarian effort to destroy the legitimacy of the established system—a series of diminutions in voting participation, party affiliation, and faith in parliamentary systems and the achievement of social goals in an honorable and honest manner—then the potential of left-wing fascism becomes manifest. This also represents a decline in traditional socialist fallback positions of mass action, mass participation, and ultimately mass revolution. That collapse of trust in the popular sectors corresponds to the collapse in party sectors. What might be called the bourgeois or political parliamentary pivot on one hand and the popular or revolutionary pivot on the other are both viewed by left-wing fascism as a snare and a delusion, a mechanism for postponing the social revolution that is going to provide the cures to all ailments and remove all the temptations of ordinary people. Left-wing fascism ultimately represents the collapse of bourgeois and proletarian politics alike.[9] It is not only the end of ideology in the traditional sense, or an end to participation in the political process, but an end of ideology even in the socialist sense of adherence to revolutionary processes that ultimately promise organized change and social justice.

End of Ideology

Left-wing fascism assaults both mass and class notions of legitimacy, both Jeffersonian and Leninist visions of the world, both the rational discourse and the popular participation models. Left-wing fascism is that unique rejection of both elements and the incorporation of nationalism from the bourgeois ideology and utopianism from the proletarian ideology. These rejections and absorptions define the four-part paradigm of left-wing fascism: for nationalism in general; for socialism in general; against parliamentarianism in particular; against organized political parties in particular.

Left-wing fascism is much more than a political psychology. It develops direct-action frameworks in terms of specific modes of insurgency techniques and connects them to the tradition of fascism and extreme nationalism. There is a strong element of racism and anti-Semitism in this movement, cleverly rendered by a "dialectical" pitting of Jews and blacks in archetypical terms. There is a further belief that the black movement must be subordinate to the class structure of American life and that blacks who see their own national destinies apart from this new movement are suspect. This leitmotiv of disdain toward successful blacks remains muted. The anti-Semitic modality is overt and made manifest first by its fashionable currency in the Soviet Union and the Middle East.[10] Historically, fascism has had a strong component of anti-Semitism: conviction of the need to liquidate the Jew as a political and economic entity and ultimately even as a biological entity. The easy glide from anti-Israeli to anti-Semitic visions has become part of the international left-wing rhetoric of our day. To move one large step further to left-wing fascism by utilizing anti-Semitism as a pivot becomes relatively simple, especially in the context of policy ambiguity concerning the legitimate claims of contending forces for national homelands.

Common wisdom has it that the most virulent forms of fascism in the twentieth century took anti-Semitic overtones. Less known but equally plain is that in light of Soviet politics from the end of World War II in 1945 until the present, anti-Semitism has been a leitmotiv of the Soviet system. There is no need here to argue whether anti-Semitism is at the center or periphery of Soviet orthodoxy. That such a controversy can even exist indicates the breadth and depth of anti-Semitism as a potent force in current affairs: it is the point at which the fascist and communist hemispheres are joined. Anti-Semitism is the cement providing a crossover from right to left in terms of both ideology and personnel.

The anti-bourgeois character of both fascism and communism in an American context has now extended to an assertion of anti-Semitism as a prototype of that anti-bourgeois sentiment. Probably for the first time, Jews rather than the customary Italians and Turks are now being blamed for drug traffic, with the consequent coming together of strange bedfellows. Again, we are led back to our prototypical organization, Lyndon LaRouche's group and its adherents. Despite the most manifest forms of racist appeal, LaRouche managed a united front with Wallace Muhammad, who in turn took the Black Muslims away from a black emphasis to an Islamic identification.

The effectiveness of the NCLC is seen most clearly in electoral activity and in the organization's success in building single-issue alliances with forces as diverse as the ultra-right-wing and anti-Semitic Liberty Lobby, the Black Muslims, and conservative-oriented Teamster union officials. . . . LaRouche and Black Muslim leader Wallace Muhammad formed an "Anti-Drug Coalition" which has spread to at least eight cities. The coalition is based on LaRouche's theory that Jews are responsible for the drug traffic. The coalition's activities include mass rallies in ghetto churches; intensive and effective lobbying for stronger narcotic laws; and seminars in inner-city high schools. Wallace Muhammad has repeatedly refused to break off this alliance despite appeals from Jewish organizations and responsible Black leaders. The coalition has attracted an amazing range of clergymen, businessmen, mayors, law enforcement officers, state legislators, Masonic leaders, and trade union officials.[11]

This indicates the emergence of a left-wing fascism that has learned to use the techniques of right-wing fascism with impunity.[12] It has also learned to appreciate the mass character of appeals to anti-Semitism. Historically, the problem of the American left has been its narrow socioeconomic base, intellectual self-isolation, and above all isolation from the mainstream of workers. It perceives the working class as ready to be tapped, but only if the tactics are appropriate to the current internal situation—one in which Jews are perceived as isolated from working-class networks, gathered in the professional and middle strata of the population, and ideologically and organizationally distanced from their traditional Democratic party moorings. Under such historical circumstances, left-wing fascist elements have seen this as an ideal opportunity to seize a political initiative and link up with social segments of the population never before tapped.

The ambiguity of the present situation harbors the sort of pseudopopulism that can easily accommodate to fascist and socialist ideals, both of which make appeals to totalitarianism in its most advanced, virulent form. Left-fascism, unlike national socialism, no longer stands for a set of rural values over and against urban corruption, or mass sentiments over and against elitist manipulation. While masquerading under populist slogans, left-fascism is highly urban and elitist. The effectiveness of such marginal movements depends heavily on the state of American national interests: whether they can be sufficiently polarized to prevent concerted policy making or sufficiently galvanized to reduce such left-wing fascist varieties of populism to manageable and nonlethal proportions.

Another serious element in left-wing fascism is its political mysticism, in which the cult of the group displaces individual conscience. Socialism becomes devoid of concrete practice or specific content. Socialism as negative utopianism becomes the order of the day. Real socialist practices are simply disregarded or at times privately rebuked. Like satanic lodges, new groups emerge with the strong feeling that Stalinism has been an oft misunderstood phenomenon that deserves to be supported once again. Just as there are cults of Hitler, there are now cults of Stalin—small bands of people convinced that history has assessed these leaders wrongly and that the source of strength of any future movement will involve a reevaluation of these former political figures.

What we have described remains a nascent movement, an ideology and organization in the making. We are not dealing with finished ideological products or large-
scale political movements capable of threatening established structures. Nor are
they necessarily a threat to classical left-wing politics. Left-wing fascism does, however, provide an answer to a question plaguing our century: In what form will fascism come to America? What will be its ideology? What will be its social message?

American fascism could provide a focus with a series of left-wing components:
minoritarianism in the form of libertarianism; fundamentalism in the form of nationalism; a defense of socialist theory with denial of socialist practice; an assertion
of nationalism and Americanism as values, with a denial of mass participation and
mass belief systems; elitism as vanguard populism; a mobilization ideology in place
of a mobilized population. These tendencies remain nascent; these fusions still remain to be crystallized in political practice. As we make attempts in the 1980s to
overcome severe economic dislocations and a breakdown of organic union manifested in a hesitant attitude toward patriotism, and insofar as we exhibit a system
with no apparent public commitment and only a series of specific egoistic requirements presumably underwritten by a doctrine of rugged individualism, while small
groups make cynical determinations for large-scale policies and structures, to this
extent we can expect to find left-wing fascism a powerful component in the political
practice of the remainder of the twentieth century.

The twentieth century is polarized into diametrically opposed secular faiths. This
dichotomy has taken hold because a century of war and genocide has given expression to competing messianic visions. After class annihilation comes classlessness,
after racial annihilation, a triumphal master race. Subordination of the person to the
collective is the common denominator. New totalitarian combinations and permutations are dangerous because they move beyond earlier hostility into a shared antagonism toward democratic processes as such. Concepts of evidence and rules of experience give way to historicism and intuition. Comfort with a world of tentative and
reversible choices gives way to demands for absolute certainty. In such a climate,
the emergence of left-wing fascism is presaged by a rebirth of ideological fanaticism. If the forms of totalitarianism have become simplified, so too has the character of the struggle to resist such trends. This awareness offers the greatest potential
for democratic survival against totalitarian temptation.

The United States has been singularly prone to look benignly upon the forces of
left-wing fascism because it so adroitly managed to escape the real thing, namely,
European fascism on one side and Soviet totalitarianism on the other. As a people,
Americans are thus more ready to assume the best, not only in people but in extrem-
ist propaganda systems. As a result, the process of intellectual cauterization against
such extremisms was also an overseas, "foreign" import. The migration phenomenon, with messages delivered by the victims of totalitarian systems, has become the
essential source of resistance to the series of insidious and insipid banalities that go
under the label of left-wing fascism. The work of Arendt,[13] Halevy,[14] Lichtheim,[15]
Reich,[16] and Talmon,[17] however different in intellectual disciplines and cultural
backgrounds, spoke the identical message on one key fact: the integral nature of the

totalitarian experience and the fusion of Left and Right sentiments in converting such sentiments into systems.

The experiences of World War II, when conflict displaced fusion and nationalist ambitions preempted totalitarian tendencies, had the effect of crystallizing differences rather than similarities between fascist and communist regimes. These differences between regimes, nations, and cultures were authentic. However, with the removal of the European wartime experiences in space and time has also come the dismantling of traditional barriers between extremes of left and right. Their capacity to come together in a set of manifest hatreds for minorities, masses, and ultimately for democracy does not signify the end of ideological disputations characteristic of the century, but only a clearer appreciation that such distinctions among the enemies of democracy weaken the chances for the continuing survival, even slight expansion to new lands and nations, of societies in which every individual counts as one: no more and no less.

18. Multiplication of Marxisms

This essay addresses three related questions: first, whether Marx's writings contain a scientific method applicable to both natural and social science, that is, is Marxism a universal world view or specifically a social philosophy? Second, what is the essential character of Marxist epistemology? Third, how do we arrive at truth, and who has the right to proclaim which version of Marxism most accurately interprets the scientific method?

The problem presents itself as a conflict between metaphysical and positivist interpretations of Marxism: between the view that philosophy is or is not a separate science characterizing reality as a whole. To clarify the issues, we shall set out what we consider to be the basic features of Marx's epistemology, and then compare them with later developments in Marxist thought. Basically, we shall argue that the dialectics of Engels and the materialism of Lenin were both the result of an attempt to convert Marxism into a general scientific theory equally applicable to the natural sciences and social sciences.

Engels repeatedly defined the dialectics as "the science of the general laws of motion and development of nature, human society and thought." With this definition, practically the entire range of knowledge falls within the scope of dialectics. Engels's elaboration and extension of Marx's essentially economic analysis of social change led him to suggest that the materialist conception of history was based on a set of immutable laws which could be applied to both the physical universe, the biological realm, and the social world. One author's earlier view was that Engels misunderstood Marx when he extended the dialectical analysis outside the realm of history and society. Engels completely failed to consider "the *dialectical relation between subject and object in the historical process* let alone give it the prominence it deserves."[1] Another scholar also comments that the application of the dialectics to nature results in a choice between two unattractive alternatives: it is "to read an element of purposive striving into the structure of reality: in other words, to revert to romanticism," and second, it reduces the concept of dialectical change to a tautological proposition, in which any happening whatever is equal to a qualitative change from one state to another.[2]

Largely owing to Engels's work, Marxism came to mean what Engels said it meant for several generations of orthodoxy. *Anti-Dühring* in particular was the most influential text for two generations of socialists. It contributed towards the development of scientism and positivism in both German Social Democracy and later in Soviet polemics on partisanship and objectivity in philosophy. Marx, however, nowhere set forth his views on natural science in any systematic fashion, nor did he ever speak of dialectics of nature. Marx permitted Engels, so to speak, to have the exclusive in this area.[3] According to one authority, it was Engels who, unwittingly perhaps, "established the tradition which ascribed to Marx a coherent monistic sys-

tem of materialist metaphysics in the accepted sense of this term, comprising a philosophy of nature, a theory of society and a view of history, all three derived from a
common set of first principles and logically supporting each other."[4]

Marx was empirical in his temperament as well as his thought. Throughout, he
condemned "a priori construction" and "drunken speculation." His analysis of social change arising from the interacting processes of nature, society, and human
consciousness nonetheless cannot be transmuted into an all-encompassing explanatory device. Yet, Engels undertook his study of mathematics and natural science to
convince himself that precisely such a holism could be achieved. He came to believe that

> in nature, amid the welter of innumerable changes, the same dialectical laws of
> motion force their way through as those which in history govern the apparent for-
> tuitousness of events; the same laws as those which similarly form the thread run-
> ning through the history of the development of human thought and gradually rise
> to consciousness in the mind of man; the laws which Hegel first developed in all-
> embracing but mystic form, and which we made it one of our aims to strip of this
> mystic form and to bring clearly before the mind in their complete simplicity and
> universality.[5]

Engels dampened the distinction between the unique character of social development and development in nature by minimizing the role of human volition and
maximizing the deterministic aspect of society. His historical materialism can never
adequately comprehend this; consequently his correspondence theory of knowledge
is unable to explain that consciousness is social before it is individual, that is, the
process by which knowledge is attained is always set in some concrete interactionist
context. It is ironic that Marx directed much of his attention in his early works toward a critique of classical materialism for its failure to take account of the role of
human consciousness. In fact, the origins of Marx's epistemology are to be found
both in German idealist philosophy and in his critique of mechanical materialism,
summarized in the *Theses on Feuerbach* and elaborated in other works. Bottomore
and Rubel have argued that Marx was not concerned with either ontological or epistemological problems.[6] This does not, however, render the attempt to find the nature
of his epistemology a meaningless exercise. The task is made more difficult by the
lack of any systematic exposition in his writings on this subject.

Much has been written about Marxism and the concept of false consciousness,
but little about the process of attaining true knowledge in Marxian terms. It is possible to discern three stages in Marx's thought on this subject. In the first period Marx
maintained that true consciousness could only be attained through the creative activity of man, that is, through overcoming alienation in the social process connected
with labor. In the second period, Marx revealed a preoccupation with the class character of knowing, with social sources and economic interests that define and delimit
knowledge. In the final phase, he came to believe that the attainment of true knowledge would only be possible with the revolutionary overthrow of class society, that

is, with the politicization of the working class and its vanguard. It is this latest stage which Avineri is referring to when he states that "Marx's epistemology thus conceals an internal tension. It tries to solve the traditional epistemological problems, but it tacitly holds that human consciousness could operate according to the new epistemology only if the obstacles in its way in present society were eliminated. Hence, Marx's epistemology is sometimes divided against itself: it is both a description of consciousness and a vision of the future."[7]

To begin with, it is impossible to understand Marx's epistemology outside the context of Hegel's philosophical idealism, since the foundations of his epistemology and materialist conception of history arise from his opposition to German historiography in general and Hegel's philosophy of history in particular. Philosophical idealism postulates that there are no cognizable objects outside of consciousness. According to Hegel, what appears as an external object is a projection of consciousness. Mind as self-consciousness knows the nonexistence of the distinction between the object and itself, because it knows the object as its self-alienation. The actual objective character of the object constitutes estrangement for self-consciousness. Since the object exists only as an alienation from self-consciousness, to take it back into the subject would mean the end of objective reality and thus of any reality at all. For Hegel, the highest stage of absolute spirit is attained with the abolition of alienation and the return of consciousness to itself. According to Marx, this is nothing but the self-objectification of the philosophic mind: Hegel's philosophy suffers from the illusion that the object of philosophy is philosophy itself—an illusion to which Feuerbach addressed himself by demanding a materialist interpretation of theology.

History exists so that truth can be revealed. It thus becomes a metaphysical subject of which human individuals are the mere representatives. "Hegel's view of history presupposes an abstract or *Absolute Spirit* which develops in such a way that mankind is only a Mass, a conscious or unconscious vehicle for the Spirit. Hence Hegel provides for the development of a speculative, esoteric history within empirical exoteric history. The history of mankind becomes the history of the *abstract spirit* of mankind, thus a spirit *beyond* man."[8] This point was also made in the *Economic and Philosophic Manuscripts*,[9] where Marx states that Hegel, in the *Phenomenology*, reduces the material world and the products of man's activity to mere thought entities and products of abstract mind.[10] Thought takes its own action for sensuous, real action.

Despite the severity of his intellectual assault, Marx acknowledged the seminal influence of Hegel on his thought, although he was closer in point of view to the materialist Feuerbach.[11] In 1844, in the manuscript entitled "Critique of the Hegelian Dialectic and Philosophy as a Whole," he praised Hegel's conception of the origins and development of man, that is, for his understanding that man creates himself in a historical process, of which the driving force is human labor. "The outstanding achievement of Hegel's *Phenomenology* is thus first that Hegel conceives the self-creation of man as a process, conceives objectification as loss of the object, as alienation; that he thus grasps the essence of *labor* and comprehends objective man . . . as the out-come of man's *own labor*."[12]

Hegel's error, according to Marx, lies in the fact that he sees only the positive, and not the negative, side of labor. "The only labor which Hegel knows and recognizes is *abstractly mental labor*." [13] It is only the abstraction of man's self-consciousness, not active man, who is made the subject. Man's objective essence, therefore, according to Hegel, is his alienated self-consciousness. Alienation is a purely spiritual phenomenon, whose overcoming leaves unchanged existing social and political institutions. The "negation of the negation," which at the social level may be viewed as the transcendence of alienation, permits individuals to recognize that objects that appear to exist outside the world-mind are merely a phenomenal expression of consciousness. Self-conscious man who denies the reality and independent existence of the material world confirms his abstract self as his true self. In summary, Marx says that "within the sphere of abstraction, Hegel conceives labor as man's act of self-genesis." However, this act of self-genesis appears "first of all as a merely formal, abstract act, because the human essence itself is taken to be only an abstract, thinking essence, conceived merely as self-consciousness. . . . Real man and real nature become mere predicates—symbols of this esoteric, unreal man and of his unreal nature." [14]

Marx identifies human consciousness with the practical process of man's shaping reality. Man shapes nature: reality is always human reality, or what Feuerbach properly described as anthropological philosophy. "The production of ideas, of conceptions, of consciousness is directly interwoven with the material activity and the material relationships of men; it is the language of actual life. Conceiving, thinking, and the intellectual relationships of men appear there as the direct result of their material behavior. . . . Consciousness can never be anything else except conscious existence, and the existence of men is their actual life-process." [15]

The basic premise of the argument in *The German Ideology* is that all historiography must proceed from the existence of living individuals, who are distinguished from animals not by the fact that they think, but by the fact that they have a culture, that is, produce their means of subsistence. What people are coincides with what they produce and how they produce it. When this fact is realized, history ceases to be a collection of dead facts or an imaginary activity of imagined subjects, as it is with the idealists. [16] According to Marx, history has been speculatively distorted by Hegelian idealism: historical change is not an abstract act of self-consciousness but a completely material, empirically verifiable act. The Marxist materialist conception of history, proceeding quite inexorably from the Feuerbachian legacy, "arrives at the conclusion that all forms and products of consciousness cannot be dissolved by mental criticism, by resolution into 'self-consciousness' or transformation into apparitions, specters, fancies, etc. but only by the practical overthrow of the actual social relations which gave rise to this idealistic trickery." [17]

The material world therefore exists for Marx as a necessary condition for the process of human self-awareness. It is only natural that man, as a living, sensuous being, equipped with material powers, should have real natural objects as part of his world. "A being which has no objects outside itself is not an objective being." [18] Objects in the world must become the objectification of man, assisting him in realizing and confirming his individuality. Man as a human natural being "has to confirm and manifest himself as such both in his being and his knowing." [19] It follows, therefore, that knowing cannot be limited merely to mental activity.

It was on this ground that Marx attacked those who styled themselves "Young Hegelians," and he did so by employing Feuerbach's materialism and *sans* mechanism. Marx praised Feuerbach for making the social relationship of man to man the basis of his theory, while, for his colleague Engels, his work represented the convergence of humanism and materialism in the theoretical sphere. [20] Feuerbach's most serious limitation, according to Marx, was that he saw man only as sensuous object, not man as sensuous activity. This was reflected in a materialist critique of religion and theology rather than society and economy. Feuerbach's view revealed a double limitation: first, he failed to see that the world is more than an abstract given, rather than the product of the activity of a succession of generations, continually in a process of change. Second, he did not recognize that the ultimate task of philosophy is not merely to supply an adequate cognition of the world, but a framework for changing the world in anticipated directions.

The Young Hegelians were subjected to an even more severe attack for their claims to have revolutionized philosophy when in fact they attacked not the actual existing world but merely the phases of this world, that is, of German idealism. They adopted Feuerbach's critique of the Hegelian dialectic as their own, and reduced the whole process of history to the relations between the rest of the world and their own philosophy. Bruno Bauer, for example, far from moving beyond Hegel's *Phenomenology*, had simply learned "the art of transforming *real, objective* chains existing outside *me* into *merely ideal*, merely *subjective* chains existing *in me* and hence the art of transforming all external, sensuous struggles into mere struggles of thought." [21]

Max Stirner also assumed that ideas dominated past history and that real conditions were modeled on man and his ideal conditions, that is, on the nature of man, of man as such: thus making the "history of the consciousness men have of themselves the basis of their real history." The "Critical Critics" were further rebuked for believing that they had arrived at the beginnings of knowledge of historical reality, while excluding from the historical process theoretical and practical relations of man to nature, that is, natural science and industry. For Marx, reality, viewed by classical materialism as a passive object of perception, is shaped by men and reacts to men. This is made clear in his First Thesis on Feuerbach:

> The chief defect of all previous materialism (including Feuerbach's) is that the object, actuality, sensuousness is conceived only in the form of the *object as perception*, but not *as sensuous human activity, practice* (*Praxis*) not subjectively. Hence in opposition to materialism the active side was developed by idealism— but only abstractly since idealism naturally does not know actual, sensuous activity as such. Feuerbach wants sensuous objects actually different from thought objects: but he does not comprehend human activity itself as *objective*. Hence in the *Essence of Christianity* he regards only the theoretical attitude as the truly

human attitude. . . . Consequently, he does not comprehend the significance of "revolutionary," of "practical-critical" activity.[22]

The second stage in Marxian thought was far less sanguine about the realization of knowledge through self-understanding. By the late 1850s, or what might be called the *Das Kapital* period, Marx had grown weary of the possibility of individual self-realization, or for that matter, the philosophical character of the process of knowing. He had also grown weary of labor as a sheer learning experience. Rather, he saw the problem of knowledge in terms of the problems of social systems.

Knowledge under capitalism is purely instrumental. It is a source of alienation because of its one-sided demystification of experience. Capitalism gives a scientific character to production, but does not give a scientific character to the relationships of human beings within the production process. The process of labor, which in the earlier phase was to be the source of knowledge and liberation, is thereby reduced within capitalism to an element of technology and little else.

> The development of the means of labor into machinery is not fortuitous for capital; it is the historical transformation of the traditional means into means adequate for capitalism. The accumulation of knowledge and skill, of the general productive power of society's intelligence, is thus absorbed into capital opposition into labor and appears as the property of capital, or more exactly of fixed capital, to the extent that it enters into the production process as an actual means of production. The tendency of capital is thus to give a scientific character to production, reducing direct labor to a simple element in this process.[23]

When Marx turns to the question of knowledge under communism in this middle period or economic stage, leisure and labor become factors. In a mood almost reminiscent of Aristotle, he sees the need and the possibility of leisure time for the higher activities. In the realm of communist freedom both leisure and labor define and determine the character of what we know. And in this world of communism, practice becomes equated with experimental science on one hand and historical science on the other, the latter being the accumulated wisdom of society as a whole:

> Free time—which includes leisure time as well as time for higher activities— naturally transforms anyone who enjoys it into a different person, and it is this different person who then enters the direct process of production. The man who is being formed finds discipline in this process, while for the man who is already formed, it is practice, experimental science, materially creative and self-objectifying knowledge, and he contains within his own head the accumulated wisdom of society. Both of them find exercise in it, to the extent that labour requires practical manipulation and free movement, as in agriculture.[24]

In this second stage of the Marxian vision of knowledge there is a liberating power of the economy per se. The way in which economic transformations permit exact human knowledge is no longer a matter of individual effort, no longer a matter of knowledge searching for its true opposite; but rather economic evolution, first one-sidedly through the capitalist expansion of natural science, and then multi-dimensionally through the socialist concept of the human sciences, permits a knowledge without distortion. False consciousness dissolves in practice rather than in introspective or even experiential reflections.[25]

At this time Marx came to believe that social practice had its roots and origins in work. His criticisms of Adam Smith's negative attitude towards work in the *Grundrisse* indicate a basic infusion of sociologism into the earlier materialism of the 1840s. Marx spoke of labor as an entity existing for others, or labor establishing itself objectively as its own nonbeing. Labor exists as a mere potentiality of creating values: "The entire real wealth, the world of real value and likewise the real conditions of its own realization are placed in opposition to it as entities with an independent existence."[26] The injustice of capitalism is precisely due to the deprivation of wealth from those who produce wealth—the laborers.[27]

The *Grundrisse* reveals that Marx retained his belief in the possibility of human emancipation expressed in the early writings. But his work in the interim economic period gave him a heightened awareness of the strength of the economic and ideological forces operating against labor. He became less optimistic about the possibilities of attaining liberation through labor, since the increasing mechanization of industry dehumanizes the worker and divorces him from the intellectual potentialities of the labor process. His writing at this time indicates a more sober economic view of the source of knowledge and a skeptical attitude towards the possibility of overcoming alienation through self-understanding. Knowledge and practice are still intimately related, but the emphasis is placed more upon class struggle and less upon the movement of large-scale dialectical forces. The connection between the means of production and the relations of production is still encompassed by the "dialectic of the concepts of productive force." But this is now a dialectic whose boundaries are to be determined, and which does not suspend real differences.[28] Marx came to see the question of knowledge in terms of the overall problem of social change: hence the emphasis placed on the class character of knowledge and the revolutionary practice came to be regarded as both the foundation of knowledge and the criterion of truth.[29]

In the third stage, certainly by 1875, Marx was arguing that the existence of inequality in capitalist society rendered the attainment of true knowledge impossible. In the *Critique of the Gotha Program* he maintained that equal rights for labor meant simply bourgeois rights. The rights of the workers were proportional to the labor they supplied, and labor was used as a standard measurement of worth:

> This equal *right* is an unequal right for unequal labor. It recognizes no class differences, because every one is only a worker like everyone else. . . . *It is, therefore, a right of in-equality in its content, like every right.* Right by its very nature can only consist in the application of an equal standard; but unequal individuals (and they would not be different individuals if they were not unequal) are only measurable by an equal standard in so far as they are brought under an equal point of view, are taken from one *definite* side only, e.g. in the present case are re-

garded only as workers, and nothing more seen in them, everything else being ignored.[30]

Marx consigned to the realm of necessity the sphere of productive human activity, the sphere which in the forties he had believed to be the arena where man would attain true consciousness of himself and his world. The realm of freedom began only beyond it, with the attainment of state power by the proletariat. We find therefore a concern with the attainment of state power, and, on the theoretical level, a move from political economy to political sociology. "The early Marx was anticipating the imminent rise of revolutionary 'consciousness' in response to a developing capitalism; the later Marx was investigating the lack of such 'consciousness' despite a developed capitalism."[31]

The crucial role of practice is retained throughout although the modes of practice change in the three stages. Man acts upon the world, from which he derives his knowledge of it: first, in the social laboring process; second, in the character of the class struggle; and third, in the struggle for control of state power. Action not directed towards the theory and practice of social change will lead, not to knowledge, but to the furthering of an illusory ideology. Marx's theory of knowledge is therefore closely connected to his view of history and the process of man's advancement: not economic history alone, but the relationship between political change and economic exploitation.

Marx took from Hegel the idea that reality is not a mere objective datum, but is shaped by man through consciousness, and combined it with a materialist epistemology derived from both the anthropological materialism of Feuerbach and the earlier sensuous materialism of Diderot, Holbach, and Helvétius which took full cognizance of man's role in shaping his social world. Marx could never agree that consciousness is nothing but a reflection of the material conditions of man's existence, the position later adopted by Engels and Lenin, for this view is antithetical to his belief in the possibility of human emancipation through man's active social practice. Knowledge is intended to serve the partisan interests of the proletariat, which is both the most exploited class and the embodiment of the true interests of society, so that human emancipation will follow the emancipation of the proletariat. The working class can, by its own efforts, liberate humanity, for only this class is in a position to understand the laws. "When a class attains consciousness of what it is doing, of the role it plays in production, it discovers the secret of the whole society of which it is a part."[32] This explains Marx's insistence on workers' associations as representing a constructive effort to prepare the way for self-emancipation. Productive forces and social relations, both of which are part of the development of the social individual, appear to capital only as means, but they must provide the material conditions for effecting social change on the part of the proletariat.

The objective basis of Marx's theory of social change is his analysis of man as a social animal. Men perform labor, i.e., they create and reproduce their existence in daily practice, by working in nature and eventually consciously changing it. Society and nature are part of a single system, so that social evolution is observable in the growing emancipation of man from nature and in his growing control over nature. Marx maintained that ultimately the natural sciences would lose their abstractly material or idealistic tendency and become the basis of *human* science, as they were already the basis of actual human life, in an estranged form. Natural science, through the medium of industry and technology, had already prepared the way for emancipation in economy and society: "Human history itself is a *real* part of *natural history*—of nature developing into man. Natural science will in time incorporate into itself the science of man just as the science of man will incorporate into itself natural science: there will be *one* science." [33]

This statement had led some Marxists, such as Lefebvre, to argue that "the dialectical analysis is valid for any content. . . . By incorporating the experimental sciences . . . and using them to verify itself, it can therefore discover, even in Nature, the complex but still analysable Becoming." [34] This view is mistaken, in terms of Marx at least, since his own works do not contain any basic assumptions that the acceptance of dialectical materialism is a precondition of gaining scientific truth. Marx believed in the independent existence of the external world and denied the independent existence of mind without matter, but these were not the premises from which a holistic view of dialectical materialism was inferred.

The only evidence we have that Marx embraced Engels's historical materialism or his copy of theory about sensations being images of objects in the external world comes from Engels himself (plus the fact that Marx approved the publication of *Anti-Dühring*). That Marx and Engels collaborated over a period of fifty years does not mean that their work by biographical fiat constitutes a spiritual union. This impression of intellectual commonality gained currency as a result of Engels's efforts to disseminate Marx's views over the thirteen-year period from Marx's death in 1882 to his own in 1895.

Engels made several contradictory statements about the unity of science which have implications for later disputes over the question of whether Marxism is the ultimate philosophy or the end of all philosophy. He appeared to exempt dialectics from the predicted positivistic dissolution of all philosophy, [35] and adopted a didactic approach to scientists who believed they could escape its laws:

> Natural scientists may adopt whatever attitude they please, they will still be under domination of philosophy. It is only a question whether they want to be dominated by a bad, fashionable philosophy or by a form of theoretical thought which rests on acquaintance with the history of thought and its achievements. . . . Natural scientists allow philosophy to prolong a pseudo existence by making shift with the dregs of the old metaphysics. Only when natural and historical sciences have adopted dialectics will all the philosophical rubbish—outside the pure theory of thought—be superfluous, disappearing in positive science. [36]

Engels's self-imposed adversary in the unfinished manuscripts, published under the title *Dialectics of Nature*, was narrow-minded empiricism, which he contrasted with his own modern materialism. In this work and in *Anti-Dühring*, he distinguished three fields for the application of dialectics: nature, history, and human thought. The realm of knowledge was divided into three components: the exact sciences, biological sciences, and historical sciences, with different degrees of truth obtainable in each.[37] The first group includes all sciences dealing with inanimate matter. These sciences are generally susceptible to mathemetical treatment and certain results obtained in them are final and ultimate truths. The ultimate truths found in the second group are platitudes of the type: "all female mammals have lacteal glands." But eternal truths are in an even worse plight in the historical sciences, which can offer ultimate truths of the sorriest kind, such as "Napoleon died on May 5, 1821."[38] Engels's argument for the relativity of knowledge was distorted by Lenin in favor of the Hegelian notion of the concreteness of truth.[39] Lenin argued that no particular thing can be comprehended unless it is examined in a universal context which reflects the structure of reality as a whole. Thus the determination of particular things presupposes knowledge of universal concrete principles, which are found in the laws of dialectics. On the basis of these laws, knowledge of absolutely true empirical propositions is obtainable, since if the premises are true, the conclusions must be true. His view led to latter-day claims that dialectical materialism is in possession of immutable and incontrovertible truths. The fallacious reasoning of this theory has been adequately discussed elsewhere.[40] It is sufficient for these purposes to establish a distinction between the modest claims of Marx on behalf of dialectical materialism and the grandiose claims of his followers on behalf of historical materialism.

The copy theory of perception, which maintained that sensations and concepts were "copies, photographs, images, mirror-reflections of things," was based on Engels's approach to the problem of knowledge. Engels had argued that matter not only preceded spirit, but that it was also the cause and source of the evolution of consciousness. The justification for this claim was supposed to be provided by the laws of the materialistic dialectic.[41] Engels adopted a commonsense, naively realistic approach to the problem of knowledge. He was not particularly concerned with the epistemological question concerning the relation of thought to reality, and believed that any problems which might arise could be simply disposed of. For Engels, "there was no doubt that we know things as they actually are not as they appear to us, for whatever we experience—feelings, thoughts, impulses, volitions— is the effect of the external world acting on the human brain."[42] The dialectics of the brain were only the reflection of the forms of motion in the real world: these basic laws of motion were always the same irrespective of whether they referred to the motion of physical bodies, human society, or thought. Experiment and practice, he believed, would be sufficient to overcome any objections to this theory. "Thought and consciousness . . . are products of the human brain and man himself is a product of nature, which has developed in and along with its environment; hence it is self-evident that the products of the human brains, being in the last analysis products of nature, do not contradict the rest of nature's interconnections but are in correspondence with them."[43]

Lenin claimed that his theory of knowledge extended Marxism by proving that there could be no limit to human knowledge. In his boundless enthusiasm Lenin admitted that the only difference could be between what is known and what is not yet known. He assumed that a correspondence relation existed between sensations and external reality, mediated by class interests to be sure, by virtue of which the world is knowable. Nature, which for Engels and Lenin exists independently of human beings and yet is completely knowable, was for Marx a nullity, a nothing. The humanized world is knowable because it is a world shaped by man according to his needs. In 1844, Marx wrote that "it is clear . . . that thinghood is therefore utterly without any *independence*, and *essentially vis-à-vis* self-consciousness; that on the contrary it is a mere creature—something *posited* by self-consciousness." [44] In this inheres the fundamental naturalism and antidogmatism of Marx's theory of knowledge.

Any theory of knowledge which propounds that sensations are literal copies of objects and that of themselves they give knowledge, leads toward fatalism and mechanism. It was against such mechanism that Marx had proclaimed that human beings make their own history, albeit not in ways always imagined. His theory of knowledge was based on the assumption that the world around us was not a thing given directly from all eternity, but was constantly molded by man's theoretical and practical activity.

Marx rejected the Hegelian principle that the idea and reality are identical, arguing instead that philosophic thought alone could never overcome the discrepancy between them. This goal could only be achieved through revolutionary practice, leading to the abolition of private property and the establishment of socialist society. Thus the revolutionary practice which changes the world and the knowing-process were, for Marx, inseparable. The knowing subject, in his view, should be conceived as man the socially active being, the representative of a particular social class: not as a passive recipient of sensations, which are wrought in the sense by outside causes. The destruction of Marx's original conception is most apparent in the *partinost'* view of philosophy, where it is maintained that the philosophy of dialectical materialism is the foundation of scientific socialism, providing it with a coherent world view, a criterion of truth, and a unitary method over and above the particular sciences. Through such reasoning, Marxism at one and the same time was converted into a series of dogmatic platitudes, and made inoperative in helping to explain any specific science or social science by virtue of the reentry of Marxism as an abstraction.

The universalistic tendencies in Marxism resulted in converting Marxism into a ritual rather than a science. The great advantage in seeing and judging Marxism as part of the tradition of sociology and economy is that in the crucible of testing its general propositions in the light of new findings, Marxism is preserved from ossification and obfuscation. Those who wanted Marxism as a secular new theology have given up the most vital aspect of Marxism: its ability to help, explain, and predict movements in the social world.

Marx accepted as his primary responsibility the analysis of social and economic systems, particularly how these systems become transformed over time, and how contending classes are the instruments for bringing about such changes. Although he made occasional bows in the direction of a universal world view, such as in the preface to *Das Kapital*, he never explicated a weltanschauung that would be applicable to both the physical and the social sciences. His aims were ambitious, but not grotesque: to explain the processes of social development as a dialectical movement in which human volition and conscious behavior played a vital role. He may have been a determinist, but he was not a predeterminist. He accepted the idea of laws and lawlike behavior in human events, but not as something apart from and over against the will of ordinary people. What is inexorable is made so by the fundamental relations contending social forces and classes enter into; change these forces and relationships, and the inexorable features of the laws in society likewise are subject to alteration.

What made Marx limit his effort to the social order is that man, unique among biological species, and certainly far beyond the capacity of inanimate objects, is both the subject and the object of history. At any time, he is confronted with limited or at least finite options, but he is not limited to the pursuit of any one of these options. Otherwise, the possibility of error would be closed to man, and hence the need for strategies and tactics would become superfluous—something they clearly were not in the Marxian system. The scientific interpretation of Marxism, in the work of Engels, reduces to a predeterminism, to a physicalism that eliminates the need for struggle and, hence, puts an end to the essential dramaturgy of Marxian socialism: a system that is ubiquitous, incomplete, and essentially far less open to empirical scrutiny than, say, the errors and terrors of capitalism. Thus, the volitional aspects in Marx permit precisely what the predeterminism in Engels tends to dampen: revolutionary action by exploited actors.

19. Methodology, Ideology, and Society

With the polarization of political opinions and positions in the United States, social researchers have become increasingly concerned about the political import of their work. Until recent years, most sociologists probably believed that sociology was above politics, even though sociologists had often engaged in political activity, and political and sociological discussion had often overlapped. Events have now made it impossible to leave that belief uninspected. The disclosure that social scientists have undertaken research designed to further the interests of the powerful at the expense of those of the powerless (e.g., riot control at home and civic action abroad) showed how even apparently innocent research might serve special political interests. Prison research has, for the most part, been oriented to problems of jailers rather than of inmates; industrial research, to the problems of managers rather than those of workers; military research, to the problems of generals rather than those of privates. Greater sensitivity to the undemocratic character of ordinary institutions and relationships (ironically fostered by social scientists themselves) has revealed how research frequently represents the interests of adults and teachers instead of those of children and students; of men instead of women; of the white middle class instead of the lower class, blacks, chicanos, and other minorities; of the conventional straight world instead of marginal characters; of boozers instead of potheads.

The belief that members of the sociological discipline are guilty as charged helps to account for the way many social researchers have responded to the attacks. They have not dismissed the charges. On the contrary, professional associations, scientific societies, foundations, and the periodical literature have all evaluated the political tenor of social research. Younger social researchers have debated whether it was even moral to be affiliated with social science as such. Older social scientists have researched their work and their consciences to see if, far from being the political liberals they imagined themselves, they were in fact intellectual sources of repression. As a result, a widespread emphasis on reversing earlier trends has taken place.

In the midst of these reconsiderations positions hardened. The language of scholarly journals became increasingly polemical and strident. Meetings thought to be scientific were disrupted by protest and discussion. Presidential addresses at national and regional meetings were interrupted. This was accompanied by, and in some cases was intimately connected with, political uprising on campuses. Some teachers, especially in the social science disciplines, found themselves unable to bear the discourtesies of their radical students. Some professors saw attempts to change the hierarchical relations of a department as an attack on the very idea of scholarship. They assumed that a student who attacked their ideas with vituperation was attacking rational thought, and not simply using in public a critical rhetoric usually reserved for private meetings. Often they were right. Some students seemed

intent on cutting off debate and substituting for the free play of intellect a vocabulary designed exclusively to conform to a political position. The distinction was not
always easy to make. Those making affronts were often as unsure of what they were
about as those receiving them.

In situations of collective upheaval, persons and groups move to maximize their
private interests. In this case, some social scientists tried to further their professional careers by judiciously taking one side or the other. Groups moved to secure
power within professional associations. Some radicals seriously discussed taking
over professional associations or university departments, having convinced themselves that worthwhile political goals might be served by such acts—though the
resemblance of such maneuvers to similar careerist actions by doctrinaire groups of
quite different persuasions in the same associations and departments was obvious.
Elder social science statesmen of every political stripe appeared, trying to gather
unpredictable youth into their own sphere of influence. The rhetoric of radicalism
appeared in every area of sociology.

Participants in these events found themselves confused. Members of the older
professional associations often failed to note the confusion. They saw the actions as
concerted expressions of radical sentiment addressed to their destruction. They
could not see conflicts of interests among radicals, blacks, chicanos, women, and
other liberation groups within larger political contexts. The persistent emergence of
differences among these groups made it obvious that the assertion of radical sympa-
thies guaranteed neither concerted political action nor a uniform style of social
analysis. These differences and confusions demonstrate the need for a clearer analysis of the political meaning and relevance of sociology.

A social science which is not authentic cannot be critical in any larger sense.
Moral sentiments do not determine scientific quality. The reverse is more often true:
the quality of sociological work determines the degree to which it has a radical
thrust. The isomorphism between critical and good social science is necessary to
maintain in order to dissuade those who think political sloganeering can substitute
for knowledge based on adequate evidence and careful analysis; to persuade others
that their work has suffered from a conventional social and political attitude, expressed in the way they frame problems and in the methods of research they choose;
and to demonstrate that there is a tradition of good social research worth preserving.

Good social research is intellectual work that produces meaningful descriptions
of organizations and events, valid explanations of how they come about and persist,
and realistic proposals for their improvement or removal. Research based on the
best available evidence should provide analyses that are likely to be true in the linguistic sense of not being falsifiable by other evidence, and also in the ontological
sense of being true to the world. Generations of methodologists have developed procedures and techniques by which approximate truth can be reached. The social scientist achieves partial truths, always open to correction. While methodologists have
dealt with only a small part of the problem of arriving at propositions and inferences
likely to be true, the techniques they recommend as warranted are all we have; we
will have to use them until we invent something better. With all their faults, inter-

views, participant observation, questionnaires, surveys, censuses, statistical analysis, and controlled experiment can be used to arrive at approximate truth. While the results are modest, some things are known because sociologists have employed these techniques.

Social scientists have done less well using truth to forecast accurately. While they know some things well, they predict few events with accuracy. Humanists and scientists alike complain that social science tells them only a tiny part of what they really want to know. People want to know how the world is; social investigators give them correlation coefficients. Coefficients do help us know how the world is, and one need not accept the humanistic contention that unless social science can reproduce the world in full living color it is worthless. Nonetheless, the charge stings. Social scientific knowledge about real problems in society does not take them far from chance events in the future and necessary events of the past. If essentials are left out, the work cannot pass the test that science poses for itself. Such work cannot account for much of the variance in the phenomena under study. In addition, sociological work loses its potential practical importance if it does not encompass the major processes and actors involved in those parts of the world to be changed. Therefore, work that is not true to the world has neither scientific nor practical value.

Why does so much work in the social sciences fail to be true both to its own scientific standards and to the larger world? Some radical sociologists have insisted that political ideologies blind us to the truth because our political masters have paid us to produce research that will be useful in a different direction, or (more subtly) because our standard methods and concepts, reflecting political biases and pressures, prevent us from seeing what would be politically inconvenient. Many failures in social research result from simple ignorance, having little to do with either ideological bias or utopian fantasy. But we should examine those instances in which social research has been severely blemished not so much by ignorance as by bias.

Consider the charge that the concept of accommodation, applied to racial relations, had a conservative effect.[1] It implied that blacks accepted their lower position in American society and that therefore, because blacks did not complain, the situation was not unjust. But to say that racial relations in a given place at a given time were accommodative means only that the racial groups involved had achieved a modus vivendi and does not imply that the actors were happy or the system just. Whether any or all actors considered the system pleasant or righteous is a matter for empirical investigation. If the description of the situation as accommodative were true to the world, no evidence of conflict and resistance could be discovered because none would exist. To assume consensus would be bad sociology insofar as it assumed that since there is evidence of accommodation, we can rule out the possibility of conflict. The concept of accommodation can be objectionable only if we insist that its use will necessarily cause social researchers to overlook or ignore conflict, exploitation, or resistance to change where they occur. But a full exploration of the possibilities, as in Robert Park's description of the race relations cycle applied evenhandedly, should spare social researchers such errors.[2]

Much contemporary social science research is not true even in the narrow epistemological sense. It is falsifiable by evidence contained in its own data or by evidence that could have been obtained had the investigator bothered to look for it. Social science researchers tend to ignore the degree to which they fail to abide by their own methodological standards and consequently fail to achieve the scientific rationality to which they pretend. Where sociology allows political biases and generalized expressions of wishful thinking to affect its conclusions, it lacks truth in either of the two meanings discussed.

An immense variety of political positions has been announced as critical. Since the actual consequences of the label are so important to all the people involved, one cannot expect any definition to go undisputed. But most arguments over definitions turn on questions of the means by which desired goals can be achieved or of the correct diagnosis of the ills that afflict society, rather than on the ends for which radicals, for example, ought to strive. Thus, most radicals will agree that a key feature of any radical political program is the reduction and eventual removal of inequalities in society, whether the inequality is of power, economic resources, life chances, or knowledge. Likewise, most radicals will agree that a radically reconstructed society should maximize human freedom, especially when it is conceived as dialectically related to social order.

Radicals may not so universally agree on the necessity of permanent change and revolution as an ideal. Every society and every set of social arrangements must be inspected for potential inequalities and interferences with freedom, even those which seem to conform to one or another blueprint for a socialist utopia. The radical, so defined normatively, is never satisfied, never prepared to abandon the struggle for an even more egalitarian and free society. At the least, the better is the critic of the good.

Where circumstances compel choice between individual interests, self-expression, and personal welfare, on the one hand, and social order, stability, and the collective good on the other, such a radical politics act for the person as against the collectivity. It acts to maximize the number and the variety of options people have open to them, at the expense of neatness, order, peace, and system. It regards conflict as a normal concomitant of social life and a necessary element in political action. Some definitions of radicalism are based precisely on collectivism. While looking for the convergence of personal and public goals, one is compelled to make a choice on behalf of persons. The radical sees change as permanent and inevitable, but he need not accept all changes as good. He tends to side with the powerless against the powerful, and renounce coercion, terror, and control as methods of establishing policies about society.

The posture of a critical science may or may not overlap with that of a radical politics. Critical research rests on a desire to change society in a way that will increase equality and maximize freedom, and it makes a distinctive contribution to the struggle for change. On the one hand, it provides the knowledge of how society operates, and on the basis of which a radical critique of inequality and lack of freedom can be made. On the other hand, it provides the basis for implementing radical goals, constructing blueprints for freer, more egalitarian social arrangements, the working plans for radical utopias. A critical social science looks for explanations of social life and theories of society which assume that radical change is at least possible, and resists those theories which root inequality in inescapable facts of biology or social structure.[3] Since such assumptions are seldom subjected to empirical test, a critical social science can just as reasonably assume possibilities that more conservative or pessimistic sociologies do not.

In the controversy between Davis and Moore[4] and Tumin,[5] the essential difference of opinion was not about the facts of social stratification in American life, or even over the existence of inequality. There were indeed differences of opinion at the factual level. The core controversy concerned the tendencies of American society: whether the direction of the democratic society carried with it as a central agenda item the reduction and finally the elimination of inequality; and at what costs to whom. If inequality is rooted in the nature of people, with only the forms of inequality changing and the types of oppressors shifting, then the goal of equality is itself suspect. Any critical sociology must explore the nature of inequality fully, and beyond that must at least assume the possibility of abolishing inequality as a long-range goal and describing the machinery necessary to implement a more egalitarian social order.[6]

This equation of radicalism and the search for equity itself represents a liberal bourgeois model rather than a radical paradigm. But an authentic radicalism need not, indeed should not, uphold the banner of a particular social system. The most important fact of our times is the need for a social scientific judgment of *all* available political systems. Any equation of radical perspectives with the demand for equity implies the evenhanded analysis of any claims to priority of equality in socialist systems such as the Soviet Union, no less than in capitalist systems such as the United States. To demand allegiance to any social system as the mark of a radical perspective is to ignore the one-hundred-year history of inequality within the totalitarianisms that have passed for socialism, as well as the longer history of inequality under capitalism.

The search for equity is only one side of the critical thrust. At least equal in importance is the investigation of the ability of society, as presently organized, to deliver equity. It is the assessment of that ability that divides radical and liberal analysts. The ability of established society to absorb new social demands of disenfranchised groups becomes a major concern of the radical. The historic concern of political radicalism with problems of revolution expresses a pessimistic view of the present social and economic order's ability to absorb change, which may be largely wide of the mark from a scientific viewpoint.

No matter which of these several tasks a critical social science undertakes, it finds itself providing the facts, theories, and understandings that all politics requires for implementation. For a political posture without reliable facts and analyses is no more than insurrectionary art incapable of predicting its own successes or failures. Radical social science provides relevant and trustworthy data, intellectual resources for measuring costs as well as benefits in realizing the insurrectionary act.

Critical research often creates a tension with radical politics by indicating the high cost of some desired act. For example, it may analyze the special features of the Cuban-Castro revolution and produce an explanation of why guerrilla insurgency was successful in Cuba in 1959 but tragically unsuccessful in Bolivia in 1969. It is by no means a simple matter to counsel the gathering of evidence instead of performing a revolutionary act. But the gathering of evidence distinguishes a radical social science from a radical politics, without necessarily destroying the basis for their mutual interaction.

Every group in power is bent on the protection of privilege. Therefore, every radical social science must expose the nature of such privilege, unmasking forms of domination. This unmasking process creates dilemmas. It implies a ruthless stripping away of all mystery and cant, not just that of the Department of Defense but also that of the Nation of Islam. One task of a radical social science is thus to persuade the oppressed and radicals of the need for as total a dedication to what is true as to what they may deem good. It is here too that the issues between most contemporary forms of radical social science and radical political action become enmeshed in controversy, since many forms of radical politics are themselves bound to canons of secrecy, perhaps more benign than conservative politics but ultimately no less destructive of the search for truth in society.

Every status quo—societal, organizational, or factional—thrives on myth and mystification. Every group in power—in a nation, a government, an economy, a political party, or a revolutionary cadre—tells its story as it would like to have it believed, in a way it thinks will promote its interests and serve its constituencies. Every group in power profits from ambiguity and mystification, which hide the facts of power from those over whom power is exerted and thus make it easier to maintain hegemony and legitimacy. A sociology that is true to the world inevitably clarifies what has been confused, reveals the character of organizational secrets, upsets the interests of powerful people and groups. While uncovering error does not necessarily aid the interests of those exploited by an organization or society, it does at least permit equal access to the evidence upon which action must be based. Only if sociological work is good in the sense of explaining actual relationships of power and authority can it provide a force for change. Thus, work which is true to the world and explains the actual relations of power and privilege that envelop and determine what goes on in society will be politically useful to radicals, even though (importantly) those who do such work may not themselves be committed to radical political goals.

Social scientists have experienced the difficulties that come from doing work which exposes the operations of powerful groups in society. In operating explicitly in behalf of radical goals and in cooperation with people engaged in radical political action, the social researcher will experience other characteristic difficulties. For instance, a good sociological analysis, explored fully for its political implications, may undermine one's own position of superiority and privilege. The critical social scientist will find that his scientific conservatism, in the sense of being unwilling to draw conclusions on the basis of insufficient evidence, creates tension with radical activists. This results from the differing time scales of the two activities. The social scientist takes time to collect evidence, but the political activist must often make decisions prior to the compilation of adequate evidence. Under such circumstances, the political individual will act; the social scientist can give him the best available evidence. Radical activism is not the same as the know-nothingism underlying the irrationalist will to act, but rather a recognition that action may be induced by needs that cannot possibly await the supply of the social scientist's information. The lag between action and information explains, in part, the peculiar tension between the political man and the social scientist, a tension that often leads the activist to disregard the social scientist's advice, and correspondingly, often leads the social scientist to a conservative estimate of the potential success of a dramatic political action.

Since radical politics and critical sociology are not the same, the two may conflict. What is the relation between political radicalism and social criticism? Rosa Luxemburg acted as a revolutionist and as a leader of the Spartacists of the German Left Socialist movement, but at the same time she functioned as a critic of Lenin and of the dogma of proletarian dictatorship. She did this at a moment of revolutionary euphoria when serious thinking was at a premium. It is her criticism which is now best remembered. The same can be said of Eugene V. Debs, whose importance in the Socialist movement lay precisely in his being above the fratricidal struggles for control of the Socialist party apparatus. Debs, the radical man, had little organizational impact in American socialism. Far less concerned with organization than DeLeon, Debs alone emerged as the ecumenical figure for the socialists.[7]

Radicalism entails a critique of organizational constraints. Yet revolution can only be made on the basis of a theory of organization. This is why the roles of critical researcher and revolutionary activist cause considerable tension within the person and between the organization and the individual. If the activist joins forces with other advocates for rapid change, the social scientist points out how limited the practical effects of these changes may be. The activist, achieving his goals, seeks to enjoy the fruits of his victory; the radical social scientist looks for new sources of inequality and privilege to understand, expose, and uproot.

The difference between political radicalism and social scientific criticism deserves further elaboration. While the two can be linked, they can also occur independently and are often quite distinct. Radical action and rhetoric are one thing, and a radically informed sociology is another. Confusing the two opens leftism to any professional opportunism of the moment. Political sloganeers can easily tailor their doctrine to the changing fortunes of political sects. Serious social scientists find it much harder to change their sociological practice to match their changing political beliefs. To teach the same courses in theory and method one taught twenty years ago, while shifting from support for the government to opposition, does little to change the political thrust of contemporary social science. One can use radical rhetoric and engage in radical political action while one's social science, because of its failure to be good, leaves established myths and institutions untouched. This is only the radical manifestation of the dualist distinction between fact and value adhered to by most conservatives. The values shift and become anti-establishment rather than proestablishment. But fact, or as is more nearly true, the fantasy that passes for scientific fact, remains unaltered.

The intersection of social and political analysis, the common ground which allows a characterization of various kinds of sociology as having one or another political cast, lies in their mutual concern with causes of events. It seems clear that any necessary condition for the occurrence of an event may be considered a cause of that event, at least in the limited sense that if the condition were not present, the event would not occur. From this point of view, there is an infinite or at least a very large number of causes of any event. To use a reductio ad absurdum, the presence of oxygen in the atmosphere is a cause of class exploitation, since without oxygen there would be no people, and without people there could be no exploitation. All such physical conditions of human action are, in this extended and vacuous sense, causes. In a more restricted and less trivial way, the actions of every person and group that contribute, however remotely, to a social event occurring in the way it did can be seen as a contributing cause of the event, since in their absence things would have occurred differently. To take a not-so-absurd example, the actions of slaves constitute one of the causes of slavery, since they could (and sometimes did) refuse to act as slaves (even though the price might be death).

Even though there are a multitude of causes of any event, both scientific and political analysis concentrate on only a few of them—different analyses emphasizing different causes. How do social scientists choose from among the many possible causes those they will emphasize in their political analysis or investigate in their research? Sometimes they look for those potential causes which vary, or might vary, in the specific cases observed. Thus, social scientists ignore the presence of oxygen as the cause of social events, since it is a constant in human affairs (except, of course, for those rare situations in which its presence becomes problematic, as in the recent study of relationships among the men who climbed Mount Everest). Sometimes they choose causes for investigation with an eye to the usefulness of results. Insofar as analysis is meant to be useful as a guide to someone's action, sociologists look to causal analysis for the clues as to how things might be changed, how they might be kept the same, and what the cost of either course is. These guidelines help somewhat but do not go far enough in cutting down the number of causes the analyst pays attention to. On further inspection, we can see that the assignment of causes to events has a political aspect. The way social scientists assign causes, both in setting up hypotheses to be studied and in announcing conclusions, exhibits the influence of a political point of view, however implicit or hazy.

When social scientists link a cause to an event or a state of affairs, they at the same time assign blame for it. An event occurred because certain actors did something that helped to make it occur; had they acted differently, the event would not have occurred as it did. If the event is judged to be morally or politically reprehensible, the sociological analysis, by isolating those actors as the cause of the event, blames them for its occurrence.

An analysis may also implicitly or explicitly place the blame for events on impersonal forces beyond personal control—human nature, the human condition, or the social system—and thus excuse the people whose actions appeared to be morally suspect by suggesting that they could not help doing what they did. Deterministic sociologies of every description perform this service for the villains they identify. If social research allows for choice on the part of human actors, then it can blame, by the way it assigns causes, any of the people involved, since they could have chosen not to do what they did. This has consequences for the political character of a sociological analysis. Volitional sociologies perform this service for the heroes they identify.

The analysis of causes has practical importance. When some object or action is labeled as the cause of the event or situation, the analysis suggests what would have to be influenced or altered in order to make a significant change in the event or the situation. Some things will be easier to change than others. The analysis may suggest that, under the circumstances, it is virtually impossible to change what must be changed in order to affect the situation. Alternatively, the analysis may focus on things easily changed in themselves but which have little chance of changing the situation. Every combination of the feasibility of intervention and the magnitude of the expected effect can occur in a particular analysis.

When social scientists, in their investigation of causes, implicitly or explicitly assign blame for events and when they suggest what must be done to cause meaningful social change, they speak of matters that are also the subject of political analyses. Their analyses can be judged to be radical, liberal, or conservative by the same criteria used to judge political analyses.

In general, radicals will judge analysis favorably only when its assignment of causes, and thus of blame, coincides with the established prejudices of the political group making the judgment. Radicals will denounce analyses as conservative (and conservatives will denounce analyses as radical) when the assignment of causes blames people who "don't deserve it." Similarly, radicals may criticize analyses that suggest causes which, when we take action, are too easily influenced and will not produce sufficiently profound results, or are too difficult to influence, thus leading to disillusionment and low morale.

Since radical political positions are more unusual and thus more visible in contemporary social science, it is radical social scientists who are most aware of these political connotations of sociological work. Most discussions of the problem have therefore been conducted by social scientists who conceive of themselves as radical and who therefore focus on ferreting out the political implications of work that is not politically self-conscious. In a society where some version of radical politics was more common and dominated research in an unself-conscious way, a similar critique might be mounted from the center or right. In our own society, political judgments of the results of sociological work could be easily made from those positions, though they could scarcely be designed to uncover hidden radical assumptions, since radical social scientists tend to make these quite explicit.

Examples of the political import of causal analysis are easily available. It is common knowledge that most black Americans live less well than most white Americans. Something ought to be done about it; people mostly agree on that as well.

What causes this situation? Some explanations explicitly blame the victims themselves, by finding, for instance, that their own inherited defects lead to all their trouble.[8] Many people found fault with Moynihan's explanation that some of the trouble lay in the disorganization of the black family.[9] That explanation seemed implicitly to blame blacks for their own troubles by suggesting that they need not have been so disorganized. It did not emphasize the causes of that disorganization, which placed the blame on their repression by an external, white community. The same analysis further suggested that it would be difficult to change the situation because it is quite difficult to change family patterns.

Consider the rash of ideological interpretations of student protest movements. Investigators may locate the causes of those protests in some characteristic of students themselves,[10] and thus implicitly suggest that it is the actions of students which, without the help of any of the other involved parties, produce all the trouble. Students are to blame while, by implication, others whose behavior we do not regard as a cause are not to blame. Alternatively, we can interpret campus disorders as political phenomena which arise in the same way as other political phenomena, and serve as a mechanism by which subordinate groups make hierarchical superiors pay attention to their demands for change.[11] In such a case, the difficulty can be located in the disparity between what one group wants and what the other group is willing to give, and it becomes equally possible to blame those who refuse to give students what they want since that refusal is one of the necessary conditions for the occurrence of the disorderly events.

Political and social analyses both operate under a potent constraint, which is that actions based on them should have the anticipated consequences. That remains a major test of any *scientific* proposition. If an analysis is factually incorrect, then political predictions will not come to pass and strategies will be discredited. Science will not validate propositions just because they appear ethically worthwhile; the propositions must be correct in the real world. In this sense, radicalism is a necessary, but not a sufficient, condition of good sociology.

The production of factually correct analyses involves a paradox. What social scientists need to know about any institution or organization in order to achieve radical goals is usually similar to what they must know to achieve conservative ends as well. Consider research on consumer behavior. Advertising and marketing experts, presumably lackeys for the capitalist system, have done research to discover how to make advertising more effective, that is, how to manipulate people so that they will buy what they might not have bought otherwise. Simultaneously, radicals have complained, although they have not done research on the topic, that advertising makes people desire commodities they do not need. Radicals agree that advertising works in the way marketing people say it does. Radical social scientists presumably want to know how to lessen the impact of advertising and make people's choices free; they might be interested in how the process of choice would work in a situation devoid of the artificial influence of advertising.

Apart from the difference in the moral animus of the language used by opposing groups, both conservative businessmen and radical activists need, to further their opposing ends, the same knowledge about the process by which consumers choose their products. If we had a decent theory of consumer behavior that had been empirically validated, then the radical, knowing how advertising works, would know where to intervene so that it would not work, and the marketing expert would know why his techniques fail and how to improve them. An adequate analysis of how things stay the same is thus at the same time an analysis of how to change them. Conventional, presumably conservative, analyses often fail to take into account matters radicals think important. If those matters are indeed important, then the conservative analysis which ignores them will be faulty and its predictions will not prove true.

Political commitment is revealed by the kind of causes social scientists include in their analyses, by the way blame is assigned to the possibilities of political action evaluated. It is revealed most clearly by ignoring causes conceived of as incapable of change when in fact they could be changed under certain conditions, and by regarding a situation as easily subject to change when in fact there are substantial forces perpetuating it. Such false assumptions make it likely that plans of action resting on them will fail. In fact, although it is often charged that American social science is (presumably successfully) engaged in helping oppressors keep subject populations in their place, the actions which are supposed to be based on these analyses often fail, precisely because they have failed to take into account important causes suggested by more radical sociological analyses.

For all the stated need for a more critical social science, there is little more than programmatic statements and little substantive work that has been done to fulfill the need. It cannot be that there are no critical researchers, for they have made their presence known. Indeed, even those who call themselves radical have trouble knowing what their sociology ought to look like; in fact, we can see that it often differs in no observable way from nonradical sociology. Some radicals in social science claim that there is no truly critical theory because most social scientists, being liberals or worse, are on the take from the establishment and naturally do not wish to make analyses that will subvert their own material interests. These radicals further suggest that organizations which distribute research funds and control publication are so dominated by liberals and conservatives that radical work cannot be supported or published. If we accept such statements as radical sociological work, the ease with which they too achieve publication and professional recognition suggests that they are not true.[12]

Those who conceive of themselves as radical social scientists find it hard to do identifiable research while politically neutral social scientists do research useful for radical goals (in the sense that they discover causal relationships which can be used as guides for radical political action). That demands explanation. There seem to be three chief reasons for this lack of connection between radicalism in social science and in political ideology: (1) the conservative influence of conventional technical procedures; (2) commonsense standards of credibility of explanations; and (3) the influence of agency sponsorship. Each of these, in its own way, deters a full explanation by social scientists of the range of necessary conditions that ought to be considered as potential causes of the situation studied.

Most commonly used research techniques require the investigator to have worked out his hypotheses fully before he begins gathering data. If we conceive research as testing deductions made from existing theories (wherever those theories come from), then the data one gathers must be suitable for making such tests. One restricts what one finds out to what will be relevant to those hypotheses. Experiments, surveys, and paper-and-pencil testing necessarily restrict the range of causes eventually considered, by the simple technical fact of confining inquiry to what the researcher has in mind when he plans his research. But in doing research, we often find that we have failed to take into account many variables and causes that, on the basis of early findings, we see we should take into account.

With respect to the possibility of a critical social science, what we leave out may not be important for the allocation of blame. But if what has been neglected, or made impossible to locate, is necessary to effect change, such research becomes less useful for radical political purposes by virtue of that gap. Even committed political radicals find themselves constrained by the research techniques they are familiar with. These techniques often leave out some things they would think important if they knew about them. Some techniques, indeed, require social scientists to leave out things they *know* might be important. Thus, it is difficult, though not altogether impossible, to study certain kinds of power relationships and many kinds of historical changes by the use of survey research techniques. If that is what one knows how to do, then he is stuck with what he can discover by that technique.

Another barrier to a critical social science lies in commonsense conceptions of credibility. Every theoretical stance, including those defined as radical, makes assumptions about the character of the world. In particular, the sociological view of the world usually assumes that some people are more believable than others, that their stories, insights, notions, and theories are more worthy of being taken seriously than those of others. One of the chief reasons conventional social science fails to uncover some important causes of events and situations is that it accepts the commonsense notion that the people who run organizations and are highly placed in communities know more about those organizations and communities than others, and therefore ought to be taken more seriously. The immediate effect of assuming the veracity of highly placed people is to leave out of consideration questions and problems that appear foolish from an elite viewpoint.

Conventional sociologists might, for instance, find it reasonable to ask why some schools are more effective in teaching their students than others. But it violates common sense to suggest, even though research might show it to be true, that schools actually prevent people from learning what they are supposed to learn. We have similar official versions and analyses of most social problems. When we study those problems, we find it hard to free ourselves from official analyses sufficiently to consider causes not credited in those versions. This is not to say that other causes are necessarily operative, but only that sociologists often fail to look at them because they seem unlikely or bizarre. Radical politics has its own set of official explanations, its own set of preferred causes. One can err as badly as taking these for granted as by taking conventional causes for granted.

Agency sponsorship tends to put conservative limits on the search for necessary conditions.[13] Although research is most commonly funded and sponsored by the government or foundations politically suspect from some radical point of view, the trouble does not necessarily arise from the political character of the sponsors. Rather it occurs because whatever their political persuasion when agencies purchase research they are concerned with answers to particular questions, questions which arise for them as operational difficulties. They do not wish to spend their money on meandering investigations of God knows what. Therefore, the agreement between researcher and agency typically specifies a limited area of research, the limits set by the agency's conception of what the problem is and where the causes lie. Ordinarily, the agency will not see its own operations as one of the causes of the problem, and thus those operations will not be included in the area the researcher agrees to study; by implication, he agrees not to study them.[14]

This discussion of barriers to unconventional analyses allows us to look critically at some common notions of what constitutes radical social science. Most of the common definitions of a radical style in social research bear some relation to making the kinds of analyses identified as being radical. In every case, however, the connection is contingent rather than necessary. We need to understand the circumstances under which the phenomenon in question actually leads to radical analysis and when it does not.

When one does research for a government agency, that agency will want the questions to be studied in a way that makes it difficult to come up with unconventional and radical conclusions. But refusing to accept government funds does not guarantee a radical analysis, nor is research paid for by the government by definition conservative. If a federally funded researcher has arranged conditions so that he has maximum freedom, he may very well produce critical findings. Having done so, he may find it difficult to get further research funds from the same or similar sources. The remedy for that is to travel light, to avoid acquiring the obligations and inclinations to make large-scale funds necessary.

Studying radical groups from a critical point of view, though one need not be particularly sympathetic with them to do so, may be of great use. Those groups might be exceptions to sociological wisdom, based on more conventional cases, and might make us aware of causal connections social scientists had not seen before. Thus, the study of communal living groups might allow social scientists to see certain possibilities of social organization that are ordinarily masked if we examine only longer-lasting and more stable institutions.

Personal involvement in political causes or affiliation with an organization that champions radical programs and positions does not necessarily lead one to do radical research. Such a political commitment might dispose a social scientist to search for causes and possible modes of intervention other analyses had left out. On the other hand, a radical might do research for his political allies which was no different in its style from the research economists might do for General Electric or Standard Oil. Such research might produce no more profound analysis of causes and would thus be no more useful to a political movement than market research and an investigation of how to keep the labor force happy have been for industry.

A radical rhetoric or ideological posture does not inevitably result in politically useful sociological work. Ideologically correct analyses cannot substitute for cogent, empirically verified knowledge of the world as a basis for effective action. Ideology cannot provide a workable understanding of the relative roles of China and India in the developmental process of Asia. Ideology cannot tell us how long it takes to make the transition from rural to urban life. Ideological radicalism cannot prove the merits and demerits of one or another form of economic investment. When radicalism without social science is employed as a surrogate for truth, it becomes fanaticism, a foolish effort to replace substance with style. But when these limits are understood and expressed, a radicalism informed by social science can help us measure the distance between where people are and where they want to go, i.e., between the society and the utopia.

In a period of falling expectations within the social sciences, it is perhaps time to raise the matter of priorities. It is the purpose of a meaningful sociology to demonstrate how it is that society and its institutions are on trial, and how it is that society and its organizations are undergoing crisis. When we keep this in mind and remember that social science is part of society, and that its researches in themselves mean little apart from the larger social tasks, then the sense and style of radical sociology will be enhanced, adding flesh and blood to its current programmatics and calling us back once again first to the criticism of society and second to the criticism of social science.

20. Developmental Dilemmas

The scientific study of international development involves a number of overlapping constituencies. The field was first pioneered by historians early in the century under the rubric of dynastic change. Then came the economists, who between Schumpeter in the 1930s and Rostow in the 1950s formalized the study of social transformation in terms of large-scale systems. Next came the anthropologists, who from Boas to Benedict conceptualized processes of development in relativistic "then and now" terms, but nonetheless gave development studies broad cultural dimensions absent prior to the post–World War II period. The field was then enriched by political scientists, whose profound understanding of the role of state power, policy making, and authority moved the study of international development beyond a matter of inexorable economic trends or social tendencies, and into decisions arrived at in local, national, and international exchanges.

Sociologists as latecomers in the analytic process of developing areas have not so much enriched empirical studies as they have evolved the theoretical dimensions of development. Empirical work, especially after World War II, involved attitude and motivational studies transplanted from American to overseas contexts, using scales and measures largely developed in social and clinical psychology. While these studies gave sociologists input into the analysis of international development, the transformation of these psychological studies into general theory has become a uniquely important contribution of sociologists.

The empirical contributions of sociology to the field of international development have been substantial, but they have been fixed at the level of explanation. The classics of sociology, however, make broad jumps from the data to the theory. The explanation by Marx of stages of development in terms of class formation and reformation, the explanation by Durkheim of the movement from organic to contractual foundations for establishing social solidarity, and, of course, Weber's emphasis on the role of religion and culture in creating a set of values that permit sustained growth, all are examples of such classic theoretical statements. They provide the background to most current attitudes and orientations about international development.

Seymour Martin Lipset's entrepreneurial thesis,[1] in which a deviant class of entrepreneurs creates the foundation for new values permitting capitalism to form in Latin America, is a direct descendant of the Weber hypothesis. At the other end of the spectrum is André Gunder Frank's dependency theory.[2] In this view, the underdevelopment of the Third World is explained by the overdevelopment of the First World. This approach has equally clear roots in Leninism and its theory of imperialism, if not directly in Marxism. More than any other discipline in social science, sociology may have inherited a broad nineteenth-century tradition of social theory. To that degree there is an unbroken line of theorizing about the processes of social change and international development.

Sociological Orientations Toward Development

Sociologists have played a pivotal role in the creation of three different orientations toward the study of development: what might be called the modernization, developmental, and dependency theses. These schools are characterized by the personnel involved, publications produced, the places where the work is primarily located, and above all, by the intellectual positions taken. This last characteristic, the general ideology of development outlooks, may best explain exactly what sociology has meant to the field of international development.

The *modernization* school was the most widely heralded after the Second World War. Basically, scholars such as Hoselitz,[3] Lerner,[4] and Shils[5] hold that modernization is the central source of development, just as traditionalism is the main source of stagnation, or nondevelopment. There are infinite variations on this theme; each involves an assumption that the historical transition is essentially cultural, i.e., from tradition to modernity. The motor force of this transition is the infusion of highly sophisticated mechanisms of communication and transportation. As these permeate the normative structure, the values of the society shift, and demands for participation in modern world systems accelerate.

The modernization thesis is informed by Keynesian economics, the idea of mixed economies of public and private sector bargaining for the most sophisticated mechanisms through the impulse toward modernized systems and behavior. Generally the modernization thesis sees the central change as a shift from feudal, landed agrarian economies to urban-based industrial economies. This position leads to bargaining between interest groups, and to the description of class differences in terms of leverage factors controlled by each group. Modernization is perceived as a way to achieve change without revolution or reaction. Much of the modernization literature assumes that the higher degree of social mobility, demographic controls, or information diffusion, the greater the degree of democratization of the social system. There is a strong implication that modernity is the unique and fundamental expression of democratization.

The models for modernization are the advanced Western powers, primarily those who won World War II, and stabilized capitalist democracy in the West. Modernization clearly reflects the values of the American century: aspirations of unchecked consumption, communication universals, and cultural relativisms. It represents the export of democratic individualism, of achievement-oriented societies. Continued stratification gaps, class, race, ethnic, and sexual disparities, military definitions of world realities, are magically filtered out of consideration. The entrepreneurial approach was offered for export to nations where the business classes exhibited little instinct for risk investment or technological innovation. A mechanistic restatement of egalitarian values took place, with little understanding of the exaggerations inherent in international systems created by powerful donor nations on behalf of recipient nations. The modernization school held unquestioned sway in American social science between 1945 and 1965. Even as late as the mid-1960s, the public presentation of development was dominated by a collection of statements on modernization sponsored by the Voice of America.[6] Despite the fact that it was transparently based on an exceptional set of political and economic experiences, the position remained impervious to a sense of inner strain, and failed to respond to external intellectual pressures.

The widespread emergence of authoritarian, totalitarian, and military regimes in the Third World, no less than the military emphases in Cold War politics, led to a reconsideration of modernization theory. A younger generation of theorists such as Huntington,[7] Furtado,[8] and Dumont,[9] labeled *developmentalists* despite their obvious ideological disparities, perceived a breakdown in the isomorphism between modernity and freedom. For this group, the relative position of any state or society within the international framework, or different sectors, classes, and subclasses within a state and society, affects events more than values, instincts, and attitudes. Developmentalism as a point of view simply represented a long overdue shift from psychologism to sociologism, and an emphasis on structural factors over and against personality factors.

Historical evolution was no longer presented in cultural terms of movement from traditional societies to modern societies, but rather in economic terms from colonialism to independence. Emphasis on Europe and America as models gave way to an appreciation of Asia, Africa, and Latin America for themselves. The developmental process was understood to be triangular in character: with economic classes preeminent in the formation of capitalism, political classes central to the formation of socialism, and military classes preeminent in the evolution and development of the Third World. In the developmental framework, policy became an even more important aspect of development, since questions of capitalism or socialism, democracy or authoritarianism, were all matters of choice for new nations rather than historical inevitabilities. At the same time, decisions concerning reform and/or revolution were determined by strategies and tactics, and not simply models of social change imported from earlier European frameworks.

The models for developmentalism were Third World nations which had been successful in achieving independence after the Second World War. Nationalist revolutions amalgamated what they held to be the most feasible structural components of the First and Second World. The developmentalist position took note of strong Third World political commitment to one-party rule, extensive military leveraging of the social order, and the emergence of a bureaucratic sector having a specific set of planning and developmental tasks. The Third World took its economic cues from Western society, specifically the Keynesian revolution in marketing, exchange, and circulation of capital, and a corresponding set of concerns to alleviate poverty. As a result, consummatory values and the instinct for commodity acquisitions, far from being crushed in these Third World states, emerged to full flowering. The Third World, which first appeared on the scene of history as a strange eclectic amalgamation of communist politics and capitalist economics, gradually evolved its own symmetries as well as its own structures. The developmentalist perspective responded to the stability and durability of this new situation and rejected the idea that the Third World was simply a transitional phase marching toward modernization, or for that matter, marching toward socialism. The new nations were marching, but to a beat generated by their own leaders. The analysis of this new beat gave substance to the developmentalist frame of reference.

In more recent years, the dependency school has attempted to restore a sense of holism and hegemony to the study of development. Under the guidance of Wallerstein,[10] Baran,[11] and Johnson[12] there is a much greater emphasis on power—economic and political—than on either values (modernization) or interests (developmentalism). The dependency school assumes that the state of backwardness of most Third World countries results not simply from variations in historical evolution, but from the conscious manipulation by the advanced First World of a dominated Third World. The idea of imperialism is central for the dependency school, replacing the idea of class for the developmental school, and the idea of nation in the modernizing school.

The world of dependency theorists was not so much bifurcated between modern and traditional sectors, as in the modernization school, and not so much tripartite divisions (First, Second, and Third World), as in the developmental school, but rather a unified world system that could best be understood in terms of position in the core, semiperiphery, or periphery of power and dominion. The dependency group was less interested in policy making for the Third World than the need to make revolution as a precondition for policy transformation anywhere in that world.

The dependency model took its cue from the Hobson-Lenin theory of imperialism, from the notion that cultural backwardness and economic deprivation resulted not merely from the natural histories of the Third World countries, but from excessive power in international terms, of advanced capitalist nations. If Leninism is Marxism in the era of imperialism, then it might be said that dependency theory is Leninism in the era of postindustrialism. Dependency theory was given practical impulse by the realities of adventurous American foreign policy in Latin America, involving the use of the military or surrogates in nations ranging from Guatemala, the Dominican Republic, Cuba, Brazil, and Nicaragua, to indirect participation in the management and manipulation of nearly every other regime in the Western hemisphere. Largely for this reason, the dependency school of sociology was clearly rooted in United States/Latin American relationships. The Soviet penetration of Cuba was not considered as part of such dependency. Hemispheric politics may have provided the context, but the Vietnam War provided the trigger mechanism for a general reconsideration of sociological standpoints. The conflict in Southeast Asia provided a seemingly overwhelming illustration of the United States' intervention in the affairs of dependent and small nations.

The ascendance of the dependency school, buoyed by American defeats in Vietnam and Cuba, turned out to be short-lived. The dissolution of the dependency school came slowly. The United States' defeat in Vietnam, the growing independence of Latin American nations, the expanding economic influence of the Middle East OPEC nations, were in effect defeats for the excesses of American capitalism. As a system, capitalism showed signs of being strengthened rather than weakened by new developments. Vietnam and Cambodia became proxies and client states for their larger masters, the Soviet Union and China, respectively. Latin America developed characteristics of national independence, military rule, and capitalist entrepreneurship. The OPEC nations developed their own notions of profit-sharing, and that meant investment and even takeover attempts, rather than destruction of capitalist bastions of power. The globalization of capitalism changed the ratio of power within the capitalist system, but left the system as such undisturbed. Some dependency advocates actually saw the Soviet Union falling under the sway of capitalist blandishments and multinational offerings. The dependency model provided a sensitizing agency to imbalances in world capitalist power, but little appreciation of the strengths of capitalism as a whole, or for that matter, the weaknesses of the Soviet alternative. It displayed a dazzling theoretical paradigm for the analysis of imbalances. Dependency theorists globalized the notion of equity; egalitarianism was made into a worldwide concern. It was understood that the rights of individuals and collectivities must be adhered to quite beyond the boundaries of any one given nation or economy. But the global framework continued to elude their ambitious designs.

The Ideological Institutionalization of Developmental Sociology

The degree of overlap between these schools of thought is almost as great as the sense of integration within each of them. Yet, clear lines do exist. Leading figures in the modernization school included Bert Hoselitz, Alex Inkeles, Wilbert Schramm, Seymour Martin Lipset, Kingsley Davis, Edward Shils, and Daniel Lerner. Clearly there is an age cohort involved; most of these people did their primary field research in the 1950s, although most are still quite active and vigorous. *Economic Development and Cultural Change* has been the foremost journal of the modernizing school for the past twenty-five years. There has been a tendency over time to mute the ideological assumption that modernization and Americanism are one. However, there remains a continuing and clear persuasion that national development must employ modernization in all its parts: capital intensive industry, bureaucratic politics, and mass society. That means changes in attitudes no less than growth in industrial output. The modernization school, because it developed first, and because it bore the full authority of established sociological tradition, is perhaps strongest at Ivy League schools such as Harvard and Princeton, and also at Stanford and Chicago. These more established institutions also contain important institutes for the study of world communism and European politics. This strong bias toward an American ideology fits directly into the modernizing thesis that often indicated overlapping orientations toward the developing areas. Involved was a direct confrontation in ideology and policy with Soviet power in the Third World. The modernization school, sometimes consciously, other times covertly, became party to a world struggle perceived as taking place between a democratic West and a totalitarian East. There is really no way to disengage these two aspects of modernization: sociological theory and political sentiment both underwrote the modernization thesis. The response to the Soviet challenge was real although often unstated. It extended from the presumption that authoritarianism was built into the swaddling clothes worn by Soviet infants to the high cost of goods and services within the Russian orbit.

Developmentalism involved people such as Alejandro Portes, Allan Schnaiberg, Charles Moskos, Denis Goulet, Gino Germani, Pablo González Casanova, Fernando Henrique Cardoso, and Luis Ratinoff. It was much more a phenomenon of the 1960s than of the 1950s. No doubt, it in part reflected a thaw in the Cold War, a termination of the Dulles era of confrontation in foreign policy, and the termination of the Stalin era in the Soviet Union. Developmentalism also included a much higher level of participation by scholars from the Third World, especially advanced countries of Latin America. It too developed its own publications, primarily *Studies in Comparative International Development*, which began as a monograph series in 1964 and evolved into a journal, and into *Comparative Politics* in 1969. Universities such as Michigan, Northwestern, California at Los Angeles, Syracuse, the State University of New York, and Pittsburgh, which came into prominence in the 1960s as graduate education in sociology rapidly expanded, became centers for the developmental approach in this country. These were schools that quickly developed Third World studies. This developmental model also implied increased sensitivity to problems of policy and the bargaining aspects of power relations: seeing the Third World as presented with a series of choices, decisions, and options, rather than inexorable tendencies from tradition to modernization or, as was later to be the case with the dependency model, from feudalism to socialism. The developmental school also penetrated the structural variables in each of these societies, emphasizing how the processes of electrification and energy allocation shaped the behavior and demands of masses for migration and participation.

Just as the 1950s gave rise to modernization, and the 1960s to developmentalism, the reemergence of Marxism as a respectable university framework gave direct impetus to dependency theory in the 1970s. Dependency theorists believed that the problem of international development could be best understood and examined in the bowels of multinational corporations and Western capitals rather than in backward peripheral societies. A new periodical issued by the Fernand Braudel Center (*Review*) is probably the best example of this tendency, with *Perspectives on Latin America, Insurgent Sociologist*, and *Kapitalistate* representing a similar, albeit more strident point of view. Those who carried the torch in this viewpoint tended to be younger people, led by Immanuel Wallerstein, and including Richard Rubinson, Terrence Hopkins, Gabriel Kolko, Dale Johnson, André Gunder Frank, and Susanne J. Bodenheimer among others.

Dependence theory, as already noted, leads to analysis of dependency only as a United States phenomenon, with scant attention to the Soviet Union. Hence, dependency is seen only as economic rather than political in character. Other problems have also arisen. The dependency school sometimes appears as the opposite of the modernization school, emphasizing unifying global factors, but with a strong critical posture toward the United States rather than the earlier generations' critical emphasis on the Soviet Union. There is also an ideological substitution of public enterprise for private enterprise as a mechanism for solving developmental problems, without much attention to problems of incentive, corruption, and innovation that are commonplace problems of socialist economies.

There is furthermore a transparent, but by no means trivial, sense in which the dependency thesis cannot be sustained: it does not account for the mutuality of dependencies at basic industrial levels. While the power of the United States to control major commercial markets is clear, the dependency of the United States on such Third World countries as Brazil, Thailand, Mexico, Madagascar, Guinea, Zambia, the Philippines, and Indonesia, to name only the most obvious, for mineral deposits is less clear but equally significant. Heavy import reliance for everything from industrial diamonds, graphite, mica, manganese, cobalt, tin, asbestos, and nickel, to zinc, silver, and tungsten, indicates the two-way flow of dependence. The case of petroleum is so well documented on this score that it requires no exaggerated mention.

The real issue then is not dependence, but vulnerability to outside influences. It is the instability and unreliability of the world economic order, or better, the absence of such an order which is a deep source of underdevelopment and the uneven distribution of wealth and corresponding power. The dependency model, by emphasizing historical factors only, tends to omit discussions of future prospects or even current prospects—short of revolutionary apocalypse. Hence, issues of grave concern to the Third World: leveraging, indexing, bargaining, stockpiling, government intervention in industrial affairs, simply go by the boards. The empirical, far from being enriched by the historical, is in effect swallowed whole by metahistory.

Sociology of Development and the Development of Sociology

One ultimately is left with a serious problem in the sociology of knowledge, no less than empirical analysis as such. Are we dealing with a sequence of intellectual positions moving from modernization to developmentalism to dependency, as we move from decade to decade? Or can we evaluate these positions as alternative strategies in the pursuit of scientific prediction and explanation? If sociological participation in developmental studies is simply subject to a genetic explanation, all we could possibly hope for is a more interesting theory for the 1980s and 1990s. I suspect that, in fact, the three postwar decades have outlined three policy alternatives, each of which will be tested in the crucible of events in the years ahead.

It might be the case that each position will experience modifications made imperative by certain methodological refinements, no less than political shifts in power. On the other hand, perhaps one of these three positions will triumph intellectually because it better explains events. Whatever the outcome, it is evident that what comes first need not be last; nor will that which comes last in terms of intellectual progeny necessarily be intellectually triumphant.

There are limits of interpretation and integration in the field of development studies. Even if some rough correlations are possible between conservatism and modernization, liberalism and developmentalism, and radicalism and dependency theory, as some have argued, we are still left with a scientific decision about the most satisfactory and efficacious mode of analysis. By the same token, if we shift our orientation to satisfy contemporary fashion, that is, whatever particular paradigm is most prevalent among specialists at any given period, we must still confront the matter of truth, the simple isomorphism between experience and events.

My own belief is that the developmental thesis continues to represent the mainstream of sociological good sense. It alone offers the possibility of a Third World perspective on itself and for itself. Developmentalism uniquely accounts for external pressures and internal dynamics in the growth process. The developmental framework combines the best and most advanced techniques of qualitative and quantitative research procedures, insisting as it does upon exact attention to ethnographic, linguistic, and national characteristics of those peoples and processes under investigation.[13] Developmentalism leaves open the question of the fundamental construction of social reality; in this it is like the best of sociology generally. It makes the fewest a priori assumptions as to whether economic, political, social, or military factors are central in terms of their explanatory power. Developmentalism also leaves open the possibility that priorities may shift within a nation. Policy making, evaluation studies, and reshuffling social indicators may change the very structure of the development process; and developmentalism is uniquely situated to make such adjustments. The risks of eclecticism have been duly noted by the opponents of the developmental perspective. Yet, what are the alternatives?

Modernization offers a furtive model of models, in which the measurement of development becomes the productive techniques of advanced industrial countries, their commodity fetishes, and the behavior and attitudes of the citizenry of these nonrandomly selected nations. Hence, the measurement of modernization becomes inescapably linked to a celebration of Western capitalism. Such a viewpoint is extrinsic and often alien to the self-discovered needs of developing areas themselves. Dependency theory offers a reverse side of this model of models in which the measurement of development becomes the productive techniques of advanced socialist countries, the social organization of these societies, and ultimately, the totalitarian behavior and attitudes of leaders of these countries. Moving beyond dependency becomes inexorably linked to participation in, if not the celebration of, Soviet communism. Such a viewpoint is extrinsic to and alien from the grounded growth needs of developing areas. Developmentalism as a standpoint of an ideology offers the closest approximation to the structure of the social scientific community, and to the needs of the Third World for an autonomic standpoint for assessing its own achievements and limitations. Developmentalism is the only standpoint that does not presume the Third World is somewhere in limbo—magically and mysteriously on the road to either modernization or socialization. Indeed, the road for the most part eludes analysis based on ideological assumptions. Developmentalism as a perspective takes seriously the contours of the national and regional requirements of developing regions as such. For these objective reasons, I argue that developmentalism has emerged as the master paradigm of social change in the twentieth century: the position that best satisfied the needs of social science research and political policy goals.

There is a significant but quite subjective distinction between modernization and dependency theories on one side, and development theory on the other—the level of intensity brought to bear upon the goals of a society. Modernization advocates, armed with functionalism, just know that the United States and the OECD nations represent the model of models and the future of futures. Dependency advocates, armed with historicism, know with equal or greater fervor that American imperialism is the source of all evil in the developmental process. They are perhaps somewhat less certain about which forms of socialism provide the best cure but they are not above advocating a course of action accelerating the breakup of capitalism through revolution. The developmentalists lack any synthetic a priori ideologies and are reduced to uncertainty and intellectual hedging, which hardly make for dedicated acolytes or clear-eyed emancipators. The situation might be characterized by Yeats's lines that: "the best lack all conviction, while the worst are full of passionate intensity." In the world of social science, insofar as the science part is taken seriously, the monism of the hedgehog is a dubious distinction, while the pluralism of the fox has its own merits. Modernists and dependency advocates, by disallowing that development occurs without regard to teleological visions of the future, inevitably lead the independent researcher to inquire about teleological agendas and private motives. The developmentalist perspective has not been so clearly etched on the sociological conscience as its adversaries not because of confusion or eclecticism, but because it requires that social science be performed as an act of a courage born of direct investigation, rather than an act of faith born of presumed divination.

The evolution of these three major approaches to problems of development indicates the chance nature of social theory, that is to say, how little such theories depend solely for their popularity or currency on the inner logic of scientific discourse, and how heavily on the external factors in political and economic affairs of nations and systems. Those who see in social research a rigor similar to that found in the physical sciences are inevitably disappointed and dismayed. They will be caught awaiting events to confirm their prearranged theories or helplessly watching theories go up in smoke as events disconfirm, time and again, inherited, elegantly worked out ideologies. The work of Herbert Blumer on development, much ignored even by those who take symbolic interactionist frameworks seriously, almost alone at one time appreciated the wide-open nature of social development, even to the point of questioning the legitimacy of the undertaking itself.[14]

One need not adopt an exaggerated solipsism (that Blumer lapsed into at times) about the measurement of development to realize the chance nature of large-scale social analysis. For change is not caprice, simply a consequence of strongly held differences in values, opinions, and ultimately, interests. To expect in such a world of alignment and realignment a unified approach to development would be akin to anticipating a unified attitude toward religious worship in a world of multiple theological perspectives. The tragedy of the present situation is the depth of cleavage. We are faced with three cultures rather than two. Advocates of the aforementioned modernization, developmentalist, and dependency schools have developed a case of collective hardening of the arteries to such an alarming degree, that not only are the leaders of two of these schools misunderstood, they are, for the most part, simply ignored or even at times vilified in satanic revivalist terms. Not only is the spirit of scientific accommodation often lacking, but any extension of good will to advocates of other viewpoints is often absent. This is the ultimate expression of dogmatism, to wish to expurgate chance by a politically inspired determinism having next to nothing to do with the canons of evidence or elements of experience.

The singular ray of hope is that as the 1980s progress, and the three alternative approaches to development will be looked at more closely and exactingly, the strengths and weaknesses of each will come to be measured with sobriety and decency. While still haunted by intellectual timidity and academic politesse, they will at least address theories of development as operational guidelines by which people live and not promulgate thunderous world historic judgments about how people should live.

21. Advocacy and Neutrality in Research

The relationship between social research and political partisanship is scarcely a novelty. This linkage has characterized many studies in sociology and anthropology for the last fifty years. The work of the prototypical and part-mythical post–World War I Chicago school of Thomas, Park, Wirth, Hughes, to mention but a few figures, is characterized by a keen sense of accurate reporting, a perspective on the raw materials which raised issues of stratification and societal values, and in the cases of Park and Wirth, strong political recommendations.[1] What characterized this earlier phase of social ethnography from later developments thus becomes a problem to be discussed, not simply a history to be described.

What distinguishes past from present is certainly not a matter of sophistication. It would be entirely debatable whether earlier or later forms of ethnography were more advanced. True enough, new elements arose: more refined methods of research based upon survey sampling rather than cartographic sampling; a sense of the national rather than the community context in which ethnography takes place; and an emphasis on different types of population omitted from the reckoning by earlier field studies. These points stated and registered, the heart of the matter has not yet been reached. For these are essentially peripheral distinctions, tending to indicate how strong rather than how weak linkages are between past and present.

An alternative explanation of the differences, one which underscores the basis for this effort, is the meliorative context of the old ethnography and the radical context of the ethnography which followed. Whatever differences there were in the Chicago school types, whatever designation may be assigned to them, they certainly were not revolutionary or manifestly ideological in their political orientation. They believed in the social system, in the ability of the democratic potentials of that larger system to correct problems of the subsystems, whether they were problems of deviance, minorities, or urban blight. Not so the latter post–World War II ethnographers. They tended to be less concerned with policy inputs than their forebears because they were less convinced that the system contained any solutions. Indeed, they were often convinced that the system was the problem.[2] Further, the new partisans assumed that the power alliance of the social scientist was with marginal groups whose conditions were direct evidence of troubles at the core of the system. The new social researchers were armed not simply with ethnographic description but with materials for a weakly formulated but generally leftist political critique. It was during this period, from the mid-1960s, to the early 1970s, that advocacy research came to represent a watershed in the history of social science domestic policy formulation, presaging the pervasiveness of social science language, terminology and social scientists themselves in government. For some, belief in political redress was commensurate with a profound distrust of government programs. Identification with the underdog was a means of countering oppression and avoiding personal and political compromise; there could be no policy making until global revolution arrived. But at this point, a critical problem arose: the revolution never came. Prophesies of doom remained unfulfilled, and worse, the new utopia posed by the other side, usually in the form of socialist bloc countries, failed to indicate anything better. Quite the contrary, as information filtered back, culminating in the smashing piece of ethnography by the novelist, Aleksandr Solzhenitsyn, on the Gulag Archipelago, it became evident that revolutionary posturing even less than meliorative faiths was naive, unconvincing, and offered little sustenance for the groups under the research knife. At the same time, the politicization of outsiders into interest groups obliterated the need for volunteer intellectuals. Presented with such a cul-de-sac, the heart itself had been cut from the new sociological partisans, and a consequent falloff of research in this area took place. To trace the empirical and normative characteristics of this natural history in the rise and fall of social science style of work with a political cutting edge becomes a significant aspect in the history of social research.

Research and Policy

In the general context of relevance-seeking that has characterized academic life in the postfunctionalist stage, and which achieved its maximum impact in the mid-1960s, a small but significant number of sociologists and anthropologists produced accounts of deviant and marginal groups which, as published works, successfully combined tough-minded reporting with tenderhearted indictments of social inequalities. In retrospect, the synthesis of social science and ideology achieved by Goffman,[3] Liebow,[4] Becker,[5] Lewis,[6] Lofland,[7] and Humphreys,[8] and other classic ethnographic ventures gave their authors and audience a new potential for social advocacy. The small-scale empirical study of two decades ago opened doors to political action in the name of the group described in ways in which earlier, qualitative research failed to achieve. Crossing the threshold from academic work to practical involvement in the mobilization of deviant and marginal groups proved a direct though not irreversible change of role from scientific observer to social actor.

The sharp decrease in this type of ethnography in the 1980s, and the corresponding decline of partisan roles it so well facilitates, raises abundant questions about the complex relationship between social science methods, ideological commitment, and advocacy. Paramount is the contextual question: under what circumstances does a particular kind of ideological persuasion appear to inform fully all phases of social science work, from posing the research question to proposing policy? The effect of partisanship on the quality of academic performance is one central issue, insofar as the partisan role demands zealous adherence to a cause, even at the expense of the quality of research performed.[9] Advocacy as a commitment expressed in specific acts of counsel, intercession, and public defense raises parallel questions of professional integrity in empirical research and in the use of knowledge to legitimize one or another interest.

The atmosphere in the 1980s is one of divided opinion about the uses of social science information by growing numbers of practitioners—economists, psychologists, sociologists, political scientists—actively engaged in policy-related research and analysis. Like the proverbial writer unconsciously speaking in prose, social scientists make policy all the time, even without knowing so. From one perspective, the definition and resolutions of social policy problems are best left to the government, with the social scientist offering nonpartisan information.[10] From another perspective, the social scientist preserves his or her critical expertise by maintaining university affiliation while independently addressing policy issues.[11]

However, since social scientists have served in a variety of advocacy roles, responding first to the government market in programs for the needy and then drifting towards cost-benefit assessment, this distinction between the polity and the academy is somewhat strained. To chart the huge penetration by social psychologists and sociologists of the federal bureaucracy in the 1960s is to understand how these particular personnel came to represent a constituency, and even to create an articulate interest group demanding still wider access to government. In the late 1970s and continuing into the present the larger role of institutions like Brookings, American Enterprise Institute, or the presidential Council on Economic Affairs, indicates a shift of emphasis not simply toward economists and away from sociologists, but toward a belief in a savings and work policy and away from a spending and welfare policy. Clearly, there are lags and inconsistencies in these patterns. But as an overview, it is fair to say that the period between 1960 and 1972 witnessed a large-scale sociological penetration of government, and the period from 1973 to the present saw a corresponding rise of the economic penetration of government. Of course, social scientists from the various fields can and do accommodate changing fiscal policies, but the selective emphasis contributes to the articulation of those policies.[12]

According to one set of critics,[13] the ascendence of economic theories and method has produced conflict over policy alternatives, rather than action. Constructive policy decisions are undermined by the multiple dissection of issues as if only data matter, of which there is never enough to justify action. This tendency to precise but partial analysis based on statistics alone blocks the open expression or admission of ideology, while feeding the national mood to delay innovations, for example, by introducing new and costly health and welfare programs.[14] The constraints of a savings policy have undoubtedly curtailed long-range planning and forced the translation of ideology into interpretations of statistical tables. This has not prevented thousands of social scientists from implementing, evaluating, and regulating existing programs, as well as participating in occasional dismantlings and innovations; presumably they act according to identifiable sets of social values, overt or covert. The difference under the Reagan administration, as opposed to ten or fifteen years ago, is the difficulty of predicting the responses of any group of social scientists or even individuals to a controversial issue or of placing them professionally in one or another political camp. Just as American liberalism has been eclipsed by the new mood of conservatism, the easy association of once and future academics with a presumed liberal Democratic party has vanished, leaving behind a more extensive and complex network of social science and government connections than ever dreamed of in the Kennedy-Johnson years. Both the character of government largesse and the sentiments of the recipients of such largesse have changed.

From Pragmatism to Radical Imperatives

As an empirical method, field research is sorely out of fashion except in those few select areas which involve community impact studies. The length of time it takes to do field work (a two-year immersion according to classical anthropological tenets), the high yield of qualitative information, and problems with scientific reproducibility are deficits in an information market seeking quick statistical returns and even quicker fixes. Not only the investment of protracted time, but the development of international ties and a sense of identification with the community and group members, distinguish the ethnographer from social scientists who work at a greater informational remove from the people whose behavior they study. While methods scarcely predict ideology, the association of ethnography with liberal pluralism did emerge in recent history, not in its politically quiescent form as nostalgia for the traditional community but as part of a groundswell of social criticism and interest-group support.

The first half of this century witnessed the development of a Chicago school of sociology, a tradition of investigatory field research coupled with a populist view of the social order. In the two decades following World War II, the polarization of sociology into the Columbia-Harvard camp, stressing universalistic value in the profession of sociology, and the softening orientation of the Chicago school also represented a methodological drawing of lines between the former's qualitatively geared positivism and the latter's attempts to develop a pragmatic package that contained not only hard data but also ethnographic observations and value orientations.[15]

The Chicago school of ethnography was postulated as a unique, even laudatory definition of the nature of human groups which literally dictated the researcher's relationship to such groups. At Michigan, Charles Horton Cooley's early articulation of the humanizing function of society affirmed the moral value of the community, placing ultimate worth on prolonged social interaction over substantive judgments of a group's activities as either illegal or deviant. C. Wright Mills's perception of the conservatism inherent in Cooley's community definition of moral order was perceptive: "The notion of disorganization is quite often merely the absence of that *type* of organization associated with the stuff of primary-group communities having Christian and Jeffersonian legitimations."[16] The bias favoring a notion of community order notwithstanding, detailed reporting of social cohesiveness among such unlikely populations as slum-dwellers, criminals, immigrants, and racial and ethnic minorities became a widely adopted characteristic of social research in the Midwest. Sociology as a Christian calling served to validate a highly general notion of moral order even among problem populations.

The research investigations of faculty and graduate students alike were underwritten by a belief in the responsibility of the social scientists to make a contribution to the populist revision of the notion of social order. The pragmatism of men like Louis Wirth, Robert E. Park, Walter Reckless, and Everett C. Hughes rested upon a new populist undercurrent. They wrote not only about urbanization as a source of criminal behavior, but about how crime can be minimized and channelized; not only about Negro-white relations, but about how such relations can be humanized through mutual support. Their sociological commitment was strongly influenced by their belief in political reform.

It took a major confluence of historical circumstances in the 1960s to give ethnographic information the power of generalization and to increase opportunities for the researcher to assume an activist role. Herbert Kelman concisely summarized what he experienced as the three major changes in post-war conditions in the United States which touched every area of academic work.[17] First was the weakening of barriers against speaking out as McCarthyist forces became discredited and a new generation of uncautious students forged by the civil rights movement added impetus to activism. Second, the interplay of knowledge and values was redefined as the central business of the university, with students demanding greater relevance and also with faculty taking their own political assumptions more seriously. Third, there developed a sense of urgency about social science participation in political change which complemented heightened feelings of social responsibility. The war in Vietnam, East-West nuclear confrontations, and international race and class struggles involving the Third World fueled the volatile atmosphere of the time.

The need for information about who had been bearing the burden of political and economic inequities was filled in great measure by reform-minded figures who were relatively marginal to academic life, and certainly not viewed as central to the historic evolution of sociology and ethnography. Set to wage a domestic war on poverty, the War on Poverty proceeded with practically no aggregate data identifying who the poor were, why they were poor, or what might best be done about it. In this statistical vacuum, the broad general statements of John Kenneth Galbraith,[18] Michael Harrington,[19] Dwight MacDonald,[20] and somewhat earlier, Gunnar Myrdal,[21] and Herbert Gans[22] were supported by sympathetic ethnographic accounts of disadvantaged groups.

As one important instance of this near-unanimous emphasis on enlarging equality, it should be noted that the only serious theoretical debate of any policy consequence in the 1960s concerned the culture of poverty hypothesis versus the environmental influence hypothesis. This was based largely on the formulations of anthropologist Oscar Lewis and his "culture of poverty" thesis. Detailed descriptions of the daily lives of blacks, Mexicans, Puerto Ricans, lower-class, and deviant groups provided evidence corroborating social inequities which were not only statistically undocumented, but experientially beyond the ken of most Americans. The works of Lewis in particular persuaded powerful elements of the cultivated new class that the poor lived, and that they might live better and more freely with their help. These beliefs became a matter of social convention which went far beyond either professionally defined commitments or scientifically gathered evidence.

For those ethnographers who took up the mantle of partisanship, the means for further weakening barriers against speech and activism were constructed in ideological ultimates. Myron Glazer in mandating the liberal position on activism wrote: "If those he studies cry out for liberation (the researcher) must help with that liberation—and on their terms."[23] Actual confrontation with sources of actual authority such as the police, prison systems, information agencies, and foreign government officials, matched in drama the new rhetoric of radical moral imperatives for field workers. Yet when the pertinent social science question of specific goals for social change was asked, the unmasking function of ethnographic reportage appeared to have less to do with either revolution or reform than with the capitulation of dedicated amateurs to civil servants in the business of social reform.[24]

The Declining Value of Social Science as Information

The most surprising phenomenon of the times was the rapidity with which the revelatory characteristics of social research and analysis, that aspect Peter Berger called "the first wisdom of sociology,"[25] failed as political currency. The golden age of social research as partisanship in the 1960s and early 1970s was not simply coincident with the liberalism of the War on Poverty, but more important, with the real expansion of social services predicated on the local community as the focus of programs engineered at the federal level. By the early 1970s several truths had emerged. For one, it was patently obvious that once marginal groups could generate their own framework for organization on which to base entitlement, i.e., they could make a strong bid for government recognition, representation, and support, quite without sociological advocates. The initial mobilization of ethnic groups, drug users, homosexuals, prisoners, women, and the aged may have required the legitimizing participation of social scientists, but broadening of channels of appeal appeared to eliminate the necessity for scholarly validation. Social science was thereby reduced from advocacy to testimony,[26] or sometimes testimony as advocacy.[27]

From the standpoint of American communities and organizations, political invisibility ceased to be a problem since government categories for program recipients had proliferated. The real point of tension became competition with other groups of similar outlook wishing to allocate resources, a competition which disallowed impartial, potentially critical, long-term research by social scientists and lent to marginal groups the same defensive restrictions. What Everett Hughes described as the protection of the secrets of the temple associated with bureaucratic organizations. In this changing scenario, the partisan role of the field researcher has been sharply revealed as action in the interest of others, rather than in the interests of a profession or for a larger cause or vision of society. The gentle, academic phrasing of social research as an opportunity to break down the hierarchy of credibility which slights the perspectives of the disadvantaged succumbed to external pressures from and in the name of interest groups to reconstruct social science morally and politically in the name of practical service.[28]

Some pressures came from within and relied on a moral construction of the class struggle. In the rhetoric of the late 1960s, scholarly investigations without an advocacy framework as such were denounced as rip-offs and as aiding and abetting the repression of the poor. In one of the more extreme posturings along this line, Martin Nicolaus wrote: "Sociology has risen on the blood and bones of the poor and oppressed. It owes its prestige in this society to its putative ability to give information and advice to the ruling class of this society about ways and means to keep the people down." [29] Short of a total retreat from empirical work, social ethnographers have had little choice but to let the definition of the field work contract rest exclusively with informants as they saw the potential use of social science. For social anthropologists with ties to Native American tribal organizations, there were obligatory responses to personal calls to do research on topics defined by the group, whatever the merits of the claims. [30]

In overseas work, political upheavals were invariably attended by severe indictments of the complicity of social scientists with colonial regimes. The demands of the natives took on a frightening cast: "the pacific or pacified objects of our investigation, primitives and peasants alike, are even more prone to define our field situation gun in hand." [31] At home and abroad, social investigators became identified with the translation of public service priorities to the community level, an ipso facto redemption via national government contracts or employment by local groups. The intellectual and professional price for continued ethnographic access has been high. Major comparative work, which would relieve community and small-group studies of their unstinting resistance to generalization, has not been forthcoming; nor has the successful integration of qualitative and quantitative methods or an historical appreciation of national development emerged from the numerous efforts in applied research.

Post–Vietnam War ethnography in America was hard hit by waning faith in local administration of programs for the poor, and by the expansion of PPBS (planning, programming, and budgeting system) as a predominantly cost-benefit evaluation effort of the Office of Economic Opportunity and the Department of Health, Education, and Welfare. Support for community autonomy emerged only fleetingly in President Nixon's 1972 campaign, and then with disastrous consequences, by the decentralization of the Bureau of Indian Affairs. [32] The pullback from the local community was based in part on the locus of reform moving upward from the local to the national level. More accurately, the notion of federally generated reform was abandoned even as the size of the social service administration continued to grow and federal monies continued to flow into state and local agencies.

Justification for cutbacks in certain parts of poverty programs was sought and found in the program-planning methodology, the cost-effectiveness effort instituted simultaneously with the War on Poverty. The outcome for expenditures on community and neighborhood programs consistently failed to meet cost-benefit criteria. [33] As a consequence, evaluators cast doubt upon the entire relationship between policy and social change. Results meant not simply that the poor were getting the same quality of educational and health services as the nonpoor, but that these services were meeting some new tests of effectiveness that had never before been applied. In this exercise, the poor served as pawns in the contests to reform all governmental policies, contests in which the best became the enemy of the good. Appraisals of the budget against poverty became entangled with discoveries that the links between educational spending and learning, and between medical care outlays and health, are not too clear.[34]

The command which government agency and department heads exert over research has permitted contract houses to do the bulk of policy work, if only because the intellectual fit is far better between the federal bureaucracy and Abt, Rand, or Systems Development Corporation than between the same bureaucracy and a university environment where time frames are looser and the prerogative to generate extraneous, apparently nontarget knowledge is protected. The sum effect of the increasing bureaucratization of channels of funding and program evaluation has been even sharper competition among organizations and communities acting as special interests totally resistant to nonpartisan inquiry which exposes them to closer observation. Even if the researcher is sympathetic, qualitative data by itself offers more informational chaff than grain and is virtually useless in holding the attention of officials or generating models of change.

Power and Closure in Research

The double jeopardy of the field researcher is inherent in being subject to the group's definition of issues and in being methodologically unwieldy, i.e., dealing with cultural entities rather than social aggregates; the deficit is shared less by those social scientists employing strictly quantitative methods. Nonetheless, the restraints which influence the potential for empirical research in field work have equal repercussions for other academic research ventures. The allocation of power, the definition of a situation and control of information, is a crucial matter in any inquiry; its transformations directly affect the empirical base of social science thought. The political activation of deviant groups, from homosexuals to drug users to pederasts, has profoundly changed the image of these groups from helpless, needy, submerged sectors of American society, into a series of robust interest groups, competing on an equal footing with other groups, from anti-abortionists to antinuclear energy groups. But this too signifies a deep change in the research posture that social scientists can take towards these presumably marginal groups. It raises new questions about how these groups perceive what social scientists can any longer do for them. In part, social scientists are being asked to become increasingly partisan as the price of entrance into future research projects. Increasingly, the researcher has to declare his homosexuality and not simply describe the homosexual scene. Access remains a big issue for social researchers. The social scientists for their part want the taste of victory, a sense that their activities have directly and organizationally been responsible for changes in social attitudes and political dominance. Self-declarations become a simple way to achieve both research and emotional ends.

There is a more subtle aspect to this partisan role: in every interaction the possibility always exists of going native—not only in the traditional overseas sense of becoming romantically attached to the Kwakitul or Trobriander Islanders, but in the content of beliefs in the context of advanced societal research. If an Eric Lincoln or

John Howard study the Black Muslims, the belief system of the group may well prevail, or modify, the structure of social science reporting. The normative values of the group studied, i.e., racial or religious identification in these cases, may prevail over the requirements of the research context. Social research invariably exposes the relativity of power: it turns out that welfare mothers are not as helpless and hapless as early researchers would have it. Homosexual communities are not huddling in closets of dark streets. Street gangs, in fact, have a good deal to say about turf ownership in ghettos. As a result, the researcher comes to a point where he or she must identify not so much with powerlessness as a sympathetic value, but with forms of power that have an attraction and a magnetism of their own making. The same situation holds true for overseas work. The articulation of local groups with a central government which has its own agenda for development makes scholarly investigation a personal mission on the part of the ethnographer who otherwise should be aiding agricultural development, population control, or labor organization. Advocacy for informants becomes a manifest political act, one of clear partisanship, which must often take place outside the national context in which research has been done, as in pleas for the protection of the Amazon tribes[35] or against the Indonesian government's military attacks on East Timor.[36]

The power of local groups to integrate the researcher from an impersonal scholarly model into the political model in turn connects to an entire structure of interest groups. This corresponds to the power of other bureaucratic institutions to impose all-or-nothing conditions of access: to claim allegiance or reject the intrusion of social scientific inquiry. Such regulated institutions as hospitals, prisons, mental institutions, and schools have evolved a defensive attitude toward researchers and, unless otherwise convinced, will restrict access on the basis of claims to protect inmates and clients. A nonpartisan report or survey may involve the release of particularly dangerous information if an institution is already dealing with regulatory review and is heavily dependent on government funding for its survival.

The capacity of social scientists to reveal unknown, unseen, or unexamined aspects of institutional life has been severely reduced by the compromises demanded of the researcher, such as an adherence to confidentiality which protects not primarily individual subjects, but the institution itself—under penalty of exclusion from research sites. Instead of sociological unmasking with its academic tone, journalistic exposure and legal advocacy have become the modus operandi for informing the public about what transpires behind the doors of nursing homes, schools for the retarded, and intensive care units. As one indication of the current restructuring of access, a most effective way of obtaining research information comes from participation in legal cases and court-ordered investigations.

The climate of institutional organization has been deeply affected by federal review and regulation in a way which ultimately can deny both public interest and social research. In such institutions, managerial problems, failure to deliver services, and changing definitions of problems are inadmissible because they jeopardize assessment and funding. The same problems in the private sector have fueled the activities of industrial sociologists for years and continue to do so. The public rendering of accounts takes place in a political context of intense positivism, of a decline in officially sponsored reform, in a bureaucratic context that frowns on support to such deviant projects. In other words, the source of fiscal support argues in favor of value neutrality as the sources of social pressure urge increased identification of the investigator with the investigated.

In yet other arenas where social scientists might seek information on behavior and written records, empirical data are inaccessible or, if accessible, the coercive power of the group threatens the autonomy of the individual researcher. Certain religious cults are in this category insofar as they resist inquiry or demand life membership. Government organizations, such as the Department of Defense and the Pentagon, have both the power of secrecy and general coercive power to restrict access and will therefore offer nothing but externalized, public stances on which to conjecture the internal organization of decision making.

The ideal classical component of social research—"a description of culture in such a way that we feel that we are dealing with real and specific men and women, with real and specific situations, and with real and specific tradition"—is now construed as a threat to social life, if not a violation of huddling rights to privacy.[37] Concurrently, the empirical basis of the social sciences has shifted to survey data. The repercussions for members of the different disciplines who confront science-and-values issues have been complex. The best times offered us a plurality of consulting roles in government and a profusion of research opportunities not only in federal government, but also in law and industry. Each option for engagement in public interest problems presents a secondary option to assume an advocacy position which will mitigate the struggle between nonpartisan professionalism and ideology.

The range of advocacy roles is great. We have seen and still do see in ethnographic work the singular reality in the investigatory spectrum where the hazards of sacrificing social science to political action on behalf of others become manifest. There are other varieties of advocacy which deserve discussion because they illuminate both the universality of the struggle to integrate knowledge and values, and the choice of postures which seem to resolve the dilemma; but they invariably promise more than they deliver.

First, advocacy can mean active partisanship, or more aptly, participation in political parties or causes. In the cases of earlier committed scholars such as V. F. Calverton[38] or Bernhard Stern,[39] there was a strong presumption that advocacy, as part of the tide of history, serves to inform social research and create the basis of objective truth. For others, such as Peter Berger or Murray Weidenbaum, membership in the Republican party does not guarantee such scientific truths whatsoever. In this approach, membership is simply isomorphic with the belief system of the scholar.

Second, advocacy in a slightly less obvious sense has to do with social movements that turn political, i.e., deviant movements or welfare mothers' movements. Scholars like Laud Humphreys write not only about homosexual communities, but participate in the promulgation of homophile societies. Others, like Frances Fox Piven and Richard Cloward,[40] likewise participated in the organization phases of the welfare rights movement.[41] At this level the presumption is that to write about such outside groups is to accept some mandate to participate in rectifying the problems written about.

Third, advocacy in a still weaker form has a positivist gloss: a tacit assumption that to write about outsider groups in an empathic manner invites broad support for such groups. Better ethnography in itself makes for better public relations. In this category we find academics like Howard S. Becker[42] on drug users and John Lofland[43] on cult groups. Where there is no explicit presumption of "do thou likewise" with respect to drugs or cults, there is a belief that their writings will elicit broad public support or eventual sound legislative relief.

Fourth, there are a series of scholars for whom research and advocacy have absolutely nothing organic to do with each other. Facts and values are distinct. Yet values or citizenship roles are perfectly acceptable, and carry greater weight precisely because of the presumed objectivity of the scientists involved. Hence, social scientists like Robert Bierstadt can function as members of the executive board of the American Civil Liberties Union without forfeiting any claims to objectivity in the research process.

Fifth, there are individuals who become part of the policy apparatus or the political mechanism, such as Daniel Patrick Moynihan[44] and Henry Kissinger.[45] For such people, social research is a sensitizing device and a preliminary training agency for the political life which helps make for better and richer decision making. There is a clear recognition that social science information is important, but that it remains relatively neutral with respect to mandating certain courses of action. However, the main commitment, the way in which such individuals make a living or do work is by shifting directly from an academic to a political locus, quite unlike members of the previous four categories who remain attached to academic social science research.

The types of advocacy roles a social scientist can play clearly extend in practice beyond these model categories. Therefore, the question of social science impact on policy becomes more a matter of the individual's participation in the process of decision making than of a bloc force of intellectuals whose total influence can be characterized in terms of a single ideology. The easy association of academics with liberal causes cannot be taken as a given as it was ten or fifteen years ago. The entire political base for action—the party system, the organization and relations of federal and state governments, and the needs and wants of the polity—have undergone drastic changes from Johnson to Reagan. Party affiliation no longer determines how an elected official votes on public welfare or foreign policy or how citizens judge issues or political performance. New oppositions, between the Sunbelt and the Snowbelt, between old allies and even old enemies on the international front, have evolved in innovative and unanticipated ways. In the meanwhile the education and social service sectors are at all levels, except community, more intellectually problematic than could have been imagined twenty years ago.

The lack of ideological consensus among intellectuals or the lack of intellectual consensus among ideologues is much less worrisome as a phenomenon than observable inroads on the firm empirical foundation of social science research by which informed policy decisions can be made. Closure in scholarly research opportunities, loss of comparative perspective, and emphasis on a single, quantitative methodology will have the ultimate effect on changing the nature of, rather than canceling out, social science influence in government. As Lindblom and Cohen remind us, "The continuation of research efforts is the major social science contribution to policy and to social change. . . . The principal impact of policy-oriented studies, say on inflation, race conflict, deviance, or foreign policy—including those specifically designed to advise a specific policymaker at a particular time—is through their contribution to a cumulating set of incentives for a general reconsideration by policymakers of their decisionmaking framework, their operating political or social philosophy, or their ideology."[46]

The burden of these remarks examining the historical antecedents of activism in social research is to show how different types of advocacy are employed to give social science an extra push in the direction of those values deemed beneficial to the future well-being of humankind. But despite the deep weakness in any one form of partisanship, it would be inappropriate to conclude on a note of extreme relativism. To do so would merely serve to cast doubt on social research as a whole, to accept at face value the argument that since scientists have values, all research is a priori a value saturated to a point beyond hope. More dangerous yet is to deny the universality of science, to assert instead that the essential difference between the social and physical sciences is that the former irretrievably are connected to subjectivity, relativity, and partisanship, and hence must simply be harnessed to one or another form of ideology, whether that be expressed in terms of the maintenance of divine institutions or climbing aboard a mythical railroad of history.

The scientific standpoint remains relevant for social research as it delivers messages to the political system. That standpoint is simple enough: whatever be the disputation of any court of inquiry, legal edicts, professional sanctions, political obligations, or religious persuasions, the earth will continue to orbit about the sun in terms of laws observed with respect to the motion of all celestial bodies. If one cannot seriously assert the same universal, lawlike status for findings of social research, it is still possible to come reasonably close. Ideology may remain a stimulus and a prod to good research as well as poor research; but the test of the quality of research remains the experiential context and evidential base of ethnography and inquiry generally.

If the social scientist forfeits the right to criticize the political establishment from a posture of autonomy he therefore risks becoming a handmaiden of the political apparatus, whatever the level of policy engagement. The concept of evidence on which research is based is the fundamental guarantee for professional autonomy. In its strength, it stands as a protection against the subversion of social science to a partisan model for promulgating certain kinds of persuasions and beliefs. The appeal to empirics is itself the essential, nay the quintessential, social science response to the relativity of beliefs, values, and postures found in social research. If science is the source of so many questions about the advocacy status of findings and events, it is also the source for resolving ideological disputes and partisan differences.

22. Language, Truth, and Politics

In George Orwell's justifiably famous 1946 essay entitled "Politics and the English Language," which seemed remarkably candid for the period, he barely hinted at what the rhetoric of totalitarianism was to become.[1] His concerns were expressed to different professional audiences, and with equal vigor by Harold Lasswell and Lancelot Hogben. These postwar luminaries were of a certain intellectual independence, whatever their political persuasions. Orwell's essay differs from others because he addresses not so much the totalitarian spirit, as linguistic problems inherent in the use of language by totalitarians. Thus Orwell emphasizes dying metaphors, the use of inappropriate verbs and nouns, pretentious diction, and meaningless words. But throughout there is a strong emphasis on the need to maintain language as a formal instrument of political clarity.

Orwell taught us the simple truism that tendentious writing for the most part is bad writing; and that what underwrites bad writing is in effect a political defense of the indefensible, whether it is the continuation of British rule in India, Russian purges and deportations, or the dropping of the atomic bomb. Discussion of the routine of death of ordinary people through military means becomes converted into a series of apologetics. What deeply disturbed Orwell was how political thought corrupted language; but perhaps even more, how language corrupted thought, how political thought debased language to such a degree that qualifying phrases could be used in order to rationalize the most hideous behavior. No wonder, therefore, that Orwell ends his essay not so much with a political series of considerations as with reflections of a more grammatical sort: Never use a metaphor when you do not have to. Never use long words when a short one will do. If it is possible to eliminate words, avoid them as superfluous. Never use the passive when you can use the active voice. Never resort to foreign phrases or jargon when everyday English equivalents are available. But since that famous essay of thirty-five years ago, the situation has gotten much more serious; it has become less a matter of form and more of substance.

In a unique effort to update Orwell's discussion, Walter Laqueur's own essay, "Foreign Policy and the English Language," reminds us of the term for the impoverished language: *psittacism*, or the habit of using words without thought.[2] It is a habit that is widespread in media coverage, especially in the analysis of foreign affairs; terms such as *conservative* and *liberal*, *fascist* and *communist*, *revolutionary* and *reactionary* are frequently, even invariably juxtaposed with scant reference to their real meaning. And if Laqueur is more keenly aware of language, of the intent to defraud and in so doing to manipulate entire populations, he too sees this as a problem common to the West as well as the East, among the democracies as well as the autocratic societies. Like Orwell, Laqueur sees no solutions in terms of accuracy in the use of language. The precise use of language, even if it does not guarantee correct understanding of politics, at least offers the possibility of getting things right. Laqueur sees the purpose of language in terms of eliminating an accumulated debris of more than three decades, and, again like Orwell, he sees imprecise political language as a problem primarily in the English language.

I would suggest that the relationship of language misuse to a totalitarian system is more deep-seated. The problem is not simply one of language reform, or of correcting formal or syntactical abuses, but a problem intrinsic to the nature of certain political systems themselves. In totalitarian systems language becomes debased in ways that are profound and provide limited potential for reform.

The rhetoric of totalitarianism is not a problem solely in the English language; it is a problem faced in any language insofar as such rhetoric becomes the property of a political party or a political state. The rhetoric of totalitarianism is the issue, more so than the reform of language by democracies or its corruption by authoritarians. The totalitarian system no longer sharpens, but blurs language meanings; it serves to disperse rather than concentrate thought. It does so by translating personal experience into mystical emotionalism. The rhetoric of totalitarianism is invariably global. Individual, local, even national levels of analysis must give way to a universe of complete interdependence. Mystification becomes grandiose, as in this fashionable explanation of "Who Will Bring the Mother Down?"

> There are no more "local" contradictions, and no more "economic" contradictions, in the sense that is usually meant; all of our contradictions, and the deeper they are the truer this is, have universal causes and universal effects: one baby in one room in one town who cries from hunger throws the entire history of the world into question.[3]

One distinguishing characteristic among a variety of less than democratic and even repugnant regimes is the extent to which the rhetoric of totalitarianism is either present or absent. Even under conditions of considerable repression, *El Mercurio* of Santiago, Chile, or *La Nación* or *La Prensa* of Buenos Aires, Argentina, reveals characteristics of a democratic press that simply are not to be found in the press of either Eastern Europe or Cuba. At some point one simply has to take for granted the obvious and not belabor the breakdown of meaning; and to give illustrations that are all too well known to require any further repetition is unnecessary. Let us instead try to understand and evolve the intellectual and ideological sources of the rhetoric of totalitarianism.

The rhetoric of totalitarianism is based on doctrinal considerations, or an assumption of absolute right on one side and absolute wrong on the other side. It is the epistemological absorption of Manicheanism in the political realm. As a result, every article is measured by the degree to which it exemplifies this sense of who is right and who is wrong. The certainty of knowledge of who are friends and who are enemies leads to a fragile solution in which any change in political alliance itself becomes a problem for consciousness and memory. Not having any standpoint other than rhetoric, real changes and alignments become hopelessly mired in contradictory policy outlines. Thus it is that Argentina, anathema to Cuba for twenty years, can be embraced by Fidel Castro and his nonaligned bloc overnight as a result of the crisis in the Falkland Islands. How is the same sort of fanatic absolutism to be maintained?

Here totalitarian systems have come up with what might be called a higher level of philosophic abstraction. Absolute right and absolute wrong are simply translated from one victim to another, or what one might call the higher victim. In a world in which Argentina is the highest victim, it is the enemy, but in a world in which a higher villain is ready at hand, in this case Great Britain or the United States, the main thrust of the rhetoric shifts and the former middle-range foe becomes a friend, at least in strategic temporary alliance.

Ultimately language itself becomes a tactic, having no meaning apart from political purpose. Thus Khrushchev in enunciating the doctrine of peaceful coexistence, did so in the name of Lenin.

> The Leninist principle of peaceful co-existence of states with different social systems has always been and remains the general line of our country's foreign policy. And this is natural, for there is no other way in present-day conditions. Indeed, there are only two ways: either peaceful co-existence or the most destructive war in history. There is no third way.[4]

Now it is true that Lenin asserted that there is no third way; but it is no less the case that Lenin postulated not the growth of coexistence but rather the international expansion of class struggle.

> We live not only in a State but in a *system of States*, and the existence of the Soviet Republic beside the imperialist states during a lengthy period of time is inconceivable. In the very end either one or the other will win. And before this result, a series of horrible conflicts between the Soviet Republic and the bourgeois states is unavoidable.[5]

It is evident that Lenin foresaw a period of intensified conflict between communism and capitalism, and not protracted peace. But the arsenal of totalitarian rhetoric does not and cannot admit human fallibility. No one can dare say that nuclear weaponry makes certain formulations of Lenin and others obsolete or untenable. The doctrinal fathers must retain their currency and tenable character. This is done by raising analysis from a functional to an ideological plane. Leninism is converted to a struggle between the communist and the capitalist ideologies. Loyalists are assured that communist ideas will conquer mankind. The much vaunted materialist conception of history gives way to an idealistic concept in which ideas conquer all. In this way, strategic shifts are carried forth with abandon, sometimes with imagination, while leaving untouched the pristine purity and doctrinal perfection of the founding fathers of totalitarianism.

The rhetoric of totalitarianism is underwritten by a doctrine of raw partisanship. Ontology is reduced to epistemology. The reality of the world is converted to class or race-based attitudes. History is a source of verification, not information. History not only absolves but it proves. This introduces an almost heroic element into the rhetoric of totalitarianism. For the actions of people, their very partisanship, change the nature of historical outcomes, and as a result transforms the objective conditions and objective situation. For this reason the rhetoric of totalitarianism cannot accept a purely objective notion of a truth or error; the actions people take can manufacture truth as well as error.

Sometimes events do not confirm any particular form of action, and history neither absolves nor blames but proves the partisan to be wrong. For example, the Cuban model may be perfectly reasonable in terms of Nicaragua, but it fails in terms of Bolivia. How is the failure in one situation to be dealt with, when there is success using the same model elsewhere? Simplification is a totalitarian norm. Here one has to understand that partisanship, like the notion of absolutism, permits a higher notion of heroism than pure historical success, namely, an ethical purpose sanctioned by doctrinal sources that has nothing to do with specific outcomes. One can be a hero and suffer failure at the same time; failure in this view is always considered temporary in character.

The corruption of language has as a central dynamic the manufacture not only of events but of outcomes. Thus the crushing defeat sustained by the PLO in having to evacuate Beirut and its complete inability to maintain a military capability against the onrush of Israeli military cadres are transposed into a glorious victory heralding better days ahead. The following communiqué from Fidel Castro to Yasir Arafat is typical of this kind of analysis.

> The people of Palestine have once again demonstrated their integrity and courage. Besieged by a technically and numerically superior enemy equipped with the most sophisticated war logistics—an enemy armed and advised by the United States and accustomed to obtaining immediate results from a lightning war—the people of Palestine resisted with insuperable dignity and held back the advance of the Zionist war machine. From the ruins of West Beirut and under the cross-fire of the Israeli navy, land and air forces, the military response of the Palestinian fighters supported by the Lebanese patriots never ceased. The whole world has witnessed with amazement and admiration the example of courage given by the Palestinian people defending their inalienable rights under the correct leadership of the PLO, their only and legitimate representative, and inspired by the invaluable encouragement of your presence in the front lines.[6]

Through the magic of rhetoric losing is turned into winning, and blunders are turned into bravery. Given the unidirectional nature of metahistory, the myth of people's warfare is converted into the myth of eternal progress. But unlike the Enlightenment doctrine of progress, setbacks are not part of nature but expressions of cowardice, defeatism, and betrayal of a cause. Under such punitive conditions, who would dare challenge the idea that victory and defeat are interchangeable concepts, defined by the state media?

There is really no admissible notion of long-term historical failure within the confines of totalitarianism. What one admits to is only a temporary setback, a strategic miscalculation, or a tactical blunder. The principle itself is never incorrect; the formulation is never so out of kilter with reality as to doom to defeat the ideological position or the future action. In this way, one observes a critical element in the rhetoric of totalitarianism: the breakdown of distinctions between truth and meaning, between the activity itself and how it is to be interpreted. Because there is no objective truth apart from subjective sentiment, objectivist language, language without emotion, and adjectives all become suspect, even dangerous.

It is not possible simply to implore users of such rhetoric to purify their use of language, to eliminate adjectives, or to restore a sense of the integrity of English, German, Russian, or what have you. The very essence of totalitarian rhetoric is its emotionalism, its extremism. Hence any article, essay, or book that is written in a nonemotive manner becomes dangerous, itself an item of hostility. The problem lodges in the very nature of social language in contrast to the nature of scientific language. The language of modern science is objective. In point of fact, it has very little to do with emotional diatribes or excessive appeals to any particular line of action.

The doctrine of the partisan character of knowledge is no simple assault on value-free notions of science and art. More exactly, it is a critique of objectivity as such. As early as 1905, Lenin in a tract on *Party Organization and Party Literature* formulated the position "that literature cannot be non-partisan," i.e., that it must either serve the "causes of the people" or oppose such causes. Years later, in a post–World War II environment dominated by the tasks of Soviet reconstruction, Stalin's cultural alter-ego, Andrei Zhdanov, expanded on the totalitarian theme of cultural workers being "engineers of human souls." This concept is interpreted to mean "knowing life so as to be able to depict it truthfully in works of art, to depict it not in a dead, scholastic way, not simply as 'objective reality' but to depict reality in its revolutionary development." And to those who feared a consequent reduction of language to pure propaganda, Zhdanov was especially ferocious.

> Our Soviet literature is not afraid of the charge of being tendentious. Yes, Soviet literature is tendentious, for in an epoch of class struggle there is not and cannot be a literature which is not class literature, is not tendentious, is allegedly non-political. . . . Our literature, which stands with both feet firmly planted on a solid materialist base, cannot be hostile to romanticism, but it must be a romanticism of a new type, revolutionary romanticism.[7]

It should occasion little surprise that this continues to remain the official theory of Soviet culture. More surprising is how individuals who accept this sort of analysis have scarcely bothered to inquire why, if the Soviet Union has abolished all class antagonisms and contradictions, it must continue to treat language as a tool of state propaganda. Even to make such inquiries is presumably to escape the responsibilities of socialist realism and revolutionary romanticism alike.

Much of the rhetoric of totalitarianism, especially leftist totalitarianism, is based on a concept of history as science. There is an obvious dilemma between the appeal to a heavily emotional and adjectival social language in contrast to the relatively neutral use of language in the physical and behavioral sciences. The problem has the capacity to exacerbate the disjunction between the social and scientific realms. It has led to a sharp dichotomy between the physical and social. There is no way that this problem can be overcome simply; efforts to do so have been crowned with disaster and tragedy, making the study of language itself part of the study of class, while making biology a function of racial doctrine and evolutionary theory. In other words, attempts to overcome the dualism created by the rhetoric of totalitarianism themselves lead to extraordinarily complex and at the same time unmanageable philosophical world views.

The compelling force of the rhetoric of totalitarianism, whatever its problems at the linguistic level, is that it inspires a great deal of fear in political matters. One might be labeled guilty of left-wing infantile disorders, for example, and see this as a sickness, not just a weakness. Shortcomings are defined in terms of the very rhetoric that defines success. Hence, one has to be exceedingly careful, making language even more remote from reality in totalitarian societies than in most primitive societies, for they share the absolute isolation and irresponsibility of leadership to membership.

One peculiarity in the rhetoric of totalitarianism is that similar activities are described in diametrically opposite terms. Good wars may be described as "clean," "neat," "surgical," or "humane." Bad wars are described as "sneak attacks," "brutal," "inhumane," "antipopular," and so on. Identical happenings are defined not by the character of the event but by the presumed worthiness of actors performing in them. Thus it is that the original Argentine invasion of the Falklands was described by its junta as admirable and performed with remarkable precision, even a thing of beauty. Vittorio Mussolini, the son of the *duce*, described an air attack on Ethiopia as "the magnificent sport." He had the impression of "a budding rose unfolding as the bombs fell in their midst and blew them up."[8] The very same destruction of life is defined as hideous, heinous crimes against humanity, if class or race enemies perform these acts.

What this means, of course, is that no population can describe the meaning of events for itself; it must have those events interpreted by a leadership, by a political faction. Only they can determine if an event is neat, surgical, and humane, or brutal, antipopular, and inhumane. This creates an inert, inactive mass, and has the effect of defeating even the possibility of political mass mobilization. It inhibits any notion of objective evaluation and judgment and hence inhibits the possibility of the political life as an active and open life.

Sustaining the rhetoric of totalitarianism requires denying alternative accesses to information, and even more important, alternative interpretations of events. A scientific or essentially apolitical approach establishes right and wrong. The rhetoric of totalitarianism seeks to link partisanship and science. But because partisanship is imposed by a political leadership from the top down, and science evolves through an experimental framework, oftentimes from the bottom up, the linkage is artificial and creates more dilemmas than solutions for the regime. It is no accident that the source of so much opposition to totalitarianism regimes, and certainly opposition to the rhetoric of totalitarianism, derives from the scientific and intellectual sectors. Special treatment is needed to keep such elites politically quiescent. In this sense, the rhetoric of totalitarianism is in actual opposition to the everyday functioning of the totalitarian society: it must create new elites in the very act of denouncing elitism.

It would be a mistake to think that the issues raised by the rhetoric of totalitarianism can be easily resolved by appeals to evidence or scholarship. Fanaticism underwrites the present moment in the totalitarian rhetoric. As Charles S. Peirce long ago pointed out, the method of authority, while perhaps not the best available, is certainly the most widely adhered to, followed in quick order by the method of appeal to divine authority, with the scientific method a distant third.[9] As a result, framers of this rhetoric are often led to miscalculate the decisions and behavior of the much-despised other side: too easily taking efforts at conciliation as weakness, too ready to assume that more belligerent standpoints require leaping to a warlike or aggressive attitude.

It is probably fair to conclude that there can be no lasting democratic victory against such rhetoric any more than one can hope that the world will be made up of people absolutely and unequivocally dedicated to objective fact without regard to self-interest or national interest. It would be much more reasonable to say that even if the rhetoric of totalitarianism cannot be overwhelmed by a scientific standpoint or a more balanced vision of the world, neither can the struggle itself be abandoned. Even if the struggle for a rational use of language is doomed to incomplete success, to abandon the effort itself would certainly doom us all to a complete failure, and hence to convert a long night into a much more serious situation: a world without light.

23. Moral Development and Authoritarian Distemper

As prolegomena to this essay, let it be said that it is based on the premise that the development of morals is diametrically opposed to and categorically distinct from moral education. Moreover, the pluralism inherent in this study of how morals develop over time and environments is at the opposite pole from the monism inherent in the study of how a particular form of moral education is to be imposed on the human race. It has become fashionable to decry open-ended notions of human variations, and equally in vogue to identify surviving political systems with moral purpose. Moral education, the parent of moral development, has become the rage from Peking to Cambridge. The fact that different forms of morals are being taught has seemingly been downgraded in the rush to judgment, in a widely held belief that the very instruction into the moral order is some sort of cultural universal that transcends what is specifically being taught.

One's intellectual life is privy to such a barrage of rhetoric concerning a crisis in morals, breakdown in discipline, collapse of purpose, that there is a tendency to forget the dangerous consequences of living in a society in which there is no crisis in morals—only moral certitude—and in which moral purpose is imposed by a political regime with a tenacity and ferocity that makes moral doubt, even ethical confusion, a dangerous posture. The short and long of this discussion is that those who believe in democracy must have a corresponding faith in the evolution of moral choice, and individuals who, to the contrary, believe that only instruction in moral order through a preset notion of moral development will ensure the survival of civilization, have already denied the essential premises and practices of a democratic system.

Relativists and Normativists

The problem of moral development, then, is inherent in the coupling of the two words. Few would dispute that there is such a thing as morals, and fewer still that there is another entity called education. Whether they fit together conceptually in a neat, two-tiered package becomes a large question. The present disarray of moral philosophy has contributed to the puzzle. Ethnicists are as polarized as can be. One sense of moral development is that it is an historical, evolutionary, and sociological concept of expanding rights. Relativists like Richard Brandt[1] and Abraham Edel[2] have argued this thesis. There is a diametrically opposite view of moral development, advocated by people such as Leo Strauss[3] and Richard Flathman,[4] claiming a normative, natural law foundation of human behavior, the assumption being that social obligations, like mathematical axioms, can be deduced from a set of first principles.

Underlying this debate between relativists and normativists is a disagreement about the degree to which options and choices in the world exist. For the relativists, choices are limited only by circumstances, and hence decision making about political issues is a series of historically conditioned searches for rights. For normativists, the world is far less permissive, sometimes even predetermined, and hence the real search ought to be for the foundations of obligations. At stake are a series of choices people make on the basis of fundamental, underlying premises of the rights and wrongs of behavior. For relativists, morals are constantly evolving in a wide-open universe, whereas for normativists, choices are made within well-understood, or at least well-defined, social structures. At the risk of turning a drastic oversimplification into caricature, what is good and what is evil for relativists constantly shift, often according to community norms and changing external pressures. What is good and what is evil for normativists stay the same, for people do the shifting, achieving higher or lower levels of ethical purification in the process.

Reconciliation of these two long-standing positions is in order, and many efforts in this direction are under way. The rise of both the social sciences and policy research may offer some clues to these new directions. The author proposes a retention of the normativist framework: what is good and what is evil remain essentially the same now as they were in the world of ancient Athens. To this should be added the relativistic perspective: what change drastically are the consequences of choices. Both political sociology and political psychology can shed light on the subject of moral development.

In the past, people tended to think of homicide as an evil under most circumstances, but they also thought of the arbitrary termination of life as basically a one-to-one relationship: one person destroying another person. In the twentieth century, however, homicide has been transformed into genocide. The situation is more nearly that of one nation destroying another nation. The magnitudes, technically conditioned and depersonalized, so profoundly alter the consequences of behavior, that the same moral choices have hugely differing outcomes. There are qualitative leaps in technology that make decisions about life and death critical for large numbers.

Several caveats are in order. First, if by moral development one means that a set of goals for society determined and defined by political leadership is good and that departures from those pretested, preset norms are evil, then the phrase is simply a clever disguise for totalitarian temptations; for moral development in this sense means nothing short of the total unification of a society along a certain path, road, or in conformity with a particular model. So conceived, moral development is but an Orwellian device disguising political repression. Second, and contrariwise, if moral development is viewed in a pluralistic context, as expanding possibilities for making meaningful choices, serving both personal, particular, general, and universal goods, the phrase—moral development—can be infused with democratic meaning if the prospect of the development of a moral sensibility as an attitude of individuals is introduced. The ability to place oneself in another's position, rather than moral development as measuring up to arbitrary social standards, becomes the touchstone of moral probity. At such a level, moral development is related to cognitive prerequisites for community rather than collective demands for order.

Both collective and individual standpoints must be reckoned with. Those societies that have put forth eugenic theories of moral development, such as the Nazi view of the biologically healthy individual, are clearly willing to sacrifice the individual self to the organic whole. Such moral development leads to uncritical supporting of systems and ultimately outlaws all choices and decisions as attributes of unsponsored individuals. On the other hand, if the development of morals represents a statement of how each individual is ultimately responsible for, and is a repository of, both personal and general goods, the spirit of the democratic interpretation is preserved. Whether we appeal to John Locke in the British constitutional tradition or to Mahatma Gandhi in the Hindu tradition of nonviolent resistance to tyranny, such a view of a morally centered polity—in which individuals determine their own fates—has been of great significance in the evolution of societies in both the East and West.

Moral Strategies and Strategies About Morals

Moral development can be viewed epistemologically. The process of cognition by which citizens learn to distinguish what constitutes right from wrong or good from evil is a learning situation. Moral development is a process of socialization. The literature on political socialization is by and large concerned with describing how such concepts are acquired and subsequently applied to the body politic. Studies of children's reactions to the assassination of Martin Luther King, Jr., or the late President John F. Kennedy, represent empirical studies of the process of becoming socialized into things political. The works of political scientists like Richard Dawson[5] and L. Harmon Ziegler[6] typify such orientations, and can properly be said to constitute a special sort of theory of moral development, one based on experiential adaptation, rather than a didactic set of commitments to ritualist or rote learning.

From the standpoint of political sociology, moral development can be considered moral postures that result from class, ethnic, or racial factors. Within such a social framework, moral development refers to the growth of isomorphism between human consciousness and socioeconomic interests. Specifically, moral development is viewed as a coalition of factors between a stake in a social order and perceived political and ideological responses. This aspect of moral development is considerably different from political socialization, for political sociology assumes a correlation between interests and behavior. The work of Karl Marx,[7] Karl Mannheim,[8] and Max Scheler,[9] among many others, suggests a special vision of moral development: the development of a set of moral postures based on class positioning and the effect of this on ascriptive superstructural features such as religion, culture, or race.

A third notion of moral development, evolving from the Kantian tradition of transcendental apriorism, and perhaps Platonic sources as well, considers the question axiomatically, as a process of learning to distinguish truth from falsity. In this way it is assumed that individuals come closer to identifying with the true nature of a political system as they appreciate the structure of such a system. Politics in this sense represents an axiomatic vision of the moral order. Becoming political is like becoming mathematically adroit, that is, learning about those axiomatic foundations determines the logical structure of the state (in the case of Plato) or world order (in the case of Kant).

The psychoanalytic tradition has contributed a fourth perspective on moral development. Even if the obvious moralistic biases of Freudian psychoanalytic theory are ignored, Freud—at the conscious level at least—eschewed a moral grounding for mental health or illness.[10] This is not the case with some of the new Freudians. For instance, Erik Erikson's views on the ages of man provide a clear-cut foundation to a psychoanalytic theory of moral development.[11] The ages (or better, states) are oral, anal, phallic, oedipal, latency, and puberty. Without arguing about the presumed intuitive righteousness of Erikson's ages, as some have, it can be seen that the position of Erikson on theological or political figures like Luther and Gandhi[12] indicates that the postpuberty stage—extending from roughly age fourteen to death—involves a powerful moral component of responsibility for behavior not carried or anticipated in the earlier adolescent period.[13]

This notion of anticipatory development, or more inclusive identities, implies a fusion of rational prognosis and moral rightness (or at least the absence of dogmatism) and a sensitivity to the diversity and complexity of the human personality. Whether such broad categories can be used or, if realized, can prevent an arbitrary and capricious rendering of moral behavior is a problem faced not only by Erikson, the veritable father of the theory of human development, but by the psychoanalytic tradition as a whole. While the stages of development in adolescents are essentially behavioral, and by implication not easily subject to adult criteria of morals, just how that moral self eventually penetrates human behavior remains cloudy. Freud saw in morality a transliteration of superego and censor mechanisms, but he did not say clearly how good works become a moral good. *Civilization and Its Discontents* describes the antagonistic mechanisms of work and sexuality but not how moral components infuse such broad ranging, biosocial categories.[14]

There is, in fact, a commonsensical definition of moral development all too easily overlooked among sophisticated analysts; that is, the notion of moral development as rendering instruction for those in need of it, a sort of gerontological vision of advice from the elderly or established to the youthful or ill-advised. More than one group of those who are responsible for the current revival of interest in this subject of moral development have as their hidden agenda instruction in right morals.[15] In contrast to this is a briefer, but probably equally honorable tradition in which moral education has to do with the ability of an individual to absorb new information without those hierarchical or traditional impediments otherwise known as learning.[16] The learning concept is less taken up with status considerations of who does or does not have the right to offer instruction. Learning is a process far more difficult than teaching, since it involves the far more complex art of listening rather than speaking.

If these strategies of moral development could be kept clear of each other, many problems would dissolve, along with the linguistic ambiguity and confusions created by overlapping conceptual frameworks. However, not only are these stand-points on moral development not properly distinguished, they are further saddled by the conceptual map of social psychology in which phrases like *human development* are viewed as isomorphic with moral development and, more pertinently, in which correlated concepts of cognition and judgment, description and prescription, are muddled beyond belief. As if this situation inherited from the past is not a severe enough handicap, educators have thrown in an additional phrase for good measure: moral education in contrast to affective education.[17] Here one comes full circle, with a strong tendency to equate fundamental with normative. Hence, pedagogical conservatives speak of moral education and the political order as an intertwined behavioral process summed up in the restoration of civics and civil behavior.[18] Defi-ciencies in education rather than inequalities in society are held to strict account for the current breakdown and malaise presumed characteristic of the times.

The language of breakdown and fragmentation replaces that of social structure and political system as crucial explanatory devices. As a consequence, and without too much elaboration, one can see that the ebb and flow of interest in moral devel-opment, far from being self-explanatory and transparent, is actually composed of a series of distinctive policy frameworks—some of which offer the potential for new linkages between events and ethics, whereas others offer little more than further intellectual disputation, or worse, an end to disputation in order to disguise the paucity of naturalistic solutions to long-standing human problems.

Moral Principles and Principles About Morals

Getting beyond strategies and addressing principles becomes the next and by far the most difficult step in evolving a meaningful statement about moral development. To take this giant step one must return to the classical statements on democratic political theory from John Locke to John Rawls, for the essence of that classic tradi-tion is, in fact, the linkage of politics to ethics. The fundamental debate over the relationship of personal rights to social obligations is what moral development is about, and the highest form of such development is to maintain the balance, the tension, between rights and obligations. The tension—the antithesis rather than the synthesis—is precisely what justice is about, and moral development is the wisdom to engage in the conduct of justice. To resolve in some arbitrary ultimate way the argument over rights and obligations, is to surrender the society either to the Anarch or, at the other extreme, to the Behemoth.[19] And such a resolution can be bought only at the price of democratic community. Theories that account for political obli-gation in terms of the consent of the governed are highly ambiguous and confusing. It is rarely clear whether laws are justified by the fact that they are willed by those subject to them or by the justice of what is enacted. In Locke two quite different arguments are inextricably interwoven. His aims were to defend the obligation to obey legitimate authority (that is, authority based on consent) and to defend the right to resist coercive force in the absence of legitimate authority. He based au-thority on contractual consent, but behind the contract are the laws of nature, and ultimately the standard is the "good of the community."[20] Since man in the state of nature has only as much power over others as he needs to preserve his own life, liberty, and security of possessions, this degree of power is all he can properly be asked to surrender to the state.

> Man being . . . by Nature, all free, equal, and independent, no one can be put out of this Estate, and subjected to the Political Power of another, without his own *Consent*. The only way whereby any one divests himself of his Natural Liberty, and *puts on the bonds of Civil Society*, is by agreeing with other Men to join and unite into a Community. . . . When any number of Men have so *consented to make one Community* or Government, they are thereby presently incorporated, and make *one Body Politick*, wherein the *majority* have a Right to act and conclude the rest.[21]

Locke used the term *consent* broadly. At first he insisted that it was consent only in the sense of voluntary agreement undertaken by people who knew what they were committing themselves to that made authority legitimate, but later he argued that when a man inherits property, he gives consent to the state recognized by his father. In fact, consent is given tacitly whenever a man travels on the roads, takes lodging for a week, and so on. Locke argued that by remaining within the state and accepting its benefits one tacitly consents to its legitimacy and coercion. Hume felt that as a result, Locke overlooked studying the moral justification of the right of revolution. Hume claimed that Locke avoided this dilemma by making obligation dependent on the nature of government.[22] For Hume, individuals enter society with the intention of better preserving themselves, their liberties, and their properties, and the power of the government they establish can never extend further than the preservation of the common good.

It is one thing to show that people have a right not to have a government thrust upon them before a government has been founded, and quite another to argue that no one is required to obey an established government unless he or she has agreed to do so. S. I. Benn and R. S. Peters suggest that "if consent is a necessary condition for political obligation, it would deny a government any rightful authority over anyone who dissented from the basic principles of the constitution."[23] People who reject the basic assumptions of the goals of government cannot be morally obliged to obey laws, for the laws would not be their laws. On the other hand, if consent is taken as a sufficient condition for obligation, it implies that, having once submitted, one is bound to accept the consequences thereafter. This argument is not very appealing to the person who conceives of moral development as accepting postulated goals and ideals of government but disapproving of the practices of a particular government in straying from one's perceptions of these goals.

In order to overcome these difficulties between rights and obligations, Locke was forced to find ways to prove that men have agreed to obey, even when they have not in fact done so. In the end he virtually makes obedience imply consent. Locke failed to distinguish between how political authority arises and what makes it legitimate. As John Plamenatz correctly notes, "Political authority is always limited by the ends it ought to serve, so that, where those who have this authority do not serve those ends, their subjects have a right to resist them or get rid of them." [24] Obligation depends, therefore, not on moral development but on whether the government is such that one ought to consent, whether its actions are in accord with the authority a hypothetical group of rational men in a state of nature would give to any government they were founding.

If it could be established that a given set of political arrangements deserved one's consent, would this not make moral development irrelevant to political obligation? A distinguished line of political philosophers have taken this position. T. H. Green, for example, stated that his purpose was "to consider the moral function or object served by law . . . and in so doing to discover the true ground or justification for obedience to law." Society's claim to exercise powers over the individual rested on the fact that "these powers are necessary to the fulfillment of man's vocation as a moral being, to an effectual self-devotion to the work of developing the perfect character in himself and others." [25] Thus, laws are morally justified only to the extent that they promote the self-realization of the individual, but moral development is meaningful only if it obeys laws. This circular reasoning was no monopoly of the conservatives; liberals and socialists have developed their own variations on this theme.

Harold Laski followed Green in arguing that politics is an activity in which men work through the state as an instrument of social organization to achieve personal and social fulfillment. Laski defined the state as "an organization for enabling the mass of men to realize social good on the largest possible scale." The social good becomes "an ordering of our personalities," so that people are driven "to search for things it is worthwhile to obtain, that, thereby, we may enrich the great fellowships we serve." [26] Accordingly, it must be recognized that the moral development of individuals cannot be abstracted from the general good of other people. In this way, Fabian socialism incorporated utilitarian doctrine with startling simplicity.

Explanations that suggest that the grounds of political obligation inhere in the nature and purposes of government can be criticized on the ground that it is impossible, and not necessarily desirable, to find general criteria to justify political obligation. Necessary and sufficient conditions of good government and political obligation can never be known. Only in totalitarian regimes can the aims of the state be reduced to one overriding purpose. Concepts such as the social good or the general welfare should not be conceived as something determinate. Nor should it be assumed that moral development means agreement about ultimate ends. In a sphere of activity such as politics, there can never be complete agreement about what counts as right, as there can be in other spheres or rule-governed activity. What reasons can be given for believing that a given state represents the rational will or the common good, and by what criteria is one to be guided in deciding whether particular states or institutions conform to these requirements?

Rawls's vision of justice contains a doctrine of moral development that overcomes some weaknesses of the classical arguments, but not others. Obligations are defined by the principle of fairness. They are related to institutions or practices that can be judged by principles of justice for institutions. Obligations are thus tied to the nature and ends of government. This construct is based on a variant of contract theory, which, according to Rawls, overcomes the pitfalls of the classical theories of Locke and Rousseau. This is so because the principles of justice are those that would be chosen by rational men, acting in their own self-interest, in an initial position of equality. However, the actual adoption of these principles is purely hypothetical; all that is needed for the purposes of the theory is that the principles be adopted by fully moral persons. Confusion over the questions of how authority arises and what makes it legitimate is conveniently avoided.

Rawls maintains that "a person's obligations and duties presuppose a moral conception of institutions and therefore that the content of just institutions must be defined before the requirements for individuals can be set out." The choice of principles for individuals is simplified by the fact that the principles of justice for institutions have already been adopted. Rawls uses what he calls the principle of fairness to account for all requirements that are obligations as distinct from natural duties:

> A person is required to do his part as defined by the rules of an institution when two conditions are met: first, the institution is just (or fair), that is, it satisfies the two principles of justice; and second, one has voluntarily accepted the benefits of the arrangement or taken advantage of the opportunities it offers to further one's interests.[27]

There are no political obligations for people generally, since obligations arise as a result either of voluntary moral acts, which are express or tacit undertakings, or of simply accepting benefits. The first part of the principle of fairness formulates the conditions necessary for these voluntary acts that give rise to obligations, since the content of obligations is defined by Rawls as an obedience to rules of justice that specify requirements for voluntary actions. Rawls's theory also implies that it is not possible to be bound to unjust institutions or to institutions that exceed the limits of natural duties of individuals to one another.

The principle of fairness is related to what H. L. A. Hart calls mutuality of restrictions. In this version, moral development is defined as follows:

> When a number of persons engage in a mutually advantageous cooperative venture according to rules, and thus restrict their liberty in ways necessary to yield advantages for all, those who have submitted to these restrictions have a right to a similar acquiescence on the part of those who have benefited from their submission.[28]

The moral obligation to obey rules is a function of cooperation; people who accept legislative enactments consecrate standards of behavior. This moral reason for obeying the law is distinct from other moral reasons in terms of good consequences or the principle of fairness. Further, acceptance of the law does not imply that there will be no circumstances where disobedience is justified. The obligation to obey the law on these grounds is based on rights. The law arises between members of a particular political society, out of their mutual relationships. Again, for Hart as for

Rawls, moral development is a societal balancing act preventing either the Anarch or the Behemoth from triumphing.

The principle of fairness binds only those who assume public office or state power. The implication behind Rawls's theory is that those individuals who possess the most advantages in society are those likely to accept the obligations of the state. There is a difference between institutions that apply to individuals because of ascriptive factors of birth and those that apply because individuals have done certain things as a way of advancing the ends of achievement. Thus there is a natural duty to comply with the constitution and an obligation to carry out the duties of an office. Obligation is therefore a term reserved by Rawls for moral requirements that derive from the principle of fairness, while other requirements are called natural duties.

Rawls implies that one is bound to obey the law simply because it exists. He insists that "as citizens our legal duties and obligations are settled by what the law is."[29] This is certainly true as a statement of fact. However, to fall back upon the obligatory character of law is surely to avoid the problem of moral consent. It does not solve the problem of why the presence of legitimate authority provides a ground for acting in the manner required by this authority. What the law demands and what justice requires are distinct questions, even if the two principles of justice are used by the courts to interpret and apply the law. There are two principal ways in which injustice may arise: first, current arrangements may depart from the publicly accepted standard of justice; and second, arrangements may conform to a state's conception of justice, but this conception itself may be unjust. Rawls maintains however that "when the basic structure of society is reasonably just, we are to recognize unjust laws as binding provided that they do not exceed certain limits of injustice." This is so because when one submits to democratic authority, one submits to the extent necessary to share equitably in the inevitable imperfections of a constitutional system.

This argument is also beyond democracy. It was made earlier in sociology by Robert MacIver. The notion was that traditions of loyalty include the assumption that one should extend law-abidingness beyond the limits of immediate approbation.[30] There is a danger that this line of reasoning could be carried to such an extreme that virtually no right of resistance would remain, and moral development would be restricted to blatant violations rather than to ethical decision making as a whole.

It is just too dangerous and limiting to reduce moral developments to how one defines equal liberty and fair equality of opportunity. There may be numerous occasions when resistance is justified, despite the duty "not to invoke too readily the faults of social arrangements." Civil disobedience is an appeal to the conscience of the larger society, and may be justified if the established authority is acting inconsistently with its own established standards. In this sense, moral development is equivalent to a careful weighting of individual desires and social goods, including a constant sifting of legal statutes and their impingement upon personal standards or principles. Resistance is justified by reference to social principles, that is, the two principles of justice, but not by appeals to conscience. On the other hand, some element of individualism is critical if moral development is not to be reduced simply to reasons of state or appeals to the people.

> In morals every man must be his own legislator and rely in the end on his own judgment. . . . A duty can be a moral duty, then, only if it can be shown to serve a greater good or avert a greater wrong. It is therefore a conditional, not an absolute duty, and must depend on the use to which authority is put. And this implies that though we may have an obligation to act on someone else's judgment, we have no duty to suspend judgment.[31]

That individuals cannot be deprived of the right to form their own judgments is part of any adequate definition of moral development. As Hannah Pitkin has said, "the capacity for awareness and intention is a precondition for being fully obligated."[32] It follows that one is not really obligated unless one empirically recognizes and morally acquiesces in that obligation.[33] However, obligation does not consist only of inner awareness and intentions; it also has a long-range aspect. It is concerned with the social consequences of action. In the public realm, one is confronted with official interpreters and institutions who judge actions. At times of resistance or revolution these authorities are called into question. The question then arises: Who is to decide what times are normal and which are not, or whether resistance is justified or even obligatory? If one says that each individual must decide for himself, then one denies the morally binding character of law and authority; if one says that the majority must decide, one is unable to cope with a situation where the majority is being challenged. Herein lie the limits of moral development.

There is no final answer to the problem of moral development, since one cannot hope to specify a set of necessary and sufficient conditions of political obligations for all eternity. If society is faced with an indefinite set of vaguely shifting criteria, differing for different times and circumstances, then it may often, if not nearly always, be necessary to scrutinize political relations to see whether individuals are on particular occasions justified in giving support to a measure or a government or withholding it. But in doing so, a theory of political rights apart from a corresponding theory of political obligations is resurrected. Again, moral development is the decision-making process whereby the balance of rights and obligations is maintained. If such a balance becomes impossible, then the problem of moral development becomes moot, since the choice is made on the basis of raw power—and for decision making in the absence of choice one needs counterpower, not moral standards.

Democratic Persuasions and Authoritarian Distempers

The fusion of moral development, political style, and democratic persuasion borrows from Deweyan or Meadian premises, from pragmatism as a theory of education to symbolic interaction as a theory of politics. George Mead understood democracy to mean the ability to absorb information from others—to listen before forming judgments, to take the role of the generalized other as a precondition to action.[34] In this sense, moral education for democracy entails the ability to learn how to absorb information about people with different sentiments, values, and interests. This naturalistic view is the opposite of a notion that moral education is a matter of "our" teaching "them" right values. Democracy always has had, and will continue to be plagued by, a certain ambiguity, an indecisiveness. Admitting to not knowing everything a priori is characteristic of the democratic polity.[35] The tentativeness that permits breakdown also makes possible a theory of moral development based on learning new information rather than instructing others about the virtues of old information.

A democratic theory of politics must make clear differentiation between moral development and the development of morals. Such a distinction takes on particular practical meaning, because it is primarily in the context of statist repression (or permission) that either notion (moral development or the development of morals) has ultimate significance. Moral development as a brute fact, derived from common-sense attitudes toward order and civility, is handmaiden to a panoply of authoritarian ideologies. The forms of such an ideology may be thoroughly benign, even genteel. Ultimately, however, the notion of moral development rests on the imposition of behavior through methods of authority or divinity. At the same time, the notion of the development of morals, in its nature, assumes a plurality and even a plethora of moral standards and standpoints; hence the development of any one set of morals signifies the sorts of codifications that are essential for a society's growth and survival.

The democratic persuasion is not an argument claiming the unlimited nature of moral possibilities or the impossibility of assessing relative advantages or disadvantages of one ethical framework against another. It is an assertion that moral choices are not ultimate and revealed verities that deductively or cosmologically flow from the nature of the state. Ethics can be measured by the consequences they yield to the person and society, rather than by initial goals set for the person or society. Contrariwise, activities of a routine sort are often measured by ethical standards deemed operationally satisfactory, even necessary, in specific societal contexts. The democratic position is now back in a world of discourse where the quest is for certitude rather than experience. Certitude blocks out possible lines of inquiry, and hence limits the range of experiences, while experiences tend to produce yet newer experiences and thus create the grounds for ever-increasing doubt and uncertainty. The choice is by no means an easy one to make, but the consequences have a great bearing on what citizens in a republic may expect from their polity.

Quite apart from the need to disaggregate normative and empirical frameworks to examine issues of moral development, it has become evident that the situation in theory basically mirrors conditions in world affairs. It can be said without much fear of contradiction that the twentieth century bears witness to powerful demands for life-giving egalitarianism, in both intimate and international relations, while at the same time it has exposed an underbelly of genocide and impersonal mass murder that has transformed moral issues into engineering issues; that is, questions of punishment, execution, burial, and so on are reduced to matters of cost efficiency and double-entry accountancy.[36] In European nations where deeply rooted tendencies toward egalitarianism were formerly manifest—for example, in socialist Germany and communist Russia—one often found forms of genocide raised to the highest levels of science. Of course, traditional forms of genocide can be found where one might expect, in places such as Paraguay and Uganda. In these latter instances, genocide serves to prevent contact with the developing world. But one must be cautious about offering general theories; forms of democracy are found in unanticipated places, just as genocides take place in equally unexpected nations.

Moral propositions about political systems are suspect, those about democratic systems doubly so; inherent in the concept of democracy is a sufficient latitude regarding moral ambiguity to make principles no less than strategies subject to alteration over time. From their reluctance to correct inherited forms of inequality, to a vague tolerance for all sorts of waste, democratic societies invite criticism for being morally obtuse, not to mention insulated from the needs of wide sectors of those disenfranchised from the democratic process. The search for moral first principles, based on absolute convictions as to where we come from and hence where we must go, is an inevitable offshoot of democratic society. All decry the waste inherent in interest-group politics and single-issue organizations, but few are brave enough to state which interest groups they would abolish or what particular interest group's issues they feel are frivolous and deserving of being suppressed. The potency of democratic systems only partially derives from its own principles; more pointedly, its strength derives from the dangerously limited options awaiting those who would abandon a democratic notion of moral choice.

Too often ideas of the perfect have led to intense fanaticism, to what Hannah Arendt[37] and Jacob Talmon[38] in different ways have described in terms of totalitarian democracy and political messianism. The process of perfecting is admittedly infuriatingly vague, but it provides the intellectual space that permits free people to operate effectively, if inefficiently. Holding firmly to the inefficiencies of such an open-ended notion of moral development is a costly affair in economic terms, inviting a certain amount of waste; but to achieve moral development at the price of political democracy is an unholy trade-off that assures only bureaucratic efficiency.

Several years ago, Harold Lasswell shrewdly observed that there is a linkage between personality systems and demands for severity. By extension, there is a relationship between demands for moral development as some sort of metaphysical given and the extensive network of international punishment in the form of global warfare and genocidal conflict. It is worthwhile to appreciate the degree to which concepts such as moral development are little else than disguised decisions for sanctioning norms. The warrant for such behavior deserves to be explained by social and behavioral scientists but not necessarily rationalized.

The claims of a society to impose suffering as an end in itself usually carries within itself a further compounded belief that such suffering is warranted for the maintenance of order and the establishment of first principles. But claims of this sort involve beliefs in political goals more nearly than statements of cultural universals. Comparative studies between cultures reveal the relative nature of most, if not all, universal claims. This does not imply that a society should avoid choices or that some moral systems are not superior to others against alien factors and forces. Rather, the danger inheres in the belief that somehow social ideologues can properly sanction what thousands of years of theological edicts and constraints have failed to achieve—a finely tuned theory of moral development. Again, one can scarcely find a better mentor than Lasswell in determining the limits of social science as an agenda-setting network for moral development.

> We cannot look to the behavioral scientists in their professional capacity to shoulder our individual responsibility for deciding what manner of individuality to seek in ourselves or to permit in our children, or in others whom we influence. But the growth of knowledge will expose the total consequences of conformity as well as of originality of deviation. The crude initial studies of the costs of difference will be supplemented—as indeed they are being supplemented by studies of the costs of stereotyping and conformity. Already there are indications of the latent problems that arise when talents and propensities are suppressed or repressed out of deference to the steamroller of conformity. These are the issues that rise to plague and embitter the latter years of life with a sense of estrangement from experience and a haunting sense of chagrin and guilt for a lifetime of timidity and cowardice. We are engaged in a vast reconstruction of our cultural inheritance in the light of the behavioral sciences. Our conclusion is that the impact upon primary and sanctioning norms has been to bring the practices of our civilization into somewhat closer harmony with the basic ideals of human dignity.[39]

If the democratic persuasion involves choices, then a notion of moral developments needs to be enlarged. Helen Merrell Lynd, paraphrasing Gauay, writes: "Not 'I must, therefore I can,' but 'I can, therefore I must.'" Lynd amplifies her view by noting that the scientific temper of discovery poses issues not in terms of morality and immorality, but in terms of conflicting moralities. Writing in the maelstrom of McCarthyism, she put forward the notion that the fusion of the democratic temper and scientific credo offers a solution to the dangerous quest for certainty on the one hand and the complete relativizing of values on the other. "Entering fully into the nature of contemporary conflicts calls upon one to make choices beyond coping with difficulties to gain security: beyond the polarity of good on one side, evil on the other. Acting in the faith that there may be ranges of individual and social development as yet unknown requires ability to live with ambiguity and varied probabilities and possibilities."[40] It would be difficult to find a superior foundation for democratic policy making and, at the same time, a wiser grounding of core principles from which can be derived a democratic vision of morals in development.

24. Moral Implications of Social Science Disputations

Let me state at the outset that I have great qualms with the notion of moral education.[1] At best, it is a nineteenth-century concept smuggled into ethical discourse by those who search for the City of God in the cities of men, and at worst, it is a late-twentieth-century concept appealing to fanaticisms of the worst sort. Clericalists tend to talk of moral education, secularists of education for moral choice. The kind of unease or discomfort with the concept of moral education herein expressed is not simply personal but one felt in general among serious people.

It is curious that the great thrust for reintroducing moral education derives from sources that are usually alien to the intellectual environment of the open university or the democratic persuasion at large. Reflecting upon fundamentalisms of all sorts—Christian, communist, and conservative—the demand for moral education seems to be a mandate that has little to do with democratic education and much to do with dogmatic instruction. In such a society, everything from truth to discipline "involves the idea of obedience to authority."[2]

Many scholars in the academic world, especially in naturalistic philosophy and the social sciences, are appropriately ill at ease with the notion of moral education. The phrase implies, or better disguises, much more than it can deliver. It implies a foreknowledge of what constitutes the moral ground or the normative base from which an understanding of right and wrong derives. From Plato to Durkheim normativists have written with a definite sense of the optimum social and political order, and the place of moral behavior in these orders. For the most part, social philosophers did not come to moral theory in terms of a doctrine of choice or a notion of voluntary decision. Quite the contrary, they came to social questions with powerful and often fixed apriorisms. In Deweyan terms, theirs was a quest for certainty rather than experience. In diametrical opposition to the pragmatic rebellion against the nineteenth-century absolutes of organicism in social science and idealism in philosophy, those who have renewed the quest for moral education sense what it should be: moral behavior is not experienced but is an entity mandated by the heavens, history, or biology; or, as is more often the case, by metaphysics, metahistory, or metabiology.

In the twentieth century, European social theorists like Jacob Talmon,[3] Hannah Arendt,[4] Elie Halevy,[5] and George Lichtheim,[6] among others, have understood much better than their philosophical or psychological counterparts the problem with moral education; namely, it carries within itself, no matter how genteel or clever, the totalitarian temptation: a notion of knowledge as foreknowledge. Those for whom a democratic environment remains a pledge no less than a style must pause and think carefully about the vision of moral education, above all its instructional mandates emanating from providence, history, or biology. The best way to do so is to move from the mellifluous tones of moral education as a general doctrine to the harsher tones of the moral educators and their specific messages.

That prolegomena announced, what next? Suppose there is an appreciation of the risks entailed by the claims of moral educators, where then do we go from here? It is certainly insufficient and inadequate to make a pronunciamento as if it were an analysis. The issue remains: How is the democratic persuasion transformed into moral doctrine? More pointedly, can such a transformation be either observed in the history of ideas or urged upon a present generation of social theorists who are searching for a firmer footing than the shifting sands of pragmatism but who prefer their ideas not to be cast in stone?

One course to take is represented by a theory of pure choice, or pushing ethical theory into empirical examination. This would transform ethics into a question of decision making or value theory and ultimately into a kind of laboratory of mechanical engineering: what ought to be done to bring about desired ends in terms of available strategies, tactics, and techniques. Morality would thus be reduced to engineering modes and principles, to concepts of how to manage, manipulate, and massage reality at various levels of human interactions. This interactionist approach is uncomfortable for many since it simply postpones a settlement of moral accounts by drowning ethics in an interactionist pool, with the result that judgment itself is invariably abandoned. What other options are then available? Let us start with a review of how moral education has been achieved in our century.

My presupposition is that the pragmatic rebellion against authority has been so thoroughgoing that education as such could not admit the concept of morality through its front door. Relativism became not so much a choice of values but rather a long vacation from values. But pragmatism could not avoid allowing moral education to enter (smuggled might be a better term) through intellectual back doors. In fact, its emphasis on experience and evidence invited such an approach. The twentieth century has thus witnessed back-dooring the notion of moral education in particular and moral theorizing in general. Until most recently, the word *morals* itself was considered somewhat impolitic, having yielded its princely seat to the word *ethics*, with its less instructional and more metaphysical presuppositions.

I am not trying to prove either that there was a pragmatic-liberal hegemony from World War I to the recent past or that the fundamentalist response has only now crystallized. Neither proposition is correct; pragmatic liberal approaches to social research were dominant but not unanimously adhered to. Likewise, the fundamentalist-conservative response never quite died out; and from the early 1950s it made steady inroads on social doctrines. It is the case, however, that the questioning of the liberal consensus has grown into a firm intellectual opposition. This quantitative shift has increased to a point where qualitative changes in the nature of social science itself are involved. In this sense, issues of moral judgment and education are directly impacted since the empirical rationale of ethical precepts is profoundly affected by such paradigmatic shifts in social research. We must now review how social science disputations have served to underscore current moral standpoints.

Let us examine several fields of social science and briefly review how issues of moral education are treated. The field of sociology, specifically social stratification, offers a central starting place. How does it treat the notion of moral education? Essentially by indirection. It is implied in a theory of stratification holding that the goals of equality of opportunity and the removal of inequality are central. Sociologists strongly suggest that there is a good, and it is operationally determined by the maximization of equality. They began to compile data and engage in field researches that demonstrated that vast inequalities abound in American society: racial inequality, religious inequality, sexual abuse, child abuse, agism. This is, after all, the real message of *Middletown* and *Middletown in Transition*, illustrating both the *structure* of inequality in the former and the movement toward equality in the latter.[7] The entire area of the sociology of stratification was dedicated to statistical enunciation of such moral truths. What appears as fact, namely, data on inequality, or differences in earning power and occupational roles between male and female, become readily and rapidly transformed into a statement and judgment about the need to remove inequality.

Sociology strongly implied that within its framework data on stratification are gathered and verified but that the very enunciation of such data provides bona fide evidence for the removal of inequality and a firm movement toward perfect equality. This is to be brought about through legal means, political techniques, and labor organizations. But the strong and lasting impression of most empirical studies of stratification is that one should work toward a society built on equality and not simply accept passively the description of societies that have built inequities. There may be powerful outstanding differences about how successful the United States has been in its pursuit of perfection but little serious discussion over the goals as such.[8]

If we move briefly to the area of political science, the same kind of overwhelming judgment about egalitarian goals is observed: all people should count as one, no more than one, but no less than one. Therefore, in the study of political science, whether it be pluralism in the practice of political systems, decision-making distribution on the Supreme Court, the checks and balances of Congress, or even the economic characteristics of voting behavior and mass participation, political scientists have been virtually united in their idea that the politicized individual should count as one, no more and no less. Voting rights legislation and congressional redistricting schemes are both the result of deeply rooted feelings along this line. In the words of Schattschneider, "Democracy is a competitive political system in which competing leaders and organizations define the alternatives of public policy in such a way that the public can participate in the decisionmaking process."[9] Equality of rights is constitutionally mandated. Recent Supreme Court interpretations have constantly argued the need for maximizing opportunities as a basic mechanism for insuring rights. Political science presents a continuing effort to pierce the disparity in the employment opportunities of races, the political opportunities of sexes, and the business opportunities of different religious and ethnic groups, with the omnipresent ideals of a democratic social order.[10]

A most fascinating illustration of how egalitarian modalities became dominant in social science is in the area of criminology, specifically the new criminology. Far from the late nineteenth-century tradition that sought to indicate how the behaviors of criminals differed from those of other citizens, the new criminology took the position that criminals are essentially involved in the redistribution of wealth and privilege. Hence, in its most recent version, crime is seen as a species of economic behavior or even recreational behavior. Crime is viewed as expressing a grievance, and hence belongs to the same family of social behavior as gossip, ridicule, and punishment. Ultimately, crime comes to be viewed as one or more types of behavior, helping to insure, not undermine, social control.[11] Crime is simply viewed as a normal way to evolve a doctrine of self-help. On such a pure democratic view, it is the continuum between criminal and noncriminal behavior that is central, not the nature of the criminal element. The very distinction between normal and criminal behavior is reduced to the whimsical nature of law in society. Relativism thus ends not in moral choice but in sheer intellectual nihilism.

The area of anthropology, given its powerful relativistic bias, has also contributed mightily to this same egalitarian impulse. Not only should every individual count as one, no more and no less, but each civilization should also count as one, no more and no less. In emphasizing differences between societies, cultural anthropology has also inadvertently argued against claims of moral superiority or moral inferiority.[12] There are differences between cultures; there are distinct patterns of behavior; but these culture patterns are built up over long periods of time. They cannot simply be described as being wrong, nor can advanced industrial systems be described as being right. The nineteenth-century distinction between primitive savages and modern civilized beings is an impossible hypothesis to sustain. Bronislaw Malinowski was typical: he always managed to poke fun at the notion of being civilized, while elevating savagery as a legitimate economic system in its own right.[13] His references to civilized peoples aim to convince us that the empire builders engage in a higher form of savagery unknown to most of his beloved Trobrianders. The way Englishmen behave at soccer matches, in crowd scenes, or with one another belies the notions of civility and civilization. There is little doubt that for most cultural and social anthropologists, empire builders are not only no better than primitive peoples, they are much worse. They carry within themselves the possibility of much greater destruction over a much wider geographic terrain.[14] There is furthermore no doubt that the founders of cultural anthropology shared this deep bias on behalf of the less developed and against the most developed. Not only did anthropology carry within itself the presumption of equity but the need to learn from other peoples. As a consequence, the strong relativistic impressions and egalitarian impulses are just as powerfully etched in anthropology as they are in political science and sociology. And such relativism carried the full weight and authority of ethnography, of fieldwork in faraway places.

If we turn to an area such as economics, the main practical revolution of the twentieth century, whether it be of a Marxian or Keynesian persuasion, is heavily impulsed in the same egalitarian direction. Setting aside momentarily the competitive theories of scholars like von Hayek and his more recent followers,[15] the main impulse of econometric models has clearly been the idea of a social floor and an economic ceiling.[16] The central presumption behind the post-Keynesians is to get beyond the equilibrium, beyond the world where there is no past and future and no history, and into a world of steady growth. Only such management of growth permits safety nets that do not tear and ladders that do not favor the haves over the have-nots.[17] Equilibrium is thus a function of growth, not stasis. And this means bringing ever-increasing numbers into the economic system as equal players.

There is a utopian element in this quest for economic equality, but notwithstanding the wide variations between Marxian and Keynesian concepts, the shank of the quest is unambiguous and shared by both schools of economic science. Economists for the most part have argued that people have entitlements. These entitlements come not from work but from being human. This is a radically different notion from the Ricardian free-market faith in subsistence or the Smithian notion that the degree of wealth derives only through what a person contributes to the society. Quite the contrary, the dominant mode of twentieth-century economics is that a standard of living is an entitlement by virtue of being human. Thus even the economists, who one might expect to be the toughest and roughest of customers on questions of cost-benefit analysis, are sentimentalists and special pleaders. They fervently believe that fiscal and monetary policies should be actively and continuously deployed toward achievement of full employment and price stability. Not free markets but total employment became the ethical cornerstone of the modern economic scientist.[18]

The area of psychology that has been most sensitive to this revolution in attitudes toward inequality and discrimination has been abnormal psychology. The conversion from the strong language of moral disapproval for sexual differences, a language characteristic of the European founders of the psychiatric movement, has given way to a neutral rhetoric bordering on outright approbation of different groups. What was formerly labeled infantile disorders, or the inability to transfer affections from the same sex to opposite sex, has now become simply a matter of alternative life-styles, or the ability to love, or the capacity to create.[19] Optional modes behavior displaced fixed norms as the key to the analytic quest for normality. Patterns of behavior once deemed deviant are now increasingly perceived as nothing more than an inherited bias of the professional establishments. Indeed, authority itself has come to be viewed as the enemy of mental health, to be replaced by a world in which the analyst and patient both become equals in a sharing support group, which in turn will evolve into communities and groups of different types prizing individuality and free expression.[20] Most recently, the trend has been to distinguish between life-styles and adjust to such differences as lesbianism and homosexuality rather than to presume any notions of urging individuals to find their way back into a vague social mainstream. This is yet one more illustration of the same theme witnessed in each of the social sciences: relativism in behavior rather than absolutism of moral claims; rights to those who choose to be different or cannot help themselves from being different; and a sharp opposition to differentiation or stratification because of biogenetic or socially induced differences in behavior.

The political philosopher Michael Walzer best summed up this dominant mood in social science when he recently proposed a simple, effective way to achieve equality: namely, eliminate the ability of some people to dominate their fellows. His point is not to introduce feasibility statements on how this can be brought about, or the sort of regime it would take to enforce such a canon, or the sort of national conformity needed to implement such a condition, but rather that this goal, this impulse to fairness, this "rule without domination," has been central to twentieth-century notions of moral education.[21] But increasingly a certain discomfort, even disquiet, has penetrated this former condition of near unanimity, this chorus of beliefs in equality: rewards without costs, creativity without craft, citizenship without responsibility. The core of moral discourse has so shifted from libertarian statements to egalitarian statements that a certain fear that moral commitment as such would be drowned in an ocean of economic interest groups. And so began the counterrevolution of fundamentalism, again, not as a question of formal philosophy but rather throughout the social and behavioral sciences.

When it is broadly realized that moral education in a postpostivist period of the twentieth century is not delivered by philosophers through the front door but by social scientists through the back door, the work of this latter group assumes greater investigative urgency. The moral imperatives of our epoch—rights against obligations, virtues easily articulated over and against vices, goods dictated by the marketplace over and against evils performed by pernicious planners—all seem to have unraveled. This entire moral climate underwritten by the social science community crested in the 1960s, a decade in which the Vietnam War was perceived to be an unmixed evil, in which racial justice seemed but a stone's throw away from governmental doorsteps, and in which students seemed to be on the threshold of achieving social parity with a much despised administration and wandering faculty. These simple practical beliefs for a seemingly clear-cut social world were intended to guarantee and verify equality over liberty, pluralism over power, individual welfare over competitive markets, alternative life-styles over oppressive straight styles, and happy natives over industrial slaves.

Ethical relativity seemed destined to achieve a total victory in such a social science weltanschauung. But the relative quickly turned into the absolute: the fear of old "thou shalts" of a theological sort issued into a subtle but no less demanding "thou shalt" of a sociological sort. Benefits were to be pursued without regard to costs; and rights were to be demanded from the state without regard to corresponding obligations to the state. The situation reached a point where guilt vanished and only no-fault forms of punishment and plea bargainings remained. Society turned litigious in this near-perfect atomization of responsibility. It was in such a strange climate that social philosophy and social ethics witnessed a rebirth. Normativist political science, phenomenological sociology, biological anthropology, libertarian economics, and instinctualist psychology—all began to make comebacks, albeit in more sophisticated intellectual packages. Social science, far from foreclosing on the subject of moral education, had only served to disguise and even distort long-standing controversies. A thin patina of data served to hide the same deep well from which empirical researches and moral imperatives both derived.

The area of stratification has been and remains the most sensitive in sociology. This field continues to mirror the larger concerns of American mass society for maximizing equality. Indeed, it is evident that in the past sociology anticipated and even stimulated developments in the reduction of racial, sexual, occupational, and educational differentiation. Its pioneer theorists debated the issues while its methodologists created the data base showing the extent to which inequities exist in rank, salaries, roles, and conditions. While an earlier pre–World War II generation sought to minimize any notion that sociology had anything to do with socialism, a latter-day post–World War II generation sought to make quite explicit that the two, however different in outlook and method, did come together in the need for changing society. Exaggerated (if not all) forms of inequality and differentiation in all forms of power relations were considered malevolent and counterproductive, and hence should be opposed on sociological grounds.[22]

While the accumulation of data and theory did serve to promote a strong sense of egalitarian need, the inability of Soviet society and even democratic welfare societies such as Sweden to satisfy the material and spiritual needs of their citizens began to cast doubt on a pure theory of egalitarianism or the inevitable, short-term end of stratification. Certain key figures, among them Alex Inkeles,[23] Seymour Martin Lipset,[24] and Paul Hollander,[25] began to emphasize that perfect equality not only minimized the capacity of a stifling political bureaucracy to implement its credo, but even worse, inhibited equality and stimulated a breakdown of economic growth, a weakening of technical innovation, and the serious inhibition of personal initiative. The political breeding ground in search of moral man led only to political oppression, fanaticism, and new forms of stratification based upon party elites and political indoctrination.[26] The requirements of a competitive international environment, no less than the demands of those who worked hard and produced for precisely the sort of differentials that liberal sociological premises formerly vilified, led to a broad-scale rethinking of egalitarian premises.

The sociology of stratification was confronted by certain epistemological problems that it could no longer closet; the most serious theoretical dilemma was that issues of stratification have the capacity, even the inevitability, for infinite regress. Even if one presumes perfect harmony and agreement across racial boundaries, even if sexual differentials in salaries are resolved, the demand structure for further leveling is inexorable: linguistic inequalities, religious boundaries, biological distinctions between the tall and the short, the heavy and the thin, just touch the surface of this argument by infinite regress. What began in the proletarian 1930s, a generation infused with the prospects of marshaling sociology to egalitarian ends, concluded in the 1980s in a quagmire of antilibertarian sentiments and a shrill insistence that the state could yet bail out an impossible situation.

The contradictions of supporting repressive statist measures that alone could insure any enforcement of egalitarian norms became tolerable. Inequalities between the family and the individual, straights and gays, victims and criminals, old and young, all appeared on the scene of sociology, and all were uniformly too complex to be rendered answerable in terms of egalitarian slogans. Intense conflicts between deviant and marginal groups, no less than between such groups and older establishments, became as apparent and insurmountable as the earlier struggles between powerful and powerless. Here too, the weight of social traditions, rather than the lightheadedness of a social science captured by ideological extremes, held sway.[27] Moral instruction in the need for equity only yielded serious practical problems, namely, how to weigh the relative valuational bases of equity and liberty. Solutions seemed ever more remote in theory as the 1980s wore on. The social practice of societies claiming economic equality was revealed to have no such ends but instead served only to expand to the political realm the stratification networks, whereas the social practice of societies claiming political democracy had a difficult time explaining, much less dealing with, ongoing forms of exploitation and inequality.

The rebellion against egalitarian modalities in an area such as criminology, in which the very notion of a crime was effectively done away in theory at least through the powerful juxtaposition of crimes and their victims, resulted in a whole new category of sociology called victimology. Everything from the behavior of the victim to compensation patterns decreed by law came to be reconsidered.[28] In this sense, the revolt against "the new criminology," like the revolt against social stratification as such, is a rebellion against taking for granted the routinization of crime. It is furthermore an insistence that victims no less than criminals should be treated in terms of the same background variables and rehabilitation potentials. Far from seeing crime as a form of social control, victimology has restored to the literature a notion of crime as a form of social disorganization and moral destruction.

In what must be regarded as a serious departure from conventional criminology, victimology tends to view the innocent recipients of crime as a special repository of the social goods of a moral society. The area of victimology has once again displayed the limits of moral relativism by perceiving the crime and criminals as an unmitigated social evil and the victims of crime as the carriers of essential and positive social values. But in this intellectual restoration, victimology reintroduces standards of conduct that were thought to be a closed issue. The relative nature of criminals and victims comes to be seen as a sharply bifurcated domain between evildoers (criminals) and do-gooders (victims). As the scientific issues have become more muddled by new realities, the sociological reintroduction of normative criteria for public consideration has become widespread.

The areas of abnormal psychology, psychiatry, and psychoanalysis are sufficiently intertwined so that it is appropriate simply to note that they evolved from an early absolutist and reductionist emphasis on wide-ranging categories of abnormality to a steady narrowing down of the conceptual framework to the point where abnormality itself came to be conceptually suspect, virtually drowned in a sea of alternative life-styles. As in anthropology, the nurture-nature issue tended to blur the significance of the hormonal basis of masculine and feminine motivational tendencies. At a time of sharply declining moral constraints on individual behavior, neither sociological, neurological, nor psychoanalytic explanations have been especially effective. Deviance itself has been displaced by difference. The assumption that homosexuality, for example, falls into areas of pathology came to be vigorously denied and organizationally repudiated.[29] Homosexuality in particular became a social question, even a political crusade, and in this way passed from personal trauma to public rights.

A broad-ranging survey such as this cannot possibly resolve technical issues hotly contested within each social science discipline. However, it is important to note that as social science discussions on deviance became more tolerant, the demands of the deviant community escalated—from one of equal rights, followed by empathy for open practices, and finally to social affirmation of many forms of deviant behavior formerly viewed as socially horrendous.[30] It is only at this point, the mid-1980s, that significant sectors of the social and medical sciences felt moved once again to introduce the place of different types of deviant behavior, the distinction between sociopathic and psychopathic behavior, and the place of pathology both personal and social in opting for alternative life-styles.[31] Whatever the specific merits of this labeling of deviance, it is evident that the pure empiricism of those who earlier argued for (or against) a discovery of deviance has broken down, to be replaced by a rather frank acknowledgement that moral criteria are both relevant and germane to the scientific analysis of the empirical status of social deviance or personal aggression.[32] The status of norms and norm breaking has thus come to figure prominently in the current revolt against relativism in areas impinging upon personal behavior and even individual life-styles. If the earlier patterns of the medicalization of deviance served as strong negative moral sanctions, the later socialization of deviance implied equally powerful positive moral supports. That social science is now moving beyond these earlier mechanical formulations is a matter of great significance whose consequence is only now an open intellectual agenda.

Political science has created its own equilibrium model, one that derives from Montesquieu and Locke, and has stood the field in good stead for most of the century. The grand scenario involves a belief in the plausibility of checks and balances, a society of laws and not of men, a politics of involvement from publics and responsibility from elites. It is not that the best minds in the field of political research failed to appreciate the seamier side of the political process, rather it was their unyielding belief that the system itself was largely intact and that only subsystems, like urban wards, were in disarray.

Increasingly, voices from the radical left, insistent on power, have been heard instead of the voices of authority, while others from a conservative right, for whom this inherited equilibrium denied the role of norms and values in making the political system work, have likewise been raised in protest. A veritable crescendo of voices were raised concerning the emergence of interest- and pressure-group politics, which are only remotely related to the basic goals of the democratic political process. Scholars as diverse as Marshall Berman,[33] Richard Flathman,[34] and J. G. A. Pocock[35] have speculated on a political environment in which rights go unquestioned, even assumed, whereas obligations are routinely denied an equal place in any serious analytic scheme of things political. Indeed, even the grounds for a belief in the possibility of political science have been denied on the grounds of natural law and practical politics alike.[36]

The limits of the pluralistic model were reached when, far from a polity in which everyone counts as one, it was recognized that it takes a veritable economic fortune even to run for minor public office. The stakes in a society differ with the occupational and fiscal place of the individual in that society. What this commonplace fact of life does to a pluralistic model, in which equality is presumed rather than proven, becomes a core issue for political science. Beyond that, declining participation in electoral politics, coupled with a sharp reduction in party commitment, also raises doubts that the older equilibrium model could be sustained in a society where the assumptions of representative government are subject to criticism and doubt. While some have seen this as a need to improve government by enlarging participation to formerly disenfranchised groups,[37] others saw this same situation as proof positive that populist politics creates the seeds of mediocrity, with popularity contests conducted in the media displacing sounder principles of professional politics.[38] Whatever implications are drawn, it has become evident that the relativism, pluralism, liberalism, and populism of established political science doctrines have come under severe peer review. As a result, fundamental moral imperatives thought to derive from these doctrinal verities have also been subject to reexamination.

Anthropology is perhaps the last of the major social science disciplines to discover that its moral tenets are not carved in stone. Buffeted about for nearly a half century between critics on the right, who saw anthropology as, in its very existence, an assault on industrial civilization, and critics on the left, who saw the same discipline as a veritable intellectual cockpit of cultural imperialism inside underdeveloped areas, the field itself remained strangely immune from both sorts of critiques. Since such critiques were rarely done inside the professional bastions as such, they were easily perceived as attacks on professionalism rather than science. The typical field reports inevitably emphasize the gentle nature of native peoples, the absence of strife and turmoil across sexual bounds, and romanticized broad continuities between biological and cultural formations.[39] This certainly typifies the sort of field reports issued over the years by the American Museum of Natural History and conforms to the general liberal and relativist positions of fathers and sons and mothers and daughters of the anthropology discipline.

That this position is now threatening to unravel is made clear in the new work of Derek Freeman, who confronts the work of Margaret Mead on Samoa in particular and the sociological prejudices of cultural anthropology and its forerunners (e.g., W. F. Ogburn) in general.[40] He asserts that the Samoans are intensely competitive; have a high incidence of deviance in the form of homicide, assault, and rape; and exhibit childrearing of such authoritarian sorts as to result in a wide range of psychological disturbances that result in suicide, hysteria, and jealousy. Their lovemaking, far from being casual, suffers from the cult of female virginity carried further than Western societies. This raises issues far beyond those of the nurture-nature controversies of the 1920s or the issues of improper research designs; rather, they represent a frontal assault on the moral backbone, or lack thereof, of cultural anthropology. Freeman's work, along with that of Ernst Mayr[41] and Nikolaas Tinbergen,[42] is an attack on the "doctrinal baggage" of cultural relativism and technological determinism, unrefined by authentic observation or realistic evaluation.

The ethologist must be in the forefront to restore traditional values and overcome the excesses (pollution, malsocialization) of the modern world. It is from such critical stuff that moral education is refined and restructured. For if the "universals" of ethology and biology point not to any wide disparity between "primitives" and "moderns" but to their close approximation, then the normative bases of ethical judgment must also be seen as a potential tool of cross-cultural analysis.

The science of economics, far from being unconcerned about its moral status, probably has been closer to the marrow of moral doctrine than any other social science, if for no other reason than that its founders—Smith, Ricardo, Marx, Marshall, and Schumpeter—all raised problems about the ethical claims of the capitalist market system. Behind its hard-boiled talk of equilibrium models and analysis of social program costs, there remains a strong moral imperative for the well-being of individuals; specifically, how individuals are to be made secure in a world with sharply different social classes: wage earners and owners, factory hands and industrial titans, welfare recipients and foundation directors, and so forth. Smoothing out the rough edges of difference seemed to be the essential task of the Keynesian revolution as well. Trade-offs between growth and satisfaction worked well enough in periods of sharp growth in a gross national product. But when the growth curve flattened out in the 1980s, real wealth became a constant, and all that rotated was the division rather than the size of the economic pie, then who gets what became a much harsher issue for economists no less than the economy.[43]

From social security to taxation of stocks and property, specific economic concerns began to tear at the fabric of pump-priming solutions, which were based on high taxation as an acceptable form of benign expropriation. No longer were wealthy classes willing to give up a small portion of their profits to a large number of masses to assure social tranquillity. The intensification of differences between haves and have-nots resurfaced, much to the chagrin of Keynesians who thought that governmental policies of allocation did away with such angular social differences once and for all. If the Marxians were delighted at this evident collapse of the Keynesian paradigm, it was a mixed and muted pleasure since socialist economies fared even worse in the wealth reallocation process. The latter-day Marxian saints wrongly assumed that centralization and planning would be resolved by radical reformist sectors. By their own standards, they proved unequal to the task.[44]

Economists have turned away in droves from welfare programs providing floors toward an increasing willingness to let the market create its own floors and ceilings. Reforms centered upon eliminating fiscal waste in management, reducing the size of the federal bureaucracy, eliminating bureaucratic interference in the natural ebb and flow of economies, and in general, returning to the nasty and brutish economic environment in which equality would be an outcome and not an input; a universe, which by analog, permits everyone to finish the race more or less successfully, but not tampering with the start of the race, with the natural or acquired advantages of the individuals running in the economic race. A kind of neo-Darwinian presumption crept into economic analysis, while at the allocation level laissez-faire doctrines of noninterference and nonintervention with the market became primary. From von

Mises[45] to Stigler,[46] it became clear that old economic formulas guaranteed democracy only at the cost of dooming or sharply curbing a free-market economy. The willingness conservative economists exhibited to run the political risks of subverting democracy instead of the economy was in diametrical opposition to the risks of liberal economists, who continued to be more concerned with floor questions than ceiling questions.[47]

What this suggests is not the venality or narrow-mindedness of social scientists of the present mid-1980s versus the expansive bigheartedness of social scientists of the mid-1960s. Rather, issues of social systems and moral order are now viewed as more complicated and less susceptible to quick fixes than was earlier thought to be the case. This translated into a review of moral premises upon which our society is grounded. In the world of trade-offs—decisions between alternative concepts of the good, changing standards of what constitutes virtuous behavior, different standards of the true and the beautiful—the social sciences were compelled to redirect their energies, to take much less for granted in the way of the malleability of norms than they were formerly prone to do.

This brief sociology-of-knowledge review of the social science literature suggests that issues of moral education are not fought out in classrooms on moral education but rather in research designs, experiments conducted, and theories dreamed up by social scientists. It is now apparent that the ghost in the social science machine is ethics. At the start and conclusion of every major piece of empirical research or theoretical paradigm developed by social scientists has been some driving moral imperative about personal rights, racial balance, sexual equality, or some other issue.[48] But this moral dimension has been obscured by those for whom facts speak for themselves. Along with the collapse of positivism in philosophy, functionalism has likewise suffered badly as the only available social research design.

It is better to view social scientists as sensitizing agents in moral discourse than as engineers of the soul capable of resolving inherited ethical issues. They have not been able to do so in the past and probably will fare little better in decades to come. It is hard to know whether changing moral climates compel a rethinking of social science premises or whether new discoveries in the social sciences compel a changing attitude toward particular ethical commitments and beliefs. In a sense, this is a less important distinction, less important than meets the eye. Causal priorities may be important to those who wish to claim a pedagogic advantage, but to the citizenry at large such matters of causation are entirely derivative and secondary. The main issue is now clear: How do the social sciences smuggle moral imperatives into their findings? At a technical level, the question becomes: How does the subject matter of moral education serve to sensitize social scientists to their own premises?

The ability to get beyond an epoch of ready-to-wear assumptions that social science and morality are irrelevant to one another, or at least independent of each other in development, itself marks a large step forward and upward. If this involves a return to notions of political morality no less than political economy, then so be it. This is a far more eloquent outcome than continuing to presume that moral discourse can seriously take place without reverence to the empirical findings of social science, or, just as tragically, that social science research is devoid of value contentions or value intentions. One no longer hears the positivistic claims that moral education is an impediment to research as such. Both such premises are reductionist, dangerous, myopic. Exclusivity of moral claims results in vague linguistic analysis lacking the shank of reality, whereas exclusivity of social science results in a constant repetition of past mistakes, a hubris of concreteness that requires constant revision and periodic adjustment like the Ptolemaic calendar. It can be expected that this dawning recognition of the need for cross-fertilization of social science and moral education can preserve our intellectual classes from the most serious consequences of spiritualism and reductionism alike.

Two distinguished philosophers, Abraham Edel[49] and John Ladd,[50] are searching for a "common ethic" and see "the theory of the valuational base" as the source of that naturalistic ethic. Both make an appeal to the social sciences. As Edel has observed: "We are, in short, looking to the full scientific perspective which embraces the lessons of the human sciences from biology to history, and applies them to the contemporary life of society and the individual, to help us fashion a general outlook on our world and ourselves."[51] While this ambition remains worthwhile on prima facie grounds, the problem is simply that the social sciences, far from offering any sort of unified picture from which guidelines can be drawn, are in fact deeply mired in contentious ethical viewpoints that are as old as classical discourse in philosophy. This is by no means to conclude on a pessimistic note or to assert that ethical claims are better staked out without reference to contemporary social scientific research. It is, however, to make clear that no heavenly mandates or cookbook recipes can be offered in a scientific world where ethical presuppositions are necessarily reworked constantly and under highly pressurized conditions.

Notes

1. Class Composition and Competition

1. David Riesman, *Abundance for What? And Other Essays* (Garden City, N.Y.: Doubleday, 1964); and C. Wright Mills, *Power, Politics and People*, ed. Irving Louis Horowitz (New York: Oxford University Press, 1963).

2. All references to authors and articles, unless otherwise designated, are to *The New Class?* ed. B. Bruce-Briggs (New Brunswick, N.J.: Transaction Books, 1980).

3. For a reasonable discussion arguing that forms of conflict, other than those between classes, are not only admissable, but self-evident, see Ralf Dahrendorf, *Class and Class Conflict in Industrial Society* (Stanford: Stanford University Press, 1959), 34–35, 124–29.

4. Karl Marx, *Capital: A Critique of Political Economy* (Moscow: Foreign Languages Publishing House, 1962), 3:862–63. In this connection, see the brilliant essay by Reinhard Bendix and Seymour Martin Lipset, "Karl Marx's Theory of Social Classes," in *Class, Status, and Power: Social Stratification in Comparative Perspective*, 2d ed. (New York: Free Press, 1966), 6–11.

5. Max Weber, "Class, Status, Party," in *From Max Weber: Essays in Sociology* (New York: Oxford University Press, 1946), 180–95. A reasonable comparison of Marx and Weber is contained in Tom Bottomore, *Classes in Modern Society* (New York: Pantheon, 1968), 24–25.

6. Emile Durkheim, *The Division of Labor in Society* (New York: Macmillan Co., 1933), 203–15. See also Robert A. Nisbet, *The Sociology of Emile Durkheim* (New York: Oxford University Press, 1974), especially 283–360.

7. Gaetano Mosca, *The Ruling Class* (New York: McGraw-Hill, 1939), 50–102. See also James A. Meisel, *The Myth of the Ruling Class: Gaetano Mosca and the Elite* (Ann Arbor: University of Michigan Press, 1958); and Irving Louis Horowitz, *Radicalism and the Revolt Against Reason* (London and New York: Routledge & Kegan Paul, 1960).

8. Ferdinand Toennies, *Community and Society* (New York: Harper Torchbooks, 1957), 202–47. See also Fritz Pappenheim, *The Alienation of Modern Man: An Interpretation Based on Marx and Toennies* (New York: Monthly Review Press, 1968); and, more recently, the compilation and interpretation by Werner J. Cahnman, *Ferdinand Toennies: A New Evaluation* (Leiden: E. J. Brill, 1973).

9. Irving Louis Horowitz, "Qualitative and Quantitative Research Problems in Comparative International Development," in *Social Development: Critical Perspectives*, ed. Manfred Stanley (New York and London: Basic Books, 1972), 6–38.

10. Probably the most reasoned analysis of such changing structured components is contained in V. O. Key, *Politics, Parties, and Pressure Groups*, 4th ed. (New York: Thomas Y. Crowell, 1958), 115–41. Sadly, Key failed to draw the general implications of his interest model; as a result, the integration of social class to political regimes was only vaguely drawn, and then without proper appreciation of the history of classes in American society.

11. Seymour Martin Lipset, "Socialism and Sociology," in *Sociological Self-Images: A Collective Portrait*, ed. Irving Louis Horowitz (Oxford: Pergamon Press, 1970), 143–67.

12. Daniel Patrick Moynihan, "Eliteland," *Psychology Today* 4, no. 4 (September 1970): 35–36, 66–70.

2. Holy Ghosts in Ethnic Closets

1. Pete Hamill, "The Revolt of the White Lower Middle Class," *New York Times*, 14 Apr. 1969.

2. Herbert Hill, "Racism and Organized Labor," *New School Bulletin* 28, 6 (8 February 1971).

3. Richard F. Hamilton, "Black Demands, White Reactions, and Liberal Alarms," in *Blue Collar Workers*, ed. Sar Levitan (New York: McGraw-Hill, 1971), 135.

4. Angus Campbell, *White Attitudes toward Black People* (Ann Arbor: Institute for Social Research, University of Michigan, 1971), 43–44.

5. Barbara Mikulski, "Who Speaks for Ethnic America?" in *Divided Society: The Ethnic Experience in America*, ed. Colin Greer (New York: Basic Books, 1974), 355–59.

6. Andrew M. Greeley, *Why Can't They Be Like Us? Facts and Fallacies about Ethnic Differences and Group Conflicts in America* (New York: Institute of Human Relations Press, 1969), 45–55.

7. Sar Levitan, *Blue Collar Workers: A Symposium on Middle America* (New York: McGraw-Hill, 1971), 13–20.

8. Robert Coles, *The Middle Americans: Proud and Uncertain* (Boston: Little, Brown, 1971).

9. Michael Novak, "The New Ethnicity," *Center Magazine* 7, 4 (July/Aug. 1974).

10. Thomas J. Cottle, "The Non-Elite Student: Billy Kowalski Goes to College," *Change* 3, 2 (Mar./Apr. 1971): 36–42; and idem, *Time's Children: Impressions of Youth* (Boston: Little, Brown, 1971).

11. Milton Friedman, "Kensington, U.S.A." *LaSalle College Magazine* 11, 4 (Fall 1967).

12. William J. Wilson, *The Declining Significance of Race* (Chicago: University of Chicago Press, 1978); and Charles V. William and William J. Wilson, "The Inclining vs. the Declining Significance of Race," *Transaction/Society* 15, 5 (July/Aug. 1978): 10–21.

13. John Howard, "Public Policy and the White Working Class," in *The Use and Abuse of Social Science*, ed. Irving Louis Horowitz (New Brunswick, N.J.: Transaction Books/E. P. Dutton, 1971), 65–66.

14. Richard Centers, *The Psychology of Social Classes* (Princeton: Princeton University Press, 1949).

15. Ben J. Wattenberg, *The Real America: A Surprising Examination of the State of the Union* (Garden City, N.Y.: Doubleday, 1974), 64–65.

16. Harold M. Hodges, *Social Stratification: Class in America* (Cambridge, Mass.: Schenkman, 1964), 101–6.

17. Novak, "The New Ethnicity," 18–25.

18. Greeley, *Why Can't They Be Like Us?* 46–48.

19. Novak, "The New Ethnicity," 18–25.

20. Michael Novak, "White Ethnic," *Harper's Magazine* 243 (Sept. 1971): 44–50.

21. John A. Morsell, "Ethnic Relations and the Future," *Annals of the American Academy of Political and Social Science* 408 (July 1973): 83–93.

22. Novak, "The New Ethnicity," 19.

23. Gunnar Myrdal, "The Case Against Romantic Ethnicity," *Center Magazine* 7, 4 (July/Aug. 1974): 26–30.

24. Oscar Handlin, *Race and Nationality in American Life* (Boston: Little, Brown, 1957).

25. Colin Gree, *Divided Society: The Ethnic Experience in America* (New York: Basic Books, 1974), 34–35.

26. Lee Rainwater, "Crucible of Identity: The Negro Lower Class Family," *Daedalus* 95 (1955): 172–216; and *Behind Ghetto Walls: Black Family Life in a Federal Slum* (Chicago: Aldine-Atherton, 1970), 361–97.

27. Thomas R. Brooks, "Black Upsurge in the Unions," *Dissent* 17, 75 (Mar./Apr. 1970): 125–38.

28. Bayard Rustin, "The Blacks and the Union," *Harper's Magazine* 242 (May 1970): 73–81.

29. Richard J. Krickus, "Forty Million Ethnics Rate More Than Bromides," *Washington Post*, 31 August 1969.

30. Richard J. Krickus, "The White Ethnics: Who Are They and Where Are They Going?" *City* 5, 3 (May/June 1971): 23–31.

31. John C. Leggett, *Class, Race, and Labor: Working Class Consciousness in Detroit* (New York: Oxford University Press, 1968), 144–54.

32. Peter Berger, "The Blueing of America," *New Republic* 164 (Apr. 1971): 20–23.

33. Charles A. Reich, *The Greening of America: How the Youth Revolution Is Trying to Make America Liveable* (New York: Random House, 1970).

34. Naomi M. Levine and Judith M. Herman, "The Ethnic Factor in Blue Collar Life" (National Project on Ethnic America, American Jewish Committee, 1971, Mimeograph).

35. Roberto Michels, "The Iron Law of Oligarchy," in *Political Parties* (Glencoe, Ill.: Free Press, 1949), 25–36, 365–74, 382–92, 400–408.

3. Environmental Options versus Economic Imperatives

1. Garrett DeBell, *The Voter's Guide to Environmental Politics: Before, During and After the Election* (New York: Ballantine Books, 1970).

2. Paul Swatek, *The User's Guide to the Protection of the Environment* (New York: Ballantine Books, 1970).

3. Thomas R. Shepard, Jr., "We're Going Too Far on Consumerism," *Reader's Digest* 50 (Feb. 1971): 147–50.

4. Lee Thayer, "Man's Ecology, Ecology's Man," *Main Currents in Modern Thought* 27 (Jan./Feb. 1971): 76–77.

5. Barry Commoner, "The Ecological Crisis," in *Social Responsibility of the Scientist*, ed. Martin Brown (New York: Free Press, 1971), 174–75.

6. E. F. Porter, Jr., "Built-in Loopholes for Pollution Laws," *St. Louis Dispatch*, 7 Mar. 1971.

7. Frank M. Coffin, *Moment of Totality (Development in the Decade of Ecology)*, Development Paper no. 4 (Washington, D.C.: Overseas Development Council, 1971).

8. Lewis M. Branscomb, "Taming Technology: A Plea for National Regulation in a Social Context," *Science* 171 (12 Mar. 1971): 972–77.

9. Michael Vermeulen, "How Hard Times Change Us," *Washington Post Parade*, 7 Nov. 1982, 4–7.

4. Unlimited Equality and Limited Growth

1. Gunnar Myrdal, "On the Equality Issue in World Development," *World Issues* 1 (Oct./Nov. 1976): 3–5.

2. Jay W. Forrester, *World Dynamics*, 2d ed., Wright-Allen Series (Cambridge, Mass.: MIT Press, 1973), 129–32.

3. S. M. Miller and John Hoops, "Work," *New Society* 36 (10 June 1976): 582–83.

4. "Snow Belt Seeks More U.S. Funds," *Los Angeles Times*, reported in the *Washington Post*, 24 Oct. 1976, E-7.

5. "Call to Second National Conference on Rural America," *Rural America* 1 (Oct. 1976): 1.

6. Center for the American Woman and Politics, *Report of CAWP: 1974–1975* (New Brunswick, N.J.: Eagleton Institute of Politics, Rutgers University, 1975), 6–7.

7. Hans H. Landsberg, *Energy and the Social Sciences: An Examination of Research Needs* (Washington, D.C.: Resources for the Future, 1974).

8. Leon H. Keyserling, *Full Employment with Inflation* (Washington, D.C.: Conference on Economic Progress, 1975), 9.

9. Kingsley Davis and Wilbert E. Moore, "Some Principles of Stratification," *American Sociological Review* 10, 2 (1945): 242–49. In this connection, see also Kingsley Davis, *Human Society* (New York: Macmillan, 1949).

10. Herbert J. Gans, *People and Plans: Essays on Urban Problems and Solutions* (New York: Basic Books, 1968).

11. Fred Hirsch, *Social Limits to Growth*, A Twentieth Century Fund Study (Cambridge: Harvard University Press, 1976), 12.

12. Herbert J. Gans, "The New Egalitarianism," in *Social Problems and Public Policy: Inequality and Justice*, ed. Lee Rainwater (Chicago: Aldine, 1974), 247–53; idem, *More Equality* (New York: Pantheon, 1973).

13. Alice Rossi, "Sex Equality: The Beginnings of an Ideology," in *Social Problems and Public Policy: Inequality and Justice*, ed. Lee Rainwater (Chicago: Aldine, 1974), 212–27.

14. S. M. Miller and Pamela Roby, *The Future of Inequality* (New York: Basic Books, 1970), 10.

15. Samuel P. Huntington, "The Democratic Distemper," *Public Interest* 41 (Fall 1975): 9–38.

16. Davis and Moore, "Some Principles of Stratification," 247.

17. Christopher Jencks et al., *Inequality: A Reassessment of the Effect of Family and Schooling in America* (New York: Harper & Row, 1972), 9.

18. John H. Goldthorpe, "Social Inequality and Social Integration," in *Social Problems and Public Policy: Inequality and Justice*, ed. Lee Rainwater (Chicago: Aldine, 1974), 136.

19. H. P. Chalfant, "Correlates of Poverty," in *The Sociology of American Poverty*, ed. Joan Huber and H. P. Chalfant (Cambridge, Mass.: Schenkman, 1974), 201.

20. Jackson Toby, "Poverty, Violence, and Crime in America," in *The Sociology Of American Poverty*, ed. Joan Huber and H. P. Chalfant (Cambridge, Mass.: Schenkman, 1974), 266.

21. U.S. Bureau of the Census, *Statistical Abstract of the United States: 1975*, 96th ed. (Washington, D.C.: Government Printing Office, 1975).

22. Ibid., 159–60.

23. Ibid., 160–61.

24. Ely Chinoy, *Automobile Workers and the American Dream* (Boston: Beacon Press, 1955).

25. U.S. Bureau of the Census, *Statistical Abstract*, 374.

26. Charles Kadushin, "Social Class and the Experience of Ill Health," in *Class, Status, and Power*, ed. Reinhard Bendix and Seymour Martin Lipset (New York: Free Press, 1966), 407.

27. Ibid., 411.

28. Herman E. Daly, *Essays Toward a Steady-State Economy* (Mexico City: Cidoc Cuaderno, 1972).

29. Bayard Rustin, "No Growth Has to Mean Less Is Less," *New York Times Magazine* 13 (2 May 1976): 72–80.

30. Daniel Bell, *The Coming of Post-Industrial Society* (New York: Basic Books, 1973); idem, *The Cultural Contradictions of Capitalism* (New York: Basic Books, 1976).

31. Mark Kelman, "The Social Costs of Inequality," *Dissent* 20 (Summer 1973): 291–98.

32. Myrdal, "On the Equality Issue," 4.

33. Norman Girvan, "Economic Nationalism," *Daedalus* 104 (Fall 1975): 146–58.

34. Irving Louis Horowitz, "Capitalism, Communism, and Multinationalism," in *The New Sovereigns: Multinational Corporations as World Powers*, ed. Abdul A. Sais and Luis R. Simmons (Englewood Cliffs, N.J.: Prentice-Hall, 1975), 120–38.

35. Nathan Keyfitz, "World Resources and the World Middle Class," *Scientific American* 235 (July 1975): 28–35.

36. Lester Brown, "Rich Countries and Poor in a Finite, Interdependent World," *Daedalus* 102 (Fall 1973): 153–64. See also Brown's article in *Food, Foreign Policy, and Raw Materials Cartels*, ed. William Schneider (New York: Crane, Russak, 1976).

37. Brookings Institution, *Trade in Primary Commodities: Conflict or Cooperation?* (Washington, D.C.: Brookings Institution, 1974), 28.

38. Hans J. Morgenthau, "World Politics and the Politics of Oil," in *Energy: The Policy Issues*, ed. Gary Eppen (Chicago: University of Chicago Press, 1975), 43.

39. William Schneider, ed., *Food, Foreign Policy, and Raw Materials Cartels* (New York: Crane, Russak, 1976), 52–53.

40. Irving Louis Horowitz, "Equity, Income, and Policy: Comparative Studies," in *Three Worlds of Development*, ed. Irving Louis Horowitz (New York: Praeger, 1977).

5. Winners and Losers

1. Irving Louis Horowitz, "Autobiography as the Presentation of Self for Social Immortality," *New Literary History* 9, 1 (Autumn 1977): 173–79.

2. Irving Louis Horowitz, "Historical Optimism and the Game of War," *Washington University Magazine* 34, 4 (1964); and also idem, *The War Game: Studies of the New Civilian Militarists* (New York: Ballantine Books, 1963).

3. Charles Henry Parkhurst, *Our Fight With Tammany* (New York: Scribner, 1895), 282–84.

4. William L. Riordan, ed., *Plunkitt of Tammany Hall* (New York: Knopf, 1948), 65.

5. Ibid., 11.

6. Ibid., 12.

7. Ibid., 25.

8. Ibid., 40–41.

9. Ibid., 43.

10. Ibid., 51–52.

11. Ibid., 79–80.

12. Ibid., 97–98.

13. Ibid., 118–19.

14. Alexander B. Callow, Jr., *The Tweed Ring* (New York: Oxford University Press, 1966), 73–74.

15. Joseph V. Stalin, "We Do Not Want to be Beaten," in *Russian Literature since the Revolution*, ed. Joshua Kunitz (New York: Boni & Gaer, 1948), 455–56.

16. Isaac Deutscher, *Ironies of History: Essays on Contemporary Communism* (Berkeley: Ramparts Press, 1971), 12.

17. Isaac Deutscher, *Stalin: A Political Biography* (New York and London: Oxford University Press, 1949), 378.

18. Joseph V. Stalin, "Concerning the History of Bolshevism" and "Dialectical Materialism," in *Selected Writings* (New York: International Publishers, 1942), 222–23, 406–33.

19. Robert C. Tucker, *Stalin as Revolutionary, 1879–1929: A Study in History and Personality* (New York: Norton, 1973), 458–59.

20. Nikita Khrushchev, "Secret Report to the XXth Congress of the Communist Party of the USSR," in *Khrushchev Remembers*, introduction, commentary, and notes by Edward Crankshaw, trans. Strobe Talbott (Boston: Little, Brown, 1970), 559–618.

21. Bernard Bailyn, *The Ordeal of Thomas Hutchinson* (Cambridge: Harvard University Press, 1974), x–xi.

22. Ibid., xi.
23. Ibid., 376–77.
24. Ibid., 377–78.
25. Ibid., 380.
26. Leon Trotsky, "Final Summary Speech before the Dewey Commission (1938)," in Isaac Deutscher, ed., *The Prophet Outcast: Trotsky, 1929–1940* (New York and London: Oxford University Press, 1963), 380.
27. Leon Trotsky, "Which Way Russia?" in *The Struggle Against Fascism.in Germany* (New York: Pathfinder Press, 1971), 449.

6. Presenting the Self for Social Immortality

1. Florian Znaniecki, *Social Actions* (New York: Russell and Russell, 1932), 11–17.
2. Erving Goffman, *The Presentation of Self in Everyday Life* (Garden City, N.Y.: Doubleday/Anchor, 1959), 130–31 et passim.
3. William I. Thomas, *The Unadjusted Girl*, excerpted in *Sociological Theory*, ed. Lewis A. Coser and Bernard Rosenberg, 2d ed. (New York: Macmillan, 1964), 41–44; John Sturrock, "The New Model Autobiographer," *New Literary History* 9, 1 (Autumn 1977): 51–63.
4. George Herbert Mead, *Mind, Self, and Society from the Standpoint of a Behaviorist*, ed. Charles W. Morris et al. (Chicago: University of Chicago Press, 1934).
5. Louis A. Renza, "The Veto of the Imagination," *New Literary History* 9, 1 (Autumn 1977): 1–26; Northrop Frye, *Anatomy of Criticism* (Princeton: Princeton University Press, 1957).
6. Giacomo Casanova, *History of My Life*, trans. Willard R. Trask (New York: Harcourt, Brace and World, 1966).
7. Lyndon Baines Johnson, *The Vantage Point: Perspectives of the Presidency, 1963–1969* (New York: Holt, Rinehart and Winston, 1971).
8. Marx-Engels-Lenin Institute, *Joseph Stalin: A Political Biography* (New York: International Publishers, 1949).
9. Nikita Khrushchev, *Rapport secret de Nikita Khrouchtchev sur Staline, présenté le 25 février 1957 au XX Congrès du PCUS Suivi du Testament de Lénine* (Paris: privately printed, 1970).
10. Guy Davenport, "Ernst Machs Max Ernst," *New Literary History* 9, 1 (Autumn 1977): 137–48.
11. Elizabeth W. Bruss, "The Game of Literature and Some Literary Games," *New Literary History* 9, 1 (Autumn 1977): 153–71.
12. Christine Brooke-Rose, "Self-Confrontation and the Writer," *New Literary History* 9, 1 (Autumn 1977): 129–36.
13. Roxane Witke, *Comrade Chiang Ch'ing* (Boston: Little, Brown, 1977).
14. Nikita Khrushchev, *Khrushchev Remembers*, introduction, commentary, and notes by Edward Crankshaw, trans. Strobe Talbott (Boston: Little, Brown, 1970).
15. Nadezhda Konstantinovna Krupskaya, *Reminiscences of Lenin*, trans. Bernard Isaacs (New York: International Publishers, 1970).
16. Russian Institute of Columbia University, *The Anti-Stalin Campaign and International Communism: A Selection of Documents* (New York: Columbia University Press, 1956).
17. C. Wright Mills, *The Sociological Imagination* (New York: Oxford University Press, 1959).
18. Jaber F. Gubrium and David R. Buckholdt, *Toward Maturity: The Social Processing of Human Development* (San Francisco: Jossey-Bass, 1977).
19. Irving Louis Horowitz, *Sociological Self-Images: A Collective Portrait* (London and Los Angeles: Sage Publications, 1970).
20. James D. Watson, *The Double Helix: A Personal Account of the Discovery of the Structure of DNA* (New York: Atheneum, 1969).
21. At least my informants use the word "pain" when asked to prepare autobiographical profiles for *Transaction/Society*.

7. Alienation and the Social System

1. For example, the following representative collections carry no information on alienation: Bernard Berelson and Gary A. Stelner, *Human Behavior: An Inventory of Scientific Findings* (New York: Harcourt, Brace and World, 1964); Solomon E. Asch, *Social Psychology* (Englewood Cliffs, N.J.: Prentice-

Hall, 1952); and Robert K. Merton, Leonard Broom, and Leonard S. Cottree, Jr., *Sociology Today: Problems and Prospects* (New York: Basic Books, 1959).

2. Erich Fromm, *The Sane Society* (New York: Holt, Rinehart and Winston, 1955), 120–21.

3. Melvin Seeman, "On the Meaning of Alienation," in *Sociological Theory*, ed. Lewis A. Coser and Bernard Rosenberg, 2d ed. (New York: Macmillan, 1964), 525–38.

4. Lewis Feuer, "What is Alienation? The Career of a Concept," in *Sociology on Trial*, ed. M. Stein and A. Vidich (Englewood Cliffs, N.J.: Prentice-Hall, 1963), 127–47.

5. Adam Schaff, *A Philosophy of Man* (New York: Monthly Review Press, 1963).

6. Karl Marx, *Economic and Philosophic Manuscripts of 1844* (London: Lawrence & Wishart, 1959), 67–84.

7. C. Wright Mills, *White Collar* (New York: Farrar, Straus and Giroux, 1965–66).

8. Alberto Moravia, *Man as an End, A Defense of Humanism: Literary, Social, and Political Essays*, trans. Bernard Wall (1966; reprint, Westport, Conn.: Greenwood Press, 1976).

9. Daniel Boorstin, *The Image* (New York: Atheneum, 1961), 3–6.

10. See in particular the recent collection of papers by David Riesman, *Abundance for What? And Other Essays* (Garden City, N.Y.: Doubleday, 1964).

11. Irving Malin, *Jews and Americans* (Carbondale, Ill.: Southern Illinois University Press, 1965). For an earlier consideration of Jewish alienation, see Simon Dubnow, *Nationalism and History* (Cleveland and New York: Meridian Books, 1961).

12. Gwynn Nettler, "A Measure of Alienation," *American Sociological Review* 22 (1957); and see his earlier paper, "A Test for the Sociology of Knowledge," *American Sociological Review* 10 (1945), 670–77.

13. Marvin B. Scott, "The Social Sources of Alienation," in *The New Sociology*, ed. Irving Louis Horowitz (New York and London: Oxford University Press, 1964), 239–52.

8. Futurology and Millenarian Visions

1. Norman Vincent Peale, quoted in Lowell Thomas, "What About the Future?" *Mainliner* 12, 1 (Jan. 1974): 30–31.

2. Thomas, "What About the Future?" 30–33.

3. Norman Cohn, *The Pursuit of the Millennium* (New York: Oxford University Press, 1970), 14–19.

4. Daniel Bell, "The End of Scarcity," *Saturday Review of the Society* 49 (May 1973): 49–52.

5. Leo Cherne, "State of the Nation," *Perspectives in Defense Management* (Winter 1972): 1–10.

6. George T. Harris, "Era of Conscious Action," in *Britannica Book of the Year* (Chicago: Encyclopedia Britannica, 1973), 6–14.

7. Daniel Patrick Moynihan, "Peace—Some Thoughts on the 1960s and 1970s," *The Public Interest* 32 (Summer 1973): 3–12.

8. Barbara W. Tuchman, "History as Mirror," *The Atlantic* 232, 3 (Sept. 1973): 39–46.

9. Ben J. Wattenberg and Richard M. Scammon, "Black Progress and Liberal Rhetoric," *Commentary* 55, 4 (Apr. 1973): 35–44.

10. Richard Flacks, "Making History vs. Making Life: Dilemmas of an American Left," *Working Papers for a New Society* 2, 2 (Summer 1974): 56–71.

11. Robert A. Dahl and Edward R. Tufte, *Size and Democracy* (Stanford: Stanford University Press, 1973).

12. Edward Weisband and Thomas Franck, "The Brezhnev-Johnson Two World Doctrine," *Transaction/Society* 8, 12 (Oct. 1971): 36–44.

9. Interest Groups and Political Partisans

1. Robert J. Pranger, "The Decline of the American National Government," *Publius* 3, 1 (1973): 97–127.

2. Kevin Phillips, "The Balkanization of America," *Harper's Magazine* 256, 1537 (May 1978): 37–47.

3. Henry Fairlie, "The Lost Art of Preaching," *Washington Post*, 25 June 1978. The same theme is struck in Fairlie's new book, *The Seven Deadly Sins Today* (Washington, D.C.: New Republic Books, 1978).

4. David S. Broder, "The Frustrations of Single-Interest Politics," *Washington Post*, 13 Sept. 1978.

5. Frank Trippett, "The Menace of Fanatic Factions," *Time* 112, 17 (23 Oct. 1978).

6. Tom Mathews et al., "Single Issue Politics," *Newsweek* 92, 19 (6 Nov. 1978).

7. John Hebers, "Governing America" (three-part series), *New York Times*, 12–14 November 1978.

8. Spencer Rich, "Touchy Issues Sank Conference on Families," *Washington Post*, 24 June 1978.

9. Charles Peters, "The Solution: A Rebirth of Patriotism," *Washington Monthly*, 10, 7 (Oct. 1978): 37–38.

10. McGeorge Bundy, commentary on Sanford M. Jaffee, *New Approaches to Conflict Resolution* (New York: Ford Foundation, 1978), Ford Foundation press release, 21 June 1978.

10. Bureaucracy, Administration, and State Power

1. The two most prescient sources on defining the nature of postindustrialism are: Daniel Bell, *The Coming of Post-Industrial Society: A Venture in Social Forecasting* (New York: Basic Books, 1973); and idem, *The Cultural Contradictions of Capitalism* (New York: Basic Books, 1976). For an earlier evaluation on Bell's latter work, see Irving Louis Horowitz, "A Funeral Pyre for America," *Worldview* 19 (1976).

2. Harlan Cleveland, "American Public Executive: New Functions, New Style, New Purpose," in *Theory and Practice of Public Administration: Scope, Objectives, and Methods*, ed. James C. Charlesworth (Philadelphia: American Academy of Political and Social Science, 1968), 168–78.

3. Hans Wolfgang Singer, "Multinational Corporations and Technology Transfer," in *The Strategy of International Development: Essays in the Economics of Backwardness*, ed. Sir Alec Carncross and Mohinder Puri (White Plains, N.Y.: International Arts and Sciences Press, 1975), 208–33.

4. B. Bruce-Briggs, "Enumerating the New Class," in *The New Class?* ed. B. Bruce-Briggs (New Brunswick, N.J.: Transaction Books, 1979), 217–25.

5. Max Weber, "Bureaucracy," in *From Max Weber: Essays in Sociology*, ed. Hans Gerth and C. Wright Mills (New York: Oxford University Press, 1946), 196–244.

6. See James G. March and Herbert Simon, "The Theory of Organizational Equilibrium," in *Organizations*, ed. James G. March (New York: Wiley, 1958), 84–108; and also Dorwin Cartwright, "Influence, Leadership, Control," in *Handbook of Organizations*, ed. James G. March (Chicago: Rand McNally, 1963), 1–47.

7. Irving Louis Horowitz, "On the Expansion of New Theories and the Withering Away of Old Classes," *Transaction/Society* 16, 2 (Jan.-Feb. 1979): 55–62.

8. Irving Louis Horowitz, "Methods and Strategies in Evaluating Equity Research," *Social Indicators Research* 16 (1970): 1–22.

9. Irving Louis Horowitz, "Social Welfare, State Power, and the Limits to Equity," in *Growth in a Finite World*, ed. Joseph Grunfeld (Philadelphia: The Franklin Institute, 1979), 21–35.

10. Charles E. Lindblom, "The Science of Muddling Through," *Public Administration Review* 19, 2 (Spring 1959): 79–88; and idem, "Policy Analysis," *American Economic Review* 47 (Spring 1958): 298–99. See also his most recent work, *Politics and Markets: The World's Political-Economic Systems* (New York: Basic Books, 1977), especially 119–42; and Bill G. Schumacher, *Computer Dynamics in Public Administration* (New York: Spartan, 1967), 163–71.

11. Dwight Waldo, "Scope of the Theory of Public Administration," in *Theory and Practice of Public Administration*, ed. James C. Charlesworth (Philadelphia: American Academy of Political and Social Science, 1968), 1–26.

12. Samuel B. Bacharach, "What's Public Administration? An Examination of Basic Textbooks," *Administrative Science Quarterly* 21, 2 (June 1976): 346–51.

13. Michael Crozier, *The Bureaucratic Phenomenon* (London: Tavistock, 1964); and more recently, idem, *The Stalled Society* (New York: Viking Press, 1973).

14. Nicos Poulantzas, *State, Power, Socialism* (London: NLB, 1978); and his earlier, albeit less decisive enunciation of the same theme, *Political and Social Classes* (London: NLB, 1973).

15. Ernest Mandel, *Late Capitalism* (London: Humanities Press, 1975), 405–7.

16. Poulantzas, *State, Power, Socialism*, 127–39.

17. Michael Crozier, *La Société Bloquée* (Paris: Editions du Seuil, 1970), 20; see the discussion of this in Michael Rose, *Servants of Post-Industrial Power?* (Armonk, N.Y.: M. E. Sharpe), 113–27.

18. Poulantzas, *State, Power, Socialism*, 251–65.

19. Jean-Jacques Servan-Schreiber, *The Radical Alternative* (New York: Norton, 1971), 59–61.

20. Aaron Wildavsky, *Budgeting: A Comparative Theory of Budgetary Processes* (Boston: Little, Brown, 1975), 155–57.

21. Joseph LaPalombara, *Bureaucracy and Political Development* (Princeton: Princeton University Press, 1963), 48–55.

22. Gordon Tullock, *The Politics of Bureaucracy* (Washington, D.C.: Public Affairs Press, 1964), 181.

23. William Howard Gammon and Lowell H. Hattery, "Managing the Impact of Computers on the Federal Government," *The Bureaucrat* 2 (1978): 18–26.

24. Ron Johnson and Philip Gummett, *Directing Technology: Policies for Promotion and Control* (New York: St. Martin's Press, 1979), 13–14.

25. Compare Alan Peacock, "Public Expenditure in Post Industrial Society," in *Post Industrial Society*, ed. Bo Gustafsson (New York: St. Martin's Press, 1979), 91–95.

26. Manfred Stanley, *The Technological Conscience: Survival and Dignity in an Age of Expertise* (New York: Free Press, 1978), 251–53.

27. Compare David Apter, *Choice and the Politics of Allocation* (New Haven: Yale University Press, 1979), 128–54; and Edward R. Tufte, *Political Control of the Economy* (Princeton: Princeton University Press, 1978), 110–45.

28. For strongly contrasting statements about democracy, which yet manage to appreciate the process and symbol of the entity, see Dorothy Pickles, *Democracy* (New York: Basic Books, 1970), 9–28 and 169–82; C. B. Macpherson, *Democratic Theory* (Oxford: Clarendon Press, 1973), especially 3–23 and 29–76.

11. Political Bases of Equity

1. Edward A. Suchman, *Evaluative Research* (New York: Russell Sage Foundation, 1967), 7.

2. Ibid., 1.

3. Sar Levitan and Richard Taggart, *The Promise of Greatness* (Cambridge, Mass.: Harvard University Press, 1976), 20–22.

4. Robert Havemann, "Poverty, Income Distribution, and Social Policy: The Last Decade and the Next" (Institute for Research on Poverty, Madison, Wis., 1976, Mimeograph).

5. Robert Dorfman, "Incident of the Benefits and Costs of Environmental Programs" (Paper delivered at the American Economic Association and Allied Sciences Association, National Convention, Atlantic City, N.J., September 1976), 5–6.

6. Ezra J. Mishan, *Cost-Benefit Analysis* (New York: Praeger, 1967), x–xi.

7. Ibid., 25–26.

8. Ezra J. Mishan, *The Costs of Economic Growth* (New York: Praeger, 1967), 45.

9. Mishan, *Cost-Benefit Analysis*, 75–80.

10. Richard Zeckhauser et al., *Benefit-Cost and Policy Analysis* (Chicago: Aldine, 1975).

11. Mollie Orshansky, "Poverty Income Levels by Types of Families," in *Poverty in Affluence*, ed. Robert E. Will and Harold G. Vatter (New York: Harcourt, Brace and World, 1970), 11–12.

12. M. S. March, "Coverage, Gaps, and Future Directions of Public Programs," in *Poverty in Affluence*, ed. Robert E. Will and Harold G. Vatter (New York: Harcourt, Brace and World, 1970).

13. Eli Ginzberg, "Planning Full Employment," *Society* 13, 4 (May/June 1976): 57–64.

14. Richard P. Nathan, "Evaluating Broad-Gauged, Multipurpose Grants," in *Policy Studies Review Annual 5*, ed. Irving Louis Horowitz (Beverly Hills and London: Sage Publications, 1981), 98–109.

15. Ginzberg, "Planning Full Employment," 61.

16. Ben Chieh Liu, *Quality of Life Indicators in U.S. Metropolitan Areas* (New York: Praeger, 1976), 8.

17. Irving Louis Horowitz, "Social Indicators and Social Policies," in *Professing Sociology*, ed. Irving Louis Horowitz (Chicago: Aldine, 1968), 332.

18. Liu, *Quality of Life Indicators in U.S. Metropolitan Areas*, 12.

19. S. M. Miller et al., "A Social Indicators Definition," in *Poverty in Affluence*, ed. Robert E. Will and Harold G. Vatter (New York: Harcourt, Brace and World, 1970), 18.

20. Liu, *Quality of Life Indicators in U.S. Metropolitan Areas*, 14.

21. Angus Campbell et al., *The Quality of American Life* (New York: Russell Sage Foundation, 1976), 218.

22. Ibid., 469.

23. Dorfman, "Benefits and Costs of Environmental Programs," 15.

24. W. J. Baumol, "Environmental Protection and Income Distribution," in *Benefit-Cost and Policy Analysis*, ed. Robert Zeckhauser (Chicago: Aldine, 1975).

25. J. F. Springer and E. Constantini, "Public Opinion and the Environment: An Issue in Search of a Home," in *Environmental Politics*, ed. Stuart S. Nagel (New York: Praeger, 1974).

26. United Nations, *Importance of the Future* 1, 3 (Apr. 1976): 4.

27. George Roth and George Wynn, *Free Enterprise Urban Transportation*, Learning from Abroad Series, vol. 5 (New Brunswick and London: Transaction Books, 1982), 31–38.

28. Eric Hirst, "Transportation Energy Conservation Policies," *Science* 192, 4234 (1976): 15–20.

29. "Proponents Fight to Keep Berkeley Traffic Barricades," *New York Times* 13 June 1975, 32; and more recently, George Sternlieb and James W. Hughes, "Energy Realities," in *Revitalizing the Northeast*, ed. George Sternlieb and James W. Hughes (New Brunswick: Center for Urban Policy Research, 1978), 324–44.

30. See, for instance, John Johnston, *Econometric Methods* (New York: McGraw-Hill, 1972), 1–6.

31. A. J. Harrison, *The Economics of Transportation Appraisal* (New York: Wiley, 1974), 215–17.

32. Melvin W. Webber, "The BART Experience—What Have We Learned," *The Public Interest* 45 (Fall 1976): 79–108.

33. Guy H. Orcutt, Steven B. Caldwell, and Richard Wertheimer, *Policy Exploration through Microanalytic Simulation* (Washington, D.C.: The Urban Institute, 1976), 1–2.

34. Raymond A. Bauer and Dan H. Fenn, Jr., *The Corporate Social Audit* (New York: Russell Sage Foundation, 1972), 14–42.

35. Orcutt, Caldwell, and Wertheimer, *Policy Exploration through Microanalytic Simulation*, 198–205.

36. Carol H. Weiss, "Policy Research in the Context of Diffuse Decision-making," in *Policy Studies Review Annual* 6, ed. Ray C. Rist (Beverly Hills and London: Sage Publications, 1982), 19–26.

12. From the New Deal to the New Federalism

1. Beryl A. Radin, "Sink or Swim: States Without Federal Strings, An Analysis of an HHS Experiment" (Paper delivered at the Fourth Conference of the Association for Public Policy Analysis and Management, Minneapolis, 28 Oct. 1982).

2. Lane Kirkland et al., Statements Adopted by the AFL-CIO Executive Council (Bar Harbour, Florida, 15–22 Feb. 1982) (Washington, D.C.: American Federation of Labor and Congress of Industrial Organizations, 1982), 11–19.

3. Bernard L. Weinstein, "New Federalism—or New Feudalism?" *Challenge: The Magazine of Economic Affairs* 25, 2 (May/June 1982): 38–45.

4. Sar A. Levitan, "The 1983 Budget and New Federalism: Trick or Treat?" *Transaction/Society* 19, 4 (July/Aug. 1982): 81–84.

5. Wallace E. Oates, "The New Federalism: An Economist's View," *Cato Journal* 2, 2 (Fall 1982): 473–88.

6. Kathleen Maurer Smith and William Spinrad, "The Popular Political Mood," *Social Policy* 11, 5 (Mar./Apr. 1981): 37–45.

7. James Q. Wilson, "Reagan and the Republican Revival," *Commentary* 7, 4 (Oct. 1980): 25–32.

8. John Kenneth Galbraith, "The Conservative Onslaught," *New York Review* 7, 21–22 (22 Jan. 1981): 14–15.

9. Felix G. Rohatyn, "A Matter of Psychology: Reagan's New Orthodoxy," *New York Review* 28, 6 (16 Apr. 1981): 14–15.

10. Robert L. Heilbroner, "The Demand for the Supply Side," *New York Review* 18, 10 (11 July 1981): 37–41.

11. Jude Wanniski, "A Supply-Side Foreign Policy," *American Spectator* 14, 2 (Feb. 1981): 7–10. For a more recent (and strident) attack on Reaganism from the right, see "Has Reagan Deserted the Conservatives?" *Conservative Digest* 8, 1 (July 1982): 5–44.

12. *Survey of Current Business Monthly*, Special Supplement, July 1981.

13. Irving Louis Horowitz, *Ideology and Utopia in the United States, 1956–1976* (New York and London: Oxford University Press, 1977), 427–38.

14. U.S. Bureau of the Census, "Money Income and Poverty Status of Families and Persons in the United States, 1980," *Current Population Reports*, ser. P-60, no. 127 (advance data from Current Population Survey) (Washington, D.C.: Government Printing Office, 1981).

15. Ibid.

16. Ibid.

17. David J. Teece, "The New Social Regulation: Implications and Alternatives," in *The Economy in the 1980s: A Program for Growth and Stability*, ed. Michael J. Boskin (New Brunswick, N.J.: Transaction Books, 1980), 124–25.

18. Raymond J. Saulnier, "The Reagan Administration's First Year: Pluses and Minuses," *Economic Outlook USA* 9, 2 (Spring 1982).

13. Transnational Terrorism, Civil Liberties, and the Social Fabric

1. Irving Louis Horowitz, "Political Terrorism and State Power," *Journal of Political and Military Sociology* 1, 1 (Spring 1973): 10–18.

2. Irving Louis Horowitz, *The Struggle is the Message: The Organization and Ideology of the Anti-War Movement*. Transcript of Hearings held by the National Commission on the Causes and Prevention of Violence (Berkeley: Glendessary Press, 1970), 121–42.

3. U.S. Congress, Senate Committee on the Judiciary, Subcommittee to Investigate the Administration of the Internal Security Act and Other Internal Security Laws, *Assaults on Law Enforcement Officers* (Washington, D.C.: Government Printing Office, 1970).

4. U.S. Congress, Senate Committee on the Judiciary, Subcommittee to Investigate the Administration of the Internal Security Act and Other Internal Security Laws, *Terrorist Activity* (Washington, D.C.: Government Printing Office, 1974).

5. J. Bowyer Bell, "Assassination in International Politics," *International Studies Quarterly* 16, 1 (1972): 59–82.

14. Routinized Terrorism and Its Unanticipated Consequences

1. See U.S. Congress, Senate Select Committee to Study Government Operations with Respect to Intelligence Activities, *Alleged Assassination Plots Involving Foreign Leaders: Interim Report*, 94th Congress, 1st session, 20 November 1975.

2. See U.S. Congress, Senate Committee on the Judiciary, Subcommittee on Security and Terrorism, *Terrorism: Origins, Direction and Support: Hearings*, 97th Congress, 1st session, 24 April 1981; *Historical Antecedents of Soviet Terrorism, Hearings*, 97th Congress, 1st session, 25 June 1981; *Terrorism: The Role of Moscow and its Subcontractors: Hearings*, 97th Congress, 1st session, 26 June 1981.

3. The best single source on the geographic distribution, category of attack, and number of casualties caused by terrorists is contained in National Foreign Assessment Center, *Patterns of International Terrorism: 1980* (Washington, D.C.: National Technical Information Service, 1981). This report is also available in *Defense and Economy World Report and Survey*, 20 July 1981, 46–57. Additional information is contained in "A New Surge of Terrorism" in *U.S. News and World Report*, 14 Sept. 1981; and James Berry Motley, "International Terrorism: A New Mode of Warfare," *International Security Review* 6 (Spring 1981): 93–123.

4. See Martha Crenshaw, "The Causes of Terrorism," *Comparative Politics* 13 (July 1981): 379–99; and Paul Wilkinson, *Terrorism and the Liberal State* (New York: Wiley, 1977); James Q. Wilson, "The Terrorist's Goal is Not to Solve the Problem," *Washington Star*, 19 July 1981, F:1.

5. Walter Laqueur, "The Futility of Terrorism" and "Second Thoughts on Terrorism," in *The Political Psychology of Appeasement: Finlandization and Other Unpopular Essays* (New Brunswick and London: Transaction/Holt-Saunders, 1980), 101–25.

6. Ted Robert Gurr, "Some Characteristics of Political Terrorism in the 1960s," in *The Politics of Terrorism*, ed. Michael Stohl (New York: Marcel Dekker, 1979), 23–49.

7. Albert Parry, *Terrorism: From Robespierre to Arafat* (New York: Vanguard Press, 1976), 55–56.

8. Brian Crozier, *A Theory of Conflict* (New York: Scribner, 1974), 129–30.

9. Irving Louis Horowitz, "Can Democracy Cope with Terrorism?" *Civil Liberties Review* 4 (May/June 1977): 29–37.

10. Shlomo Gazit, "The Myth and Reality of the PLO," in *International Terrorism: Challenge and Response*, ed. Benjamin Netanayhu (New Brunswick, N.J.: Transaction Books, 1981), 345–56.

11. Walter Laqueur, "Reagan and the Russians," *Commentary* 73 (January 1982): 19–26.

12. Claire Sterling, *The Terror Network: The Secret War of International Terrorism* (New York:

Reader's Digest Press, 1981); and Samuel T. Francis, *The Soviet Strategy of Terror* (Washington, D.C.: Heritage Foundation, 1981).

13. Irving Louis Horowitz, "Left-Wing Fascism: An Infantile Disorder," *Transaction/Society* 18 (May/June 1981): 19–24.

14. Sheldon Wolin, "Separating Terrorism from Radicalism," *New York Times*, 3 Nov. 1981; and Victor Navasky, "Security and Terrorism," *The Nation*, 14 Feb. 1981, 168.

15. James A. Nathan, "The New Feudalism," *Foreign Policy* 42 (Spring 1981): 156–66.

16. William R. Farrell, "Military Involvement in Domestic Terror Incidents," *Naval War College Review* (July/August 1981): 34, 56–66.

15. Revolution, Retribution, and Redemption

1. Aleksandr Solzhenitsyn, *The Gulag Archipelago, 1918–1956: An Experiment in Literary Investigation*, vol. 1: pts. 1 and 2, translated from Russian by Thomas P. Whitney (New York: Harper & Row, 1974); vol. 2: pts. 3 and 4, translated from Russian by Thomas P. Whitney (New York and London: Harper & Row, 1975); vol. 3: pts. 5, 6, and 7, translated from Russian by Harry Willetts (New York and London: Harper & Row, 1978). All quotations in this chapter are from this trilogy.

16. Marginality, Originality, and Rootless Cosmopolitanism

1. Daniel Bell, *The Winding Passage: Essays and Sociological Journeys, 1960–1980* (Cambridge, Mass.: Abt Books, 1980).

2. Hannah Arendt, *The Life of the Mind, Volume One: Thinking*, edited with a postface by Mary McCarthy (New York: Harcourt Brace Jovanovich, 1978); and *The Life of the Mind, Volume Two: Willing*, edited with a postface by Mary McCarthy (New York: Harcourt Brace Jovanovich, 1978). Volume and page numbers are given in parentheses at the end of each quotation.

3. Jacob L. Talmon, *The Myth of the Nation and the Vision of Revolution: The Origins of Ideological Polarization in the Twentieth Century* (Berkeley and Los Angeles: University of California Press, 1981).

17. Left-wing Fascism

1. Vladimir I. Lenin, *"Left-Wing" Communism, An Infantile Disorder: A Popular Essay in Marxian Strategy and Tactics* (1920) (New York: International Publishers, 1940), 10–11.

2. Leon Trotsky, *The Struggle against Fascism in Germany*, with an introduction by Ernest Mandel (New York: Pathfinder Press, 1971), 437–43.

3. Christopher Hitchens, "Eurofascism: The Wave of the Past," *New Statesman* 231, 18 (29 Nov. 1980): 567–70.

4. Theodor W. Adorno, "On the Fetish Character in Music and the Regression of Listening" and "Commitment," in *The Essential Frankfurt School Reader*, ed. Andrew Arato and Eike Gebhardt (New York: Urizen Books, 1978), 270–318.

5. See Carol White, "The Rieman-LaRouche Model: Breakthrough in Thermodynamics," *Fusion* 3, 10 (August 1980): 57–66; and Steven Bardwell and Uwe Parpart, "Economics Becomes a Science," *Fusion* 2, 9 (July 1970): 32–50.

6. Norman Kogan, "Fascism as a Political System," in *The Nature of Fascism*, ed. S. J. Woolf (New York: Random House, 1968), 11–18.

7. Irving Louis Horowitz, "Preface to the Paperback Edition of Radicalism and the Revolt Against Reason—Then and Now," in *Radicalism and the Revolt Against Reason* (Carbondale and Edwardsville: Southern Illinois University Press, 1968).

8. Harvey Kahn et al., ";NCLS/U.S. Labor Party: Political Chameleon to Right-Wing Spy," *The Public Eye* 1, 1 (Fall 1977): 6–22.

9. Lionel Abel, "Our First Serious Fascist?" *Dissent* 27, 4, whole no. 121 (Fall 1980): 430–36.

10. Roger S. Gottlieb, "The Dialectics of National Identity: Left-Wing Antisemitism and the Arab-Israeli Conflict," *Socialist Review* 9, 5, whole no. 47 (Sept./Oct. 1979): 19–52.

11. Russ Bellant, Susan Gluss, Eda Gordon, Harvey Kahn, and Mark Ryter, *National Caucus of Labor Committees: Brownshirts of the Seventies* (Arlington, Va.: Terrorist Information Project, 1977).

12. Arnold Beichman, "The Myth of American Fascism," in *The Heritage Lectures*, no. 7 (Washington, D.C.: Heritage Foundation, 1981), 1–22.

13. Hannah Arendt, *The Origins of Totalitarianism*, new ed. (New York: Harcourt, Brace and World, 1966).

14. Elie Halevy, *The Era of Tyrannies* (New York: New York University Press, 1966).

15. George Lichtheim, *Collected Essays* (New York: Viking Press, 1973).

16. Wilhelm Reich, *The Mass Psychology of Fascism* (New York: Farrar, Straus and Giroux, 1979).

17. Jacob L. Talmon, *The Myth of the Nation and the Vision of Revolution* (Berkeley and Los Angeles: University of California Press, 1981).

18. Multiplication of Marxisms

1. George Lukács, *History and Class Consciousness* (London: Merlin Press, 1971), 3.

2. George Lichtheim, *Marxism* (London: Routledge & Kegan Paul, 1961), 254; also, Sidney Hook, *From Hegel to Marx* (London: Victor, 1976), 75–76.

3. David Joravsky, *Soviet Marxism and Natural Science* (New York: Columbia University Press, 1961), 6. Also, A. A. Zhdanov, *On Literature, Music, and Philosophy* (London: Lawrence and Wishart, 1959), 50; and George L. Kline, "Recent Soviet Philosophy," *Annals of the American Academy of Political and Social Science* (Jan. 1956): 126–38.

4. Z. A. Jordan, *The Evolution of Dialectical Materialism* (London: Macmillan, 1967), 11–12.

5. Friedrich Engels, *Anti-Dühring* (Moscow: Foreign Language Publishing House, 1959), 17.

6. T. B. Bottomore and Maximilian Rubel, "Introduction to Karl Marx," in *Selected Writings in Sociology and Social Philosophy*, ed. T. B. Bottomore (London: Penguin, 1965), 63.

7. Shlomo Avineri, *The Social and Political Thought of Karl Marx* (Cambridge: Cambridge University Press, 1970), 69.

8. Karl Marx, "The Holy Family" (1845), in *Writings of the Young Marx on Philosophy and Society*, ed. Lloyd D. Easton and Kurt Guddat (New York: Doubleday/Anchor, 1967), 382.

9. Karl Marx, *Economic and Philosophic Manuscripts* (1844), ed. Dirk J. Struick (New York: International Publishers, 1957).

10. Ibid., 176.

11. Karl Marx, *Capital* (London: George Allen and Unwin, 1974), xxx.

12. Marx, *Economic and Philosophic Manuscripts*, 177.

13. Ibid., 177.

14. Ibid., 188.

15. Karl Marx and Friedrich Engels, "The German Ideology," in *Karl Marx: Selected Writings*, ed. David McLellan (Oxford: Oxford University Press, 1977), 161.

16. Ibid., 162.

17. Ibid., 168.

18. Ibid., 181.

19. Ibid., 182.

20. Marx, "The Holy Family," 388.

21. Ibid., 379.

22. Ibid., 400–401.

23. Karl Marx, *Grundrisse: Foundations of the Critique of Political Economy*, trans. Martin Nicolaus (New York: Random House, 1973), 704.

24. Ibid., 148–49.

25. Irving Louis Horowitz, "Socialism and the Problem of Knowledge," in *Essays on the Future of Socialism*, ed. B. P. Parehk (London: Croom, Helm, 1974).

26. Marx, *Grundrisse*, 100.

27. Allen W. Wood, "The Marxian Critique of Justice," *Philosophy and Public Affairs* 1, 3 (Spring 1972): 242–82.

28. Marx, "Theses of Feuerbach," in *Karl Marx: Selected Writings*, ed. David McLellan (Oxford: Oxford University Press, 1977), 156–58.

29. Marx, *Grundrisse*, 109.

30. Karl Marx, "Critique of the Gotha Program," in *Karl Marx on Revolution*, vol. 1 of *The Karl Marx Library*, ed. Saul K. Padover (New York: McGraw-Hill, 1971), 488–506.

31. Leonard Krieger, "Marx on Engels as Historians," *Journal of the History of Ideas* 14 (1953): 397.

32. Sidney Hook, *Towards the Understanding of Karl Marx* (New York: John Day, 1933), 159.

33. Marx, *Economic and Philosophic Manuscripts*, 143.

34. Henri Lefebvre, *Dialectical Materialism* (London: Jonathan Cape, 1969), 107.

35. Engels, *Anti-Dühring*, 40.

36. Friedrich Engels, *Dialectics of Nature* (London: Lawrence and Wishart, 1941), 243–44.

37. Engels, *Anti-Dühring*, 122–29.

38. Ibid., 125.

39. Vladimir I. Lenin, "Materialism and Empiro-Criticism," in vol. 13 of *Collected Works* (London: Lawrence and Wishart, 1938), 114–30.

40. Z. A. Jordan, *Philosophy and Ideology* (Dordrecht: D. Reidel Publishing Co., 1963), 324.

41. Gustav A. Wetter, *Soviet Ideology Today* (London: Heinemann, 1960), 490.

42. Jordan, *Philosophy and Ideology*, 324.

43. Engels, *Anti-Dühring*, 55.

44. Marx, *Economic and Philosophic Manuscripts*, 180.

19. Methodology, Ideology, and Society

1. Gunnar Myrdal, *An American Dilemma* (New York: Harper & Bros., 1944).

2. Robert E. Park and Ernest W. Burgess, *Introduction to the Science of Sociology* (Chicago: University of Chicago Press, 1921).

3. Irving Louis Horowitz, *Professing Sociology: Studies in the Life Cycle of a Social Science* (Chicago: Aldine-Atherton, 1968).

4. Kingsley David and Wilbert E. Moore, "Some Principles of Stratification," *American Sociological Review* 10 (Apr. 1945): 242–49.

5. Melvin W. Tumin, "Some Principles of Stratification: A Critical Analysis," *American Sociological Review* 18 (Aug. 1953): 387–93.

6. Arthur J. Vidich, Joseph Bensman, and Maurice R. Stein, *Reflections on Community Studies* (New York: Harper & Row, 1964).

7. Ray Ginger, *The Bending Cross* (New Brunswick, N.J.: Rutgers University Press, 1949).

8. William Ryan, *Blaming the Victim* (New York: Pantheon, 1971).

9. Lee Rainwater and William L. Yancey, *The Moynihan Report and the Politics of Controversy* (Cambridge, Mass.: MIT Press, 1967).

10. Lewis S. Feuer, *The Conflict of Generations* (New York: Basic Books, 1969).

11. Howard S. Becker, "Introduction: The Struggle for Power on Campus," in *Campus Power Struggle*, ed. Howard S. Becker (Chicago: Aldine, 1970).

12. Martin Nicolaus, "The Professional Organization of Sociology: A View From Below," *Antioch Review* 29 (Fall 1969): 375–87.

13. Herbert Blumer, "Threats from Agency-Determined Research: The Case of Camelot," in *The Rise and Fall of Project Camelot: Studies in the Relationship between Social Science and Practical Politics*, ed. Irving Louis Horowitz (Cambridge, Mass.: MIT Press, 1967).

14. Anthony M. Platt, *The Politics of Riot Commissions* (New York: Collier, 1971).

20. Developmental Dilemmas

1. Seymour Martin Lipset, *Revolution and Counterrevolution: Change and Persistence in Social Structures* (New York: Basic Books, 1968).

2. Andre Gunder Frank, *Latin America: Underdevelopment or Revolution* (New York and London: Monthly Review Press, 1969).

3. Bert F. Hoselitz, *Sociological Aspects of Economic Growth* (New York: Free Press, 1960).

4. Daniel Lerner, *The Passing of Traditional Society* (New York: Free Press, 1964).

5. Edward A. Shils, "Intellectuals in the Political Development of the New States," *World Politics* 12, 3 (Apr. 1960): 329–68.

6. Myron Weiner, ed., *Modernization: The Dynamics of Growth* (London and New York: Basic Books, 1966).

7. Samuel P. Huntington, *Political Order in Changing Societies* (New Haven: Yale University Press, 1968).

8. Celso Furtado, *Development and Underdevelopment* (Berkeley and Los Angeles: University of California Press, 1964).

9. René Dumont with Marcel Mazoyer, *Socialisms and Development* (New York: Praeger, 1973).

10. Immanuel Wallerstein, *The Modern World System: Capitalist Agriculture and the Origins of the European World-Economy in the Sixteenth Century* (New York and London: Academic Press, 1974).

11. Paul Baran, *The Political Economy of Growth* (New York: Monthly Review Press, 1957); see also Paul Baran and Paul M. Sweezy, *Monopoly Capital* (New York: Monthly Review Press, 1966).

12. Dale L. Johnson, James D. Cockroft, and Andre Gunder Frank, *Dependence and Underdevelopment* (Garden City, N.Y.: Doubleday, 1972); see also Frederick Stirton Weaver, "Capitalist Development, Empire and Latin American Underdevelopment," *Latin American Perspectives* 3, 4 (Fall 1976): 17–53.

13. Stanley deViney and John Crowley, "Universality of Modernization: An Empirical Critique," *Studies in Comparative International Development* 13, 2 (Summer 1978): 23–29.

14. Herbert Blumer, "The Idea of Social Development," *Studies in Comparative International Development* 2, 1, whole no. 15 (1966): 3–11.

21. Advocacy and Neutrality in Research

1. Edward Shils, "The Confluence of Sociological Traditions," in *The Calling of Sociology and Other Essays in Pursuit of Learning*, ed. Edward A. Shils (Chicago and London: University of Chicago Press, 1980), 134–64.

2. Kathleen Gough, "Anthropologie et Impérialisme," in *Anthropologie et Impérialisme*, ed. Jean Copans (Paris: François Maspero, 1975), 70.

3. Erving Goffman, *Asylums: Essays on the Social Situation of Mental Patients and Other Inmates* (Chicago: Aldine, 1962).

4. Elliot Liebow, *Talley's Corner* (Boston: Little, Brown, 1967).

5. Howard S. Becker, *Outsiders: Studies in the Sociology of Deviance* (New York: Free Press of Glencoe, 1973).

6. Oscar Lewis, *La Vida* (New York: Random House, 1968).

7. John Lofland, *Doomsday Cult: A Study of Conversion, Proselytization, and Maintenance of Faith* (Englewood Cliffs, N.J.: Prentice-Hall, 1966).

8. Laud Humphreys, *Tearoom Trade: Impersonal Sex in Public Places* (Chicago: Aldine, 1970).

9. Howard S. Becker and Irving Louis Horowitz, "Radical Politics and Sociological Research: Observations on Methodology and Ideology," *American Journal of Sociology* 76, 1 (July 1972): 48–66.

10. Daniel P. Moynihan, *Maximum Feasible Misunderstanding* (New York: Macmillan, 1969); and Harold Orlans, *Contracting for Knowledge* (San Francisco: Jossey-Bass, 1973).

11. Irving Louis Horowitz and James Everett Katz, *Social Science and Public Policy in the United States* (New York: Praeger, 1975), 159–78.

12. Irving Louis Horowitz, ed., *Constructing Policy: Dialogues with Social Scientists in the Modern Political Arena* (New York and London: Praeger, 1979).

13. Steven E. Rhoads, *Valuing Life: Public Policy Dilemmas* (Boulder, Colo.: Westview Press, 1980); and Paul F. Lazarsfeld and Jeffrey G. Reitz, *An Introduction to Applied Sociology* (New York: Elsevier, 1975).

14. Henry J. Aaron, *Politics and the Professors: The Great Society in Perspective* (Washington, D.C.: Brookings Institution, 1978), 16–64.

15. Irving Louis Horowitz, "Social Science and Public Policy: Implications of Modern Research," in *The Rise and Fall of Project Camelot: Studies in the Relationship between Social Science and Practical Politics*, ed. Irving Louis Horowitz (Cambridge, Mass.: MIT Press, 1967), 339–76.

16. C. Wright Mills, "The Professional Ideology of Social Pathologists," in *Power, Politics and People: The Collected Essays of C. Wright Mills*, ed. Irving Louis Horowitz (New York and London: Oxford University Press, 1963), 525–52.

17. Herbert C. Kelman, *A Time to Speak: On Human Values and Social Research* (San Francisco: Jossey-Bass, 1967), 300–305.

18. John Kenneth Galbraith, *The Affluent Society*, 2d rev. ed. (Boston: Houghton Mifflin, 1969).

19. Michael Harrington, *The Other America* (New York: Macmillan, 1962).

20. Dwight MacDonald, *Discriminations: Essays and Afterthoughts* (New York: Grossman, 1974).

21. Gunnar Myrdal et al., *An American Dilemma: The Negro Problem and Modern Democracy* (New York: Harper & Bros., 1944).

22. Herbert Gans, *Urban Villagers: Group and Class in the Life of Italian Americans* (Glencoe, Ill.: Free Press, 1962).

23. Myron Glazer, *The Research Adventure* (New York: Random House, 1976), 160.

24. Alvin W. Gouldner, "The Sociologist as Partisan: Sociology and the Welfare State," *American Sociologist* 3, 1 (Feb. 1968): 103–16.

25. Peter L. Berger, *Invitation to Sociology: A Humanistic Perspective* (Garden City, N.Y.: Doubleday/Anchor, 1961).

26. Lawrence Rosen, "The Anthropologist as Expert Witness," *American Anthropologist* 79, 3 (Sept. 1977): 555–78.

27. Howard S. Becker, "Whose Side Are We On," *Social Problems* 14 (Winter 1967): 240–41.

28. Marvin Wolfgang, "The Social Scientist in Court," *Journal of Criminal Law and Criminology* 65, 2 (June 1974): 239–47.

29. Martin Nicolaus, "Remarks at the American Sociological Association Convention," *American Sociologist* 4, 2 (May 1969): 154–56.

30. June Helm, "Long-Term Research Among the Dogrib and Other Dene," in *Long-Term Field Research in Social Anthropology*, ed. George M. Foster (New York: Academic Press, 1979), 145–63.

31. Eric R. Wolf, "American Anthropologists and American Society," in *Reinventing Anthropology*, ed. Dell Hymes (New York: Random House, 1969), 257–58.

32. Jeanne Guillemin, "Federal Policies and Indian Politics," *Society* 17, 4 (May 1980): 29–34.

33. Rita D. Berkson, "Community Health Centers After Fifteen Years," *Health/PAC Bulletin* 12, 6 (1980): 6–14.

34. Robert J. Lampman, "What Does It Do for the Poor? A New Test for National Policy," *Public Interest* 34 (1974): 74–75.

35. Shelton H. David, *Victims of the Miracle: Development and the Indians of Brazil* (New York and Cambridge: Cambridge University Press, 1979).

36. Shepard Forman, "Human Rights in East Timor," *Society* 15, 5 (July 1978): 78–80.

37. Paul Radin, *The Method and Theory of Ethnology* (1933; reprint, New York: Basic Books, 1965), 22–46.

38. V. F. Calverton, ed., *The Making of Man: An Outline of Anthropology* (New York: Modern Library, 1931).

39. Bernhard J. Stern, *Historical Sociology: The Selected Papers of Bernhard J. Stern* (New York: Citadel Press, 1960).

40. Frances Fox Piven and Richard Cloward, *Regulating the Poor: The Functions of Public Welfare* (New York: Pantheon, 1971).

41. Guida West, *The National Welfare Rights Movement: The Social Protest of Poor Women* (New York: Praeger, 1981), 292–94.

42. Howard S. Becker, *Outsiders: Studies of the Sociology of Deviance* (New York: Free Press of Glencoe, 1973).

43. Lofland, *Doomsday Cult*.

44. Moynihan, *Maximum Feasible Misunderstanding*.

45. Henry Kissinger, *The White House Years* (Boston: Little, Brown, 1971); idem, *Years of Upheaval* (Boston: Little, Brown, 1982).

46. Charles E. Lindblom and David K. Cohen, *Usable Knowledge: Social Science and Social Problem Solving* (New Haven: Yale University Press, 1979), 5–6.

22. Language, Truth, and Politics

1. George Orwell, "Politics and the English Language," in *In Front of Your Nose*, vol. 4 of *The Collected Essays, Journalism, and Letters of George Orwell*, ed. Sonia Orwell and Ian Angus (New York: Harcourt, Brace and World, 1968), 127–40.

2. Walter Laqueur, "Foreign Policy and the English Language," *Washington Quarterly*, 4, 1 (Winter 1981): 3–12.

3. Martin Nicolaus, "Who Will Bring the Mother Down?" in *Readings in U.S. Imperialism*, ed. K. T. Fann and Donald C. Hodges (Boston: Porter Sargent Publisher, 1971), 293.

4. Nikita Khrushchev, "Speech to the Twentieth Congress of the Communist Party of the USSR" (15 February 1956), in *Peaceful Co-Existence: An Analysis of Soviet Foreign Policy*, ed. Wladyslaw W. Kulski (Chicago: Henry Regnery Co., 1959), 129.

5. Vladimir I. Lenin, *Collected Works* (*Sochinenia*), in *Peaceful Co-Existence: An Analysis of Soviet Foreign Policy*, ed. Wladyslaw W. Kulski (Chicago: Henry Regnery Co., 1959), 131.

6. Fidel Castro (Ruz), "Message to Arafat," *Granma* 17, 36 (30 August 1982).

7. Andrei A. Zhdanov, *Essays on Literature, Philosophy, and Music* (New York: International Publishers, 1950), 12–13.

8. Laura Fermi, *Mussolini* (Chicago: University of Chicago Press, 1961), 324–25.

9. Charles Sanders Peirce, "Three Methods of Fixing Belief," in vol. 5 of *The Collected Works* (Cambridge: Harvard University Press, 1931–58), 233–48.

23. Moral Development and Authoritarian Distemper

1. Richard B. Brandt, *Freedom and Morality* (Lawrence: University of Kansas Press, 1976); idem, *Ethical Theory: The Problems of Normative and Critical Ethics* (Englewood Cliffs, N.J.: Prentice-Hall, 1959).

2. Abraham Edel, *Ethical Judgment: The Use of Science in Ethics* (Glencoe, Ill.: Free Press, 1955); idem, *Method in Ethical Theory* (Indianapolis: Bobbs-Merrill, 1963).

3. Leo Strauss, *Natural Right and History* (Chicago: University of Chicago Press, 1953); idem, *What is Political Philosophy?* (Glencoe, Ill.: Free Press, 1959).

4. Richard E. Flathman, *Political Obligation* (New York: Atheneum, 1972).

5. Richard E. Dawson and Kenneth Prewitt, *Political Socialization: An Analytic Study*, 2d ed. (Boston: Little, Brown, 1977).

6. L. Harmon Ziegler, *Interest Groups in American Society* (Englewood Cliffs, N.J.: Prentice-Hall, 1964); idem, *The Political Life of American Teachers* (Englewood Cliffs, N.J.: Prentice-Hall, 1967).

7. Karl Marx and Frederick Engels, *The German Ideology* (London: Lawrence and Wishart, 1970).

8. Karl Mannheim, *Ideology and Utopia: An Introduction to the Sociology of Knowledge* (New York: Harcourt, Brace and World, 1968).

9. Max F. Scheler, *Formalism in Ethics and Non-Formal Ethics of Values: A New Attempt Toward the Foundation of an Ethical Personality*, 5th rev. ed. (Evanston, Ill.: Northwestern University Press, 1973).

10. Philip Rieff, *Freud: The Mind of the Moralist* (Garden City, N.Y.: Doubleday, 1961).

11. David Elkind, "Erik Erikson's Eight Ages of Man," in *Readings in Human Development: Contemporary Perspectives*, ed. David Elkind and Donna C. Metzel (New York: Harper & Row, 1977), 3–11.

12. Erik H. Erikson, *Young Man Luther: A Study of Psychoanalysis and History* (New York: Norton, 1958); idem, *Gandhi's Truth: On the Origins of Militant Nonviolence* (New York: Norton, 1969).

13. Erik H. Erikson, *Childhood and Society*, 2d ed. (New York: Norton, 1963).

14. Sigmund Freud, *Civilization and Its Discontents*, trans. James Strachey (New York: Norton, 1962).

15. Robert L. Ebel, "What Are Schools For?" in *Readings in Human Development: Contemporary Perspectives*, ed. David Elkind and Donna C. Metzel (New York: Harper & Row, 1977), 12–16.

16. John Dewey, *Democracy and Education: An Introduction to the Philosophy of Education* (New York: Macmillan, 1917).

17. Lawrence Kohlberg, "Development of Moral Character and Moral Ideology," in *Review of Child Development Research*, ed. Martin Hoffman and Lois Hoffman (New York: Russell Sage Foundation, 1964), 398–401.

18. For a behavioristic summary of the cognitive standpoint on moral development, see Lawrence A. Kurdek, "Perspective Taking as the Cognitive Basis of Children's Moral Development," *Merrill-Palmer Quarterly* 24 (Jan. 1978): 3–28.

19. Irving Louis Horowitz, *Foundations of Political Sociology* (New York and London: Harper & Row, 1972).

20. John Locke, "Second Treatise," in *Two Treatises of Government*, ed. Peter Laslett (Cambridge: Cambridge University Press, 1960), sec. 163, p. 94.

21. Ibid., sec. 95, p. 348; see also sec. 119, p. 366.

22. David Hume, "Of the Original Contract," in *The Social Contract*, ed. Ernest Barker (New York and London: Oxford University Press, 1946), 221–22.

23. S. I. Benn and R. S. Peters, *Social Principles and the Democratic State* (London: George Allen and Unwin, 1959), 322.

24. John Plamenatz, *Consent, Freedom and Political Obligation*, 2d ed. (New York and London: Oxford University Press, 1968), 230–31.

25. T. H. Green, *Lectures on the Principles of Political Obligation* (London: Longmans, 1895), 29–41.

26. Harold Laski, *A Grammar of Politics* (London: George Allen and Unwin, 1970), 25.

27. John Rawls, *A Theory of Justice* (Cambridge: Harvard University Press, 1972), 110–12, 114–17.

28. H. L. A. Hart, "Are There Any Natural Rights?" in *Political Philosophy*, ed. Anthony Quinton (New York and London: Oxford University Press, 1968), 61–62.

29. Rawls, *A Theory of Justice*, 349–51.

30. Robert M. MacIver, *The Modern State* (New York and London: Oxford University Press, 1926), 154.

31. Benn and Peters, *Social Principles*, 326–27.

32. Hannah Pitkin, "Obligation and Consent," in *Obligation and Dissent*, ed. Donald W. Hanson and Robert B. Fowler (Boston: Little, Brown, 1971), 41–44.

33. Burton Zwiebach, *Civility and Disobedience* (New York: Cambridge University Press, 1975), 169–200.

34. George Herbert Mead, *Mind, Self and Society: From the Standpoint of a Social Behaviorist*, ed. Charles W. Morris et al. (Chicago: University of Chicago Press, 1934); see also Anselm Strauss, ed., *On Social Psychology: Selected Papers* (Chicago: University of Chicago Press, 1964).

35. Ralph Barton Perry, *General Theory of Value* (Cambridge: Harvard University Press, 1926); idem, *Puritanism and Democracy* (New York: Vanguard Press, 1944), 589–609.

36. Irving Louis Horowitz, *Genocide: State Power and Mass Murder*, 2d ed. (New Brunswick, N.J.: Transaction Books, 1977).

37. Hannah Arendt, *The Origins of Totalitarianism*, rev. ed. (New York: Harcourt, Brace and World, 1966).

38. Jacob L. Talmon, *The Origins of Totalitarian Democracy* (London: Secker & Warburg, 1952); idem, *Political Messianism* (New York: Praeger, 1960).

39. Harold D. Lasswell, "The Choice of Sanctioning Norms," in *On Political Sociology*, ed. Dwaine Marvick (Chicago: University of Chicago Press, 1977), 348–65.

40. Helen Merrell Lynd, *On Shame and the Search for Identity* (New York: Second Editions, 1961), 181.

24. Moral Implications of Social Science Disputations

Based on a lecture delivered 2 February 1983 to the special project on "Moral Education and Moral Philosophy," sponsored by the Exxon Corporation and supervised by Abraham Edel and Elizabeth Flower of the Faculty of Arts and Sciences, Department of Philosophy, University of Pennsylvania. All rights to reproduce or republish these lecture notes are reserved by the author. [Draft version: 23 March 1983]

1. Irving Louis Horowitz, "Moral Development, Authoritarian Distemper, and the Democratic Persuasion," in *Moral Development and Politics*, ed. Richard W. Wilson and Gordon J. Schochet (New York: Praeger, 1980), 5–21.

2. John Wilson, *Discipline and Moral Education: A Survey of Public Opinion and Understanding* (Windsor, Berks: NFER-Nelson Publishing Co., 1981). Far more revealing still is Wilson's reply to D. W. Livingstone's review of this work, "Reply to Livingstone's 'On Moral Philosophy and Educational Practice,'" *Curriculum Inquiry* 13, 1 (Spring 1983): 95–97.

3. Jacob L. Talmon, *The Myth of the Nation and the Vision of Revolution* (Berkeley and Los Angeles: University of California Press, 1981).

4. Hannah Arendt, *The Origins of Totalitarianism*, new ed. (New York: Harcourt, Brace and World, 1966).

5. Elie Halevy, *The Era of Tyrannies* (New York: New York University Press, 1966).

6. George Lichtheim, *Collected Essays* (New York: Viking Press, 1973).

7. Robert S. Lynd and Helen M. Lynd, *Middletown: A Study in Contemporary American Culture* (New York: Harcourt, 1929); and idem, *Middletown in Transition: A Study in Cultural Conflicts* (New York: Harcourt, 1937). My discussion of the Lynds' work is contained in the *International Encyclopedia*

of the Social Sciences 18, ed. David L. Sills (New York: Free Press, 1971), 471–77.

8. See, for example, Kingsley Davis, "A Conceptual Analysis of Stratification," *American Sociological Review* 7 (1941): 309–21; Kingsley Davis and Wilbert E. Moore, "Some Principles of Stratification," *American Sociological Review* 10 (1945): 242–49; and for a rebuttal, see Melvin Timin, "Some Principles of Stratification: A Critical Review," *American Sociological Review* 18 (1953): 387–94. For a fuller discussion of these issues in "classic" form, see Reinhard Bendix and Seymour Martin Lipset, *Class, Status, and Power: Social Stratification in Comparative Perspective*, 2d ed. (New York: Free Press, 1966).

9. E. E. Schattschneider, *The Semisovereign People: A Realist's View of Democracy in America* (New York: Holt, Rinehart & Winston, 1960), 141.

10. David B. Truman, *The Governmental Process: Political Interests and Public Opinion* (New York: Knopf, 1951).

11. Donald Black, "Crime as Social Control," *American Sociological Review* 48 (February 1983): 34–45.

12. Ruth Benedict, *Patterns of Culture* (Boston: Houghton Mifflin, 1934); and *Anthropology Today: An Encyclopedic Inventory*, ed. A. L. Kroeber (Chicago: University of Chicago Press, 1953).

13. Bronislaw Malinowski, "The Primitive Economics of the Trobriand Islanders," *Economic Journal* 31 (1921): 1–16.

14. Sol Tax, ed., *The People vs. The System: A Dialogue in Urban Conflict* (Chicago: University of Chicago Press, 1968).

15. Friedrich A. von Hayek, *The Constitution of Liberty* (London: Routledge & Kegan Paul, 1960); and Milton Friedman, *Capitalism and Freedom* (Chicago: University of Chicago Press, 1962).

16. See, for example, John Maynard Keynes, *General Theory of Employment, Interest and Money* (London: Macmillan, 1936); and Oskar Lange, "On the Economic Theory of Socialism" (in two parts), *Review of Economic Studies* 4 (1936): 53–71; (1937): 123–42.

17. Joan Robinson, *The Accumulation of Capital* (London: Macmillan, 1956); idem, *Economic Heresies: Some Old-Fashioned Questions in Economic Theory* (London: Macmillan, 1971).

18. Abba P. Lerner, *The Economics of Employment* (New York: McGraw-Hill, 1951); idem, *Everybody's Business* (East Lansing: Michigan State University Press, 1961).

19. Erich Fromm, *The Art of Loving* (New York: Harper & Row, 1956); idem, *The Sane Society* (New York: Holt, Rinehart & Winston, 1955).

20. Carl B. Rogers, *On Becoming a Person: A Therapist's View of Psychotherapy* (Boston: Houghton Mifflin, 1961); idem, *Becoming Partners: Marriage and Its Alternatives* (New York: Delacorte, 1972).

21. Michael Walzer, *Spheres of Justice: Defense of Pluralism and Equality* (New York: Basic Books, 1983).

22. Ted George Goertzel and Albert J. Szymanski, *Sociology: Class, Consciousness, and Contradictions* (New York: Van Nostrand, 1979); and Ted George Goertzel, *Political Sociology* (Chicago: Rand McNally, 1976).

23. Alex Inkeles, *Social Change in Soviet Russia* (Cambridge: Harvard University Press, 1968); and Alex Inkeles and Raymond Bauer, *The Soviet Citizen: Daily Life in a Totalitarian Society* (Cambridge: Harvard University Press, 1959).

24. Seymour Martin Lipset, "Economic Equality and Social Class," *Equity, Income, and Policy*, ed. Irving Louis Horowitz (New York: Praeger, 1977), 278–86.

25. Paul Hollander, *Soviet and American Society: A Comparison* (New York: Oxford University Press, 1973); idem, *Political Pilgrims* (New York: Oxford University Press, 1981).

26. Robert A. Dahl, *After the Revolution? Authority in a Good Society* (New Haven: Yale University Press, 1970); and David Lane, *Politics and Society in the USSR* (New York: Random House, 1971).

27. Allan C. Carlson, "Sex According to Social Science," *Policy Review* 20 (Spring 1982): 115–39; and Steven Goldberg, "Is Homosexuality Normal?" *Policy Review* 2 (Summer 1982): 119–38.

28. Frank G. Carrington, *The Victims* (New Rochelle: Arlington House, 1975); Emilio C. Viano, "Victimology and Its Pioneers," *Victimology: An International Journal* 1, 2 (1976): 189–92; Israel Drapkin and Emilio C. Viano, *Victimology: A New Focus*, 5 vols. (Boston: D. C. Heath, 1974–75); and Emilio Viano, *Victims and Society* (Washington, D.C.: Visage Press, 1976).

29. Alan P. Bell and Martin S. Weinberg, *Homosexualities* (New York: Basic Books, 1980); and Martin S. Weinberg and Colin J. Williams, *Male Homosexuals* (New York: Oxford University Press, 1974).

30. Laud Humphreys, *Out of the Closets: The Sociology of Homosexual Liberation* (Englewood Cliffs, N.J.: Prentice-Hall, 1972).

31. Steven Goldberg, *The Inevitability of Patriarchy* (London: M. T. Smith, 1977); and idem, "Is Homosexuality Normal?" *Policy Review* 21 (Summer 1982): 119–38.

32. Konrad Lorenz, *On Aggression* (New York: Harcourt, Brace, 1974); and idem, *Behind the Mirror* (New York: Harcourt, Brace, 1977).

33. Marshall Berman, *The Politics of Authenticity: Radical Individualism and the Emergence of Modern Society* (New York: Atheneum, 1970).

34. Richard Flathman, *Political Obligation* (New York: Atheneum, 1972).

35. John G. A. Pocock, *Politics, Language and Time: Essays on Political Thought and History* (New York: Atheneum, 1971).

36. Harry V. Jaffa, *Equality and Liberty: Theory and Practice in American Politics* (New York: Oxford University Press, 1965), 209–29.

37. Benjamin Page, *Who Gets What From Government?* (Berkeley and Los Angeles: University of California Press, 1983).

38. Nelson W. Polsby, *The Consequences of Party Reform* (New York: Oxford University Press, 1983).

39. Margaret Mead, *Coming of Age in Samoa: A Psychological Study of Primitive Youth for Western Civilization* (New York: William Morrow, 1928).

40. Derek Freeman, *Margaret Mead and Samoa: The Making and Unmaking of an Anthropological Myth* (Cambridge: Harvard University Press, 1983), 281–302.

41. Ernst Mayr, *The Growth of Biological Thought: Diversity, Evolution, and Inheritance* (Cambridge: Harvard University Press, 1982).

42. Nikolaas Tinbergen, *The Animal in Its World: Explorations of an Ethologist, 1932–1972*, 2 vols. (London: George Allen and Unwin, 1972–73).

43. E. J. Mishan, *Introduction to Normative Economics* (New York: Oxford University Press, 1981); and idem, *Cost-Benefit Analysis*, expanded edition (New York: Praeger, 1976).

44. Evsei Grigor'evich Liberman, *Economic Methods and the Effectiveness of Production* (White Plains, N.Y.: International Arts and Science Press, 1972); see also Kent Gardner, "The Formulation of Economic Policy in the Soviet Union: The Political Evolution of Libermanism" (Ph.D. dissertation, University of North Carolina at Chapel Hill, 1972).

45. Ludwig von Mises, *Theory and History: An Interpretation of Social and Economic Evolution* (New Haven: Yale University Press, 1957); and idem, *Socialism: An Economic and Sociological Analysis* (New Haven: Yale University Press, 1951).

46. George J. Stigler, *The Citizen and the State: Essays on Regulation* (Chicago: University of Chicago Press, 1975).

47. Gunnar Myrdal, *The Challenge of World Poverty: A World Anti-Poverty Program in Outline* (New York: Pantheon, 1970); and idem, *Against the Stream: Critical Essays on Economics* (New York: Pantheon, 1973).

48. David L. Featherman, "Social Mobility: Opportunities are Expanding," and Sidney M. Willhelm, "Social Mobility: Opportunities are Diminishing," *Transaction/Society* 16, 3 (March 1979): 4–17.

49. Abraham Edel, *Anthropology and Ethics: The Quest for Moral Understanding* (Cleveland: The Press of Case Western Reserve University, 1968).

50. John Ladd, *The Structure of a Moral Code* (Cambridge: Harvard University Press, 1957).

51. Abraham Edel, *Analyzing Concepts in Social Science*, vol. 1 of *Science, Ideology, and Value* (New Brunswick, N.J.: Transaction Books, 1979), 276–77.

Index

Irving Louis Horowitz is Hannah Arendt Distinguished Professor of Sociology and Political Science at Rutgers University and editor-in-chief of Transaction/SOCIETY. He has held major visiting professorships at Stanford, Wisconsin, California, Princeton University's Woodrow Wilson School of Public and International Affairs, and Washington University. He has also held overseas appointments at the London School of Economics, the National University of Mexico, Queen's University in Canada, and the Hebrew University in Jerusalem where he was distinguished lecturer in the American Civilization program.

Professor Horowitz's earlier writings on political sociology include *Radicalism and the Revolt against Reason*, *Three Worlds of Development*, *Beyond Empire and Revolution*, *Ideology and Utopia in the United States*, and *Foundations of Political Sociology*—which has since appeared in German, Spanish, and Italian language editions. Prior to this book, his most recent work is *C. Wright Mills: An American Utopian*.

of related interest

HETERICK MEMORIAL LIBRARY
306.20973 H816w   onuu
Horowitz, Irving Lo/Winners and losers :

3 5111 00157 8867